Rae
Days

Thomas Walkom

KEY PORTER BOOKS

Canadian Cataloguing in Publication Data

Walkom, Thomas L. (Thomas Lawrence) 1950-
  Rae Days

Includes index.
ISBN 1-55013-598-8

1. Ontario - Politics and government - 1990-
2. New Democratic Party of Ontario. I. Title.

FC3076.2.W35   1994   971.3'04   C94-931450-1
F1058.W35   1994

The publisher gratefully acknowledges the assistance of the Canada Council, the Ontario Publishing Centre and the Government of Ontario.

Excerpts from "We're in the Same Boat Now" by Bob Rae have been reprinted with the author's permission.

Key Porter Books Limited
70 The Esplanade
Toronto, Ontario
Canada M5E 1R2

Printed and bound in Canada

94 95 96 97 98   5 4 3 2 1

Table of Contents

For C.

Preface

THIS IS A BOOK ABOUT BOB RAE'S NEW DEMOCRATIC
Party government in Ontario—what it did, what it didn't do, and why.
From both necessity and choice, it is not a blow-by-blow chronical.
Instead, it focuses on those elements crucial to the Rae experiment.

What makes this experiment particularly important is that it marks a
defining moment in Canadian politics. Around the globe, democratic
socialist parties are trying to rethink their roles in a world where the
left has gone out of fashion. Until now, Canada's NDP has been able to
avoid addressing such matters. However, Rae's government has forced
the issue. It is re-inventing social democracy on the run. Its often
bizarre and contradictory actions are throwing the NDP, and many of
those who regard themselves as left-leaning Canadians, into confusion.
After Bob Rae, this country's politics will never be the same. This book
is about that too.

What follows is based, in part, on my six years as a political columnist at the Ontario legislature—first for *The Globe and Mail*, currently
for *The Toronto Star*. As well, I have interviewed dozens of people over
the past twelve months specifically for this project. Many, for reasons
of loyalty to the government, fear of being fired or just plain discretion,
asked not to be identified by name. Others were less hesitant. Notes at
the end of the book identify sources, except those for which anonymity
was required. Obviously, information from unnamed sources has been

treated with care and was used only when there was sufficient reason to accept its authenticity. Such is the nature of political journalism.

While most involved in the Rae government have been happy to be interviewed, there have been a few exceptions. Most revolve around Rae himself.

For a showman, Rae can be a most private person. At times, he likes to unburden and explain himself. At other times, he resents any questioning of himself or his thinking. Initially, it seemed, I would be dealing with the former Rae. In the fall of 1993, he told me he would be pleased to be interviewed for the book. A few weeks later, however, I was informed by Peter Mosher, Rae's press secretary, that the premier had changed his mind. Mosher said he did not know why. Further inquiries in January 1994 produced the same answer. (Later, the premier was gracious enough to give me written permission to quote from his song "We're in the Same Boat Now." I do thank him for that.)

I ran into similar problems with some of Rae's friends. Author Michael Ignatieff explained from London that he had become uneasy about speaking of his old friend. Rae, he said, was easily wounded; even the most innocuous statements from one who knew him as well as Ignatieff might cause Rae grief. "We were young and vulnerable together," Ignatieff said by way of explanation. Nonetheless, he said he would check with Rae. Unless the premier objected strenuously, Ignatieff said, he would agree to be interviewed. As a journalist himself, he said, this was his bias.

I contacted Ignatieff a week later in Toronto. He had just had dinner the night before with Rae and his wife Arlene. No, Ignatieff said, he would not be available for an interview. No, he said, it had nothing to do with a request from Rae; it was Ignatieff's own decision.

Other Rae friends were less hesitant. Some insisted on not being identified. Others—including Jonathan Guss, John Honderich, Esther Myers, and Lenny Wise—were willing to be interviewed at length and on the record. I would like to assure Rae, should he ever read this book, that all of his old friends expressed affection and loyalty for their comrade. Should anything in this book suggest otherwise, it is undoubtedly the result of my poor writing skills rather than their intent.

Luckily, Rae was not entirely an unknown quantity to me. I have followed his political career for twenty-six years since he was student politician at the University of Toronto and I a first-year reporter on the campus newspaper, *The Varsity*. For part of the time that Rae was federal NDP finance critic in Ottawa, I was *The Globe and Mail*'s parliamentary correspondent covering finance. Later, when he was opposition leader at Queen's Park, we would discuss social democracy. Occasionally, he would send me copies of his most piquant speeches or writings. Information from our conversations over this period is woven into this book and, I hope, adds some depth.

On the whole, the premier's cabinet colleagues have not been shy. I would like to gratefully acknowledge the co-operation of the following ministers (past and present): Floyd Laughren, Evelyn Gigantes, Howard Hampton, Ruth Grier, Dave Cooke, Frances Lankin, Brian Charlton, Bud Wildman, Peter Kormos, Marilyn Churley. I attempted to get Citizenship Minister Elaine Ziemba's views on some of the controversial issues explored in Chapter 11 below; alas, she was unavailable. I do, however, apologize to other ministers who would have liked to have been interviewed; there was simply not enough time.

I am also grateful to the following (in no particular order) from the government, the NDP, labour or elsewhere who were willing to give up their time to help in this endeavour and who are willing to have their names appear in print: David Reville, Mel Watkins, Richard Johnston, Anne Creighton, Judy Darcy, Lynn Spink, Julie Davis, Janet Solberg, Kathleen O'Hara, Michael Decter, Rob Mitchell, Sue Colley, Peter Warrian, Rod Mickleburgh, Walter Curlook, Stephen Lewis, Dick Proctor, Graham Murray, Steven Langdon, Karen Mock, Jeff Henry, Bob Parkins, Julie Mason, Chuck Rachlis, Ellen McKinnon, Kimble Sutherland, Bob White, David de Launay, Gordon Wilson, Mike Rachlis, and, of course, Isabel Archer.

My colleagues and friends in *The Toronto Star* legislative bureau and the Queen's Park press gallery have been generous with their help—particularly Derek Ferguson, Anne Dawson, Kelly Toughill, Leslie Papp, Matt Maychak, Bill Walker, Richard Brennan, Jim Coyle, Robert Fisher, and Amelia Cassela. My thanks go to the *Star*'s editor, John Honderich, who encouraged this endeavour and gave me three months leave to write it. Key Porter has proven to be an enthusiastic publisher. Susan Renouf, the editor-in-chief at Key Porter oversaw this book; she has been a pleasure to work with. Beverley Beetham-Endersby did the actual editing of the manuscript and made useful suggestions. The staff of the Legislative Library at Queen's Park were, as usual, both friendly and helpful.

I should also give special mention to Floyd Laughren who, one day over a beer, suggested I write this book. Laughren pointed out that Karl Marx would have had an interesting time trying to figure out the Ontario NDP government. While I can't claim to be Karl Marx, I too have had an interesting time.

My mother, Phyllis, sparked my interest in both journalism and politics. Her newspaper columns (from the Kirkland Lake *Northern Daily News* of the early 1950s) are still among the cleverest I have ever read. Thanks also to my long-time friend Linda McQuaig, whose own work proved useful in this endeavour and who helped orient me in the bizarre world of book publishing.

Finally, there is Charlotte Montgomery—fellow reporter, partner in adventure and general co-conspirator; a political journalist who knows both Ontario and the NDP. I've profited greatly from her experience and insights. Moreover, she encouraged me to take on this project and kept me going when I wanted to drop it. She read and commented on every dreary draft of every chapter. She is also married to me and (this sounds like a cliché but is true) has put up with the weird moods that seem to affect people who write books. My thanks to her know no bounds.

1

The New
New Democrats

OCTOBER 25, 1993 — ELECTION NIGHT IN CANADA: ACROSS
the country, Conservative MPs were going down to defeat. In Quebec,
the separatist Bloc Québécois had come from nowhere, a phenomenon
not seen since Réal Caouette's Créditistes had swept out of the
province's hinterland in the 1960s. From their base in the West, the
zealots of Reform were blazing a path across English Canada. Over top
of them all were Jean Chrétien's Liberals, the government party determined to govern again.

For the media, the most dramatic stories were the rise of the Bloc;
the Reform breakthrough; and the defeat, personal and political, of
Conservative leader Kim Campbell. The woman who, just a few
months earlier, had been the darling of the pundits, lauded as the bright-
est politician since Pierre Trudeau, had been defeated in even her own
Vancouver constituency. The Campbell story seemed to combine all of
the elements of classic tragedy—hubris, a dramatic rise, a humiliating
fall, even a hint of sex.

But, in English Canada, the real story of the federal election of 1993
was not the decimation of the Conservatives. All that had happened
here was that one right-of-centre party had been edged out by another.
Outside of Quebec, the Reform Party would battle with the Conservatives to become English Canada's opposition to Chrétien's Liberals.

Rather, the real story of 1993 was the virtual elimination of the
social-democratic left from Canadian politics. Audrey McLaughlin's

New Democratic Party had gone into the election with forty-three seats; it emerged with nine—too few even to maintain official-party status. In Ontario, all nine New Democrat MPs lost their seats, and the party's share of the popular vote crashed to an almost unbelievable 6 per cent. Even in Nova Scotia, never fertile ground for the NDP, the popular vote was higher.

In the Southern Ontario auto-manufacturing city of Oshawa, NDP supporters were particularly bitter as they watched the election-night results roll in. Oshawa had symbolized the NDP's hopes—a working-class city of trade unionists who voted for Canada's only serious left-wing party. Oshawa had produced Ed Broadbent, the salesman's son who had gone on to become a professor of political science and head of the federal party. The riding had been NDP since 1968. When New Democrat Mike Breaugh, Broadbent's successor, won Oshawa in a 1990 by-election, no one was surprised.

Breaugh had been a provincial politician, a New Democrat MPP in the Ontario legislature. He had left provincial politics largely because he couldn't stomach his leader, Bob Rae. Ironically, Breaugh had bailed out just before the upset provincial election of 1990, which had brought Rae to power in Ontario. Even more ironically, the actions of Rae's provincial New Democratic government since 1990 had helped to ensure Breaugh's humiliating federal defeat in 1993.

For in Oshawa, the NDP did not come second, not even third. It came fourth—after the Liberals, after Reform, even after the Conservatives. Union members who used to vote NDP made no secret of why they had abandoned the party: they didn't like the Rae government. "It's time the party showed Rae the plank and told him to jump," Brian Nicholson, an Oshawa NDP city councillor, told the press on election night. From Windsor, defeated New Democrat MP Steven Langdon called on his old comrade-in-arms, Rae, to take responsibility for the débâcle and quit. In Toronto, Mel Swart, a former New Democrat MPP and the man who in 1982 had nominated Rae to be leader of the Ontario party, held a formal press conference to disown the Ontario premier. The federal election was the final straw. "The people of Ontario, and even Canada, considered the Rae government to be the example of what to expect from the NDP," Swart said. "Because Bob Rae and no one else [in the party] had a platform across Canada. He made the news across Canada. . . . Rae should resign."

Inside the large, pink sandstone Ontario legislative building known as Queen's Park, Rae adamantly denied all responsibility for the collapse of the federal NDP in Ontario. Canadian voters, the premier argued, had repudiated not the NDP but the Conservatives. The NDP casualties were simply collateral damage, innocent bystanders trampled by the voters on their way to the Liberals. "The reality is that the Liberal party was chosen as the vehicle," he told reporters. "The corporate agenda of the Tories, a very right-wing agenda ... was defeated."

While it was true that many factors beyond the actions of the Ontario government accounted for the collapse of the NDP federally, Rae's explanation was a little too pat. In fact, Ontario voters had not voted against the right. About 40 per cent had cast ballots for either the Reform Party or the Conservatives. Indeed, the Tories — whose agenda Rae claimed had been defeated — picked up 18 per cent of the Ontario popular vote, triple that won by the NDP.

During the election campaign, NDP officials had made no secret of the Rae effect on party fortunes. The party's central campaign office acknowledged privately that the actions of the Ontario government — its recent tax hikes (the largest in provincial history), its decision to roll back public-service wages through a so-called social contract, its many snafus and cock-ups, its broken promises — were contributing to a loss of support from traditional NDP voters.

True, the actions of other NDP governments had not helped. In Saskatchewan, Premier Roy Romanow's New Democratic government was closing hospitals. In British Columbia, Premier Mike Harcourt's NDP government was locked in a bitter battle with environmentalists over logging in Clayoquot Sound. But the NDP's share of the popular vote in those provinces had not dipped as precipitously as it had in Ontario.

What's more, the Rae effect had spread beyond Ontario. Throughout the federal election campaign, the NDP's central office received disturbing evidence that the Rae government's record was hurting the party in other provinces. In Newfoundland, New Democrats using the public-service cut-backs of Liberal premier Clyde Wells to attack Chrétien were dogged with questions about Bob Rae's social contract. In other provinces, long-time New Democrats cited Rae's record as justification for voting against the party. The explanations were varied and often surprising. In one focus group done for the federal party, a Saskatchewan voter said he was no longer voting NDP because Rae had abolished the oath of allegiance to the Queen for Ontario police officers.

"The effect extended far beyond Ontario's borders," said Dick Proctor, provincial secretary for the Saskatchewan NDP and former federal secretary of the national party. "I get letters cancelling Saskatchewan NDP memberships because of things that Rae has done."

Rae's national influence stemmed in large part from the fact he was a consummate media performer. The Ontario premier was well loved by television producers for his ability to deliver short, crisp sound-bites. Rae, in turn, liked nothing better than exposure in the national media. He had never abandoned his love of the national political stage. As well, interviews on cross-Canada radio and television allowed him to escape a Queen's Park press gallery he often seemed to find parochial, disrespectful, and unappreciative of his statesmanlike qualities.

Throughout the summer of 1993, Rae had appeared often on the national television news, expounding on his social contract, his new views of social democracy, his commitment to fiscal conservatism. In fact, Rae's appearances had become so frequent that an irritated Roy Romanow finally telephoned to ask him to stop. As the Saskatchewan premier later confided to an associate, every time Rae appeared on national television the NDP's popularity in the West dropped.

What party officials and NDP voters found so disturbing was that Rae's government had effectively redefined social democracy. New Democratic governments had had their scraps with labour before. Indeed, such scraps had led to the 1982 defeat of Allan Blakeney's NDP government in Saskatchewan and the 1975 defeat of Dave Barrett's NDP government in British Columbia. But Rae's social-contract battle with Ontario's public-sector unions had become one of epic proportions. To anyone who would listen, Rae insisted he was not simply rolling back public-service wages like other premiers, not just saving money, but that he was redefining the whole nature of collective bargaining. His social contract, he told supporters, would serve as a model for labour relations across Canada. Every time Rae made that claim, trade unionists in the NDP, most of whom were committed to free collective bargaining, winced.

Similarly, other NDP governments had been fiscally conservative. But no government in Canada—Liberal, Tory, or NDP—had been as tough as Rae's. In 1993, Ontario's NDP government had slashed spending and raised taxes to a degree unmatched elsewhere in the country— more than Brian Mulroney's Conservatives had ever done, more than Jean Chrétien's Liberals or Ralph Klein's Alberta Tories would do the

following year. And the Rae government had carried out its mission
with the fervour of the recent convert, loudly contradicting everything
the NDP had ever said about economic management and the priorities
facing a country caught in depression.

Other NDP governments had tried to make peace with business. But
none had done so with such a combination of enthusiasm and naïvety as
Rae's. On the one hand, the Ontario NDP government won the lasting
enmity of Ontario business by changing provincial labour law to suit
the trade unions. On the other, the government made unprecedented
concessions — usually secretly — that were worth tens of millions of
dollars to some of the most profitable companies in the world, the drug
multinationals.

Other NDP governments had broken promises, but when Rae's government shattered pledges the NDP had made in opposition, it did so
almost gleefully. The government did not back away from public auto
insurance just because the timing was bad. It did so because, as government figures would insist privately, it had decided that public auto
insurance and a host of other long-held NDP policies were impractical,
wrong-headed — even silly. "That was then," opposition MPPs would say
mockingly, as Rae abandoned this or that promise from his opposition
days; "This is now." Indeed, the implication of the government's flip-
flops was that virtually everything the NDP had stood for prior to September 6, 1990, the day the party won power in Ontario, was invalid.

The NDP had been founded on the premise that it would be different.
Throughout the depression of the early 1990s, the federal party argued
that there was an alternative to the slash-and-burn strategy of what it
called "neo-conservative orthodoxy." Liberals or Conservatives might
say the country had to accept double-digit unemployment, that the only
action governments could take was to reduce public-sector deficits in
order to get their fiscal houses in order — that there was no choice. New
Democrats, however, had always insisted that politics allows choices —
that unemployment, not the deficit, could be made the country's highest
priority; that the neo-conservatives did not have a monopoly on truth.
McLaughlin's 1993 election campaign was centred on this theme.

Rae's government was a living rebuke to McLaughlin, a disavowal of
this, the cardinal assumption behind the NDP. "We had no choice,"
Ontario NDP ministers would say as the government backtracked on its
promises. "There was no alternative." In effect they were saying that
the neo-conservatives had been right all along — that fundamentally

there is only one way to govern, that there are no choices, that an NDP government can never be much different from any other. Through its actions and words, the Ontario government had pierced to the core not only the NDP but all Canadians yearning for an alternative to business-as-usual politics.

Most in Rae's government had never intended to reinvent their party. In the end, they did so on the run, under the pressure of events and in the cauldron of daily governance. By the dying months of its first term, the government's official line was that everything it had done was strictly in line with party principles. Rae was fond of comparing his actions to those of Tommy Douglas, the CCF-NDP's first leader to win power.

But, to most outside the closed circle of Queen's Park, it was clear that, after five years of Rae in power, the New Democratic Party—federally as well as provincially—would never be the same. To Julie Davis, the Ontario Federation of Labour's secretary-treasurer and president of the provincial party, the scale of change forced by the Rae experience would be of a magnitude unseen since 1960 when the old Co-operative Commonwealth Federation and the Canadian Labour Congress united to form the NDP.

"It will certainly force a review of its [the NDP's] relationship with labour," Davis said. "And because this is Ontario, and because it's so big and because it is the home or headquarters of most of the unions in this country, it's going to have an impact far beyond our borders. B.C. had that kind of evaluation; Saskatchewan had that kind of evaluation. But it never left those provinces. This is going to be an evaluation for the country ... in much the same way as happened in 1960 with the creation of the new party [the NDP].... I think this will be on the same scale."

In part, as Davis noted, interest in the Rae experiment stemmed from Ontario's importance in Canada. Even in recession, it was the wealthiest province, with the most sophisticated economic structure and the largest share of the country's population. But, in large part, the widespread interest flowed from the NDP's own expectations. As a party rooted in prairie populism, the NDP expected to win power from time to time in Saskatchewan and Manitoba. It had been pleased to win power twice in British Columbia. But the resource nature of the B.C. economy and its sharp class cleavages always made that province seem so different from the rest of the country. Ontario would be the real test.

Indeed, within the NDP, strategists had often argued over which victory would be more important for the party—a win nationally, or a win in Ontario. Many felt that victory in Ontario, in the country's economic heartland, could establish the NDP's credentials once and for all as a serious, social-democratic party.

To the discomfiture of many, the Rae victory seemed to have produced a cuckoo in the nest. Ontario's government was not a bold example of social democracy in action but of the left in retreat.

"I was excited when they won," said former NDP federal secretary Dick Proctor. "The glow carried on for several months. . . . Disillusionment started to settle in a year later." What dampened the glow for Proctor was the Ontario NDP government's decision on the first anniversary of its election victory to scrap its push for public auto insurance. Proctor was at an NDP finance meeting in Winnipeg when news of the auto-insurance reversal was released. "We had a very vigorous debate. There was a real feeling from [New Democrats from] across the country that Ontario had let the side down."

By 1994, some of the NDP's most respected figures had quietly retreated in disgust from the Rae government. "I'll put up a sign in my yard [for the next Ontario election]," said one, "but I won't lift a finger otherwise." Others were saying that any attempt to rebuild the federal party after the 1993 election débâcle would have to wait until after Ontario voters had given their verdict on the Rae government. Janet Solberg, former Ontario NDP president, put it bluntly: "Nobody cares what happens in Saskatchewan. Nobody cares even what happens in B.C. When we got elected here in Ontario, people cared. It was an experiment. Bob Rae might say to himself, 'What we do in Ontario doesn't matter in Manitoba.' But it has a resonance across the country. . . . People do take notice. It's not just what's going to happen here in Ontario. I think it's got a profound impact across the country."

Others, however, felt the Rae government was a breath of fresh air — that it had swept away stale ideological shibboleths which had long comforted a party smugly satisfied with its status as perpetual opposition and self-appointed conscience to the nation. The Rae government, these New Democrats argued, had proved that the NDP could govern Canada's largest province during hard times in a practical fashion and achieve real, if limited, goals.

To historian and former NDP official Desmond Morton, the Rae experience demonstrated how the party had been able to adapt to what he called Ontario's progressive-conservative political culture. Morton lauded Rae's efforts and chided those unionists who viewed Rae as a "capitalist stooge." Ross McClellan, a former New Democrat MPP and one of the chief political operatives in the Rae government, put it this way: "We will never go back to easy advocacy of all issues for all people. For some people, that's painful but it's part of the reality of becoming a party that is actually capable of governing. We're not going back to the NDP of the period [from] 1930 to 1990."

What Rae himself thought of this remained unclear. In his public pronouncements, he was careful to insist on the intellectual links between his government's actions and long-held principles of the NDP. In his own private thoughts, however, he must have known those links were being put under unbearable strain.

To one long-time associate adept at reading the premier's complex mind, Rae was trying to create a new NDP, one which would gradually abandon its old-fashioned socialist and labour roots and embrace instead the interests of the broader middle classes. This new party, the associate went on, would not be like the existing Liberal party, which Rae had turned from in his youth and which he still thought corrupt. Rather, it would be a real liberal party, a pure liberal party—the kind of liberal party which, until he unexpectedly won power in 1990, had existed only in Bob Rae's imagination.

2

A Liberal in Sandals

EVERYONE WHO KNOWS BOB RAE HAS A STORY. MOST BEGIN with a bow to his brainpower, for Rae is bright. But then the stories veer quickly off into the quirkier aspects of his personality: his legendary inability to make small talk; his sudden bouts of vague abstraction, which suggest, at the precise moment when his attention is most needed, that he has gone into private communion with an unseen being; his insistence (his friend Lenny Wise calls it his "obsessiveness") on seeing the fine print, on knowing how everything—absolutely everything—works.

Example: In 1989, as leader of the opposition, Rae, two fellow New Democrat MPPs, two aides, and a reporter are touring Native health facilities in the bleak communities of Ontario's James Bay coast. Native health is a good issue for the NDP and a good way to get press coverage for an opposition leader at an otherwise quiet time. But, during a tour of the Fort Albany nursing station, Rae suddenly stops. "What's that?" he asks, pointing to a ladder and a trap door in the ceiling. "The attic," he is told. As the party turns into another part of the station, someone notices Rae is missing. They retrace their steps, and there he is— halfway up the ladder, poking his head into the attic. He just had to see.

Former press aide Rob Mitchell tells of travelling with Rae after the NDP's disastrous showing in the 1985 Ontario election. On this day, the two were in a small town in northwestern Ontario, where, after delivering his speech, Rae was scheduled to dine with the local NDP riding executive. The speech was stirring. But, before sitting down to dinner, Rae told his hosts he had to nip upstairs to his hotel room to make a telephone call. The group waited. And waited. After an hour, Mitchell was sent up by the now-ravenous riding executive to inquire discreetly after their leader. "I knocked at the door; he answered in his pyjamas, his toothbrush in his hand," said Mitchell. "He had completely forgotten. He was always doing stuff like that."

With his few very close friends, Rae is usually not so distracted. He is warm and witty—able and eager to talk about some of his most private anguishes and fears. And he can be spontaneously emotional. One friend was slightly taken aback when Rae, as a gesture of gratitude during a particularly difficult period, suddenly kissed him full on the lips.

With others, however, including those aides and co-workers not within this small circle of friends, Rae is remote, aloof—almost cold. "He doesn't talk to very many people," said Lenny Wise. "Even when he's talking to people, he doesn't really." Others concur. "Someone once said Bob is only comfortable with those under five or over seventy-five," Lynn Spink, at one time Rae's executive assistant, said as she tried to explain her former boss. "Except when he's on stage, giving a speech, or at the lectern—then he's completely at ease."

"He's very good with people he has absolutely nothing in common with—like old people or black people," said another former aide. "But generally, his people skills are terrible. He has this terrible habit, when you're talking to him, of not looking at you—of staring off into space. At first you think: 'Oh, it's that he's captivated by what I'm saying and is thinking up a profound reply.' But then he never says anything—just keeps staring."

Unlike most politicians, Rae never developed a capacity for making others feel comfortable in his company. Just having lunch with him could be excruciatingly uncomfortable. Rae would wolf down his food, apparently in an effort to end the ordeal as quickly as possible. Only if the conversation turned to abstract ideas did he relax.

"As a kid the one thing I loathed—and I still loathe them—was the cocktail party, and my parents had them all the time," Rae told a journalist early in his political career. "But what you learn as you become more involved in public life is that other people feel as uncomfortable as you do."

In fact, few people seem as uncomfortable in one-on-one situations as Rae. This inability to relate to individuals extended even to his own cabinet and caucus. During his eight years as opposition leader in Ontario, Rae was never fully integrated into the small NDP caucus. "Caucus members would get together in [Windsor MPP] Dave Cooke's office and shoot the breeze and have a drink," recalled Rob Mitchell. "But Rae was never there. And people would kind of make fun of him."

As premier, Rae's congenital inability to communicate drove his cabinet crazy. By the second year of government, even long-time loyalist Ruth Grier complained to friends that Rae wouldn't speak to her. Rae's aloof manner particularly irked his attorney general, Howard Hampton, who took it as a sign of arrogance.

Where Rae shone, however, was in moments of personal tragedy. When aides or associates suffered loss—such as the death of a family member—the otherwise awkward Rae seemed to show intuitive understanding and tact. He had experienced his own share of personal sorrow; grief in others seemed to allow him to momentarily connect, to exhibit the feelings he usually kept bottled inside. "When my father was seriously ill, Bob sent flowers to him in the hospital and wrote me a really nice note," said Anne Creighton, a Rae aide during the opposition years. "And it was the same when anyone in the office was seriously ill—he was genuinely compassionate. It wasn't forced or fake."

Robert Keith Rae was born August 2, 1948, the third of four children. He was born into a family that—while not rich—had become middle class and comfortable. Rae's father, Saul, was a rising star in Canada's Department of External Affairs. Bob Rae grew up in a home where the up-and-coming mandarins of the day were frequent visitors. Talk in the Rae household turned naturally to politics.

However, one element of his life that Saul Rae did not talk about much in those days was his own father, for Saul Rae's father had been born Jewish. And in the Anglo-Scottish, anti-semitic foreign service of 1940s Canada, Jewishness was not an asset.

For turn-of-the-century Canada, the story of Willy Cohen and Nell Rae was not atypical. Cohen, a tailor with an interest in natty clothes and the racetrack, came from a Lithuanian Jewish family that had emigrated to Scotland. There, he had met and married Nell Rae, a Glasgow shipyard worker's daughter. As Bob Rae later explained to *Toronto Star* reporter Judy Steed, a mixed marriage was not greeted with pleasure in Presbyterian Scotland. So Willy and Nell left for Hamilton, Ontario, in 1912 to start a new life under a new name— hers. When Saul was born in 1914, it was as Saul Rae, not Saul Cohen.

Soon, the family was completely assimilated into Anglo-Canadian society.

At some point, Willy Cohen just stepped out of the picture — rarely to be mentioned again. His family was not wealthy, but Nell Rae was tough. Bob Rae's friend Jonathan Guss would later describe her as "the Mammy Yokum of the family — tough, outspoken, no pushover ... [who] started with nothing and lived to 107." Nell Rae made do, in part, by putting her children into show business. Grace, Saul, and Jackie (who later became a well-respected songwriter) performed song-and-dance routines in all the major vaudeville houses of Toronto. They called themselves the Little Raes of Sunshine.

Later, after selling shoes for a year, Saul entered the University of Toronto. Bright and ambitious, he crossed the Atlantic to earn a doctorate at the University of London. Overseas, he met Lois George, a doctor's daughter from a conventional, upper-middle-class English family. Years later, Esther Myers, Bob Rae's first serious girlfriend, would remember Lois's mother, Mildred, as "lovely, very genteel," a person who, to Myers, "represented an era that was dying."

Saul and Lois married in 1939. A year later, he joined the Department of External Affairs and began globe-trotting. John was born in Algiers in 1943, Jennifer in Paris in 1945, Bob in Ottawa in 1948, and David in Washington in 1957.

To be in the federal bureaucracy in the 1940s and the 1950s was to be Liberal. It was not a question of partisanship but of common sense. Liberals had reigned in Ottawa since the mid-1930s, and it seemed that they would rule for ever. In the early 1950s, Saul Rae served as special assistant to then Secretary of State for External Affairs Lester Pearson. He represented Canada in Vietnam and was, in 1956, appointed to the coveted post of ambassador to Washington.

As a child, Bob Rae is remembered as bright but not terribly athletic. He attended elementary school in Ottawa and Washington. When Saul Rae moved to Geneva as an ambassador to the United Nations there, Bob enrolled in its prestigious International School.

At home, the Rae family was both close and closed. "In this family, having a personality of your own was considered a major attribute," explained Jonathan Guss. "You were supposed to do things, to perform, to keep up." Performance — in the theatrical sense — seemed to be the key. To Guss, this explained in part Rae's continuing attempts to be a songwriter as well as a politician. "He probably wants to be a

Renaissance man. Don't make fun of him for that. But I think that's partly it. . . . He always wants to do two things at once, to work on two tracks." Indeed, for Bob Rae, the highest praise may have been that bestowed by his uncle Jackie at Nell Rae's funeral in 1994. Young Bobby, the old vaudevillian said, had definitely outperformed them all; as premier, he had reached the pinnacle of performance.

Each summer, Saul and Lois would take the children to the family cottage on a private island in Big Rideau Lake, south of Ottawa. The island was to be for family only; outsiders were not welcome. Lenny Wise remembers that, even as a married adult, Bob Rae had to wait until his parents left the island before he could sneak friends over to share a weekend.

Among the children, Bob (or Bobby, as he was known in the family) had the most difficulty with his older brother, John. The two are close, but John—taking his position as the eldest son seriously—was often disapproving of his younger brother. Between the two, a friendly rivalry developed, which carried on into adulthood. John was a force in the federal Liberal party and a long-time ally of Jean Chrétien. Later executive vice-president of the giant Quebec firm Power Corp., John dismissed as nuts his younger brother's decision to run for the NDP in 1978.

The competitiveness between the two brothers reached baroque proportions after 1987 when David, the youngest Rae, developed an aggressive form of lymphatic cancer. Doctors concluded that a bone-marrow transplant might help David—but that it would work only if donor and recipient were absolutely compatible.

"There was a kind of rivalry between Johnny and Bob over who would provide the transplant," recalled a friend later. "And when the doctors told Bob it was him, that only his marrow was compatible, he was really excited. He wasn't just excited because he might save David's life—although obviously he wanted to do that—but because it was his marrow that was being used and not Johnny's."

Lenny Wise, who stayed close to Bob throughout the entire ordeal of David's sickness and eventual death, remembered it the same way. "They both wanted to be the one—perceived as the one—who helped to make an attempt to save their brother's life," he said.

Within the family, Bob was closest to his sister, Jennifer. Fiercely protective of her younger brother, she worked on all of his campaigns. Like John and the rest of the Rae clan, Jennifer gravitated naturally to the Liberals. She was a close friend of Jim Coutts, at one time the powerful principal secretary to former prime minister Pierre Trudeau. Jennifer also dated Trudeau in his bachelor days, before dropping him to take up with someone else.

Bob Rae's relationship with his parents seems to have been more difficult. There was genuine affection and respect, but to Rae's friends it seemed that a distance existed between the parents and their second son.

"His parents know him the least," said Wise. "He's confided in them probably less than anybody alive." Parental influences left their mark, however. From his mother, Bob Rae developed a strong and abiding interest in religion and ethics. His father left him with an instinctive sympathy for the ideals of Pearsonian Liberalism—based on the principles of public service, a professional state bureaucracy, and rational management leavened with a dose of compassion.

Having not been born into privilege himself, Saul Rae believed that all of his children should develop self-reliance. In 1974, Bob returned to Canada from England, having just come through one of the darkest periods of his life, a black depression. He was out of work and out of money, sleeping on the couch of one friend, D'Arcy Martin, and allowing another, Lenny Wise, to buy his meals. In typical fashion, Wise recalled, Rae never asked his friends for anything; instead, he put himself in a situation where they might offer. According to Wise, Rae never considered asking his parents for a loan during that difficult period. "He never took money from his parents, ever. And if he had asked, they would have said: 'Why don't you earn it yourself.'"

Part of Rae's problem with his parents seems to have stemmed from their attempt to hide Saul's Jewish background. Not until he was seventeen did Bob Rae find out his grandfather had been a Jew. Later, he confided to Lenny Wise that he had been surprised and upset—surprised that there was a whole side of his background of which he knew nothing, upset that his parents had kept this information from him.

In part, it was Willy Cohen's gambling habit that had made him a non-person in the family of Saul and Lois Rae. But, in part, it was his religion. "They were ashamed of the Jewishness of the grandfather," said Wise—and Rae himself was ashamed of their shame. "That's when he went through an identity crisis," explained Jonathan Guss.

From then on, Rae became increasingly interested in things Jewish—Jewish philosophy, Jewish humour. Wise speculated that it was Rae's newly found sense of his own past that drove him, as an undergraduate at the University of Toronto, to try to date only Jewish women. To Guss, however, this was an extreme interpretation. "He's not Jewish. He's Anglican. He learned everything he could about Judaism, wrapped his mind around it, his heart around it—and then he went back to being Bob."

By 1966, the University of Toronto was on the edge of ferment. Thanks mainly to events in the United States—the growing antagonism to the Vietnam War and the student revolt at Berkeley, California—activism was about to become a trend at Canada's largest university. The Vietnam War plus somewhat vague concepts of student power and social justice would dominate the U of T campus for most of the next decade.

Into this politically charged milieu Bob Rae found himself thrust—an outsider in a university that, while large, was still composed of cliques; an eighteen-year-old who, because of his European education, was enrolled straight into second year. "I was always something of an outsider because of my upbringing, because I didn't grow up in one town," Rae explained to one reporter. "I didn't go to a public high school. I didn't grow up in a neighbourhood. I think there was a feeling that I had to prove myself in any crowd of people, or else they would somehow feel I was odd or terribly different."

But, at the same time—and this would repeat itself throughout his adult life—he was an outsider with insider connections. Graham Fraser, a childhood friend from Ottawa, was already working at *The Varsity*, the university student newspaper. Soon, Rae would be writing pithy book reviews for the paper. Fraser also mentioned Rae to a friend of his, another active student at University College's Sir Daniel Wilson Residence, named Jeff Rose.

Rose was already a well-known figure on campus. He and Michael Ignatieff, who, like Rae, was a diplomat's son, were involved in organizing annual teach-ins, massive events at the university's Varsity Arena, where controversial speakers would debate major world issues. Rose and Ignatieff pulled Rae into helping organize a teach-in on China that year. The next year, Rae helped his friends by doing public relations for a teach-in on religion and international affairs.

Rae was also determined to involve himself in the family business of entertainment. His father, Saul, had, during his student days, produced the *UC Follies*, an annual satirical review at U of T's University College. Bob Rae tried out and won for himself a part in the *Follies*, impressing a twenty-six-year-old wiseacre named Leonard Wise, who would become one of Rae's long-time friends. In later life, Wise would get great pleasure out of describing his first impression of the man who became Ontario premier. "He looked like a bit of a drip ... not particularly tall; not particularly distinguished-looking; not particularly anything. He'd got glasses, blond hair; he'd got a pale face. Looked like nothing special."

Indeed, the *UC Follies* experience was vintage Rae, exemplifying the tremendous gap between his private and public personas. In rehearsal, Rae—given the secondary role of the straight man in a two-person skit with Wise—was indeed nothing special. But on opening night, with an audience watching, Rae suddenly blossomed. As a public speaker, he had a showman's instinct for both timing and audience reaction. And that night, the straight man used both to steal the skit, leaving Wise shaking his head in amazement. "He doesn't look like much," Wise recalled later. "But he's very clever and very subtle.... You must not underestimate him.... You can't underestimate him or he'll kill you. He's very good at what he does."

By 1968, Rae had used these public skills to become a well-known figure on the university campus. He, Rose, and Ignatieff had developed reputations as campus intellectuals. With his tweed sports jacket and longish—but not too long—hair, Rae certainly looked the part. Ignatieff wrote eloquent essays on topics of world importance for *The Varsity*. Rae, who by 1968 was the campus newspaper's book editor, concentrated more on pithy, clever reviews. While other students might be frying their brains with LSD or watching hockey on television, these three were part of a small group that would stay up all night arguing about philosophy, religion, and politics. Rose argued the socialist position, Ignatieff was a Liberal, and Rae a liberal with doubts.

At the same time, Rae had also involved himself in the heady world of university politics. As his friend Ignatieff would note later, Rae "is fiercely ambitious." In 1968, Rae was elected to the university's Students' Administrative Council. There he developed a reputation as a moderate who could bridge the gap between the increasingly militant student left and those who were more conservative.

None of this put him at the forefront of student politics. Indeed, Rae scored second to last among the five council members elected from University College. He was dismissed as hopelessly bourgeois by those on the increasingly fashionable student left. And even among moderate student leaders, he was outshone by the student council president, a serious, articulate New Democrat named Steven Langdon.

However, as a student, Rae already demonstrated characteristics he would develop as a mature politician. First, he had an innate sense of caution. The late 1960s was a time for getting caught up in enthusiasms—be it for drugs or revolution. But Rae remained ever so slightly square. Unabashed admiration of Maoist China, for instance, although fashionable at the time, disturbed him. In *The Varsity*, he mused about the problem of allowing sentiment to cloud analytical judgment, noting that "compromised intellectuals seem to be a universal phenomenon."

Second, he got along with the enemy. Campus politics in the late 1960s had turned into a polarized confrontation between students and administrators over who would run the university. To his colleagues on the student council, Rae would give ringing speeches about student power. But university authorities, such as U of T president Claude Bissell, knew him as someone they could talk to. Rae's friend Graham Fraser later described him as "the kind of radical university administrators liked to deal with." Years later, as an aspiring politician hoping to win a Commons seat for the first time, a surprised Bob Rae would open his mail to discover a campaign contribution cheque from his old sparring partner, Claude Bissell.

Third, and most important, Rae was fascinated by abstractions. For most undergraduates, the entire issue of governance—how much say students had in running the university—was remarkably arcane and ultimately irrelevant. But student power fascinated student politicians, and none more than Rae. As a member of the Students' Administrative Council, Rae helped to negotiate, with university administrators and faculty, the creation of a new Commission on University Government. He then ran for, and was elected as a student member of, that commission. It deliberated and came up with a series of recommendations that ultimately formed a new basis for running the University of Toronto. This new formula was complicated, received massive attention from the campus press, opened up countless new possibilities for student politicians, and ultimately made absolutely no difference to the lives of most on campus. It was a perfect trial run for Rae's later constitutional jousts.

Meanwhile, events outside the university were beginning to shake Rae's instinctive liberalism. The Vietnam War seemed to exemplify what could happen when well-meaning liberal Democrats got caught up by a system bent on war and profit. Moreover, Vietnam struck a personal chord with Rae. Saul Rae had been a Canadian diplomat on the

International Control Commission which, in the 1950s and 1960s, had tried to mediate the escalating war in Vietnam. By late high school, Rae was becoming increasingly critical of the way the American—and Canadian—governments viewed the conflict in Vietnam. This, as he said later, brought him into direct conflict with his father.

In university, the distance between the Liberal politics of Saul Rae and his son's small-l liberalism widened. Reviewing a book by *New York Times* journalist James Reston, Rae wrote admiringly of the veteran reporter's old-fashioned "tweedy liberalism." Still, Rae continued, this kind of liberalism may no longer be enough. "The strength of the military-industrial power establishment makes old liberalism's approach somewhat dated and inadequate." For James Reston, Rae might well have substituted his own father.

However, the appearance of Pierre Trudeau briefly rekindled Rae's faith in the liberalism of the Liberals. To many young Canadians, Trudeau represented a real break with the past. In 1968, Rae and fellow *Varsity* staffer Rod Mickleburgh journeyed to Ottawa to work for Trudeau in the Liberal leadership convention. The pair ended up helping to put out Trudeau's campaign newsletter. Michael Ignatieff, meanwhile, was a Liberal delegate at that convention for Trudeau. In the election campaign that followed, Rae worked for Charles Caccia, a Toronto Liberal candidate who would later become a Trudeau cabinet minister.

However, the love affair with Trudeau did not last long. A few months after the 1968 election, Rae wrote a scathing essay in *The Varsity*, taking to task both Trudeau and the Liberal party. The election, he said, had revealed the Liberals were bereft of ideas. "There was no redeeming social content in Mr. Trudeau's speeches...." Rae wrote. "Instead of talking about mountains to climb, wars to win and diseases to conquer, Mr. Trudeau talked about the limitations of government, about people helping themselves, about pragmatism, pragmatism, pragmatism.... Mr. Trudeau, for all the fire of his youth ... is an intellectual conservative. His is a legal mind, his intellect austere. He sees things legally and institutionally."

Rae went on to mock Trudeau for sacrificing principle to this so-called pragmatism: "To those who criticize the Canadian government for its complicity in the Vietnam War, Mr. Trudeau talks about economic realities"—the jobs that flowed to Canadians from producing war material for the United States. But to Rae, this was bogus, another example of

Trudeau's ability to reduce issues to their most absurd extremes in order to win debate. "Patent nonsense," Rae called it. "Canada would not be reduced to a state of complete economic and physical degradation if it started asserting its economic and political independence."

Worse still was Trudeau's insistence on what Rae called the "rhetoric of limitations." Faced with the problem of unemployment, the Liberal government insisted it could do nothing. "The unemployment evident last summer and clearly in store for this winter has been met by cutbacks in government spending and determined attempts to balance the budget," Rae noted, adding "Whatever happened to that great Liberal John Maynard Keynes?"

That such a bankrupt party could sweep the country was a victory of style over substance. Certainly Trudeau was Canada's most interesting political leader; that was a given. Indeed, Rae took time to scold the New Democrats for their "almost unbearable self-righteousness" and for their refusal to challenge Trudeau with equally attractive politicians. "There is no reason apart from sheer blind stubbornness why the Canadian left should be stuck with leaders sounding (and looking) vaguely like Beatrice Webb...." he wrote. "The grey old spinster with wire glasses and sneakers has become the national image of the NDP."

Still, Rae concluded, progressives — presumably including himself — had been sucked in. "It is a sad reflection on the intellectual sterility of Canadian politics that so many sympathizers of the NDP came around for Mr. Trudeau in 1968: the only explanation — apart from his position on Quebec — is that the man was so much more intelligent and tough-minded than anything Canadians had been exposed to in living memory.... But surely the infatuation with intelligence should come to an abrupt halt. Those interested in radical social change and reform should no more look to Mr. Trudeau than the Progressives and CCFers looked to Mr. [William Lyon Mackenzie] King.

"For Willy King is alive and well, jazzed up and wearing sandals. The language is new ... but the message is the same. Go slow; don't take chances and whatever the cost stay away from basic principles."

Rae's essay was an early and devastatingly accurate portrayal of Trudeau's own form of individualistic liberalism. Ironically, the same characteristics he found so objectionable in Trudeau — the elevation of pragmatism over abstract principle, the "infatuation with intelligence," the triumph of business-as-usual — would end up being the hallmarks of Rae's own time in power.

Later in life, Rae would confide to aide Rob Mitchell that he had been seriously involved with only two women—one of whom he married. That one was Arlene Perly, a vivacious and popular drama student at the University of Toronto who also wrote occasionally for *The Varsity*. Rae knew her there, but never, it seems, had the nerve to ask her out on a date. Indeed, according to Lenny Wise, Rae's terrible luck with women was one of the foundations of their friendship. "When you have two guys striking out regularly, you have something in common." Wise maintained that one of the reasons why Rae never got anywhere was that he seemed to be attracted only to middle-class, Jewish women. And at that time, the women he asked out were interested in dating only middle-class, Jewish men. "Oh, we couldn't go out with Bob—he's not Jewish; that was the routine," said Wise.

Until 1969: that was Rae's last year at the University of Toronto. It was also the year he went on an exchange weekend to Harvard. Rae had met Jonathan Guss on a previous Harvard exchange, two years earlier. The two would become fast friends. But this time, he met someone even more important—Esther Myers, his first serious girlfriend.

Myers had been active in the campus Jewish student organization, Hillel. It was there she met and briely dated Lenny Wise. In fact, for a while, Myers dated both Wise and Rae who developed a fierce, if friendly, rivalry.

"I can remember once walking along the street with Esther," recalled Wise later. "I had her hand and I was pulling her over to my side, and he kept pulling her over to his side. It was a tug of war, which is childish. I know that it happened. I know also that we were pushing for her to make a decision."

For Myers, a serene brunette who later taught yoga in Toronto, there was no contest. She and Rae, she said, knew they were soul mates from the first time they set eyes on each other. "We just met and were attracted to each other.... It didn't have to do with having a lot in common and getting to know each other better and all that kind of stuff."

Luckily, both were already planning to go to England the following year. Rae had won a coveted Rhodes scholarship to study at Oxford. Myers was planning to do graduate work in philosophy in London. She was quickly swept into Rae's circle. He took her to the family cottage on Big Rideau, where she met his parents. He also introduced her to his brother David and sister, Jennifer. "She was fun," recalled Myers. "They're alike in many ways.... That was at the stage when you could

sit on Jennifer's front porch and she'd say 'Pierre called yesterday.'"
Back on the campus, Rae, Myers and Michael Ignatieff—Rae's roommate—spent much of their time together.

Myers went to England that summer. But instead of entering graduate school, she took a job as a social worker in London. Rae followed in the fall and took up his studies at Oxford. On weekends, he would come down to London to see Myers. He introduced her to his grandmother, Mildred George, and to his old friend Jeff Rose.

Rose had gone to England a year ahead of Rae to study at the London School of Economics. But, swept up in a new bout of student activism, he had quit university to study on his own. It was a heady time of ideas and more ideas. By 1970, Rose had moved from London into a small cottage near Oxford. Myers would later remember him sitting in the cottage, madly working away at what she laughingly referred to as "the next major philosophic work."

That lasted for a year. Then Myers's mother became ill, and Esther increasingly depressed. By the end of 1970, she had joined a group centred around radical psychotherapist R.D. Laing. At a time when most psychiatrists were still prescribing pills or electro-shock therapy for depression, Laing was unique. He taught that individuals were actually no crazier than society as a whole; rather than suppress mental anguish, the affected person should try to work through it.

Working through her depression was a full-time occupation for Myers. By 1971, caught up in her own problems, she drifted away from Rae and his circle.

Meanwhile at Oxford, Rae was wrestling with his own problems. Partly under the influence of Jeff Rose, he was moving intellectually into the orbit of social-democratic thinkers. This led him into an investigation of Beatrice and Sidney Webb, central figures in the turn-of-the-century Fabian Society—that group of middle-class intellectuals who had provided much of the ideological content of the British Labour Party. For his Bachelor of Philosophy degree, Rae submitted a ninety-eight-page dissertation that was a fundamental—and at times scathing—revision of the conventional Labour view of the Webbs.

The intellectual left, Rae wrote, had tended to idolize the Webbs. In fact, they were racists and middle-class élitists, contemptuous of much of the working classes they claimed to represent.

For the Webbs, Rae continued disapprovingly, socialism was both the logical extension of nineteenth-century liberal capitalism and a way to prevent this national degradation. Their "socialism ... was not a revolt against efficient management, large organizations or the complex division of labour, but in some sense their rational extension." This in turn meant that socialism, as defined by the Webbs, was not directed against the middle classes. In fact, it was in the interests of these classes to embrace scientific socialism, for otherwise the poor might seize power themselves.

As for the poor, they were not one homogeneous group. The Webbs had concluded that some were "innocent," others "hardened vagrants." Poverty should be dealt with not by handing out money indiscriminately to all the poor but through a minimum, or guaranteed, annual income at a level sufficiently low so as not to encourage malingering. Indeed, the poor had as much of an obligation to society as society to the poor. Social programs should not be universal, the Webbs wrote. Society's money should be granted only to those poor who agreed to use it for moral improvement.

"Their [the Webbs'] appeal," wrote Rae, "was addressed to the middle classes, and indeed, to the governing section of the upper middle class." The Webbs saw their Fabian platform as one that was above petty partisan squabbling, for it was concerned with "the efficiency of the country as a whole." Trade unions, while deemed necessary by the Webbs, were useful only if "workers and consumers worked in a partnership." To implement this program, the state had to rely not on the poor or working classes but on a new breed of neutral civil servants, "disinterested experts and scientific intellectuals." In the political arena, these were to be joined by professional politicians whose task would be as much to educate their constituents as to listen to them.

Throughout his thesis, Rae's reaction to the Webbs was one of mild distaste. Certainly he was appalled by their reliance on racism, eugenics, and the sense that history was moving towards an inevitable end. But he also argued that the pair had fundamentally confused any kind of state collective action with socialism. "This is mistaken," Rae wrote, "because it blurs important distinctions as to why the state has decided to interfere, what kind of policy it is implementing and in whose general interest this intervention is carried out." Although Rae does not state so directly, throughout his thesis there is an assumption that different classes have antagonistic interests. The Webbs' early insistence that state action could represent all, he wrote, "accounts in some part for their facile optimism."

In fact, this failure to acknowledge different class interests, Rae

wrote, permeated Ramsay MacDonald's Labour government of 1929.
MacDonald, in an ill-advised effort to protect the British pound, had broken with his own party's policies to form, in 1931, a coalition government with the opposition Tories. The result was to split and cripple the Labour Party for a decade. (The pound, incidentally, ended up being devalued anyway.)

Sidney Webb himself was a minister in the 1929 government and, Rae wrote, placed more faith in his civil servants than in his party's platform—with disastrous results. His timidity was reflected in the rest of the MacDonald government as it tried to deal unsuccessfully with the crisis of the 1930s.

"The determination to occupy the middle ground only resulted in the Conservatives effectively emasculating even the smallest reform," wrote Rae. He quoted with approval economic historian R.H. Tawney's 1932 assessment of the MacDonald government: "The Labour Party," Tawney had written, "is hesitant in action, because divided in mind. It does not achieve what it could, because it does not know what it wants. It frets out of office and fumbles in it, because it lacks the assurance either to wait or to strike. Being without clear convictions as to its own meaning and purpose, it is deprived of the dynamic which only convictions supply. If it neither acts with decision nor inspires others so to act, the principal reason is that it is itself undecided."

Rae was also critical of the way the Webbs approached welfare reform. Their division of the poor into deserving and undeserving, as well as their insistence that recipients of welfare be forced to improve themselves, smacked of paternalism. "There is remarkably little in the Webbs' argument which would appeal to the working class, or, indeed, to the unemployed," he wrote. Indeed, the manner in which the Webbs couched their brand of socialism offended Rae. Their reliance on so-called science and on technocratic solutions ignored fundamental human values, such as dignity and equality.

"The Webbs were insensitive to very real problems for socialists, to 'abstractions' like freedom and equality," Rae wrote. While their critique of the inequities of capitalism was "an example of social criticism and analysis at its finest," the theory they espoused—of gradualism and the commonality of interest among classes—possessed a fundamental weakness. That weakness was their conviction—which Rae believed misplaced—that, eventually and inevitably, socialism as they defined it would triumph.

"Once the belief in inevitability had [*sic*] disappeared," he warned, "the socialism of gradualism can easily become that of accommodation and opportunism." That, he noted, was precisely the fate that had befallen Ramsay MacDonald's Labour government. Its accommodation with its enemies among the owning classes, its failure to articulate and stick to its own set of socialist principles, doomed it to irrelevance, extinction, and ignominy.

Many of Rae's criticisms of the Webbs stuck with him through his later political career. His mistrust of received socialist ideology — including public ownership as an end in itself—remained. So did his insistence that politics must reflect fundamental liberal human values. As he told *The Toronto Star*'s Judy Steed later, the élitism of the Webbs continued to offend him.

Yet much of what he found disturbing about the Webbs ended up resurfacing in Rae's own actions once he took power: the reliance on professional civil servants; the emphasis on pitching social democracy to the middle classes; the insistence on social partnerships and the refusal to acknowledge that different groups in society—business, labour, the rich, the poor—could have fundamentally different interests.

At Oxford, Rae was scathing about the Webbs' approach to welfare reform, their division of the poor into deserving and undeserving, and their insistence that relief be granted only to those willing to undertake self-improvement. Yet this was precisely the kind of welfare reform his government would end up contemplating.

Rae's ideological journey at Oxford, from being a small-l liberal with misgivings to becoming a sceptical social democrat, had profound repercussions in his own psyche. On the one side were the expectations of his family—that he gain a doctorate and then pursue a noble career in academe, the public service, or legitimate (that is, Liberal) politics. On the other was the spirit of the times. Britain, with its explicit system of class distinctions, offended Rae's liberal sensibilities. The effete and cloistered nature of Oxford academic life began to seem increasingly irrelevant.

"I wanted to break out of the mould," Rae said later. "If you grow up a certain way, you're stereotyped, limited. I didn't want to live like that, in a box." After finishing his thesis on the Webbs in 1971, Rae told reporter Jeffrey Simpson, he "began to feel slightly out of touch." This worked itself into a full-blown depression.

"I felt a kind of depression and uncertainty about myself that I had never felt before," Rae said later. "It lasted for about a year. I went to a psychotherapist twice a week."

For about two years, Rae wandered the world, both literally and spiritually. He visited friends in North America and Europe, working as a lecturer at the London School of Economics and Massachusetts's Radcliffe College. He talked to friends constantly about his doubts, his dilemma, the blackness that had descended on him. He abandoned plans to go for an Oxford doctorate and decided to be content with the lesser, although still prestigious, Bachelor of Philosophy degree.

"He needed to talk," said Jonathan Guss, who at the time was a diplomat at the Canadian embassy in The Hague. Rae, he said, would come to visit and stay up all night talking with either Guss or Leslie Milrod, Guss's wife. They would talk about the condition of the world and whether it was possible to change the state of people's existence.

"I was feeling lost," Rae would say later. "The idea of going on and trying to achieve great academic goals didn't seem worthwhile. I had no sense of direction."

But there seemed to be no way out. By 1973, he was in London, where he worked for about eighteen months with squatters, first at a legal-aid clinic and later with tenants. "There were a lot of London flats that were not being used properly, that were being left empty," he said later. "I learned how to change locks; I found I was good with a screwdriver."

He re-established contact with Esther Myers. "I think leaving Oxford left him in a kind of limbo," said Myers later. "If not this, then what?"

Myers was still part of the group around R.D. Laing, a school which believed that the psychological problems of individuals were grounded in the contradictions of society. Indeed, many British Laingians were doing the same kind of work as Rae—toiling with the poor, in part as an attempt to sort out their own lives.

Initially, Rae's work with the homeless seemed to make him even more depressed. "Close up and seeing how people had to live, it must have done him in," said Lenny Wise. "He had led a privileged existence. Even though his parents aren't rich, they had always lived in beautiful houses supplied by the federal government. And he had servants.... Now he was living in the streets of London and seeing what people really lived like." Myers, who herself had done social work in London, had similar memories: "He'd be in direct contact with that kind of poverty, and it's wrenching."

Guss, however, describes this as a pensive, rather than a black, period for Rae. "It was natural for the era. It was probably formative for him. It was when he stopped being what some had come to perceive as an extremely bright egghead, bordering on the arrogant. He came out a much more sensitive and sensible person who just dealt with people straight up."

Others who knew him then say that Rae's psychological depression was deep, black and long-lasting—a profound crisis of self-identity during which he did not know who he was or what he stood for. Even Myers, who had gone through a similar experience herself, said Rae's depression was worse.

Rae would later talk of that experience as an epiphany. Working with the poor, he said, once again gave him a sense of purpose. Talking to a journalist a few months before he was elected premier, he recalled meeting a Mrs. Blair during his London period. "She was having some problems, but she was strong. The next time she came in, she was in tears; she had broken down. And I helped her."

By 1974, he was back in Canada—penniless and without a job. But the conflict between his old and new values, his family's expectations and his recent experience working with the poor, his ambitions and his social conscience were at least partially resolved. He would do good, but as a social democrat rather than a Liberal. He would go to law school. And he would enter politics—but not in the easy way. He would not—as his brother John had done—operate through the governing Liberals. Rather, Bob Rae would take the harder route. He would join the NDP. It would be his crown of thorns, his expiation, his sacrifice.

Upon returning to Canada, he looked up old friends. Initially, he bunked in with D'Arcy Martin and Anita Shilton. Martin had been a fellow member of the University of Toronto's Commission on University Government.

Rae also contacted Lenny Wise, who eventually helped him move from Martin's home to a succession of dreary rooming-houses. Rae managed to pick up an old piano, however, and would spend hours in his room, playing and composing songs.

At law school, he used his facility with languages to do legal-aid work for immigrant workers. One evening in 1975 or 1976, Rae found himself at a crowded house party in Toronto's east end. The music was loud, the room smoky. But over in a corner was someone Rae had known through the U of T student left, a journalist named Bob Parkins.

Parkins remembered Rae as a somewhat preppy undergraduate. But
he had always liked him. Moreover, by huddling with Rae, he could
avoid being drawn into interminable discussions about Maoism and
Angolan politics, a fate that always seemed to dog him at these kinds of
parties in the mid-1970s.

Rae explained his predicament. He was a social democrat now, he
said, anxious to connect with the Canadian labour movement. But he
didn't know anyone in labour. Could Parkins help?

Indeed, he could. Parkins played hockey once a week with a group of
old friends. One was Peter Warrian, a former student radical who had
headed the Canadian Union of Students when Rae was involved in
student politics. Warrian now worked for the United Steelworkers of
America, a union with close ties to the NDP. Parkins would mention
Rae's name.

Warrian too might well have been surprised that the Rae he had
known in student days was now a social democrat. But Rae was smart
and, thanks to his efforts with immigrant workers, had credentials. The
Steelworkers were happy to have the young law student article with
their general counsel.

Rae had now made a connection with organized labour. The next
step was the NDP itself. Here, the intermediary was to be Lenny Wise.
Although not a New Democrat himself, Wise knew all the people at the
centre, particularly the Lewis family. He had worked on campaigns for
both David Lewis, the federal leader, and his son Stephen. He also
knew Janet Solberg, Stephen's sister and a former president of the
Ontario NDP, as well as their brother Michael, a party organizer with
ties to the Steelworkers.

Wise took Rae to NDP headquarters and introduced him to all there.
Later, Wise recalled it as a disaster. "I introduced him to the whole
shebang—the mafia, the NDP mafia—who completely ignored him.
One hundred per cent. Completely, completely ignored him. They
didn't want to meet him; they didn't want to know him; they couldn't
give a shit about who he was." Finally, Michael Lewis reluctantly agreed
to take Wise and his friend to lunch. "So, he takes us to lunch, plunks us
in a restaurant, sits down at a table, and promptly runs off to say hello to
all his union buddies, leaving us sitting staring at each other."

At the time, many in the NDP were suspicious of this golden-haired
convert to social democracy, this Liberal diplomat's son who seemed to
be coming on so fast. "I'd been an organizer for the party from 1975 to

1977, and I'd never met him before," said Richard Johnston, a former MPP who ran against Rae for the Ontario NDP leadership.

Indeed, many New Democrats remained suspicious. "He engenders a lot of personal antagonism," explained Janet Solberg, who, in 1991–92, would work for Rae. "I think that's so unfair. Maybe [it's because] he has less connection with the party and the labour movement than others." She laughed. "You know he was a labour lawyer once, for six days or something. Six minutes."

Rae himself was aware of the shallowness of his NDP roots. Attacks on his Liberal background, he told a reporter in 1980, "used to bother me because I think anyone is sensitive about criticism about which they feel insecure. And if you feel, as I felt, that I was something of an outsider, then it makes you nervous. I used to think, 'What if everyone believed that I was some kind of weird fop who, by some sort of mistake, had gotten involved.'"

By 1978, however, Rae had come to the notice of both the NDP brass and political journalists. John Gilbert, the New Democrat member for the Toronto riding of Broadview–Greenwood, had been appointed to the bench, and a federal by-election was being called. Within the NDP, Broadview–Greenwood was known as a safe seat. Whoever took the party's nomination would almost certainly win a place in the House of Commons.

Rae had still not made much of an impression on the NDP establishment. "I don't remember Bob being thought of as anything other than a good candidate then," recalled Stephen Lewis, who at the time was stepping down as leader of the Ontario party. "He was not yet seen as the bright light he would later become." But John Gilbert was impressed and, while officially neutral, let it be known that the young articling law student was his choice. To make the point clearer, Gilbert's wife explicitly supported Rae.

Still the Broadview–Greenwood nomination was not a cakewalk. Rae was up against former MPP John Harney and veteran NDP feminist Kay Macpherson. Luckily, Rae also had the talents of his sister, Jennifer. Making use of a wide network of friends and acquaintances — many of whom usually voted Liberal — she managed to stack the nomination meeting with the new, younger professionals who were moving into the riding. "She rounded up hundreds of people," recalls Lenny Wise. "And we stuffed them into a high-school auditorium." Rae won the nomination. As expected, the NDP won the by-election.

Bob Rae arrived in Ottawa less as a new boy in the world of federal politics than as someone who had finally, after a long and circuitous detour, arrived back home. In the Commons, he was precocious and always quotable. Lines that he had used with great effect back in his old debating days at university—such as "You can't just sit down and discuss a menu with a bunch of cannibals"—were welcomed, particularly by a jaded parliamentary press gallery that had become weary of the Trudeau Liberals.

Indeed, Rae's university experience was perfectly suited to Parliament, where members are expected to excoriate each other in public but get along in private. In university debating—at which Rae excelled—the paramount skill is to be able to argue, at a moment's notice and with great conviction, any side of any issue, no matter how absurd. Rae could do this and was quickly appointed his party's finance critic, even though—as he acknowledged later—he and his principal aide, Arlene Wortsman, had only three university economics courses between them.

Whether Rae truly believed in what was then the NDP's economic platform—massive government spending to create jobs, interest-rate and price controls, public ownership in the energy sector, and radical reform of the corporate-income-tax system—is now unclear. Certainly, he did not follow any of these prescriptions upon winning power in Ontario a decade later. But, at the time, he certainly sounded as if he meant what he said.

Still, there were warning signs. Travelling by taxi on the way to an Ottawa television studio, Rae and Conservative finance critic John Crosbie amused each other by engaging in the old debating trick: Rae argued for Tory economic policies; Crosbie took the NDP side. Once at the studio, they reversed positions and, before the cameras, went at each other hammer and tongs—Rae for the New Democrats, Crosbie for the Tories.

Rae's retreat, once in power, from so much of what had been the received NDP doctrine he used to argue for so eloquently has been taken by some New Democrats as evidence that he was never serious—that social-democratic politics was always to him a debating game, an intellectual exercise. Others are more charitable. "His actions and his arguments are not always in sync," said one who has worked with Rae. "He's not always consistent. Sometimes, he just follows an argument to its logical end because he gets carried up in it. But it's more than arguing just for the sake of arguing, more than just debating. He can believe in what he says *for that period of time*."

By 1979, his political career in hand, Rae turned back to his personal life. His attentions were now focused on Arlene Perly. She was to be his second serious romance.

Although Esther Myers had returned to Canada in 1975, her relationship with Rae had never been revived. Myers, who had returned because her mother was said to be near death, made a stab at contacting her old boyfriend. "I was upset at the time and sort of hanging around, doing nothing," she said. "I had one contact with him then for help, and he said: 'Look, get a job.' And it was really helpful, just in terms of giving me something pragmatic to do."

Except for a note several years later when he was premier, this was the last real contact Myers had with Rae. "He's got his life now," she mused later. "An old girlfriend around is hard to put together with that. I think it's unfortunate. I know Arlene. She and I have no problem.... But I think it's hard for him, and therefore he kind of kept a distance. I mean, he's a good friend and a loyal friend ... [but, for him,] it's a question of keeping things in compartments. And he wants to keep the compartment of his marriage intact."

As well, Myers felt she reminded Rae too much of his year of psychological turmoil in England: "I'd seen him in that dark period. He didn't like to be seen that way."

Unlike Myers, Arlene Perly was active in both labour and NDP politics. In fact, she had joined the NDP before Rae. Perly had become an Air Canada flight attendant while working on her M.A. in drama at the University of Toronto and was actively involved in her union. There she met Julie Davis, a labour activist who would later become Ontario NDP president.

However, Perly also had a busy social life. During the week, she would study for her M.A. and work as a teaching assistant. She always had a boyfriend. On weekends, she would fly off to London or Paris as part of her Air Canada job. "I used to worry that the engineers who had me as their drama teaching assistant would run into their serious, feminist lecturer as a flight attendant on an air trip and flip," she told a reporter later. "Those were still the days when we would see how short we could get away with wearing our uniform skirts."

Rae's approach to Perly was, as usual, complicated. He pursued her with both vigour and reluctance. Apart from anything else, winning Perly's hand appealed to his competitive instincts. Perly was attractive, and Rae, as she told a reporter later, was "one of those people who get

better-looking over the years." As well, according to her friend Lenny
Wise, she was dating two other men at the time Rae appeared on the
scene. Finally, there was the religion problem. Perly was Jewish; Rae
Anglican. "Her parents were not thrilled," said Wise. As Rae confided
to one old comrade during that period, his relationship with Arlene was
troubled. Still, he was not about to give up. In 1979, Rae bet Wise one
dollar he would marry Perly within a year.

To other friends, however, Rae had been expressing reservations
about marriage. He had just come to Ottawa and was leading an active
and draining political life. Would marriage fit into this life? Would it be
fair to Arlene to ask her to marry him? What if she accepted? Rae
dithered. His Ottawa friends pressed him to marry Perly. She was, they
said, perfect. Eventually, he decided. In 1980, Lenny Wise received a
telephone call. It was Rae. All he said was, "You owe me a dollar."

By 1981, life seemed golden for Rae. He had kept his seat in the
election of the previous year and was beloved by the NDP. He was
smart; he made sense; and—miracle of miracles—with his quick wit
and bright quips, he could make the television news. As a student, he
had once complained that "the grey old spinster with wire glasses and
sneakers has become the national image of the NDP"; now, Rae himself
was managing to change that image.

As well, he and Perly quickly involved themselves in the business of
making a family. That summer, their first daughter, Judith, was born, to
be followed over the next four years by Lisa and Eleanor. Summers
were spent with Lenny and Sandy Wise at a rented cottage in Muskoka.
Rae's circle of friends expanded. In Ottawa he and John Honderich,
then parliamentary bureau chief for *The Toronto Star*, had become fast
friends. Honderich would later become editor-in-chief of the *Star*, the
country's largest newspaper. At Lake of Bays, Wise introduced Rae to
Brian Segal, who would later become publisher of *Maclean's*, the
country's largest news magazine. Rae also kept up his childhood friendship with Graham Fraser, later to be Ottawa bureau chief for *The Globe
and Mail*.

Rae was a keen and skilful tennis player. Soon he was playing tennis
regularly with other up-and-coming young professionals. He had good
contacts; he had respect; and—if he could wait a few years—he also
had the best chance of replacing Ed Broadbent as federal NDP leader.

It was into this Eden that Stephen Lewis, Gerry Caplan, and others
connected to the Ontario party came calling. Lewis, who had recently

stepped down as leader of the Ontario NDP, was a kingpin in the party, with close ties to organized labour and the entire Eastern New Democratic establishment. Caplan, a former federal secretary of the NDP, was a skilled political operative and Lewis loyalist. They had an offer for Rae—a tempting one that he would find hard to refuse.

The Ontario party, Rae was told, was in disastrous shape. Under Michael Cassidy, the leader who had replaced Lewis in 1978, it was going nowhere. Cassidy, a humourless former financial journalist, had no ability to communicate, no pizazz, and now—thank God—he had agreed to step down. Yet the Ontario NDP held great potential. It had been the official opposition in 1975—a position its federal counterpart had never come close to reaching. With luck, hard work, and a new, bright leader, they told Rae, the NDP might win power in Ontario. Rae, they said, should be that leader.

Rae was unsure. He liked the federal stage, felt comfortable in Ottawa. He liked talking about the grand issues of the day—monetary policy, macro-economic policy, the constitution. He knew nothing of the Ontario party and little about Ontario issues. He was happy.

But the pressure kept up. It was his duty, he was told. It was his fate. And if he became leader of the Ontario NDP, he might—he just might—end up as premier.

3

Party Animals

FOR THE NDP, THE NIGHT OF SEPTEMBER 6, 1990, WAS a scene of crazy jubilation. After decades in opposition and two near misses, the party had finally—finally—won power in Canada's largest province. At Rae's victory party, upstairs in La Rotonda banquet hall, on Toronto's Dufferin Street, the high and mighty of the NDP came to pay homage. Stephen Lewis and his wife, Michele Landsberg—up to this point at least, acknowledged within the NDP as the First Family of Ontario socialism—made their way up the stairs and through the milling crowd. For Lewis, there was a bittersweet element to the euphoria: more than a decade earlier he had hoped to be the one to make the historic breakthrough, and the failure rankled yet. Still, the NDP was his party and Rae a leader whom he had been instrumental in putting into place. The grin splitting the shark-like face that had once delighted political cartoonists was genuine. Landsberg, *The Toronto Star*'s pugnacious feminist columnist, was less enthusiastic about Rae; he was a bit too know-it-all for her taste. But the new premier seemed sincerely interested in the kinds of women's issues that moved Landsberg; and his caucus contained some strong new feminist members. So she, like her husband, was smiling.

Sprinkled throughout were other NDP luminaries, such as Canadian Auto Workers chief Bob White, Leo Gerard of the Steelworkers, Ontario NDP president Julie Davis. All were there to see the man they regarded as their premier in his first moment of glory. Over the next four years, many would become bitter critics of the government.

But that evening, there was no hint of the trouble to come. At the front, Rae, wearing the double-breasted blue suit that had become the trademark of his campaign and flanked by his wife and his sister, Jennifer, took the accolades with careful humility. During the campaign, Rae had savagely attacked the personal integrity of his Liberal opponent, David Peterson. But, on this night, vitriol was to be put aside. Peterson, Rae said, had waged his campaign with dignity, adding, "We've been there ourselves." The lesson of this campaign, he told the crowd, was that public trust must be earned. "We did not expect this result," he added.

Indeed, he had not. As Rae would admit later, he had been prepared to call it quits after the 1990 campaign, resign the leadership of his party, and retreat to something more cerebral. Perhaps he would write a book, he had told associates. And to this end, throughout 1989, Rae had been puttering away at a word processor in the corner of his office, trying to put into written form his thoughts on social democracy and the future of the NDP. "What We Owe Each Other," the result of this musing, was a rambling document linking Rae's reflections on the Fabians (from his Oxford Bachelor of Philosophy thesis) and his thoughts on his brother David's death. It touched on Native rights, the environmental movement, and the power of love. But a hard-edged political manifesto it was not. Nor, to be fair, was it meant to be. Rather, "What We Owe Each Other" seemed to be the swansong of someone who, at a fundamental level, felt he had failed in politics, who felt his party had failed and was trying to figure out why. Unfortunately for the NDP in 1990, it was virtually the only political program the party possessed.

The Ontario NDP, like its federal counterpart, had its roots in the Great Depression of the 1930s. Populist parties had long existed in Ontario. The great wave of rural populism which had swept North America during the late nineteenth and early twentieth centuries had brought the United Farmers of Ontario (UFO) into being. In combination with independent Labour MPPs, the United Farmers swept to power in 1919, in the midst of a post-war recession. But the farmer-labour government soon collapsed, torn by the contradictions of its constituent groups and lacking a clear platform that would give it reason for existence. By the 1930s, most UFO politicians, except for a few diehards, had been swept into the provincial Liberals.

The Co-operative Commonwealth Federation (CCF) was determined
to avoid the ideological fuzziness of its populist predecessors. The plat-
forms of the CCF, particularly the Regina Manifesto of 1933, established
it, intellectually at least, as a socialist party in the so-called scientific tradition of European social democracy. It would have a program, based on
public ownership of vital industries, peaceful parliamentary democracy,
and planning. Its base would be the farmers, who wanted better prices;
working people, who wanted jobs; and, in the words of the Regina Manifesto, "all who believe that the time has come for a far-reaching reconstruction of our economic and political institutions."

The Ontario CCF was quickly organized along similar lines. The CCF
had been set up as a decentralized party, dominated in large part by its
provincial organizations. But the struggles of the federal and Ontario
organizations quickly became intertwined. Not only was Ontario the
electoral and economic powerhouse of the Dominion, but both parties
faced the same internal divisions — between farmers and labour,
between purists who wanted to build a truly socialist party and those
who wanted parliamentary seats, between Toronto intellectuals who
contributed much of the ideological verve of the new party and almost
everyone else. By 1934, the fractious Ontario CCF was deemed too
radical by the national party. Federal leader J.S. Woodsworth moved in
and disbanded the provincial leadership.

The Ontario CCF's first high point came in 1943. Riding on wartime
disillusionment with the old-line parties, the CCF had become Ontario's
official opposition, with thirty-four seats. In 1945, under the leadership
of Ted Jolliffe, it seemed poised to seize power from George Drew's
Conservatives. But in the campaign, Jolliffe charged that the government was using the Ontario Provincial Police to infiltrate the CCF. His
strategy backfired. In the ensuing election, the CCF was reduced to an
eight-seat rump. The party recovered its official-opposition status again
in 1948. But in the 1952 election, it crashed again, emerging with only
two seats.

In 1953, federal leaders parachuted Donald MacDonald into Ontario
with the task of rebuilding the provincial party. It was no easy job.

MacDonald was by no means a doctrinaire socialist. As a young
man, he had flirted strongly with the idea of running as a Conservative,
but during the Depression was instead drawn into the CCF. A practical
man, MacDonald set out to rebuild the Ontario CCF along lines that
would make sense to the majority of voters. Party policies during the

MacDonald period were moderately collectivist; the CCF called for public health insurance and public ownership of the natural-gas distribution system. But MacDonald was perhaps best known for his humanist instincts—his emphasis on prison reform, for instance. As well, he effectively hammered away at the ruling Tories over a series of conflict-of-interest scandals, ranging from natural gas to land development.

MacDonald set a tone for the Ontario CCF-NDP that persisted into the 1980s: it was to be the party of a few moderate but dearly held principles; it would stand up for the dispossessed; it would have moral integrity.

But MacDonald fell victim to the urge for youth and change which swept Canada in the late 1960s. In 1961, the CCF had been reconstituted as the NDP. That change brought organized labour more directly into the running of the party; adherents hoped that, in return, the new party would gain the votes of unionized workers. In 1968, Canada went through its own belated version of Camelot with the election of Pierre Trudeau. By 1970, the Ontario NDP figured it was its turn. In a carefully engineered coup, MacDonald was replaced with thirty-three-year-old Stephen Lewis.

Lewis was from a different milieu. Articulate, passionate, and possessing an appreciation of his own political and oratorical qualities, Lewis had grown up with social democracy. His grandfather had been a socialist in Russian Poland; his father, David, had been the motive force behind the 1961 merger of the unions and the CCF.

Stephen; his brother, Michael; and his sister, Janet Solberg, became legendary in the NDP. Along with allies such as Gerry Caplan, the Lewises organized ridings that had never been organized, developed campaign strategies that had never been tried. Aided by their father's strong ties to the labour movement, they dominated the back-rooms of NDP conventions—twisting arms, doing deals, arranging outcomes. In 1968, Stephen was dispatched to Vancouver to persuade federal leader Tommy Douglas to make way for David Lewis (Douglas refused and held on until 1971). In 1970, Lewis's manoeuvrings in Ontario were more successful. Donald MacDonald stepped down, and Lewis, with a studied appeal to the left of the party, took over the Ontario NDP.

The party Lewis inherited was itself in the process of becoming re-invigorated. The so-called Red Belt around the nickel mining town of Sudbury had produced three MPPs—Bud Germa, Elie Martel, and Floyd Laughren—firmly on the left of the party. Germa was an old-time

socialist, a smelter worker with no love for either civil servants or the
academic theorists who frequented the NDP. Laughren would later fondly recall him as a "real hard-hat." Martel, a gruff, opinionated ex-teacher, was able to flourish as NDP House leader in the clubby back-rooms of Queen's Park, making deals with his Liberal and Tory counterparts while at the same time regularly calling for the national-ization of the giant Sudbury nickel mine owned by Inco Ltd.

Laughren, a community college economics teacher and son of an illiterate farmer, was the most easy-going of the Sudbury trio. But he was just as much a left-winger. For Lewis, trying to do the familiar NDP balancing act of soft-pedalling left-of-centre policies to a conservative electorate, the three were constant burrs beneath the saddle.

At the same time, Lewis's NDP had drawn to it a combination of activists and eccentrics. Millionaire Morton Shulman, for instance, used his position as the NDP member for High Park to carry on his various crusades against organized crime and corruption. Shulman, who entered the public eye as Toronto's fighting coroner (and became the model for a successful CBC television series), was adept at political theatre. At one point, he scandalized even the loose decorum of the leg-islature by brandishing a .22-calibre automatic rifle.

Coming into the 1970s, the NDP—particularly in Ontario—was torn by one of the grand ideological debates that have resurfaced throughout the party's history: Should it return to the more socialist roots of the Regina Manifesto? Or should it continue to water down its socialist content in the hope of winning more parliamentary seats? The debate over the Waffle group (so called because its adherents argued that, if they had to waffle, they would waffle leftwards) also split the party along one of its perennial fault lines, eventually pitting the Toronto intellectual wing (plus a strong contingent in Saskatchewan) against the parliamentary and union leadership.

In terms of content, the Wafflers were hardly extreme. They called for limited public ownership, along the lines of the Regina Manifesto, plus a strong dose of economic nationalism. Initially, in fact, the Waffle attracted a good many from the party establishment, such as future federal leader Ed Broadbent and Lewis loyalist Gerald Caplan, both of whom later dropped out.

But more important than the Waffle's content was its style. It was suffused with the energy (and arrogance) of the student movement of the late 1960s. Wafflers were determined to contest what they regarded as the tired old shibboleths of the parliamentary NDP. Their nationalism (and hence their suspicion of international unions) did not endear them to Canada's labour leaders.

In April 1971, Waffle leader Jim Laxer challenged Stephen Lewis's father, David, for the leadership of the federal party. To the consternation of the party establishment, Laxer placed a strong second. The Ontario election a few months later was marked by infighting between Wafflers and other New Democrats. Finally, in early 1972, Stephen Lewis decided to make his move against a faction which, to him, had become a party within the party. That March, he launched a blistering attack on the Waffle. An investigation into the faction was ordered by the party's Ontario executive. At a meeting of the NDP Provincial Council in Orillia that summer, the issue came to a head. Whether the Waffle was purged, as its adherents charged, or whether it simply chose martyrdom over compromise, the result was the same. The faction was, to all intents and purposes, eliminated from the Ontario NDP.

Individual Wafflers, such as economist Mel Watkins and Laxer, drifted back into the margins of the party (Laxer later drifted out again). But the intellectual focus provided by the Waffle, a focus which allowed the NDP to challenge the increasingly conservative ideology of North American society, was gone. There would still continue to be a left caucus within the NDP. But increasingly it would become marginalized, discounted by the majority of the party as a refuge for Trotskyists and malcontents.

Instead, the Ontario party attempted to latch on to some of the concerns popular with an urban electorate. Lewis campaigned furiously against urban development of farmland in Southern Ontario and clearcut logging in Northern Ontario, policies which probably won the NDP few friends in northern and rural areas but which were popular in downtown Toronto ridings. More importantly, he focused public attention on occupational health and safety.

With the trade unions still unable to deliver their members at election time, the NDP became increasingly concerned with courting single-issue voters. Anyone with any beef against any government could be sure to have a friend in the NDP. It supported residents east of Toronto who didn't want a second international airport built in their region. It supported residents west of Toronto who didn't want the existing international airport expanded. And it supported aircraft workers who wanted anything built that would increase the demand for airplanes. It supported environmentalists who wanted the province rid of pop in cans. And it supported Hamilton steelworkers who made, and wanted to keep making, those cans. It supported anti-nuclear activists, determined to shut down the province's atomic generating stations, and it supported the unions whose workers were employed at these stations. It supported small business, while at the same time calling for a steep hike in the minimum wage, the policy that small-business owners hated most. As the NDP accelerated its drive to attract interest groups, its vinyl-covered policy binder—the pride and joy of members who believed their party alone had a real program—became a bewildering array of contradictory resolutions.

On the broader front, however, the NDP had increasingly less and less to say. Public auto insurance remained a bulwark. The party talked vaguely of an industrial strategy and of developing secondary industry in the North. But since Ontario remained prosperous during the 1970s and 1980s, and since the party's own polls showed that voters didn't trust it with money matters, the lack of a clear economic program caused the NDP little concern. More worrisome was the party's continuing inability to get elected.

In 1975, the Ontario NDP had become the official opposition again. In part, this was the result of fortuitous vote splits. But, in part, it was believed to be the result of the party's new, moderate, interest-group approach. When the minority Tory government finally fell in 1977, many in the party were convinced that their chance had come. "People firmly believed we'd form the government," said David Reville, who later became an MPP himself.

However, the ensuing 1977 election was a psychological disaster for the NDP—in Reville's words, a "huge disappointment." The party dropped only five seats in the legislature; but it lost its coveted status as official opposition. Lewis, who was deemed to have erred during the campaign by downplaying party policies in order to appear more moderate, resigned. Looking for a replacement, the party establishment and the trade unions gathered behind Hamilton MPP Ian Deans.

Meanwhile, the left, including ex-Waffler Jim Laxer, united behind Ottawa MPP Michael Cassidy, a former financial journalist accurately described by NDP historian Desmond Morton as a "decent, utterly uncharismatic figure, quite unable to rally the party's dispirited membership." A Cassidy victory seemed so improbable, recalled Charlotte Montgomery, at the time a *Toronto Star* reporter covering Queen's Park, that many union delegates simply didn't bother showing up to vote.

But to the surprise and horror of the NDP leadership, Cassidy managed to beat out Deans. For many in the party, the Cassidy period was a bad dream, an interregnum best forgotten.

Another election defeat in 1981, this time involving the loss of twelve seats, gave the party a chance to end the interregnum. Cassidy resigned as leader. From inside the caucus, Richard Johnston emerged as the candidate of the left. The charming, twice-married Johnston, who had succeeded Lewis as MPP for Scarborough West, was opposed by Port Arthur MPP Jim Foulds.

However, Lewis and the party leadership weren't satisfied. What was needed, they felt, was a candidate who was firmly on the moderate wing of the party but who possessed a personality that could appeal to the media. And who better than Bob Rae, the federal caucus finance critic, a man whose one-liners brought joy to the Ottawa press corps?

In 1981, over dinner at the home of *Toronto Star* reporter Rosemary Speirs, Lewis, Michele Landsberg, Gerry Caplan, and labour lawyer Howard Goldblatt pressured Rae to run. Initially, he had been reluctant. A group from Ontario, including MPP Dave Cooke, had already journeyed to Ottawa to woo him, and at first Rae had refused. After all, he was doing well in Ottawa, was comfortable with federal issues, and saw himself as a potential successor to federal NDP leader Ed Broadbent.

By the time of the Toronto dinner, Rae was more amenable to the idea of tackling the Ontario leadership. Appealing to a combination of duty and vanity, Lewis and the others made their points: Rae had to enter the race to save the Ontario party; the most important provincial component of the NDP needed someone who was thoughtful, committed, impressive, interesting, and a good communicator. Moreover, Broadbent might hang on for a long time, denying Rae a chance at the federal leadership. And the most important point: after four decades in power, the Ontario Tories were ripe for a fall; the provincial Liberals were nowhere; with the right leader, the NDP was almost sure to form the government.

This time, the party and union establishment were not prepared to risk a Cassidy-style upset. With the support of the Lewises and labour leaders such as Canadian Auto Workers chief Bob White, Rae quickly became the front runner. He was also an impressive candidate. Janet Solberg, who as an Ottawa riding association president had been charged with dragooning delegates into Rae's camp, remembered him as being "head and shoulders above the others." Rae won the leadership handily. All he needed was a seat in the legislature.

However, a strong streak of parochialism runs through Queen's Park. The victory of this glib outsider had left a residue of bitterness. Many New Democrat MPPs never accepted Rae's victory. Initially, no one would resign his or her seat to accommodate the new leader. The two MPPs whose ridings overlapped Rae's federal constituency refused point blank. For eleven months, the new NDP leader remained outside the legislature, fuming. Only when the ever-loyal Donald MacDonald agreed to resign from his seat in Toronto's York South riding was Rae able to enter the Ontario legislature as a sitting MPP.

It was not Ottawa. In the world of Ontario provincial politics, Rae's father, family, and federal Liberal connections counted for nothing. There were no wrinkled retainers to welcome him home, no statesman-like journalists appropriately respectful of his academic credentials. The more down-home reporters of Queen's Park were more likely to ask the new NDP leader why he thought he was so smart. In Ottawa, Rae's one-liners had headed the evening television news. At Queen's Park, they often fell flat. In the legislature, back-bench Tories in loud suits mocked him mercilessly.

Inside his own caucus, the new leader had few friends. His social awkwardness kept him aloof from his more sybaritic colleagues. For, by the 1980s, the opposition New Democrats had become party animals. At gatherings, Toronto MPP David Warner (later Speaker of the Legislature) might climb on top of a television set to do Al Jolson imitations. From time to time, a handful of members (two of whom later became senior cabinet ministers) would repair to the apartment of one of their number to smoke marijuana.

And they partied. In 1989, after one particularly raucous evening, Toronto MPP David Reville was persuaded to let an inebriated out-of-town colleague sleep it off on his living-room couch. Wakened in the middle of the night by a loud noise, Reville looked out his window. His caucus mate—who would later be named a cabinet minister—was standing on Reville's front porch, clad only in his underwear, urinating down the steps.

The division between leader and caucus extended beyond play. Richard Johnston and Oshawa MPP Mike Breaugh had never accepted Rae's leadership. Johnston became a focal point for internal opposition and, until he quit the legislature in 1990, delighted in mau-mauing Rae.

Bud Wildman, an intense member from the northern riding of Algoma, took no pains to hide his ambition or his disapproval of Rae (Wildman would say later that it was only in government that he came to truly appreciate his leader). Even Floyd Laughren, who later became a Rae loyalist, admitted it took him some time to get to like his leader. "Bob never enjoyed the luxury of working with a caucus that liked him," Rae's press aide, Rob Mitchell, said later.

The 1985 election, the first under the new leader, eroded Rae's stature further. In spite of their bright, new, media-wise leader, the NDP had once again come in third. Moreover, the biggest gains had been racked up by David Peterson's Liberals.

David Peterson! Many in the NDP had only contempt for the soft-spoken London businessman. Rae thought him intellectually thin and made little attempt to hide this opinion. Indeed, to most political watchers at Queen's Park, Peterson seemed a most unlikely person to bring the Liberals to office after forty-two years in opposition. Pleasant but dull, he was an indifferent speaker and, in the legislature, a lacklustre opposition leader. But behind the scenes, Peterson and his team had reforged the Liberals from a rural Grit rump into an urban vote machine. In the mid-1980s, the handsome, greying Peterson—the sleeves of his snowy white shirt rolled up, his red tie loosened—seemed to capture the mood of Ontario.

What is often forgotten is that David Peterson's Liberals didn't win in 1985. They placed second. Frank Miller's Tories, while not winning a majority, picked up more votes than any other party. In normal times, the Conservatives would have formed a minority government. This would have lasted until the opposition parties combined to force another election. Thanks to the frustrations within the NDP, these were not normal times.

David Reville was a fledgling New Democrat MPP in 1985. An active and popular downtown Toronto alderman, Reville had grown up in a privileged family. After attending Upper Canada College, a private school, he had followed the normal route of members of the Toronto élite—Trinity College at the University of Toronto, and then law school. After that, it was assumed, Reville would follow in the footsteps of his father, a judge. But somewhere along the track, Reville derailed. At law school, he tried to kill himself. At age twenty-two, he was declared a manic depressive and locked up in a psychiatric hospital. Later, after he was out, Reville became a plumber, a crusader for mental health, and a member of the NDP. As he explained to Canadian Press reporter Beth Gorham in 1989: "I became a New Democrat because I was mentally ill." What he meant, Reville explained later, was that, as a mental patient, he had finally understood what it was to have no power. And he wanted to change a system that kept so many people powerless.

Coming from the raucous but fairly straightforward world of Toronto city politics into the dark and Byzantine manoeuvrings of the Ontario NDP caucus was an eye-opener for Reville. Many in the caucus felt they had been cheated twice from government. They wanted to form a coalition with the Liberals—supporting Peterson in exchange for cabinet posts. Another group wanted the party to follow normal practice and give conditional support to the Conservatives, who, after all, had gained a plurality of the vote. Yet another faction wanted the NDP to support neither, to let matters unfold day by day.

At the same time, there were the usual post-election recriminations: Whose fault was it that the NDP had not done better? In caucus, Johnston was sniping at Rae; Laughren and Wildman were slugging it out over who would get the post, coveted by northern members, of natural resources critic. "Laughren and Wildman hated each other," Reville later recalled.

Underneath, two forces were at play. First, there was the desire for power. The NDP caucus had not so much a coherent agenda as a set of specific, single-issue agendas—from environmental protection to pay equity. Members were frustrated by years in opposition; they wanted a chance to put their ideas into practice.

Second, there was a debate over which of the old-line parties was the real enemy. It had been NDP folklore that the Liberals were the true scoundrels. Under Stephen Lewis's leadership, the party's overall strategy had been to attack the Liberals, displace them, and consign them to the oblivion they seemed to so richly deserve.

But a newer generation of New Democrats found the Tories more odious than the Liberals. The caucus research office, for instance, was impressed by stands the Liberals were taking on matters such as the environment. To these people, continued support of the fossilized Conservative regime, particularly under a right-of-centre premier such as Frank Miller, seemed anathema.

Rae was more sympathetic to the Liberals. But he was unsure about coalition. As a student of history, he understood the dangers of allowing one political party to be subsumed inside another. At a caucus meeting, members were polled. Coalitionists were strong but did not form a majority. Rae liked the idea of coalition. But, according to Johnston, initially at least, Rae stayed on the fence. To Johnston, this was classic example of Rae's inability to seize the moment. To Reville, it was another example of the insanity of the caucus he had just joined: "I didn't know what to make of it; I was just astounded by it; I found the whole thing bizarre. We had absolutely no information on other coalition governments, how they had worked or not worked. I asked people about that and they just said, 'Never mind.'"

In any case, coalition soon became moot. The party leadership, including Stephen Lewis, had gotten wind of the scheme. To Lewis and federal leader Ed Broadbent, formal coalition was a prescription for the political suicide of the NDP.

With the coalition option removed, the caucus embraced the next-best thing — the idea of a political accord. The notion of a written contract — committing the New Democrats to support whichever party promised to implement the NDP's policy prescriptions — appealed to Rae's legalistic mind. It also appealed to union leaders in the party. Rae announced his caucus would be taking bids from the Liberals and Conservatives. But as journalist Rosemary Speirs has chronicled in *Out of the Blue*, her book on the end of the Tory regime, the NDP was never interested in a deal with the Conservatives. Rae himself felt it was important to put an end to Conservative rule. A deal, brokered by the NDP member Ross McClellan and Peterson's key aide, Hershell Ezrin, was soon signed.

Much later, Rae would brag about how the two-year accord allowed him to "bring in reform with the Liberals." But in 1987, the direst warnings of the pessimists seemed to have been borne out. True, the NDP's social agenda had dominated the Peterson government's first term. Laws putting in place such path-breaking programs as pay equity for women were passed under NDP pressure. Indeed, the NDP was able to put into place more of its agenda in two short years than ever before. Ironically, the NDP also put more of its agenda into place with the Liberals governing than it did later during its own time in power.

However, the New Democrats got no credit. Ontarians thanked Peterson instead. When the next election came in 1987, Peterson's Liberals were swept back into government with the largest majority in provincial history. The NDP, while hanging on to official-opposition status, was cut back from twenty-three to nineteen members. Even McClellan, a key architect of the accord, lost his seat.

To many in the NDP, the 1987 election result was a devastating political indictment of the decision to prop up the Liberals. The New
Democrats had created a monster; mumbling, ineffectual David Peterson had been transformed by power into one of Ontario's most popular
premiers. "Bob came out of the election really low," veteran NDP campaign organizer Sharon Vance said later.

Those New Democrat MPPs remaining gnashed their teeth and calculated pension benefits, trying to determine when would be the best
time to leave politics. Oshawa MPP Mike Breaugh was the first to go,
leaving in 1990 to enter federal politics. By midsummer, Richard Johnston and David Reville had decided not to run again. Johnston was sick
of it; Reville wanted to do something useful. Even Floyd Laughren was
preparing to leave after nineteen years in politics. Peterson had already
offered him a job should the Liberals win the next election. (The only
reason Laughren didn't quit in 1990, he said later, was that the election
was called before he had time to do so.) Rae's principal secretary,
Robin Sears, who had masterminded the 1987 campaign, had already
left to take a plum patronage post offered by the Liberals.

Meanwhile, Rae seemed increasingly out of touch with daily politics.
Already, he had been hit by twin tragedies. In 1985, a few months after
the election, Arlene Perly Rae's parents were killed in a car crash. In
1989, Rae's younger brother, David, died, after a two-year fight against
lymphatic cancer.

The death of Al and Hannah Perly had devastated their daughter.
Lenny Wise would later recall being telephoned at midnight by Rae.
His parents-in-law were dead, he told Wise, and Arlene, dazed with
grief, had disappeared. "It was just absolute craziness," said Wise later.
"We had to drive off and try to find her, me and Bob.... Everyone's
driving all over the place and it's just like craziness." Arlene would later
tell *Toronto Star* reporter Judy Steed: "I lost three years out of my life."

Meanwhile, nothing was getting better at Queen's Park. The death of
Tommy Douglas in 1986 had shaken Rae. The young NDP leader had
known Douglas in Ottawa and had regarded him as a mentor. An aide later
remembered Rae in tears. "Tommy always advised me not to run for the
Ontario leadership," Rae was saying between sobs. "And he was right."

As the pressure grew, Robin Sears began to make increasing use of
Rae's old friend Wise: "Robin used to call me in," recalled Wise.
"[He'd] say, 'Lenny, you got to get him [out of here].' And I understood
what he meant because he [Rae] would be wigging out. He'd be acting

crazy. The pressure would be getting to him and he'd be starting to act strange. . . . Robin would say 'Just take him out of here; take him for a walk; make him laugh. . . .' He always wanted to go to the cafeteria, for some reason, to get an egg sandwich. . . . An egg sandwich and a glass of milk was his obsession; that was all he ever seemed to eat. And we would go for a walk. Just to get away. And I would make him laugh. And he would forget for a moment. That was basically my job."

At Christmas 1987 came another crisis. This time it was Rae's brother, David. Bob Rae got the news of his brother's illness by telephone while on holiday in Florida with Arlene and his friends the Wises. "He was crying on the phone," said Wise. "He was telling me he [David] was finished."

For Bob Rae, the slow deterioration and death of his brother was a wrenching experience. In an attempt to arrest David's cancer, Bob underwent a painful bone marrow transplant operation. Even that did not work. The sickness and eventual death of his younger brother seemed to make Rae more pensive, more withdrawn. The NDP leader began to concentrate his mental energies on the plight of those he saw as truly dispossessed, Native people and urban black immigrants.

According to Rob Mitchell, it was during this period that Toronto black activists, such as Dudley Laws and Lennox Farrell, began to have more influence with Rae. Their arguments—that Ontario society was systemically racist—seemed to appeal to him. Evidence showed up in small ways. In one instance, Mitchell recommended that Rae be wary of involving himself in the controversy surrounding the police shooting of a Mississauga black teenager. Rae was a cautious man, and normally this kind of advice would have reflected his own instincts. But the new Rae had become more aggressive. "You're racist," he snapped at his press aide.

Aides joked that they could tell where Rae's focus was by the pictures on his office wall. If they were of Martin Luther King Jr., he was thinking black; if Native art, he was thinking Indian. A 1989 trip to some of the grim aboriginal settlements on the James Bay coast convinced him that Indians did indeed live in a form of colonial servitude. Later that year, Rae made a decision to get himself arrested along with Indians and environmentalists opposed to the logging of old-growth forests near the Northern Ontario town of Temagami. He was indeed arrested. But, unlike some of the other protestors, who faced jail and fines, he was never charged.

With the fall of the Soviet Union, Rae travelled to Lithuania (the original home of his grandfather Willy Cohen) to view firsthand the travails of yet another nationality struggling to escape what he would later call the "jackboot" of colonialism. "Bob's a black Lithuanian now," his aides would say.

Back in his office, Rae would peck away at a word processor, trying to put these disparate thoughts into the written form that would eventually become "What We Owe Each Other." In particular, he tried to link individual love — the feeling people have for each other — with socialism, as a form of institutionalized mutual caring. More hard-edged New Democrats blanched whenever Rae would bring up the topic; reporters were prone to sneer. During one trip with the press, Rob Mitchell was horrified to see Rae's briefcase fly open and Erich Fromm's *The Art of Loving*, a pop-psychology book, spill out. Mitchell quickly pounced to recover the book before any reporter could see it.

In 1989, Ed Broadbent resigned as federal NDP leader. Suddenly Rae had a way out of what, for him, had become the Appalachian backwater of Ontario politics. Rae's principal secretary, Robin Sears, urged him to try for Broadbent's job. Also supporting a Rae candidacy were the pillars of the NDP establishment — Bob White, Leo Gerard, Stephen Lewis, Gerry Caplan, Janet Solberg, Michael Lewis, former Saskatchewan premier Allan Blakeney, Roy Romanow, Manitoba NDP leader Gary Doer, and Nova Scotia NDP chief Alexa McDonough.

Only David Agnew was reluctant. Agnew had worked with Rae in Ottawa and by 1989 was one of his more trusted aides. If Rae took over the federal party, Agnew warned, the expectations would be enormous. He couldn't hope to live up to them. It would be like Ontario in 1982 all over again; he would be trashed.

Besides, Rae was told, he might not even win the federal crown. Western New Democrats wanted one of their own. Former B.C. premier Dave Barrett was thinking of entering the race. If he did so, and took votes from labour delegates, he could spoil it for Rae. Stephen Lewis was dispatched to try to persuade Barrett not to run. He failed.

By October, speculation about Rae's future had reached a crescendo. Most in the caucus were sure he was going to go. On his way to northwestern Ontario to address a meeting of Indian chiefs, Rae suddenly decided he had to make up his mind. He called an emergency caucus meeting and headed back to Toronto.

Assembling in the opposition caucus room of Queen's Park on the night of October 5, NDP members awaited Rae's return with some antic- ipation. Johnston, Wildman, and Ruth Grier were already planning their campaigns for the Ontario leadership. Wildman and Grier were also secretly investigating the idea of a deal to support each other against Johnston in any leadership convention.

But Rae was late. His airplane had run into bad weather. The extra time, as he explained later, gave him time to think and rethink. By the time he reached Queen's Park, Rae was ready to announce his decision. He would stay in provincial politics.

Reporters outside the caucus room heard a ragged cheer. But when the members emerged, their faces said it all. Wildman was particularly grim; Johnston had left by a back door; only Grier seemed genuinely pleased. The New Democrat MPPs again cheered, but with little enthu- siasm, their leader's decision to stay on.

While Rae grappled with his own demons, little else was happening in the NDP caucus. By 1990, most MPPs had become cynical and dispir- ited. Rather than attempt to cobble together coherent positions, they had concentrated almost exclusively on scoring political points in the media. Faced with a choice between working the issues or working scandals, they chose scandals.

"I thought we were posturing just for the sake of posturing—just obstructing," said Richard Johnston later. "We were living off the battles of the CCF of earlier generations. No one was examining what we believed in.... I don't know exactly when, but at some point, we lost it. You have to believe in something, or you've lost it. And we lost it."

Even Rae supporters such as David Reville felt a similar malaise: "I was health critic," said Reville later. "I was pressured to scream at the government because a woman had to go to Buffalo to have her baby delivered because of complications. Actually, I thought it appropriate she went to Buffalo rather than have Ontario spend millions putting special obstetrical equipment in all our hospitals. I tried to resist that pressure, but you couldn't.... I had to worry that Ernie Eves [the Tory health critic] might get ahead of me. He might ask a question in the legislature about some fat executive who didn't get his triple heart bypass on the same day. What should I do then? Should I attack the government too?"

Most of the time he, and other members, did attack the govern- ment. The standard opposition position—any enemy of the govern- ment is a friend of mine—was accelerated. In concert with religious fundamentalists, the NDP fought the idea of allowing stores to open on Sunday. On health policy, it supported both expanding hospital services and reducing them in favour of community-care alternatives. On auto insurance, it supported lower rates, public ownership, and the right of accident victims to sue, without bothering to see how the three could tie together. Too often, it wound itself into knots, simultaneously support- ing contradictory positions that could not work together—at least not without more thought than the NDP caucus was willing to give.

"It was the desperation of an opposition party," said Reville three years later, when, as a senior aide to Premier Bob Rae, he reflected on his past. "I think you get captured in opposition, just like in government. . . .

"This was a small group of people who had had good intentions and spent their lives trying to make things fair. But we didn't have a fucking idea what it meant. We had the passion and theory. But we didn't have a fucking idea how to make things work. And we still don't."

4

Wackos from Outer Space

ON OCTOBER 1, 1990, THE PREMIER AND HIS NEW CABINET were officially sworn in at the University of Toronto's Convocation Hall — a place where, as an undergraduate and student politician, Rae had already scored so many triumphs. From the balconies of the giant auditorium, NDP partisans cheered their favourite ministers as they stepped up to take the oath — Sudbury's Shelley Martel, Welland's Peter Kormos, Rae himself. There was no presentiment then that, within three years, Martel would be politically disgraced, Kormos fired from cabinet, and Rae disowned by most of the labour movement. On stage, a children's choir sang the Depression hit "Side by Side."

Rae himself spoke to the emotion of the moment. "I am very, very proud," he said. "I'm especially proud that so many members of my family are here. Especially proud of the fact that we're able to have this ceremony in this hall, which has such special meaning for my father and me.... The joy is, perhaps, greater because it was so unexpected."

Indeed, it *was* unexpected. And that alone made the task facing the new government even more daunting. For the NDP was entirely unprepared to take power in Ontario. When the election had been called in the summer of 1990, neither Rae nor anyone else had given the New Democrats a remote chance of winning. "I thought we'd keep enough members to maintain party status," an astonished Richard Johnston said later. "But not many more."

Rae himself had been preparing to fight, lose gracefully, and call it

quits. Holidaying at his summer cottage on Big Rideau Lake just prior
to the election call, Rae had confided to his wife, Arlene, that this campaign would be his last as Ontario leader. As he acknowledged later, in
some ridings the party had gone to great lengths just to find NDP candidates willing to run.

How true. In Peterborough, novice Jenny Carter ran under the NDP
banner. Not only did she win, she was put into cabinet as Rae's Energy
minister. Honest to a fault, Carter told reporters that her husband, Cyril,
a professor at Trent University and an expert on nuclear power, should
really be the minister. After all, she explained, he knew so much more
about energy than she.

In the rural riding of Lambton, near Sarnia, NDP candidate Ellen
MacKinnon had developed a case of what she later called "stage fright"
early in the campaign. "I was at an all-candidates meeting and I
couldn't see the questioners," she recalled. "It made me really nervous."
During the evening, she was asked a long, complicated question about a
proposed landfill site that might be used to take Toronto garbage.
Tongue-tied, MacKinnon answered in eight short words: "No garbage.
Not here. Not now. Not ever." Later, the former municipal councillor
would laugh about the incident. "A lot of people came up to me afterwards and said they liked that answer. They could understand it."

MacKinnon's riding association had told the candidate that
she could relax, that she had absolutely no chance of winning. But,
much to her surprise, MacKinnon and seventy-three other New Democrats did win, providing Rae with a solid majority in the legislature.

The New Democrat MPPs who assembled at Queen's Park after the
September 1990 election were a mixed lot. Only five were lawyers. Of
the sixty newcomers, only fourteen had any experience as elected
politicians on municipal councils or school boards. Marion Boyd, the
executive director of an advocacy clinic for battered women, had taken
a London seat from the elegant David Peterson. Tony Martin, an anti-
poverty activist, had won the northern riding of Sault Ste. Marie.
Kimble Sutherland, a twenty-four-year-old former student-council president, had been selling hot dogs to minor-league-baseball fans in
London's Labatt Park.

Putting together a cabinet was an exercise in making the best from
thin gruel. Virtually every member of the old caucus who had bothered
to run was assured a cabinet seat. Only Brian Charlton was left out.
Charlton, energy critic in opposition and the logical choice for Energy

minister, had committed the sin of presumption. He had commented on what he might do as minister before Rae announced his cabinet. For that, the Hamilton MPP was banished temporarily to the back-benches.

But even with nearly every experienced MPP in cabinet, approximately half of the ministry posts remained empty. Most of the neophyte MPPs were virtual unknowns. In the end, the remaining twelve ministers were picked for the usual political reasons that go into Canadian cabinet-making—with one significant exception: Rae's cabinet would contain proportionally more women than any other in Canadian history. Zanana Akande, a Toronto high-school principal and one of the NDP's high-profile candidates in the election, was assured a seat in the ministry. The fact that she was the caucus's only black helped her nail down a senior post as Minister of Community and Social Affairs. Frances Lankin and Anne Swarbrick fit three criteria: they were female, well connected to the labour movement, and from Metro Toronto. The thirty-six-year-old Lankin, at one time a prison guard, and a former negotiator for the Ontario Public Service Employees Union, was particularly ambitious. In 1985, she had unsuccessfully contested the Riverdale nomination against David Reville. She was also a close friend of Julie Davis, president of the Ontario party, secretary-treasurer of the Ontario Federation of Labour, and chair of the NDP's victorious election campaign. Rae made Lankin chair of the cabinet's Management Board, a low-profile but tricky job and one that put her in charge of her old civil-service comrades. She would prove to be one of the most competent members of Rae's cabinet.

Other ministers seemed to be chosen almost at random. Rosario Marchese was to be the Metro Toronto's Italian Canadian in cabinet as Culture minister. Peter North, a carpenter from Chatham, could shore up cabinet representation from the rural southwest—until this point a desert for the NDP. As well, North's adoptive mother was a Native Indian, which would round out the cabinet's racial and ethnic balance. Rae figured—inaccurately, as it turned out—that, as head of the minor Tourism ministry, the thirty-year-old newcomer couldn't get into much trouble.

More difficult than the cabinet, however, was the structure of government itself. Rae's NDP had little idea of how the bureaucracy worked or how legislation was implemented. Being a sensible person, Rae turned to others who did know, such as former Saskatchewan premier Allan Blakeney. Former Ontario NDP leader Stephen Lewis was drafted to head a transition team that that would make recommendations on how to organize the affairs of government. Lewis's sister, Janet Solberg, was tasked with finding suitable New Democrats to act as political aides to the ministers.

Rae was determined to rely on trusted colleagues for his office. David Agnew would continue as his principal secretary, the top aide. Former MPP David Reville would babysit the caucus and carry out special projects for the premier. Chuck Rachlis, the NDP's research director in opposition, would handle economic matters in the premier's office. Ross McClellan, the former MPP who been instrumental in forging the 1985–87 accord with the Peterson Liberals, would be put in charge of policy. Personable, fiercely partisan, and prone to scheming, the former social worker would emerge as one of the most influential figures in the government.

Others less well connected to Rae were imported. Carol Phillips, the assistant to Canadian Auto Workers head Bob White and wife of former NDP federal secretary Gerry Caplan, would handle patronage. New Democrat perennial Norm Simon, still known by some of his high-school chums as Nooky, would be the official communications strategist. Lynn Spink, a labour consultant who at one time had worked with Rae's old chum, Jeff Rose, would act as Rae's executive assistant, accompanying him everywhere. Child-care activist Julie Mathien would cover social policy for the premier. Canadian Press reporter Laurie Stephens was hired to handle relations with the cantankerous Queen's Park press gallery. Former Stephen Lewis aide Melody Morrison would work under Agnew and later succeed him as principal secretary. In mid-1991, lawyer Hilarie McMurray, a former aide to Ed Broadbent, was brought on to deal with justice matters and solve all manner of political crises. Reville would later call her the "government's best political junkyard dog."

Interestingly enough, within four years, five of these senior Rae aides—Rachlis, Phillips, Simon, Spink, and McMurray—had left the NDP government.

To Agnew and McClellan, the new government's key organizational task was to avoid what they saw as the fatal flaw of the Peterson government—its lack of central direction. Once the discipline of the 1985–87 accord had been removed, McClellan argued, individual ministries had begun to make policy at the behest of their own particular special interest groups rather than for the government as a whole.

McClellan was determined that this drift should be not be repeated. In his view, the central institutions of the government—the premier's office and the cabinet office—should be responsible for driving policies developed by cabinet; the job of the line ministries would be to put these policies into place.

To McClellan, Lewis, and many others in the NDP, two things had to be accomplished if this strategy were to succeed. First, the bureaucracy had to be tamed. Strong political aides in the line ministries would ensure that the civil servants were carrying out government policy and not the internal agendas of the bureaucracy. Second, a strong policy unit had to be created at the centre to formulate and coordinate the government's overall strategy.

Lewis was intrigued by the way successive Saskatchewan NDP governments had employed planning secretariats. These were made up of politicized civil servants working in the central cabinet office and charged with riding herd over the bureaucracy. Lewis had worked briefly on former Saskatchewan premier Tommy Douglas's planning board in 1956. He argued that Rae should create such a board in Ontario.

In fact, Lewis saw a role for himself as a key player in this kind of operation. The former Canadian ambassador's experience at the United Nations, however, had taught him that visibility was not necessarily commensurate with influence. As he confided to friends later, if he were offered a position, he wanted it to be one that would allow him to exercise influence effectively, not just make eloquent speeches.

Rae, however, disagreed on both counts. He was reluctant to be seen politicizing the civil service; thus, he decided against a Blakeney-style policy secretariat. While he did offer Lewis a job—to head up a recovery secretariat in the cabinet office—it was not the kind of influential post the former NDP leader wanted. (Indeed, Rae is reported to have noted to aides that Ontario had room for only one premier.) Lewis turned the job down.

Canadian Auto Workers chief Bob White was another who turned down a job offer from the Rae government. This one was to coordinate industrial strategy and would carry the rank of deputy minister. "I didn't want to leave labour," explained White, who later was elected head of the Canadian Labour Congress. "I didn't want to become a senior bureaucrat in government.... I thought I'd get pigeonholed into some office."

Under the Liberals, cabinet secretary Peter Barnes had been working on a scheme to make the civil service more efficient. To the incoming

NDP, however, the plan looked like so much gobbledy-gook—plenty of flow charts but no action. Agnew figured the government's energy would be better spent on substantive issues. One key NDP figure later described the reason for leaving the civil service alone in 1990: "We just didn't know enough about government. Everyone seemed to have his own agenda—it was hard to know who to listen to. In 1990, it was enough to get accustomed to governing without throwing the civil service into a tizzy."

Barnes's exercise was summarily scrapped. Ironically, two and a half years later—in the midst of political and economic crisis—the idea of restructuring the civil service wholesale would be resurrected.

Rae was aware of the need to maintain control of government. But he was also wary of upsetting bureaucrats who could so easily sabotage him. Initially, therefore, he was reluctant to make sweeping changes. Barnes was kept on as the province's top civil servant: in part, to reassure the bureaucracy that the NDP did not intend a purge; in part, because Rae—the son of a bureaucrat—appreciated the value of a non-partisan civil service. Moreover, he rather liked Barnes, a Briton who had once served as a colonial civil servant in Kenya.

As for strengthening central control, again Rae moved cautiously. There were only two institutions which the new government could have used to control the agenda of government—the cabinet office and the premier's office. The former is made up of career civil servants, the latter of partisan political aides. Canadian precedents existed for using either.

In Ontario, four decades of Tory rule had so blurred the distinction between partisan politics and sound administration that the civil servants of the cabinet office had ended up doing both. Peterson's Liberals had reintroduced the distinction between politics and the civil service by separating the premier's office from the strictly civil-service cabinet office. But, to the incoming NDP, the cabinet office under Peterson had atrophied. "It was just a place that arranged meetings and made coffee," said one senior Rae aide later.

Initially, Rae kept the essential distinction between premier's office and cabinet office. The premier's office would exercise political control over the government. But the cabinet office would also be strengthened and given a specific mandate to guide the actions of the line ministries. As one of the premier's aides explained later, just the fact that the cabinet office was known to have a mandate seemed to make a difference in the hierarchical Ontario civil service: "You can't imagine the absolute terror you can strike into people's hearts by just phoning them."

For his window into the mysteries of the civil service, Rae chose to rely on a small number of NDP bureaucrats, some of whom, ironically, had been hired by the eclectic Peterson. Initially, these were Michael Mendelson—promoted to deputy cabinet secretary under Barnes— and Marc Eliesen, the deputy minister of Energy. Eliesen, former research director for the federal NDP, had been the head of Manitoba Hydro under the New Democratic government of Howard Pawley. In the beginning, his job was to help the new premier make his way through bureaucratic minefields. Over the next two years, Eliesen's star would rise and then dramatically fall. In his place, two other ex-Manitoba bureaucrats—deputy health minister Michael Decter, and to a lesser extent Treasury board secretary Jay Kaufman—would come to rank highly in the premier's regard.

Mendelson too had worked as a Manitoba bureaucrat under the NDP. In part, Mendelson's job was to keep an eye on Peter Barnes. His more important contribution, however, was to restructure the cabinet office into a functioning body that could centrally oversee the work of individual ministeries. By 1993, Mendelson was one of the most powerful functionaries in the Rae government; he and McClellan had become the gatekeepers, the ones whose approval had to be gained before any proposal could even be discussed at the cabinet table.

Later Rae hired his old university chum Jeff Rose, a former president of the Canadian Union of Public Employees (CUPE), as deputy minister of Intergovernmental Affairs, the ministry handling constitutional negotiations. Rose's role in government, however, seemed to remain oddly constrained. As a personal friend of the premier, he had access that few others enjoyed. In his own sphere of intergovernmental affairs, he dominated. Rose was responsible for Ontario's position in the constitutional talks leading up to the 1992 referendum on the Charlottetown Accord. Later, Rose convinced Rae to campaign publicly against Ottawa, over both the North American Free Trade Agreement and federal cut-backs in provincial transfer payments (the latter became known as Rae's Fair Share campaign).

In other areas, though, Rose either had little clout or chose not to use what little he did possess. He told friends he played no role at all in the 1993 decision to impose a social contract on public-sector workers— even though one of the major unions involved was his own CUPE. When senior bureaucrats and aides got together to plan the major issues of the day, Rose was often not invited.

To keep both ministers and bureaucrats in line, key aides were hired centrally and dispatched to ministerial offices. The idea here was to emulate the NDP's election-campaign structure, one in which candidates did not choose their campaign managers but were assigned them by party headquarters. In elections, this allowed the NDP's central organization to ensure that its candidates didn't do anything too nutty. The hope was that a cadre of experienced aides working with inexperienced ministers could perform the same service for the government.

In theory, all of this should have worked. In practice, very little did.

The premier's office was to be the central political organ. At the centre of it was Agnew, who, next to Rae, was the most important figure in government.

Agnew's father had been the last editor-in-chief of *The Telegram*, one of Toronto's great newspapers, which had folded in 1971 only to be resurrected as a feisty tabloid named *The Toronto Sun*. Later, when events began to sour for the Rae government, critics would whisper that Agnew had never really been a New Democrat, that his class background was one of privilege, that he was even related to the Eatons of department-store fame. The Eaton connection did exist, but it was remote. Agnew's maternal great-grandmother was a sister of Lady Eaton; occasionally the Agnews would be invited to the Eaton estate for family gatherings. But, as David would wryly tell friends, he wasn't "in the will."

It was true, however, that Agnew had never joined the New Democrats before going to work for Rae. He had never joined any political party. All he had ever wanted, he would say later, was to be a newspaper reporter. During high school, Agnew had worked summers as a sports reporter for *The Toronto Sun*. After high school, and while attending university, he worked for the St. John's *Evening Telegram*.

Agnew had also worked for Rae briefly in 1979, as a parliamentary intern. After that, he returned to reporting for Canadian Press in Ottawa and was preparing to go to Vancouver when the news cooperative, in one of its periodic belt-tightening moves, cut back staff. Instead, Agnew was dispatched to CP's bureau in Edmonton. He was dissatisfied enough with Edmonton that when, in the spring of 1981, he got an offer to be Rae's executive assistant, Agnew accepted. It would be, he figured then, a good break for one or two years.

But the years dragged on. When Rae won the 1982 Ontario leadership,

Agnew followed him to Toronto. In early 1990, after what was described as a power struggle between Agnew and then principal secretary Robin Sears, Sears quit to take up a government job with the Liberals. Agnew became Rae's principal secretary, his most influential aide.

Those who worked with Agnew and Rae remarked on their similarity of temperament. Some called Agnew a clone of the premier. But this was probably unfair to both. Agnew was far more relaxed than Rae, less forced. While both possessed a spare, dry wit, Agnew was more natural, less of a showman, less reliant on audience applause. Outside of work, Rae and Agnew rarely socialized. As Agnew explained to an associate once: "We don't go bowling together."

At the same time, like his predecessor, Sears, Agnew could be more ruthless than his somewhat sentimental boss. When faced with a choice between kindness and advancing the interests of Rae, Agnew would almost always choose the latter.

"David is just as controlling [as Sears]," said Janet Solberg, who has worked with both. "But he wears it less on his sleeve."

Where Rae and Agnew were similar was in their tendency to be cerebral, cautious and conservative. Unlike Rae, however, Agnew always seemed to understand this about himself. In his opposition days, Rae would sometimes forget, fancying himself an environmental crusader or black-rights activist. During these periods of experimentation by his boss, Agnew would keep his own feet firmly on the ground. In 1989, when Rae proposed he be arrested during an anti-logging blockade, it was Agnew who advised against it. Rae did not take his advice that time.

But, by the election campaign of 1990, Rae had decided he was sick of pretending to be someone else. He would accept himself for what he was—a man in a suit. He turned to one aide to outfit him appropriately (Rae is colour blind). And he turned to Agnew to run his campaign. Once Rae won power, it was Agnew he wanted to head up the premier's office.

Under the master plan, this office was supposed to function as a central, political coordinating body for government. Instead, like most premiers' offices, it soon became consumed with dousing political brush fires.

"It didn't work terribly well as a whole," according to Janet Solberg, who in late 1991 did a six-month stint in the premier's office. "I'm not sure anyone knew what anyone else was doing.... At the beginning, and I guess even now, it was just such a bunker mentality. At the beginning, because there was so much to do and we were all new to it. And now, because people feel so under siege from all directions. . . .

"I might be completely wrong, but I reckon the day I left, if you'd asked David Agnew what I did, he wouldn't have been able to tell you."

Dominating the premier's office were the personalities of Agnew, Rae, and McClellan. To David Reville, the office was dysfunctional. To Solberg, the "isolated atmosphere" within it too often resulted in bad political judgment. "Bob is very much a person who thinks through things himself," she said. "I think David is very much the same. They're both very smart. They probably think of all the angles. But it's not my style of working. And I think it probably permeated the atmosphere in the premier's office."

To Lynn Spink, the premier's office seemed dominated by an overwhelming sense of arrogance under siege. What surprised her, and eventually rankled so much that she quit, was the assumption that anyone who criticized the government—particularly anyone who criticized from the left—was a dangerous and ignorant fool. Agnew and McClellan, Spink said, would dismiss Canadian Labour Congress chief Bob White and Judy Rebick, former head of the National Action Committee on the Status of Women, as "liabilities—with contempt and disdain. Frances [Lankin] was seen as a liability because she was too close to the unions. All of these people were treated as impediments."

For their part, McClellan and many around him were astounded by what they saw as the incompetence within the civil service. Even those more sympathetic to the bureaucracy were amazed by the amount of time needed to do the simplest things. "Unbelievable," said Solberg. "It's a miracle that anything gets done. And I'm not blaming the civil service; that's just how things are. . . . It's really a berserk system."

Mistrust of the bureaucracy was not limited to the premier's office. Many political aides come to government from a lifetime of opposing authority. Kathleen O'Hara, press attaché to Northern Development minister Shelley Martel, recalled her first meeting with a senior NDP aide: "I told him I'd spent a month in the Don Jail [on contempt-of-court charges for handing out leftist newspapers]. He said, 'Oh, when were you there?' He'd been in the Don too on a political charge. It was like old-home week."

From the beginning, political aides and the permanent civil service were in conflict. To labour and other social-action groups, the senior bureaucracy had always been the enemy, the self-satisfied fat cats who always managed to persuade their political masters why change was impossible. The attitude of many NDP and labour figures was succinctly expressed by Ontario Federation of Labour chief Gord Wilson: "I told Ross McClellan that I think what the government should do [to take control] is take six deputy ministers to the front steps of the legislature and hang them. And not cut them down for a week. Let them hang there and rot."

In fact, as some NDP aides who later joined the civil service found, the reality was far more complex.

For most civil servants, in fact, the NDP victory was a welcome breath of fresh air. This had less to do with ideology and more with human nature. Like most people, civil servants prefer action to inaction. The NDP promised action. Following Rae's victory, bureaucrats sought out copies of the NDP election platform, "Agenda for People," and began to devise new policies that would fit in. "There was hope for change and a willingness to work with the NDP, which the NDP tragically failed to work with or understand," one senior civil servant said later. "There was an expectation that this government would be sympathetic to government programs. We were disabused of that very rapidly."

Part of the problem lay with the fact that many New Democrats had never worked in large organizations. The intrinsic slowness of bureaucracy confounded and frustrated political aides. The immediate reaction of many was that it was a plot directed against the NDP.

"What became apparent to us all was that we were part of the enemy," said a senior bureaucrat, reflecting on the government's time in office. "We were not to be trusted. We did not belong to the club. Our ideas were not worth listening to.... We were as foreign to the NDP as the bankers of Bay Street."

Much of the hostility was focused against Peter Barnes. Some aides saw him as a Machiavellian *Yes, Minister* figure, deliberately setting out to sabotage Ontario's brave social-democratic government. Some saw him as merely ineffectual. In particular, senior bureaucrats would say later, Ross McClellan seemed to mistrust Barnes. His British accent, his colonial background, his sleek, tailored look, seemed to represent everything the NDP was against.

In fact, Barnes had grown up in more straitened circumstances than Rae himself. But that didn't seem to matter. Barnes, and the bureaucracy in general, became convenient scapegoats for the NDP government's failure to do what it had promised.

Among those who liked to bash civil servants, the exception—initially, at least—was Rae. But for the civil service, all of that changed in January 1993 when, in a rambling speech to University of Toronto business students, the premier started taking his own pot-shots. The time had come, Rae said, to shake up the civil service. It was inefficient, out-of-date. Bureaucrats working "with quill pens" in the bowels of the government would have to shape up.

In some sectors of the civil service, this became known as "the quill pen" speech. For many—already demoralized by the NDP—it really burned. One senior official would later call it "a seminal moment for the bureaucracy."

The NDP government's sense of contempt for the bureaucracy was an important backdrop to its 1993 decision to impose wage roll-backs on Ontario public servants. For, by 1993, the NDP government—in spite of its rhetoric about the value of the public sector—shared the bias of most Canadians: to wit, that civil servants are overpaid and underworked.

For the cabinet, the first few months of power were a blur. Meetings of the Policy and Priorities Board, the smaller inner cabinet, could last from 8:00 a.m. to 10:00 p.m.—in part because of the NDP's decision-making process. Unlike most governments, this was not one in which the premier necessarily had the final say. Theoretically, Rae could be— and occasionally was—on the losing side of debates.

To Dave Cooke, initially Rae's Housing minister, some new ministers were becoming overly involved in picky questions: "There was a real need to try to get people to get away from getting into real bureaucratic detail and get more into talking about the politics of the situation," he said later. "Frances [Lankin], for example, is an incredible person in terms of being able to pick up detail and really get into the nitty-gritty. For others of us, that's not something we either want to do or could do.... At some point, it was getting too blurred [between] who was the politician and who was the bureaucrat."

Relations between bureaucrats, aides, ministers, and the premier's office varied from ministry to ministry. Cooke, for instance, would later say that he got on well with his civil servants: "I've always believed in the bureaucracy, even though it's frustrating on occasion that things take a little bit of time.... Sometimes, the time it takes to go through the process is good. It gives real opportunities to think through the policy implications.... No matter what happens in the next election, I have more respect for the bureaucracy now than I've ever had."

For Attorney General Howard Hampton, however, life was not as simple.

Hampton, a thirty-eight-year-old lawyer from northwestern Ontario, and Rae had never clicked. The son of a paper-mill worker, Hampton grew up in a small town, later attending Dartmouth College on a hockey scholarship. Rae, the son of a diplomat, grew up in world capitals before going to Oxford on a Rhodes scholarship.

To Hampton, this difference in background explained a great deal: "No, I don't feel close to the premier. But then I don't know anyone in the cabinet or caucus who does. Sometimes weeks will go by and we won't talk. And then suddenly he'll send me a note or call.... We don't have a relationship of animosity. But we're not close.... I consider myself to be a politician who works mainly on the basis of instincts. I rattle something around in my head until it feels right. And when it feels right, experience has taught me that, 99 per cent of the time, I'm right to do it. Bob's a very analytical individual. Some would say he comes from an intellectual background rather than a working—certainly not a working, small-town background. So it's no secret. We often disagree on a lot of issues. I would say, of all people in the cabinet we are probably on opposite sides of issues."

Hampton had not expected to be named to the prestigious post of attorney general. In part, as he explained later, he knew that he wasn't popular with what was called the Toronto left-wing bar—mainly civil-rights and defence lawyers. To some Toronto lawyers, Hampton seemed a rube.

"Their hope was that whoever got the AG's job would be someone close, someone they knew, someone they felt comfortable with," said Hampton. "That didn't happen. Though I met a lot, often with lawyers who were so-called NDP lawyers... I wasn't one of the gang."

Many in the Toronto left-wing bar did have an agenda, which they saw as making the justice system fairer. Initially, some tried to work through Rae directly. Lenny Wise remembered being telephoned by civil-rights lawyer Clayton Ruby early in the mandate. Ruby said he needed to talk to the premier but didn't know how to get through. Could Lenny give him Rae's home telephone number? Wise did, but only after swearing Ruby to secrecy. No one was to know how he obtained the number. What Wise did not say was that Rae's home number was listed in the Toronto telephone book.

To some in Hampton's office, however, the agenda of the Toronto left-wing bar seemed to be one of vengeance—getting back at certain Crown attorneys or officials. Hampton was suspicious, therefore, when Rae appointed Mary Hogan, a provincial court judge popular among Toronto NDP lawyers, as his deputy minister. "The feeling was," said one government figure close to the decision, "that 'we'll put Hampton in there as the figurehead, and Mary will be the real minister.'"

Soon, there was almost open warfare between Hampton and his deputy. The flash point was Hogan's decision to appoint Michael Code, an associate of Clay Ruby, to be assistant deputy minister in charge of criminal law.

Code was acknowledged to be a brilliant appellate defence counsel, one who had argued and won complex cases before the highest courts. Hampton, however, wanted to promote a Crown prosecutor from inside the ministry. The dispute was finally referred to Rae, who told Peter Barnes, his top civil servant, to come up with a solution. Hogan won, and Code was appointed. But the Hampton– Hogan relationship continued to deteriorate. The attorney general began to freeze out his deputy from key decisions.

"You have to have a really strong level of trust between a deputy minister and a minister," explained Hampton later. "And we lost whatever level of trust we had." Finally, Hogan quit. Later she was reappointed to the bench.

Meanwhile, the chaos of ministers' offices, the failure to even return telephone calls, had angered the party apparatus. As well, rank-and-file members were miffed. Rae, in an effort to be non-partisan, was not appointing enough New Democrats to patronage posts to suit his party. In 1991, party president Julie Davis, provincial secretary Jill Marzetti, and former party president Janet Solberg met with Agnew to complain.

"It's not as if we were going to put a neurosurgeon on the Egg Marketing Commission or something," said Solberg later. "There were pig farmers who were New Democrats who felt they ought to have a chance. Bob had this public-service thing—'Don't ask me for a job; I'm not here to give New Democrats jobs.' And so that was infuriating to all of us because they were appointing more Liberals or Tories.... And again it's not a matter of people wanting a turn at the trough. It's our people, saying, 'We're just as qualified as Liberals or Tories; give us a chance.'"

One unintended result of this meeting was that Solberg went to work for Rae. But the chaos inside government continued. By 1992, it was clear that the NDP's original plan of maintaining centralized control over government was in a shambles. Under attack from business, its own supporters, and much of the public, the NDP seemed to be barely riding the tiger of government, much less directing it. To Solberg, there was no sense of consistent overall strategy. As Sue Colley, the senior political aide to Frances Lankin, would put it later: "The NDP took legislative power but they never took political power."

Bureaucrats remained puzzled by the cabinet's consensual style of decision making. At times Rae would be on the losing side of a debate inside cabinet. Civil servants, who expected the premier to have the final word, could never get used to this. A decision in late 1993 to give the NDP caucus a veto over cabinet decisions confused the civil service even more. Bureaucrats who had managed to work an issue through cabinet committee, cabinet office, the premier's office, and cabinet itself, now could see their efforts exploded on the caucus-room floor.

For Michael Decter, who until he resigned in 1993 had been one of Rae's most trusted and influential bureaucrats, the government continued to experience a vacuum at the centre: "It's not clear who the buck stops with.... You can have a lot of people at the centre talking to themselves and that's not really like having control of the government."

To Decter, this stemmed in part from Rae's own remote, personal style. "The premier is not connected to it. He's the least connected.... There just isn't someone home in the way you'd expect from a government.... It's like the centre isn't. I mean, it's there, but it's not as thoroughly there."

As well, said Decter, the cabinet suffered from its own inconsistency: "I've been at cabinet meetings successive days where you'd think they had collective amnesia. They agree to something one day, and the next day not only do they agree to something different but it's like they don't remember there was the discussion."

The government's difficulties weighed on Rae. At times, he seemed depressed. Occasionally at night, his old friend Lenny Wise would come over to visit. The two would sneak out the back door of Rae's comfortable West Toronto home, hop over his back fence to avoid the Ontario Provincial Police bodyguards keeping watch at the front, and sit on a bench in a small park nearby, just talking. On occasional Sundays, Rae, who along with three old friends from law school had formed a gourmet cooking club, would relax with good food and some non-government conversation.

"After coming to power, it took him a while to realize how you change things," one of the premier's associates said later. "I think he realized in the second year that one of the best ways to influence government was not by being a politician but by being a long-term civil servant.... Maybe he thought he should have gone the academic and civil-service route, that he had made the wrong choice."

But by late 1992, Rae had decided he had to act. If he couldn't be both premier and top civil servant himself, he would do the next-best thing—appoint someone like him to head the bureaucracy. His first choice was Michael Decter, but Decter refused. So Rae did what he had perhaps wanted to do all along. He appointed his alter ego and chief political aide, David Agnew, as cabinet secretary. Barnes, who by this time, was virtually frozen out of major decisions became deputy minister of Industry. Agnew became Ontario's top civil servant. To aides in the premier's office, the decision made sense. "Bureaucrats want clear instructions," said one. "[Agnew] knew what was going on in the premier and cabinet's mind and would be a good transmitter."

By this time, both Rae and Agnew had become convinced they should restructure the civil service. The consensus at the centre was that the government was suffering from a surfeit of ideas, what one senior aide called a "politically overactive thyroid." One way to restore control was to merge ministries and reduce the number of ministers. "If there were fewer people protecting their turf, there would be better decision making," explained one influential NDP figure later.

Rae, always intrigued by grand schemes, liked the idea. After all, as a New Democrat he believed in government; he ran a government; what better legacy could he bequeath than to make that government more efficient. What's more, it would look good. The NDP was always accused of supporting bloated bureaucracies; Rae would be different. He would trim his.

Throughout that winter, schemes of amalgamation and superministries were bandied about. But the final result, as so often happens with grand reorganization schemes, was both more and less than had been envisaged. Rae wanted to trim ministerial dead wood from his cabinet. But he couldn't bring himself to fire ministers. Instead, he demoted three—Allan Pilkey, Richard Allen, and Karen Haslam—to the position of junior minister. These juniors collected reduced ministerial salaries. But, except for special occasions, they were not allowed into the weekly cabinet meetings.

Rae's most important aim on the ministerial front, however, was to shift Ruth Grier from the Environment portfolio to Health, and Frances Lankin from Health to Industry.

Grier, a committed environmentalist, had made the mistake of trying to carry out the promises she and the NDP had made in opposition. To that end, one of her first acts as minister in 1990 had been to reopen a controversy which the Liberal government had just succeeded in quieting—where to put Toronto's garbage. The Liberals had decided to set up a landfill dump in neighbouring Durham without going through a full environmental-assessment hearing. But the NDP had fought the Liberals on the Durham dump—and won seats in the region for their pains. Grier cancelled the Liberal scheme.

Meanwhile, Metro Toronto's government had planned to ship its garbage north, to the small mining town of Kirkland Lake. To many in Kirkland Lake, the garbage plan was seen as a job-creation measure. But Grier, pushed by the caucus's northern members, such as Shelley Martel, and holding to the environmentalist principle that regions should take care of their own waste, said no to that. The NDP had long opposed burning garbage, so Grier killed that idea too. Instead, she set up a new Interim Waste Authority to locate dump sites around Toronto.

By 1992, Toronto was still producing tonnes of garbage, there was nowhere to put it, and Grier's efforts to find a dump site had raised a storm of outrage in communities all around the city. Whereas the garbage policy of the Peterson Liberals had angered residents in just a few communities, the NDP's Interim Waste Authority managed to alienate voters in fifty-seven.

In the end, the NDP government ended up authorizing not one but three new landfill sites around Toronto. One was just eight kilometres from the Durham dump site the NDP had campaigned against in 1990. Another—on prime farmland north of Toronto—was slated to be the largest in North America. Grier aides would later blame the bureaucrats. But she wore the political responsibility.

As well, the NDP's environmental principles were proving to be incompatible with the new, business-oriented philosophy of the government. Early on, Grier's ministry, supported by the premier's office, killed a proposed housing project in downtown Toronto, one that was to have been built on former industrial land. The ministry made the valid point that the area was filled with toxic industrial waste which would have to be cleaned up—at a cost of $180-million—before any housing

could be built. Grier had followed NDP policy, but the government's
actions didn't help the depressed Toronto construction industry.

In early 1993, Grier's ministry released tough new draft regulations to limit the amount of chlorine that pulp-and-paper mills could dump into lakes and rivers. That too was NDP policy. But industry didn't like it and the regulations were eventually weakened. For a government determined to put economic growth ahead of environmental concerns, Grier had become an obstacle to be removed.

With Lankin, the situation was more complicated. Lankin had shown herself to be Rae's most competent member of cabinet. Indeed, the former labour negotiator, with her ties to the unions and the women's movement, was also a potential challenger to Rae for leadership of the NDP. As unions and the NDP rank and file became increasingly disgruntled by the government's shift to the right, the possibility of an eventual leadership review, once remote, had become more likely.

What's more, Lankin had stymied the plan of her deputy, Michael Decter, to end universal free drug coverage for those sixty-five and over. Decter wanted to go ahead with his plan, and Rae backed him.

At the same time, the idea of handling a major economic ministry intrigued the ambitious Lankin. Rae and Agnew felt they needed someone to repair strained relations with business and transform the moribund Ontario Industry ministry into a vehicle for economic renewal. Who better than the government's most competent minister?

Publicly, Grier put on a good face about giving up Environment. Privately, she was devastated. "I now know how a foster child feels when the Children's Aid knocks at the door and takes him from one family to another," she said later. Lankin's reaction, however, was mixed. She had told Rae she did not want to be moved. But the siren call of running what, at the time, was billed as an economic superministry appealed. Finance minister Floyd Laughren recalled later that Lankin initially seemed enthusiastic, even though he warned her about the pitfalls of her new ministry. For, in Ontario, the Industry ministry can be a political dead end. Whereas the Health minister is always on television, the Industry minister usually spends her time travelling to small towns, handing out cheques to obscure manufacturers of plastic piping, or announcing vague industrial strategies that few reporters understand, and even fewer cover. Lankin soon found all of this out herself.

Grier, aides said later, burst into tears when told she was being shifted. Whatever you do, she told the premier, don't let them ship

Toronto's garbage to Kirkland Lake. Faced with the spectacle of one his most loyal supporters so distraught, Rae acquiesced.

A few days after the announcement of the shuffle, Bud Wildman, the new Environment minister, arrived at Rae's home to talk about his new job. He found the premier busy packing his van to go to his cottage for the weekend. In the living-room were Agnew and Ross McClellan. Wildman had been told of his shift only at the last minute. But he was philosophical. At least, he told Rae, he could reverse the decision on Toronto garbage and arrange to have it shipped up to Kirkland Lake. That might win some northern votes. Everyone looked embarrassed. "We're staying the course on environment," Rae told Wildman. Ruth Grier's tears had undone one of the few rationales for the cabinet shuffle.

But the most important element of Rae's reorganization was his decision to make Agnew cabinet secretary, the province's top civil servant. Bureaucrats worried that Agnew's appointment was the ultimate attempt to politicize the civil service. In fact, it was the opposite. It was the bureaucratization of politics. By placing his most trusted aide in charge of the civil service, Rae had given deputy ministers—the top bureaucrats—direct access to his ear. Political aides soon noticed that the lines of power no longer went through the ministers to Agnew and the premier's office and finally to Rae. Instead they went from the bureaucracy to the deputies such as Jay Kaufman and Michael Mendelson, to Agnew and McClellan, and thence to Rae, effectively bypassing the politicians. Melody Morrison, who replaced Agnew as Rae's principal secretary, instituted the practice of having the premier meet with his most senior ministers—Floyd Laughren, Frances Lankin, and Dave Cooke. But even this was not enough.

In the end, the structure of government created by the Ontario NDP government was both close to, and far removed from, the one Ross McClellan had originally envisioned. The government was indeed centralized—nothing could make it to the Policy and Priorities Board without clearance from McClellan and Mendelson. Even cabinet office bureaucrats had to vet their suggestions with the pair before being allowed to comment on proposed policies.

At the same time, however, centralization had not—as McClellan had originally hoped—given a particularly socialist cast to the government. Centralization had just made it centralized, focused on one person—Rae—and coordinated by those who had his trust. With few exceptions, these were not members of his cabinet. They were bureaucrats and subordinates—Decter, Kaufman, Mendelson, McClellan, and, in his role as cabinet secretary, Agnew.

The explanation lies, in part, in the personality of Rae. Aides and ministers alike found him open to all, but close to none. At one point, Grier became so distressed that she phoned friends to seek advice on how to deal with a premier who was becoming increasingly otherworldly. Rae had no cronies in government—no single group to whom he could turn during the tight moments and ask for frank political advice. There could be no collective political structure overseeing the Ontario government, because, at the most fundamental level, Rae the loner didn't know how to create one.

True, he was no tyrant. In cabinet, he might lose specific debates. He often changed his mind. But that very inconsistency was his edge, for it kept others off balance. Typically, he would absorb advice and ideas and then, with little or no warning, announce his view. Rae's policy flip-flops took not only the Ontario public but many of his own top aides unawares. Some of his oldest friends had no idea where his ideas came from; it was as if his mind were a black box, impenetrable from the outside, processing information and spewing out decisions that often seemed at odds with one another.

"We are not wackos from outer space," Rae insisted early in his term. Later, as his government's economic policy moved back and forth across the ideological map, he was moved to say: "My brain has not been captured by alien forces." Not everyone was convinced.

5

Revenge of the Pink Ladies

AUGUST 1991: AS MEMBERS OF THE CABINET'S POLICY AND
Priorities Board straggled into Queen's Park, they could reflect on nine long and difficult months in office. Business was still in an uproar over the government's first budget, a modest attempt to counter the economic recession. The recession itself showed no sign of abating. Already, one minister had been forced to resign, and one fired. As well, the public had watched the farce of Rae accepting the resignation of two additional ministers, only to reverse himself minutes later after a plea for clemency from, of all people, the leader of the Liberal opposition.

And then there was auto insurance.

Since the 1940s, public insurance had been the signature of CCF and NDP governments. Public health insurance—medicare—had been the first battle. Once it had been accepted nationwide, provincial New Democrat organizations turned their attention to auto insurance.

Like medical insurance, auto insurance makes economic sense if organized as a public monopoly. Insurance is about risk. An insurer who can draw on the whole population—good drivers as well as bad—is able to minimize risk and use his capital most efficiently. These so-called economies of scale inherent in public auto insurance monopolies had already borne fruit in four provinces. Thanks to NDP governments, Saskatchewan, British Columbia, and Manitoba enjoyed full public auto insurance. The Parti Québécois had also introduced partial public insurance to Quebec. In all four provinces, the efficiency involved in moving from a multitude of private companies to a single insurer had significantly reduced premiums paid by drivers. Indeed, so popular was public auto insurance that, even when the NDP and the PQ lost power in the West and Quebec, their successors refused to undo what had been done.

For the insurance industry, Ontario was to be the last stand. Ontario was the country's largest insurance market. It was also headquarters for most of the nation's domestic insurance industry. Skyrocketing car insurance premiums had already made the industry unpopular with the public in the mid-1980s. The Peterson Liberals had made an abortive effort to freeze and then regulate rates. But a massive lobbying effort by the powerful industry through their Insurance Bureau of Canada had whipped the Liberals back into line.

In 1989, the Peterson government revamped Ontario auto insurance along lines favoured by the insurers. In particular, the rights of accident victims to sue in court were sharply curtailed. That action, the insurers estimated, would save them million of dollars in claims. The savings from this so-called no-fault system went straight to the bottom line of the insurers; they in turn made a gentleman's agreement with the Liberals to keep rate increases moderate.

With premiums affordable, most drivers were content. The deal worked out by the Liberals and the big insurance companies left only accident-victim groups and personal-injury lawyers fuming. And the NDP.

Rae's surprise victory in 1990 was greeted by the insurance industry as a nightmare come true. For years, public auto insurance had been a trademark of the party. Mel Swart, the veteran MPP from Welland–Thorold, a gritty working-class riding in the Niagara Peninsula, had made public auto insurance the crusade of his life. During the 1987 election campaign, public auto insurance had become the crusade of the entire NDP. When Swart retired from politics in 1988, his successor, Peter Kormos, took up the cudgel.

Kormos was a raunchy young lawyer with a liking for fast cars and a knack for gleaning publicity. He'd been a rebel since high school, when he was suspended for leading a student strike. In the fall of 1988, Kormos arrived at Queen's Park ready, as he told reporters, to "rattle the cage." Auto insurance would be his instrument.

Kormos's NDP colleagues at Queen's Park weren't quite sure what to make of their new caucus mate. Although the New Democrats were much like anyone else in terms of personal morals, they tended to project a prudish public image, a remnant from their social-gospel roots in the old CCF. In this category, at least, Kormos didn't seem to fit. Favoured with a shock of sandy hair that stood straight up at the back, he resembled a kind of hopped up Woody Woodpecker. Kormos was mouthy, drove a Corvette instead of a K-car, wore cowboy boots rather than Birkenstock sandals, and preferred *The Toronto Sun* to *Canadian Dimension*. He was a working- class boy who didn't mind showing off that he'd made good. And his constituents in the pool halls, grimy factories, and doughnut shops of Welland and Thorold loved him for it.

Rae didn't exactly approve of Kormos. But he hoped to make use of the thirty-six-year-old lawyer's energy in the NDP campaign for public auto insurance. Energy is what Kormos had. He showed just how much in April 1990 when he managed to carry on a one-person, one-month filibuster against the Liberal government's plan for no-fault insurance. On one day, he talked for seventeen hours straight, using the technique of both the modern telethon host and the old-time carnie to appeal directly to those Ontarians watching on cable television. It was a public-relations coup for the NDP. But by the end of it, both Rae and Kormos had committed the party firmly to two things.

First, an NDP government would reintroduce the right of accident victims to sue (lawyers call this the restoration of tort rights). Second, an NDP government would introduce public auto insurance during its first term. During the course of the 1990 election campaign, Rae spelled out both of these promises in blood.

Those who have been through the experience of government say that the time for bold action is at the start. Former Saskatchewan NDP premier Allan Blakeney, for instance, has written that a government must launch any new program as quickly as possible because "the public does not like change." After its first year, a government—any government—gets worn down by the business of governing. Unless it has a clear, sharp agenda, unless it starts that agenda rolling on day one, it is likely to find its term over with nothing to show.

In the case of auto insurance, it seemed as if Rae were taking Blakeney's advice. Kormos was named minister of Financial Institutions in charge of the project, a clear signal that the government was serious. Rae told the province that his government was committed to both public auto insurance and the restoration of the right of accident victims to sue; all that remained was to find the right model. Would it be

B.C.–style insurance, Quebec-style insurance? Something in between?

All was not as it seemed, however. For, while Rae had made the ebullient Kormos minister in charge of auto insurance, he had also set up a special division in the cabinet office. Whether Rae did this because he didn't trust Kormos with the auto-insurance file is unclear. The result was that, for the first four months, the effort was split. On the one hand was Kormos with his ministry. On the other was the cabinet-office operation reporting to Rae. The private insurance industry was able to use this rivalry to slow down the government even further and, in the words of one of its lobbyists, "screw it up a bit."

At the same time, bureaucrats within the Ministry of Financial Institutions were uneasy about the NDP plans. They had already been through this exercise once with the Liberals and felt that the NDP dream was hopelessly naïve. Restoring the right to sue would increase costs and cause premiums to rise; the efficiencies of public insurance would cause costs and premiums to fall again. To drivers, the net gain would be zero. Where was the political rationale?

Scenario after scenario was tried. Perhaps the government wouldn't reintroduce full tort rights for accident victims; perhaps only personal liability insurance would be nationalized, with private companies continuing to provide coverage for damage and collision. Perhaps the government wouldn't run the system at all but would let some politically appropriate company such as a cooperative run it for them.

Throughout, there were clashes between Kormos and the bureaucracy. In particular, he became alarmed at the close ties between some of the senior bureaucrats running the insurance operation and people in the private industry itself. "I had guys in the industry calling me up and telling me what we were doing before I knew," he said later. "I was very paranoid."

Even after Rae abolished the parallel cabinet-office operation in January 1991, appointed Blair Tulley as deputy minister of Financial Institutions and, on paper at least, handed the entire file over to the ministry, the battles continued. Kormos was sure the bureaucrats were trying to sandbag his demands to come up with a system that combined public insurance and tort rights. The bureaucrats in turn insisted that he was trying to square the circle.

"I was the minister, but that meant nothing," Kormos said later. "Tulley took his instructions from the premier's office and the cabinet office." Indeed, the two central offices did continue to involve themselves

in what was still considered the government's most high-profile initiative. That might have worked out if Rae and Kormos had communi-
cated more. But they didn't. They were two existential loners in
different planetary orbits. "In the six months I was there, I never talked
to Bob Rae once," said Kormos.

Whoever was at fault, the upshot of the infighting was that work on
the auto-insurance project ground to a halt. All of this took valuable
time. By the government's figuring, it would take three years to get a
public system operating properly. At best, that would leave one year
to win political points for the new system before another election.
With every month of delay, that period of potential political credit
was being eroded.

The delay also gave the insurance companies time to mobilize. One
of the key auto-insurance players during the Liberal period had been a
thirty-eight-year-old Haileybury native named George Cooke. Cooke
had worked at the short-lived Auto Insurance Board before joining then
Liberal treasurer Bob Nixon as a special assistant. Better than anyone
else inside or outside government, Cooke understood the political and
financial elements of the auto-insurance monster.

After the Liberal government fell, Cooke had gone to work for lobbyist S.A. Murray Consulting Inc. In one of its smartest moves to date,
the Insurance Bureau of Canada asked S.A. Murray—and George
Cooke—to set matters right. With contacts throughout the Treasury
and the Ministry of Financial Institutions, as well as in the insurance
industry generally, Cooke quickly came to know as much about the government's plans and problems as the government itself. In some cases,
he knew more. He also knew where the NDP was vulnerable politically.
That was on the issue of jobs.

By the summer of 1991, the insurance companies—through the
Insurance Bureau of Canada and S.A. Murray—were beginning to
score political points with the public. The Liberal no-fault scheme, with
its restrictions on the right to sue, had sent insurance profits climbing.
That meant the insurers could make money without bumping up premiums. Keen to smooth relations with a public that didn't much like insurance companies, the insurers kept their rates in line and, in some cases,
even lowered them.

At the same time, the insurers began to present themselves as
humane firms, interested in stopping public insurance not for crass,
commercial reasons but only because of their overriding interest in the

welfare of their employees. Public insurance, they warned, would cost some of these employees their jobs.

This, of course, was true. In fact, the whole point of public insurance is to create savings for the consumer by eliminating wasteful duplication. That, in turn, means eliminating jobs that duplicate each other, making the whole system more productive. What made public insurance more costly for Ontario, the insurers argued, was the large number of head offices in the province. Public auto insurance in B.C. might cost the jobs of a few workers in the field. Public insurance in Ontario, the industry claimed, would cost up to 10,000 head-office jobs.

As an argument from some of North America's largest financial industries, this was steeped in hypocrisy. For these were the same firms which, in the name of efficiency and productivity, happily fired their own workers. As Andrew Rogacki, president of Progressive Casualty, noted at the time, the private insurers were preparing to rationalize and trim their labour forces themselves in a few years. But these would be productivity gains and lay-offs to increase private profits—which were all right. Productivity gains in a public enterprise, apparently, were not.

Hypocritical or not, the strategy worked. In a province with tens of thousands out of work, the idea that a government might deliberately put workers on the dole made headlines. The government, already on the defensive, retreated into itself. Rather than counter industry claims about the perfidy of public insurance, the government kept silent, insisting that it would not comment until the cabinet made up its mind.

That was becoming increasingly difficult. In March, Kormos had been fired from cabinet. The whisper campaign had become extreme. Anonymous denunciations to the media dredged up old controversies from his past. Already, Kormos was openly hostile to some of his fellow ministers—particularly Lankin and Swarbrick. Publication of the fact that one of his top aides had once been convicted of wife assault did not endear Kormos any further to his female colleagues.

Meanwhile, Rae—even though he had long been aware of the so-called revelations about Kormos's past—was becoming alarmed. The premier had been warned that the Welland MPP would be a loose cannon in cabinet. He was beginning to think the Cassandras were right. On March 18, 1991, twelve days after Kormos infuriated his cabinet colleagues by posing, fully clothed, for a *Toronto Sun* beefcake shot, Rae fired him from cabinet.

To replace Kormos in the auto insurance portfolio, Rae brought in

Brian Charlton, now thoroughly chastened after his initial exclusion from cabinet. Charlton personally supported public auto insurance. But, in cabinet, he carried little clout. He was not even on the Policy and Priorities Board, the inner cabinet.

As well, auto insurance still did not belong to the minister of Financial Institutions; it was the property of the inner cabinet, and particularly the property of Rae. Charlton's job was to present the options and implement whatever Rae and cabinet decided. Ever a good soldier, that is what he would eventually end up doing.

The key problem that Charlton and his staff faced was the same one that had bedevilled the government all year. Both Rae and Kormos were publicly committed not only to government-run insurance but to the restoration of the right of accident victims to sue. The bureaucrats had told the government that these two aims were politically incompatible: public insurance would lower insurance premiums; restoration of tort rights would drive them up again.

Kormos, refusing to give up, had merely sent the bureaucrats back to try again. But Charlton soon came to the opinion that the bureaucrats were right. He favoured a partial no-fault public system that officials said would save drivers money on their premiums. But every time the scheme came to cabinet, Rae—conscious that his personal credibility was on the line—wanted to add in more tort rights. These, in turn, would eat into the per-driver savings.

Meanwhile, both David Agnew, Rae's principal secretary, and Ross McClellan, his senior policy aide, were getting cold feet. The job losses involved seemed too politically difficult. Charlton countered that significant savings would offset any political damage caused by phasing out insurance workers. As well, he pointed to the credibility issue. "In the context of this whole question of keeping your promises ... it just became very symbolic," Charlton said later.

But Agnew and McClellan remained unconvinced. Later, Janet Solberg would remember McClellan's conversion from public insurance: "Ross said: 'Remember when the insurance companies used to say to us, let them do it in Saskatchewan; let them do it in Manitoba; let them do it in B.C.; Ontario's different. Well, they were right.'"

By this time, after start-up costs, severance packages, and tort rights had been factored in, the potential savings Charlton was promising had been whittled down to $100 per car owner per year. "That was lower than what people would have liked," said Charlton later.

Inside the inner cabinet, Health minister Evelyn Gigantes remained sceptical about the government's ability to implement in a timely way a public insurance scheme that worked. "I had watched a system incapable of getting out a new health card," she said later. "And I kept saying to my cabinet colleagues, 'I want to tell you how difficult it is to put out a good system of health cards, and I want you to understand how much more difficult it's going to be when you're looking after all those auto insurance policies.' It was going to take two and a half years to get it in place, which meant we would have to go through the shedding of 5,000 jobs in the industry and we would have very little time for the system to prove itself before the election."

The propaganda campaign of the insurance lobby was also beginning to take effect. Initially, lobbyist George Cooke had warned his clients to go slow, to wait until after the first NDP budget before aggressively taking on the government. All indications from his Treasury and financial contacts were that the budgetary deficit would be huge. This, Cooke advised the insurers, would end the public's honeymoon with the NDP and leave the government politically vulnerable.

He was right. The government's announcement in April that its deficit had tripled, to almost $10 billion, was not well received by the public. By midsummer, the honeymoon was definitely over. The insurers had already produced detailed estimates of potential job losses public insurance might cause. Cooke urged them to hammer home a simple point: women comprised 70 per cent of the insurance workforce; therefore, any lay-offs caused by public insurance would hit women.

The industry moved its campaign into high gear, targeting female ministers and prominent women in the NDP. It was then that George Cooke produced the pink ladies. It was a masterful stroke.

The pink ladies, as they called themselves, worked for the insurance companies. They had been told that public auto insurance would cost them their jobs and were understandably upset. So it didn't take much for George Cooke and the rest of the lobby team working at S.A. Murray to persuade female insurance workers to bring their concerns to the people who counted at Queen's Park. S.A. Murray provided the transport. If a demonstration was in order, S.A. Murray provided the placards, tastefully and professionally done in pink.

The pink ladies visited, among others, Julie Davis. Davis was at the time both secretary-treasurer of the Ontario Federation of Labour and president of the Ontario NDP. She had never been excited about public auto insurance. And while she was clearly aware that the pink ladies were there at the behest of their employers, she was also concerned about what the government had in mind for the women it knew would be laid off.

"It certainly led me to ask a lot of questions about . . . what would we do with these people," she said later. "And I couldn't get answers."

The pink-lady argument was also making Women's minister Anne Swarbrick rethink public insurance. And it spoke directly to Rae, who had gone out of his way to make sexual equality a watchword of his government.

But Rae was also firmly committed to public insurance, or at least so it seemed. Early in July, the premier gave a stirring speech to staffers working on the auto-insurance brief. The government was going ahead, he said. It knew public insurance was the right thing to do, and it was going to do it.

That was before the full might of the pink ladies had been unleashed. By late July, the auto-insurance debate within the NDP was taking on the colouring of a women's issue. At one meeting, Davis, Ontario Federation of Labour president Gord Wilson, Canadian Union of Public Employees head Judy Darcy, and other labour leaders sat down with government figures to discuss auto insurance. Wilson argued strongly in favour of going ahead with public insurance. Davis was by this time opposed. Darcy too did not see public insurance as a top priority.

"It made some economic sense not to go ahead," said Davis later. "And this was the big issue for me. My position on it was 'Who cares?' Boy was I wrong. . . . Who knows where my head was?"

By the time the inner cabinet met in early August, the dynamics had shifted dramatically. At that meeting, and for the first time, Rae himself openly questioned the wisdom of proceeding with public insurance. Of the eight-member inner cabinet, only Tony Silipo, the newly appointed Management Board chair, spoke in favour of forging ahead. Those present knew that the decision had been made; public auto insurance had been killed.

A few days later, George Cooke organized the largest pink-lady demonstration to date. S.A. Murray made sure the press was present when 5,000 ordinary, polite, but worried working women—with pink ribbons and pink signs—paraded in front of Toronto City Hall, pleading with the leader of Ontario's first social-democratic government not to throw them out of work.

It took six more weeks for the dénouement to work itself out. The final decision was taken by cabinet on September 6, 1991, one year to the day from the NDP's smashing electoral victory. Meeting at a resort in the Georgian Bay holiday town of Honey Harbour, the cabinet thrashed out the final arguments.

Northern Development minister Shelley Martel and Silipo spoke in favour of public insurance. Charlton too still wanted to go ahead. But another strong supporter of public insurance, Attorney General Howard Hampton, was not there. At the urging of Rae's office, he was thousands of kilometres away, attending a federal-provincial Justice meeting in Yellowknife. Hampton had not been told that auto insurance was even on the agenda for Honey Harbour. When he discovered the decision had been made without him, he was furious.

"But as I thought about it," he recounted later, "I realized that, since we seemed to be stalled on the issue of auto insurance, and had been stalled on the issue of auto insurance for twelve months, I should have realized that that indicated we weren't going ahead."

In cabinet, Martel made an impassioned plea not to abandon the central plank of the party's platform. But, with Rae and Treasurer Floyd Laughren opposed, she, Silipo, and Charlton were outgunned. Throughout the meeting—and the meeting with the NDP caucus that followed directly after—Martel sobbed softly.

In order to soothe ruffled feelings, the government decided it would say it was not abandoning public auto insurance, just postponing it. But speaking to reporters, Rae was far more blunt. He said his government had no intention of revisiting the issue. After complaints from the caucus and party, he would later hedge that to say the government had no intention of revisiting auto insurance in its first term. But it was clear that, for Bob Rae at least, public auto insurance in Ontario had become a dead issue.

The decision stunned New Democrats across the country. Federal and provincial party officials attending an NDP finance meeting in Winnipeg were dismayed. "It was a very vigorous debate," recalled Dick Proctor, at the time federal secretary for the NDP. "There was a real feeling from across the country that Ontario had let the side down." Howard Pawley, the former Manitoba NDP premier who, as a minister in 1970, had braved business opposition to pilot public auto insurance into law in that province, was openly critical: "[David Peterson] finished his term with nothing to show the electorate; he hadn't delivered on what he had promised. It was the key to his defeat. And now the NDP is doing the same thing."

In Ontario, the auto-insurance decision would raise the first questions inside the party about Rae's leadership and the direction of the government. "This is escape from power," said an angry Peter Kormos. "A real crisis not for the public but for our traditional supporters."

Later that fall, party and government leaders would have to scramble to prevent a meeting of the NDP's governing provincial council, attended by a strong phalanx of public-insurance supporters, from getting out of hand. In just over two years, Mel Swart—former MPP, long-time Rae supporter, and the man who had made public insurance his calling—would be demanding the premier's resignation.

"Symbolically, it [the auto-insurance decision] spoke to people who were both party members and party supporters in a far more negative way than I'd ever expected," said Julie Davis ruefully some two years later.

But on September 6, 1991, all of this was a long way away. Back at Honey Harbour, key aides—including Rae policy adviser Ross McClellan—met to discuss the aftermath of the announcement. At one level, there was a sense of relief; at least a decision had finally been made on the troublesome insurance issue. But then someone asked a question: "If we don't do public auto insurance, what will we do? What will people remember us for? What will be our signature?"

Around the room, there was dead silence. No one had thought of that.

6

The Casino Economy I: Not Much Coherent Thinking

FOR ANY GOVERNMENT, THE QUESTION OF LEGACY IS important. Not the legacy over which future generations of historians will argue but a more immediate, practical legacy: How, in future elections, will voters remember the government's time in office? Politicians sometimes refer to this as a government's signature. For Rae's NDP, the capitulation on public auto insurance meant there would be no obvious signature, no symbol to take to the public at the next election and say: Look, this is what we are all about.

By the end, Rae was arguing that his government would be remembered as a pioneer in areas of economic and social policy—the first government in North America to institute a meaningful employment equity law; the first government in Ontario to pass legislation protecting the wages of workers whose employers go bankrupt; the government which tried to rationalize welfare, training, and its own operations in an effort to restructure the way business is done in the province.

For some Ontarians, Rae's so-called social contract—the get-tough legislation that rolled back public-service wages—will be remembered as the government's signature. But it is likely that more will remember the NDP as the party that brought casino gambling to Ontario.

The decision to legalize casinos touched on almost every important element of the Rae government—its preoccupation with debt and consequent mad scrambling for revenues, its almost macho willingness to jettison old NDP assumptions which no longer seemed to fit, the casual way in which it could make important decisions.

In opposition, the NDP had fought the creation of lotteries, denouncing games of chance as a tax on the poor. In May 1990, then opposition MPP Floyd Laughren had attacked government attempts to use lottery profits to supplement the province's consolidated revenues. "Essential services should be funded by the tax system of this province, not through games of chance," he said then. "This anti-gambling approach has been the basic thrust of our political movement since it was founded in the Depression," added Mike Farnan, another New Democrat MPP.

The party itself had no policy on casinos—a fact which the government would use to justify its actions—mainly because no one in the party had ever assumed such a policy would be needed. Neither did it have a policy on human sacrifice. In so far as anyone in the NDP had ever thought about such issues, most in the party assumed they were opposed.

While most NDP objections to gambling were based on questions of equity—the tax-on-the-poor argument—Rae's critique was fundamentally moral. To Rae, the casino encouraged the worst kind of human instinct, unalloyed greed. During the merger mania of the 1980s, he liked to use the casino as the ultimate symbol of an economy gone wrong, one in which companies gambled away the future of their workers just for a chance at speculative profits. "The casino economy is a travesty of an efficient and productive economy," he said in 1986. An NDP government, he told the Ontario Federation of Labour, would replace this casino economy with one which rewards not greed but enterprise. In his 1990 treatise, "What We Owe Each Other," Rae made his moral critique of the casino explicit—it divorced reward from effort: "The casino plays on greed. The sense of the ultimate chance, the hope against hope that the spin of the wheel or the shot of the dice will produce instant wealth, instant power, instant gratification. The work ethic 'steady as you go' appears alongside as fundamentally boring, goody two-shoes values." Such moral issues were not insignificant to Rae, who believed that social democracy—if it were to have any meaning—had to encompass humane values.

All of this changed in 1992 when, with little warning and no consultation, the government announced it would authorize casinos. Rights to run the first casino, in Windsor, would eventually be awarded to a glitzy Las Vegas–style consortium which, according to the government's own documents, at one time had "a lot of mob involvement" before being cleaned up in the 1970s. More casinos, the government indicated, were likely to follow.

The casino plan—first indications of which were revealed by *The Toronto Star* in March—was entirely unexpected. Government backbenchers had not been warned. Even the cabinet member nominally in charge of gaming, Consumer and Commercial Relations minister Marilyn Churley, was caught off guard. On April 22, she denied reports the cabinet had finally authorized a casino. Eight days later, Treasurer Floyd Laughren announced the NDP was getting into the casino business.

Editorial cartoonists were delighted, the general public bemused, and some long-time New Democrats horrified. Under Rae, the Ontario NDP had become known for the moral—almost sanctimonious—approach it took to such issues. And now casinos? Some New Democrats ripped up their party cards. Mayors of other hard-hit towns scurried to lobby for casinos in their districts; the chief of police in Peel Region just outside of Toronto warned publicly that the decision would bring more organized crime to Ontario. Rural members of Rae's caucus were uneasy, with many New Democrat MPPs upset that they had not been properly consulted. Eventually one rural government backbencher, Victoria–Haliburton MPP Dennis Drainville, bolted the caucus over the casino issue to sit as an independent.

Where had the casino decision come from? Why had Rae and the NDP been able to reverse themselves so easily? In part, the answer lies in practical politics. Windsor–Riverside MPP Dave Cooke, then minister of Municipal Affairs, was under attack in his riding and wanted a popular issue on which he could be re-elected. But in a broader sense, the casino decision was indicative of the Rae government's entire approach to economic policy. Its roots lay in the economic philosophy—or lack thereof—that the NDP brought to government.

By the end of 1990, members of Rae's government knew Ontario was in crisis. It was something the NDP had always predicted but never really expected: a full-scale economic depression, aggravated by the particularly unfortunate timing of the Canada–U.S. Free Trade Agreement and the Bank of Canada's obsession with combating inflation through high interest rates. Clearly, jobs and the economy—matters the Ontario NDP had paid far too little serious attention to, and about which it had almost no ideas—would be the priorities. But what could the government do?

At the centre of all this was Floyd Laughren, the man Rae appointed deputy premier and treasurer. Laughren was widely respected within the NDP. The left saw him as one of theirs. He had, for instance, supported Richard Johnston against Rae in the 1982 Ontario NDP leadership race—an acid test for those on the left of the party. At the same time, the right—including Rae—appreciated Laughren's openness and pragmatism. Although he had an ideology, he was no ideologue.

Laughren had been born in Shawville, Quebec, a dirt-poor, anglophone and ferociously anti-French community of loggers and farmers. At the age of five, he had become seriously ill. But with few medical services in Shawville, his father, a farm labourer, had moved the family to Southern Ontario.

Floyd Laughren grew up with little interest in politics. "My dad was 100 per cent illiterate," he explained later. "And there were never any newspapers in the house, so I was not even remotely politically involved." Nonetheless, his upbringing left him with a great respect for education. He went to the Ryerson Polytechnic Institute in Toronto and then, after six years in retail business, enrolled at York University and obtained a B.A. In 1969, he got a job teaching economics at Sudbury's Cambrian College. It was Sudbury—a hard-rock Northern Ontario city whose landscape is still scarred from early nickel mining and smelting—that politicized Laughren. "It may sound naïve," he said later, "but I was really taken aback by the desolation in the Sudbury community. There were no monuments to wealth, other than the desolation—inadequate roads, no parks, inadequate public infrastructure. It was truly remarkable. And the pollution in those days was just awful. That was step one."

Step two in the radicalization of Floyd Laughren was the federal government's 1969 white paper on tax reform. In 1967, a federal royal commission on taxation under the chairmanship of Kenneth Carter had called for full-scale reform of a system heavily biased in favour of the wealthy. The white paper, issued by then federal Finance minister Edgar Benson, was an attempt by the federal Liberal government to figure out how it could deal with Carter's far-reaching recommendations. Business was unsure how to approach the tax-reform proposals. In Sudbury, the Chamber of Commerce asked Cambrian College for someone who could offer a seminar on the Benson white paper to local business people. Laughren volunteered. "It really was a great experience," he said, "because they didn't like what was going on [in the current tax system] either, especially small business.... So they learned and I learned. . . . The combination of that plus the environmental pol-lution really got me thinking."

Laughren started to attend NDP meetings. A provincial election had been called for 1971. But, in Nickel Belt, the constituency just outside Sudbury, tensions within the NDP riding association were high. Sudbury had just come through a fierce union battle between the left-leaning Mine, Mill and Smelter Workers and the more conservative United Steelworkers of America. The NDP nomination in 1971 was being contested by two people—one Mine-Mill, the other Steel. The party wanted a compromise candidate. Laughren was persuaded to stand. He won the nomination and, to his surprise, the election.

In opposition, Laughren soon won a reputation as a leftist. Much to the dismay of Stephen Lewis, then Ontario party leader, Laughren and his two Sudbury colleagues, Elie Martel and Bud Germa, kept punching holes in the NDP's attempts to soft-pedal socialism. In particular, the trio wanted Inco Ltd., Sudbury's largest nickel producer, nationalized, a demand which sent chills down corporate spines.

Rae's decision to appoint Laughren treasurer in 1990 renewed those chills. At the time, business and their spokesmen were urging Rae to act as his own treasurer. But many New Democrats remembered the British Columbia precedent. B.C.'s first NDP premier, Dave Barrett, had insisted on being his own Finance minister, a decision widely believed to have contributed to the downfall of his government.

Rae also heeded the advice of Julie Davis, party president and secre-tary-treasurer of the Ontario Federation of Labour. "We know things are bad and they are going to get worse," she told the premier shortly after the 1990 election victory. "And when you have to make those tough economic decisions, far better for you that the party has someone who they've seen as being on the very far progressive wing of the party saying things the government has to do."

Three years later, this advice would backfire as Rae and Laugh-ren—citing economic necessity—bucked Davis and the rest of the province's labour leadership to overturn public-sector union contracts. "God knows, I didn't anticipate things would be nearly as bad as they are," Davis said then. "But I thought at the time it would be good for Bob, if there were going to be tough decisions—and I was thinking more along the lines of things they wouldn't be able to do because of the economy—there would be Floyd there beside him, agreeing with him . . . [and] that would lend credibility broadly across the party."

The transformation of the man jokingly referred to by his children as "Pink Floyd" into a typically conservative Ontario treasurer puzzled people across the ideological spectrum. "The great question to me in all of this is Floyd," said Davis three years into the government's mandate. Walter Curlook, chairman of Cambrian College when Laughren was a radical economics instructor there, was equally surprised. In 1993, he had nothing but praise for the one-time scourge of capitalism, calling him "one of the most pragmatic treasurers we've ever had." By this time, Curlook was vice-chairman of Inco Ltd., the company Laughren had once wanted to nationalize.

The explanation behind the mysterious conversion of Floyd Laughren, and behind the consequent and equally puzzling conservative economic stance of the Rae government, includes many factors. But two stand out: the nature of the economy the government faced upon taking power; and the perennial failure of the NDP, both federally and provincially, to develop a coherent and practical program for dealing with that economy.

In previous postwar recessions, Ontario had managed to avoid massive dislocation through what was, for Canada, a uniquely diversified economic structure. Southern Ontario contained a manufacturing base protected by tariffs and special trade agreements, the most notable of these being the Canada–U.S. Auto Pact. In the North, a resource sector produced minerals and lumber products for export. In the past, when northern resource industries had gone into a slump, southern manufacturing took up much of the slack. And vice versa.

However, beneath the surface of this seemingly auspicious marriage between manufacturing and resource industries were serious structural weaknesses. The problems of the protected, and generally foreign-owned, manufacturing industry had been well known since the late 1960s: plants were old, production lines small and inefficient. Most important of all, their existence was too often dependent on the good-will of head offices domiciled in the United States.

Less well understood was the vulnerability of the auto economy. By the late 1980s, autos and auto parts had become the province's largest export; entire towns and regions were dependent on auto manufacturing. But the auto economy depended on the continued existence of the Auto Pact, a unique political arrangement that gave Canada special status in the U.S. market. If that status were to be altered by the United States (either through weakening the Auto Pact or expanding it to include other nations able to produce more cheaply and efficiently than Canada), the province's entire economic structure could be placed in jeopardy.

All of this would have caused the provincial economy trouble eventually. The actions of the federal Conservative government in the late 1980s accelerated the process and turned eventual trouble into an immediate economic crisis.

Some analysts still argue that the 1989 free-trade pact with the United States will ultimately turn out to be economically beneficial for Canadians. They may be proven correct. What is clear, however, is that the federal government, and free-trade boosters generally, grossly underestimated the immediate damage the deal would wreak on the economy of the Canadian heartland. Throughout Ontario, plants closed or relocated production south of the border; without tariff protection, there was no reason for them to stay.

More ominously, the Canada–U.S. deal signalled trouble for the Auto Pact, providing for it to be phased out over ten years. As if to emphasize the point, Canadian parts manufacturers began to shift production to the *maquilladora* zones of Mexico to take advantage of cheap labour there. Auto-related plant closings hammered small towns and cities throughout Southern Ontario. In communities that had been well-off—such as Collingwood, St. Catharines, and Windsor—the unemployment rate soared.

Meanwhile, the Bank of Canada, the country's semi-autonomous central bank, was making the situation even worse. Since the early 1980s, the Bank had been obsessed with fighting rising prices. But by the end of the decade, the central bank's then governor, John Crow, was determined to ratchet the inflation rate down to zero. Zero inflation was to be achieved by choking off the economy through high interest rates, until unemployment reached such a level that those still working would be unable to win wage increases. With wage increases at zero, prices would soon follow suit and inflation would be licked.

Crow's strategy worked only too well. In 1990, Canada had the dubious and unusual honour of entering economic recession before the United States.

For Ontario, the result of federal trade and monetary policy was devastating. Through free trade and high interest rates, Ottawa had brought both rapid structural change and deliberate deflation to the Ontario economy. Either one alone would have caused widespread unemployment. Together, they were disastrous.

That was what Bob Rae's NDP inherited.

Throughout his mandate, Rae would rail at Ottawa for this unhappy state of affairs. And it is true that the economy the NDP took over was by no means its fault. What was less forgiveable, though, was that the new government had absolutely no strategy for dealing with an economy in free fall. For a party that had been born in the Depression of the 1930s, with the express purpose of ending the misery of unemployment and destitution, this failing was—to say the least—ironic.

For most of this century, economic thinkers trying to come to terms with unemployment have divided along two lines. One broad strand argues that joblessness is the result of structural failings in the economy. The other holds that joblessness is more a function of the business cycle, those periodic booms and busts which punctuate a capitalist economy. During a slump, these demand theorists argue, consumers and business stop spending. This, in turn, throws even more out of work. The resulting unemployment, however, can be alleviated by a government willing to take up the slack in demand—either by spending money or by cutting taxes.

During the early part of the century, structuralists dominated the discussion. Those on the right argued that unemployment resulted when human beings tried to interfere with the perfect workings of the impersonal market; in particular, they targeted labour unions, minimum-wage laws, government regulation, farm price support, tariffs, and anything else that interfered with the theoretical ability of markets to reach an optimum situation.

The broadly defined left, to which the CCF belonged, saw the problem in the structure of capitalism itself, a structure which resulted in periodic and devastating slumps. To the non-Marxist left, the anarchy of the private market was the cause of unemployment. Logically, therefore, a planned economy—one that regulated production to avoid booms and busts—was the answer.

However, the Depression of the 1930s brought the demand theorists, the other broad strand, to the fore. Usually associated with the English economist John Maynard Keynes, demand economics dominated Western thinking of all political stripes in the post-1945 period.

For the CCF-NDP, the postwar period was a time of breaking with, or at least downplaying, its socialist roots. The emphasis on public ownership and a planned economy was watered down during the 1950s and 1960s. Eventually, all that was left of the party's structural critique of capitalism was a vague distrust of monopolies, banks, and foreign multinational companies. Public ownership was to be limited to very specific key industries deemed to operate more efficiently under monopoly conditions, such as health or auto insurance. Otherwise, structural problems were to be dealt with by regulation.

At the same time, the party found the tenets of Keynesian thinking attractive. First of all, it was respectable—even Richard Nixon had declared himself a Keynesian. Second, it seemed to hold a practical answer to the problem of unemployment—an activist government should be able to counter the problem of rising joblessness by cutting taxes, spending money, or lowering interest rates.

But as the Polish economist Michael Kalecki pointed out in a prophetic article written in 1943, Keynesian economics contained its own contradictions. An economy near the full-employment point limited the ability of employers to use fear of joblessness to squeeze wage concessions from their workers. In other words, Keynesian economic policy allowed more power over wages to be shifted to workers and unions. By limiting the force of the savage deflationary recessions which had once ravaged the industrial world, it allowed price inflation to run out of control.

By the 1970s, conservative structural economists had made a comeback. In particular, monetarist theorists associated with the U.S. economist Milton Friedman held sway. Monetarists maintained that government could control the price level only through the creation of money, that everything else government attempted—from regulation to counter-cyclical Keynesian-style spending—was counter-productive. Finally, monetarists argued that unemployment was a structural problem which could be solved only when the familiar impediments (minimum wages, unions, farm price supports, regulation) were removed.

At the same time, a new form of old conservative economic thinking—one opposed to virtually all forms of public spending—was gaining strength. These radical conservatives, encouraged by a real and growing fiscal crisis among Western governments, argued that "unproductive" government borrowing used up valuable capital that might otherwise go to "productive" private investment. Moreover, government spending on programs such as welfare and unemployment insurance kept wages from falling sufficiently. Here, the monetarists and the radical conservatives had a convenient marriage of the minds.

By the early 1980s, the twin themes had become the industrial world's new orthodoxy. Together, they were referred to as "neo-conservative economics." They did fit together neatly. A monetarist central-bank policy aimed at curbing inflation could, and did, lead to widespread unemployment in Canada, the United States, and Britain. Massive unemployment reduced tax revenues, thus exacerbating the fiscal crisis facing governments. This in turn gave governments the necessary excuse to cut back the kind of expenditures—on programs such as welfare and unemployment insurance—which kept up wages and which were decried by monetarists and radical fiscal conservatives alike.

True, the new solutions resulted in higher unemployment. Yet if the public could be persuaded that inflation and government debt rather than joblessness were the real bogeymen, political support could be obtained for this harsh medicine.

Only at one level did the aims of the monetarists and the radical fiscal conservatives clash. The Bank of Canada's anti-inflationary, high-interest-rate policy raised the government's own borrowing costs significantly and caused the federal debt to mushroom. By 1990, Ottawa was paying an estimated $7 billion extra each year in debt-interest charges because of central-bank policy.

This contradiction did not bother the federal Conservative government. For, no matter what was said publicly, debt reduction and inflation fighting were never the ultimate goals. What linked the two schools of neo-conservative thought was their mutual desire to transform the wage structure—to lower the cost of labour. Neo-conservative spokesmen referred to this as becoming "globally competitive."

In the mid-1980s, the Bank of Canada could use inflation as an excuse to put downward pressure on wages, as it raised interest rates, and thus unemployment. By the early 1990s, when inflation was effectively licked, the federal government could then turn around and use public debt as an excuse to continue the same kinds of wage-squeezing policies.

Throughout most of the 1980s, the NDP stayed aloof from this new conservative interest in structural economics. One of the most consistent fighters for orthodox Keynesian economics was Rae, who, as a federal MP, had been his party's finance critic. With unemployment at about 7 per cent in 1981, Rae lambasted the ruling federal Liberals for what he called their "Tinkerbell economics. We have a government which has introduced a budget which does not take into account the tragedy of unemployment.... This budget says, in effect, there is nothing we can do. We do not have solutions to your problem. We cannot deal with the problem of recession."

A year later, as Ontario NDP leader, he heaped scorn on the Conservatives of Premier Bill Davis for using the deficit as an excuse to ignore the jobless. "The government can do some things," Rae said then. "It can intervene."

Indeed, the only new thinking going on inside the NDP at the time was at the margin. Jim Laxer, academic and ex-Waffler, the man who had once challenged the NDP establishment from the left, was becoming increasingly concerned with problems of debt and deficit. In 1983, Laxer, then federal research director, wrote a devastating critique of NDP economic policy. The party, he said, could no longer rely on Keynesian prescriptions. It had to recognize that government debt was a problem, that governments could no longer spend money helter-skelter. Economic problems, he went on then and in later articles, were structural. What was needed was an overall strategy for dealing with the economy, and a partnership between business, labour, and government to put that strategy into practice. "The alternative to neo-conservatism," Laxer wrote in 1988, "involves the creation of an economic partnership among business and government, and in most cases, labour."

In effect, Laxer was recommending what the theorists call a corporatist state, where the major components of society act together for the good of the corpus or body politic. Corporatism had been a theory of the right in the pre-war period and adopted by, among others, the Italian Facists. But Laxer could point to social democracies, such as Sweden's, which used elements of corporatism to regulate their economies.

Initially, Laxer's critique met with scorn from his party. The unions in particular saw an attack on Keynesian thinking as an attack on full-employment policies. As Laxer later wrote bitterly, no one attacked him more than Rae, the establishment Keynesian. Laxer himself left his job, and eventually the NDP, occasionally returning from self-exile in the south of France to issue a stinging critique of his former party. But ideas similar to his lived on, to resurface in the oddest of places.

One such place was the union movement itself. Within the major unions, a struggle was developing over the issue of worker involvement in management and ownership—what Rae's government would later call "partnership." One camp argued that the battles over wages which had characterized unionism in the 1940s, '50s, and '60s had become passé. At a time of slower growth, there was simply less to go around—

unless both labour and management changed their approaches. That change meant dealing with the organization of the workplace. Unions should strive to involve themselves in the running of companies through co-management. This would be democratic, allowing workers more control over their lives. It would also be productive, since co-management and co-ownership would encourage efficiency and productivity.

The other camp, however, argued that co-management was ultimately a dead end—a ruse by capital to entice labour into giving up hard-won gains.

However, labour–management partnership—or bilateralism—was winning favour among the labour leadership. The Steelworkers had found this particularly useful in their dealings with employers. By 1988, the Ontario Federation of Labour was agitating for new bilateral business–labour organizations, sponsored by, but not including, government. Their model, set up by David Peterson's Liberals, was the Workplace Health and Safety Agency, a government-sponsored organization run jointly by employers and the unions. In the summer of 1990, the unions lobbied for and won a commitment from Peterson that his government would set up a new organization to oversee industrial training, the Ontario Training and Adjustment Board. The new body would be another example of co-management. It would be run by constituent groups—representing business, labour, and others—rather than the government alone. But it would be financed by government.

By 1989, the New Democrats had realized they were lagging behind in terms of economic ideas. "There was not much coherent thinking," said Chuck Rachlis, at the time director of research for the NDP caucus. "No one thought we'd ever win, so it wasn't a priority.... We tended to do the things which interested us, like tax reform, and ignored the rest." As Laughren acknowledged, ideas that did exist—such as strategies for encouraging secondary manufacturing—had been rendered virtually impossible under the terms of the Canada–U.S. Free Trade Agreement. To rectify this situation, he assembled a group of left-wing intellectuals and asked them to submit ideas as to where the party should go.

The thinkers themselves included more than the usual collection of NDP professors. Nationalist economist Mel Watkins, who in spite of his connection with the Waffle had made his peace with the party, was invited. But so were leftists such as Marxist political scientist Leo Panitch and the prolific York University professor Danny Drache, both of whom, in the past, had been considered a little too piquant for the

NDP. From the other side, the group included David Wolfe, a University
of Toronto political scientist with only limited connections to the party.

The thinkers were asked to write papers on different aspects of social-democratic economics. "It was like a graduate seminar," Watkins recalled later. "Floyd [Laughren] was very open, not ideological at all in party terms." Unfortunately, most of the left thinkers didn't bother to put much effort into their papers. Watkins recycled an old paper he had done for something else, as did Panitch and Drache. "If anyone had thought they [the New Democrats] were going to win power, we would have been more serious," said Watkins.

Three of the participants did take the exercise seriously, however. One was Riel Miller, a bright young economist who had organized the event for Laughren. A second was Isabella Bakker, a York University political scientist and Miller's wife, who had agreed to compile the ramblings of the leftist academics into a coherent summary. ("She did an excellent job," said Watkins. "She pulled common threads from the discussions that we weren't even aware were there.") The third was Wolfe. Wolfe had already been involved in the debate over trade-union strategy. His paper called on the NDP to take its head out of the sand and accept the *fait accompli* of free trade. Both Wolfe and Miller would end up in senior economic-policy positions during the first years of the Rae government.

Miller, a Ph.D. graduate in economics from New York's New School of Social Research, had worked at the Paris-based Organization for Economic Cooperation and Development under Canada's Sylvia Ostry. To their friends, Miller and Bakker were the model, modern social-democratic couple—well dressed, attractive, intellectual. His self assured, analytical style was well-suited to the senior common rooms of the university. But, in politics, it often grated. "He's very bright," said Watkins, who worked with Miller in the anti–free trade movement of 1987, "but he has a tremendous capacity to irritate people."

As an economist, Miller had little time for the Keynesianism which had become NDP orthodoxy. Instead, he was more of a grand, conceptual thinker—intrigued by the growth of new, information-based service industries, interested in a form of social-democratic economics that would emphasize cooperation and flexibility. Other parties already had their Riel Millers; indeed, the Peterson Liberals had set up an advisory body called the Premier's Council, devoted to ideas of competitiveness, cooperation, and flexibility. But inside the NDP, Miller was something of a novelty.

In their 1989 thinkfest, the left academics had been asked to cover the usual gamut of NDP interests—immigrants, tax fairness, industrial strategy. What they came up with, however, as reflected through the prism of Bakker's summary, was quite different. The key paper was Wolfe's. He argued that international competition and free trade left the NDP with only two choices: it could ignore the rest of the world and try to isolate itself from it; or it could get into the game. Wolfe's preference was the latter. The NDP, he said, should accept the internationally competitive world of free trade rather than fight it; Ontario's strategy should focus on restructuring the economy away from older industries and towards newer ones that produced high value-added commodities (and thus permitted high wages) able to compete internationally. Other papers took a similar tack. Echoing the old Tory refrain, one thinker argued that the NDP had to concentrate on producing wealth, not just distributing it. Others called for a new commitment to training, as well as cooperation among labour, business, and government. Still another argued that welfare had to be seen as an integral part of economic policy, not merely a residual program for the poor.

Overall, none of these ideas was new. Most were versions of the structuralist strand in economics: if government has a role to play, it is in changing the fundamental way in which the economy works rather than fiddling around trying to boost consumer demand. As well, most were influenced by the critique of Keynesian economics which had begun on the right in the 1970s. As Bakker put it in her summary: "With Keynesianism now in ashes, economic recovery means potentially a new way of doing things that goes beyond a fine-tuning of capitalism."

In hindsight, several points stand out about the Ontario NDP's 1989 attempt to rethink its economic policies. First, most participants appeared to assume that the booming economy of the 1980s would more or less continue—a perhaps not-unreasonable assumption in 1989. The compilation document set out a strategy for making a growing economy wealthier; it had nothing to say about rejuvenating an economy caught in the crisis of severe depression. Second, there were serious gaps. Papers that the caucus had asked for—on taxation, investment policy, the role of unions, privatization of public industries, and the deficit—were never delivered. Given that these would be among the most vexing problems the NDP would face on taking power, the gaps were unfortunate. Third, the tenor of the ideas that were presented—with their emphasis on wealth creation through training, cooperation, and linking social programs such as welfare to the needs of the economy—were remarkably similar to ideas already well accepted on the right and centre-right. In the United States, similar ideas, under the name of neo-liberalism, had taken hold of the Democratic Party. In Canada, they were articles of faith among both the federal Liberals and the Mulroney Conservatives. Ironically, the Ontario NDP's new ideas were also not too far removed from the Laxerite heresy of 1983.

The broad policy discussion which these papers was supposed to generate inside the NDP never jelled. In part, it was the fault of the thinkers themselves. Most had been diligently impractical, remaining on high levels of abstraction. "I don't think in my twenty years of politics, I had as much frustration as I had with that exercise," Laughren said later. "We worked extremely hard on that. We really did. We agonized over it."

In the end, Laughren found it too vague: "There was nothing I felt I could go to the party with; we hadn't been able to come up with anything ... around which people could rally. Not a question of left-wing, right-wing, anything like that—but a simple economic message that would say, 'This is where we are at and where we want to go.'"

Rae remained interested, nonetheless, and tried to keep the process going. The party's provincial council discussed Bakker's summary document, but again there was no focus. "The discussion was all over the map," recalls one participant. "A lot of it was traditional NDP left rhetoric."

In March 1990, Miller drafted another economic-policy document based on the thinkers' symposium. Keynesian economics, he wrote, was dead. Social democrats could no longer rely on the state to redistribute income from an ever-increasing pie. The trick was to figure out how to make the pie grow in a manner that was non-exploitative. "Once again, the sources and character of wealth creation, the supply side, are the central concerns of socialist policy." The aim of NDP economic policy, Miller wrote, should be to introduce "policies which use democratic means to build both social and private productive potential." What he called "social productivity" would not be a measure of simple efficiency but of "well-being" and would be created through "collective investment." To usher in an era of social productivity, the NDP should begin by establishing a network of "social contracts" with "representative organizations" such as unions, the women's movement, environmentalists, and aboriginal groups. These social contracts would not be in the European style—agreements over wages, employment, and inflation. For these kinds of social contracts were too often one-sided, penalizing workers. Rather, the NDP should negotiate specific social contracts about "tangible legal rights and economic and social programs." Areas to be negotiated would include pension-fund management, labour relations, environmental policy, training, and public services. These contracts would, in turn, demonstrate to the electorate the NDP has "clear, analytically sophisticated and openly negotiated policies which show how we would manage the economy credibly."

Miller's draft was also considered too vague. Throughout the summer of 1990, the NDP's economic-policy review continued to flounder. Research director Chuck Rachlis wrote another draft. Versions were circulated throughout the party, but nothing caught fire. In midsummer, Rachlis, Miller, and David Wolfe were asked to draft yet another version. They met once with Rae and made preparations to release the NDP's latest thoughts on economic policy in August. But, on July 30, Premier David Peterson called the election. The NDP's attempt to figure out an economic policy ground to a halt.

At one level, the NDP's economic-policy exercises were spectacular failures. The party went into the campaign with no platform—on the economy or anything else. Indeed, the document which eventually became the party's entire platform—the "Agenda for People"—was written over a weekend in mid-campaign by Chuck Rachlis and David Agnew. Even then it was written for the most cynical of reasons: the press had begun to notice the party had nothing to say.

Certainly, few would ever refer again to the 1989 thinkers' exercise. But that did not mean it was without influence. Almost by default, it ended up shaping the way the NDP government would approach the economy. For one thing, the NDP had no other ideas. For another, the key players in the rethinking exercise all found themselves, initially at least, playing important roles. Riel Miller became chief economic-policy adviser to Laughren, the new treasurer. David Wolfe was brought in as secretary to the cabinet's Committee on Economic Development. Rachlis, politically the most practical of the three, became economic-policy adviser in Rae's office.

Elements of this half-completed economic-policy exercise continued to bubble to the surface during the government's term. The emphasis on long-term structural change, on training, on productivity—all became hallmarks of the new government, as did its mistrust of Keynesian economics. (Ironically, the NDP abandoned Keynesianism, a set of policies specifically designed for economic depression, just at the moment when it might have been useful.) Even the government's controverial social contract with the public sector was previewed, albeit in a far different form.

More important, the weaknesses of the rethinking exercise—its abstract nature, its failure to deal with the specific problem of mass unemployment, its deafening silence on issues of deficits and public finance—also remained with the government. By the end of its term, the NDP government had developed a long-run strategy for handling some of the structural weaknesses of the Ontario economy. But it could never deal with the recession; it could never figure out how to even begin putting more than half-a-million jobless back to work.

7

The Casino Economy II: Pink Floyd Meets the Debt Wall

ON THE AFTERNOON OF APRIL 29, 1991, TREASURER FLOYD Laughren rose in the legislature to deliver his maiden budget. A budget is a government's economic blueprint. It explains its intentions in the all-important area of finance, borrowing, and taxation, and how, if at all, it hopes to influence employment. As the first budget of the first NDP government to win power in Canada's largest province, Laughren's performance was watched, particularly by business, with more than the usual interest.

Laughren was proud of the document that had been crafted. It had clearly defined the enemy — recession — and equally clearly spelled out an answer — government action. Other governments might concern themselves with deficits, said Laughren. The NDP government, however, was different. "We had a choice to make this year," he told the legislature defiantly. "To fight the deficit or fight the recession. We are proud to be fighting the recession." With Ottawa and every other provincial government concentrating on deficit reduction, Laughren hoped this rhetoric would demonstrate that Queen's Park was indeed in different hands.

At the same time, he knew the concrete measures he was proposing were far from radical. The budget contained almost no tax changes and little new discretionary spending to combat the dramatically worsening unemployment picture. Sure the deficit would go up, but this was hardly the government's fault. How could it keep its finances in line when unemployment, and the consequent fall in tax revenues, meant there was so much less money coming in?

What captured headlines, however, was the deficit figure. Laughren was predicting a $9.7-billion shortfall for 1991—up more than three-fold from the previous year. Business commentators were outraged. "It is nothing less than astonishing that a major Canadian government would deliberately and proudly set out to double the public debt within four years, raise already high tax rates, contribute to national inflation and colonize an even larger portion of the economic landscape for government activity," wrote one. The federal Tories, sensing a way to discredit their NDP foes, weighed in. Newspaper tycoon Conrad Black thundered that he would eschew Ontario investments as long as the province was ruled by an NDP government, a pledge he broke a scant seventeen months later when he purchased a chunk of the Southam newspaper chain.

Soon, the first Laughren budget had entered political mythology as an example of the way not to go, a warning to those who would buck the economic orthodoxy that governs the Western world. Commentators compared it to French president François Mitterrand's abortive attempt in the early 1980s to unilaterally stimulate the economy of his country, an attempt that led to a flight from the franc, devaluation, and a hasty U-turn by the Socialist government. Even two years later, in the lead-up to the 1993 federal election, then Tory prime minister Kim Campbell harkened back to Laughren's 1991 budget as a disaster that had destroyed business confidence in Ontario.

In fact, the Laughren budget caused none of these problems. Foreign investment continued to flood into Ontario. The dollar went up. According to the Conference Board of Canada, a middle-of-the road economic think tank, the Laughren budget of 1991 marginally helped to push up growth and employment across the country. Overall, it was probably the most useful economic action taken that year by any Canadian government.

To those who asked where the $10-billion deficit came from, Laughren could have truthfully answered: the recession took most of it. An analysis of the province's finances shows that plummeting tax revenues and rising welfare costs would have created a deficit of more than $8 billion even if the government had done nothing. Over the year, 250,000 Ontarians had lost their jobs, and the unemployment rate had climbed to a post-Depression high of almost 10 per cent. This devastating unemployment had caused tax revenues to drop off dramatically.

At the same time, welfare spending was exploding. Federal changes to the Unemployment Insurance Act had pushed more of the jobless more quickly onto the welfare rolls. Federal cost-cutting measures had unilaterally reduced Ottawa's share of Ontario's welfare bill. The result was that the burden was falling squarely on the province. Caught between falling tax revenues and rising welfare spending, the Ontario deficit shot up.

But critics of the NDP government ignored these reasons for the deficit. They also ignored the fact that, compared with those of most other provinces—and certainly compared with those of the federal Conservative government in Ottawa—Ontario's finances were still in good shape. In relative terms, its debt was low.

The word "relative" is key, for what matters in public finance is not the absolute size of a government's debt but its ability to service that debt—that is, pay the principal and interest owing each year. Using that measure, Ontario was in relatively good shape. Even after Laughren's $10-billion announcement, interest charges on Ontario's debt counted for about twelve cents of every tax dollar received. By contrast, interest charges on the federal debt—in spite of the fiscally conservative rhetoric of the Mulroney government—accounted for thirty-four cents of every tax dollar received.

Few critics paid attention to those facts. Instead, most played to the popular stereotype of the NDP: It spends like there is no tomorrow; it can't manage the store. Even Mulroney had the brass to criticize Laughren for the "burden you are placing on your children and grandchildren." Few pointed out the blatant hypocrisy of this statement.

Unfortunately for the government, Laughren and his staff seemed incapable of countering the attacks. Most governments introducing controversial measures release a flood of background information. At best, this is context; at worst, hyperbole. The 1991 Laughren budget had virtually none. Reporters asking how Ontario's debt compared with that of other provinces were told by Treasury officials that no analysis had been done. In fact, officials were reluctant to release financial information about other provinces (all of which is public) for fear of offending fellow bureaucrats in other capitals. Laughren himself made no attempt to disaggregate his $10-billion deficit into a cyclical component (that caused by the recession) and an active component (that created by deliberate government action). Those who wanted to make those kinds of distinctions had to find the information themselves. And few did.

Instead, the government seemed to think it could counter all opposition by repeating the mantra: We are fighting the recession, not the deficit. Throughout the early part of the summer, both Rae and Laughren gamely made the argument. It got nowhere.

It got nowhere because the government was not really fighting the recession, or at least not vigorously. Laughren and Rae were reluctant to stimulate the economy full bolt. The government wanted the credit for fighting unemployment; but it wasn't sure it wanted to spend the money necessary to do that. Indeed, since coming to power, it had not been sure what to do.

One of Rae's first actions as premier had been to reveal the state of the province's books. The departing Liberals had promised a balanced budget for 1990. Instead, the deficit would hit what was at the time a record high of $3 billion. Rae chided the Peterson Liberals for not levelling with the voters. His was the standard strategy for any new government: Come in, announce the cupboard is bare, and blame the previous tenants.

What the new government failed to do, however, was come to terms with the question of how to handle deficits in the midst of economic depression. Should it follow the lead of every other Canadian government and slash spending in order to curb the deficit? Or should it do what Rae and NDP orthodoxy had always said a government should do in such circumstances—use the fiscal capacity of the state to pump money into the economy and create jobs?

In cabinet, a minority argued that the province was entering a more serious economic crisis. "The Treasury people were coming over and saying, 'It's a recession; Ontario will bounce back,'" recalled Attorney General Howard Hampton. "Some of us were saying, 'Hey, this is not just a recession.'" But for Laughren, the advice from Treasury was comforting. If the recession was short-lived, then he could afford to engage in some Keynesian pump-priming without too much risk.

A trip by Rae and Laughren to New York that fall only reinforced the treasurer's views. Newly elected Canadian government leaders always journey to New York to pay homage to the moguls of world capital. Laughren and Rae were no exception. They even sat, stony-faced, through a Manhattan dinner party, hosted by the province's agent general and former *Toronto Star* love columnist Joan Sutton Straus, in which they were treated to a menu featuring "The Sky Is Not Falling Chicken" and "Socialist Spuds" (Rae didn't appreciate

101
*The Casino
Economy II:
Pink Floyd
Meets the
Debt Wall*

the humour; by spring, Sutton Straus was no longer agent general). Laughren was anxious to see more than moguls, though, on this, his first visit to New York. One afternoon, he played hookey from a meeting with the editorial board of *The Wall Street Journal* to tour Harlem. The third-world conditions horrified him. "I'd never comprehended the enormity of the erosion," he said later. "It was so appalling, and the thought of us ever slipping into that was so abhorrent that, if it took deficit financing to stop that, then I would do deficit financing."

The first New York visit was also an indicator of the kind of pressures the NDP government would feel from financial markets. Both the premier and the treasurer realized they could not ignore those who liked to eat "Socialist Spuds" at Joan Sutton Straus's. But, at this early stage, they resisted being captured by the financial markets. Stepping out on the tarmac at Toronto's Island Airport after the 1990 New York trip, Rae took a deep breath and said to his executive assistant, Lynn Spink: "What I need is a busload of Steelworkers yelling 'Get back in the real world.'"

So the government would fight the recession. But how much? "Rae believed the deficit and debt were not unimportant," said one senior aide later. "But he didn't believe it was the number-one problem. The social-democratic bias—our bias—had been to fight unemployment. ... That was the bias of the first budget. We were trying to walk that walk."

Prior to the NDP victory, the Treasury's budget office, headed by assistant deputy minister Michael Mendelson, had been preparing an ambitious economic stimulus plan to counter the recession. Under Rae, in his new role as deputy cabinet secretary, Mendelson continued to promote the idea. The government, he said, should pump an extra $2 billion into the economy even if that did push the deficit higher. Laughren adviser Riel Miller also favoured economic stimulus, but to a lesser degree. Miller, the dapper left-wing New School intellectual, had been brought into Treasury by Laughren specifically to keep the ministry bureaucrats off balance, a feat they sometimes felt he accomplished too well. For Miller, the real challenge of the budget was not in the deficit but in laying out a framework for long-term social-democratic reform of the economy. To that end, he devoted most of his efforts to drafting a paper based on the NDP discussions of the previous two years and eventually released as Budget Document E. Budget Document E continued with themes of structural change and the need for innovation. But, to Miller's irritation, once published it was virtually ignored—both inside and outside government.

103
The Casino
Economy II:
Pink Floyd
Meets the
Debt Wall

Prior to the 1991 budget, Laughren and Rae had called in a group of nine economists for advice. "It was clear they already had decided to have some kind of stimulative policy," University of Toronto economist Mel Watkins, one of the participants, recalled later. "It was also clear that very few in that room understood the seriousness of the recession. Treasury seemed to think they were dealing with a short-run recession: Stimulate a bit and then forget it. "

In the end, this misreading was the undoing of the 1991 budget. The government decided it would take a Keynesian tack. But it did so with little enthusiasm. "We weren't trying to spend our way out of recession, no matter what everyone said," explained one senior aide later. "We didn't think we could do that." None of the cabinet wanted the government to use its full fiscal might against the recession. But no one had any other ideas.

The result was the worst of all worlds—a budget Keynesian enough to anger business but not stimulative enough to do much good. After tax increases and previously announced programs were counted in, the budget called for about $350 million in net new spending on a budget of $53 billion—enough to spark only about 15,000 new jobs in the economy. In a province where 250,000 jobs had been lost over the past year, this was small beer.

The ferocity of the reaction against the budget took the government by surprise. By 1991, it had become accepted wisdom in both business circles and the media that government debt was bad. However, the Rae government did not understand how deeply this neo-conservative orthodoxy had seeped into society. It did not understand that nerve—and lots of it—was required to run an economic policy directly counter to the perceived wisdom of television and radio talk shows.

The Rae government did not have that kind of nerve. Beyond the level of rhetoric, few in the NDP regime were committed to the stimulative economic policy of the 1991 budget. It had just been something to do. When presented with concerted and logical opposition to that policy (and neo-conservatives are not illogical), the government simply folded.

For a while, Rae and Laughren kept up their defence—that they were fighting the recession, not the deficit. But soon they lost heart. Polls showed support for the government plummeting as a result of the budget. "Politically, it was a disaster," said a senior aide. "There was a strong sense out there that we were doing something wrong. Unless we could sell the story that we could manage the place, we wouldn't get the keys again."

Inside government, the search was on for scapegoats. The 1991 budget was officially deemed a public-relations disaster rather than a policy flop. Eventually both Jackie Boyle, the director of communications in Treasury and Dianna Rienstra, the head of NDP caucus communications, would be blamed for the budget and purged.

By the fall of 1991, the government's rhetoric had switched right around. Rae and Laughren no longer talked of fighting recessions rather than deficits. Instead, like the federal Tory government in Ottawa, the NDP now talked of the need for fiscal responsibilty, deficit control, and rebuilding the economy through the efforts of the private sector.

"The one thing I learned from the first budget is that you can't do it on your own," Rae told Global Television's Robert Fisher. "You've just got to be working with other governments because, if you're out there on your own, the costs are just too high." Laughren was blunter. "It wasn't working," he explained two and a half years later. The recession was longer and deeper than he had first anticipated. "To me," Laughren went on, "'91 up to the spring of '92 wasn't too bad. We still thought we were going to come out of it. Once we got into '92 and into the fall of '92 ... things really started to sink in: This was not a recession like other recessions."

The 1991 budget was the NDP government's first and last attempt to deal boldly with the immediate crisis of unemployment. After that, convinced of its own impotence, it retreated. All that it was prepared to do was spend the usual sums on public works, such as road repairs, bridges, and sewers.

Typically, any Ontario government spends about $3 billion annually on such capital projects. The NDP government boosted this total somewhat, reaching $3.6 billion in 1993. But mainly it concerned itself with repackaging in a jazzier format programs that were, in large part, business-as-usual. Fixing potholes and building sewers became something called Jobs Ontario Capital. An existing plan to build non-profit housing became Jobs Ontario Housing. Eventually, a small program to finance projects such as local hockey rinks was hived off as a separate Jobs Ontario Community Action.

By late 1993—in the light of Jean Chrétien's victory federally—the

Ontario NDP government realized that its array of job projects could be a ticket to re-election. Rae travelled the province, cutting ribbons for projects such as court-house renovations. The pre-election slogan, worked out by communications adviser Jean-Guy Carrier, was "Putting Ontario back to work." As one political aide said later, "Even I can't believe in that."

105
The Casino
Economy II:
Pink Floyd
Meets the
Debt Wall

Few did. Most in government who worked in the economic field were convinced the province could do little to alleviate the immediate unemployment crisis. The best that could be done was to prepare for an eventual economic recovery. To this end, the NDP government's real economic policy would consist of three arms: emphasizing long-term structural reform through initiatives such as training; encouraging the private sector in the hope that it might create jobs; and controlling the deficit.

The decision in September 1991 not to proceed with public auto insurance made a convenient breaking-point for the government. Public auto insurance represented the old ways—going it alone, antagonizing business. The new NDP would instead cooperate with business. Rae had articulated this theme in a speech to the Ontario NDP convention earlier that year when he had laid out his economic agenda: to create wealth, encourage efficiency, work in partnership with private business, and concentrate on training. With public auto insurance out of the way, he was able to add a fifth pillar: the province would control its finances. A few days after public auto insurance was scrapped, Floyd Laughren was asked by reporters whether the NDP had sold out. "Not yet," Laughren replied, laughing. "But it's early in the mandate."

Policy makers began to concentrate on long-term structural issues—the kinds of things the NDP had been groping towards in its abortive thinkers' conference. Key areas would include training, investment, and industrial strategy. None of these ideas was novel. Liberal and Conservative governments had long ago come to similar conclusions. But, for some in the NDP government—such as Laughren policy aide Riel Miller—the challenge would be to imbue these standard ideas with social-democratic content.

Training, for example, was to be a priority. The NDP would follow through with a plan of the Liberals and create a new, autonomous board—the Ontario Training and Adjustment Board. The new Ontario board would take government training money and deliver it through a "partnership" structure, one made up of representatives from business, labour, and interest groups. Such a concept appealed to business and labour, both of whom wanted control over public training money. It could appeal also to the interest groups within the NDP. No longer would training come under control of a government responsible to an elected majoritarian legislature. That was an example of the old democracy. Instead, the board would be run by representatives, often self-appointed, from social sectors deemed important—teachers, aboriginals, francophones, the disabled, racial minorities, and women, as well as business and labour. It would exemplify sectoral, or stakeholder, democracy.

On the investment front, the NDP would ape Quebec, which, under a provincial Liberal government, had developed the Caisse de dépôt et placement du Québec as a vehicle to mobilize pension funds for investment. The Caisse, however, had an advantage. Since 1965, it had been the repository for contributions under the Quebec Pension Plan, that province's version of Ottawa's Canada Pension Plan. Ontario did not have the same kind of access to the pension contributions of its citizenry. Instead, the NDP hoped to mobilize the pension monies of the province's almost one million public servants as well as any willing private-sector unions to create an ambitious $2-billion Ontario Pension Investment Fund. To Ross McClellan, one of Rae's key political aides, the pension fund would replace public auto insurance as the NDP's signature—the policy that would define the Rae government in the mind of the electorate. Much of the work on the fund idea would fall to David Wolfe, the University of Toronto academic seconded to the cabinet office. The fund seemed precisely the kind of thing Wolfe had talked about in 1989—a mechanism for encouraging investment in the high-technology industries of the future.

Finally, the government would have an industrial strategy. The idea of an industrial strategy can cover much ground. Many governments claim to have such strategies. The most successful, however, have been those of governments which profess not to—notably the U.S. government, which funds high-technology industrial development through its defence budget, and that of Japan, which allows a kind of business–bureaucratic oligarchy to determine government and industrial policy.

In July 1992, after much discussion, the NDP produced its industrial strategy, a forty-three-page document entitled "An Industrial Policy Framework for Ontario." The document reiterated much of the received wisdom of the 1990s—that industry should become more competitive to meet "global change" and "new challenges," that

Ontario should move to a high-value-added economy, that business and labour should work together in "partnership" to permit "adjustment."

107
*The Casino
Economy II:
Pink Floyd
Meets the
Debt Wall*

Ironically, the NDP industrial strategy was less interventionist than that of the previous Liberal government. The Liberals had talked of using the state to develop and support specific leading-edge, high-technology industries. The NDP industrial strategy talked instead of "supporting winning activities"—such as innovation, training, and technological development. "The winning activities approach," the document explained, "doesn't require the government to pick winning industries or champion companies of the future, something experience suggests that markets can do much better than governments."

As such, in terms of its approach to state involvement in the economy, the Rae government was far closer to the Mulroney Tories than to the old NDP. Both the Rae and Mulroney governments saw their role as limited to providing the right climate for business—what the NDP industrial strategy document called "the competitive fundamentals."

In practical terms, however, the new structural strategy produced few dramatic results. The new training board, for instance, ended up essentially as a bureaucratic reorganization. Before the NDP came to power, civil servants had worked for something called the Ministry of Skills Development. Now they worked for something called the Ontario Training and Adjustment Board.

Whether the new board would prove more successful than its predecessor in equipping Ontarians with the skills needed in the new economy proved impossible to judge. In the midst of depression, neither the new nor the old economy needed workers. The newspapers carried letters from and stories about those who, after being laid off, were retrained in one field, laid off in their new job, retrained again, and so on.

Nor did the new industrial strategy produce many practical results. This was by design. The government, anxious not to spend money, had decided its industrial strategy would be an approach rather than a specific initiative. If there had been much activity going on in the Ontario economy, the NDP industrial strategy might have guided the government in deciding where to concentrate its efforts. But since there was little industrial activity, and since the government—following the débâcle of the 1991 budget—was reluctant to spend money to create any, an industrial strategy was of little use.

The proposed pension investment fund too withered away. In April

1992, the government announced it planned to raise $2 billion from private- and public-sector pension funds to invest in high-technology industry. But the bold hope of creating an Ontario version of the Caisse de dépôt was sandbagged by the public-service pension funds. Most made it clear they wanted to invest the pension contributions of their members in vehicles that yielded the highest and safest returns. These apparently did not include an investment fund run by an NDP government and geared to financing high-risk, high-technology industries. By 1993, the proposed $2-billion fund had shrunk to a $70-million venture-capital pool which, in partnership with large private investors, would provide management advice to small firms. Some analysts argued that the shrunken version was probably a good idea, that it filled a specific gap in private capital markets. But a signature policy — a bold initiative designed to show just what a social-democratic government could do if given the chance — it was not. It had taken more than two years to carry out.

Where the Rae government did make strides was in the area of cost-cutting and government rationalization. This was odd only because it was a field to which the NDP in opposition had paid absolutely no attention.

Traditionally, Ontario governments adopted a casual view of government spending. True, there might be periodic cut-backs and freezes, but overall there was no particular system to determine what the government spent and why it did so. A strong treasurer might exercise veto power over new initiatives. But once past this initial hurdle, they would usually continue, unimpeded.

However, by 1990, there was growing pressure within the senior ranks of the civil service to rationalize and cut the size of government. "The New Democrats inherited a mess," said one highly placed bureaucrat. "Ontario before Rae was like Ottawa in the early days of Lester Pearson, in the 1960s. There was absolutely no fiscal management. . . . No one knew what anything meant. If you asked, 'Why are we continuing to do this or that?' no one knew. It was all arbitrary."

Initially, the new government was equally casual. In 1991, the government increased grants to municipalities, hospitals, and schools by 8.2 per cent. The same year, it awarded a 5.8 per cent pay increase to its own civil service.

By late 1991, all of this came to an abrupt halt. The government had already created a new Ottawa-style Treasury Board to oversee spending.

Cut-backs, the cabinet decided, would be the order of the day. However, instead of making arbitrary, across-the-board cuts, ministers were told to comb their departmental estimates line by line, identifying items that could be shaved.

For the rank and file of the civil service, it was quite a reversal. During the first year of government, bureaucrats had been trying to use the NDP's 1990 election platform, "Agenda for People," as a guide to what they should do. In fact, some eager bureaucrats had even started designing programs that seemed to match the agenda. But the September 1991 decision not to proceed with public auto insurance ended that phase. "After that, nobody ever referred to the 'Agenda for People' again," said Sue Colley, one of the new government's most senior political aides during the 1990–93 period. Instead, the new marching orders to the bureaucracy were: Find money.

To some dissenters inside government, the new emphasis on fiscal restraint represented the victory of a conservative bureaucracy over a confused NDP. "The bureaucrats started working on their right-wing agenda—welfare cut-backs and government downsizing—within six weeks of the government taking office," said one senior official. Others, such as Rae aide Janet Solberg, saw it not as an overt bureaucratic conspiracy to defang the NDP but as a failure of the cabinet to resist the almost natural imperatives of government. Governments of all political stripes tend to get caught up in worrying about their finances, she said, for this is one of the few things they think they can control.

Behind the lust for cash was the deficit. In August 1991, Rae had told his staff that the NDP was determined to hold the line: The deficit would not be allowed to rise over $10 billion.

In part, this was a rational reaction to the real problems of raising money. Ontario's credit rating had already fallen a notch from triple-A. If it were to fall much farther, certain types of financial institutions would no longer be able to buy provincial bonds. The government would be forced to offer an extra quarter percentage point or so in interest to attract other lenders. In part, however, Rae and Laughren were determined to show their critics that the NDP could handle government finances—that, if necessary, it could be as tough as any Conservative or Liberal government.

Yet the economy was not making this task easy. By 1991, the unemployment rate in Ontario had risen to over 10 per cent. Government tax revenues continued to fall; welfare costs to the province were still rising as more and more jobless workers went on the dole. It was in this environment that the notion of legalizing casinos took hold.

Gambling, through the government-run Ontario Lottery Corporation, was already a small but growing source of government revenue. The province also permitted charities to hold small-scale casino, or so-called Monte Carlo, nights.

By 1990, gambling was on the increase in North America, as cash-strapped governments looked for ways to increase revenues. Casino gambling had become a respectable and profitable big business. Several U.S. states, anxious to get a cut of the take, had legalized the practice.

In Canada, Manitoba had already opened a glitzy, government-run casino; Quebec was considering the idea. As the Ontario government struggled through its new spending-cut exercise, the idea of cashing in on the casino craze seemed increasingly attractive.

In fact, casinos are not necessarily the money machines that governments expect—at least, not in the long term. First, the economics of casino gambling is fairly straightforward: It is a form of entertainment. A dollar spent at a casino means one dollar fewer spent on some other form of entertainment—be it theatre, cinema, or horse-racing. In other words, casino gambling, in economic terms, is part of a zero-sum game.

Second, casinos will reap huge profits for their owners and tax windfalls for the state only as long as competition is restricted. Profitablity stems from the casino's quasi-legal status. Once casinos exist everywhere, profit margins—and tax revenues—will fall to normal levels.

For a government interested in cashing in on casinos, the trick is to ensure that most customers are from outside its borders (so as not to take away money from other forms of entertainment in the province) and to be one of the first into the game.

The NDP government paid little attention to nay-sayers. What captured the imagination of Rae, Laughren, Cooke, and a small coterie inside the premier's office was the chance to bring in revenues. And why not? What was wrong with gambling? Why should the government pass moral judgment on something that thousands of Canadians already did for pleasure? Rae's critique of the casino as a symbol of greed was quickly forgotten.

The gambling idea had begun with a proposal from the government-run Ontario Lottery Corp. to set up electronic slot machines, also called video lottery terminals (VLTs), in corner stores. Cabinet was cool to the idea. But then, as Cooke explained it, "A couple of us said, 'If we're thinking about VLTs, why not casinos?'"

In February 1992, senior Rae aide Ross McClellan ordered the bureaucracy to give top priority to producing a policy paper on casino gambling. For a government that could take months or even years to produce the simplest policy, the casino process was lightning swift. In March, *The Toronto Star* reported that cabinet was considering a proposal to permit six casinos across the province. This only increased the pressure. A Windsor entrepreneur had already been lobbying for a casino in the hard-hit auto town. When Windsor boosters learned the cabinet was considering casinos, they turned up the heat on local MPP Dave Cooke, one of the more powerful figures in the cabinet. More cautious voices in government, such as Consumer and Commercial Relations minister Marilyn Churley, persuaded the cabinet to back down from immediately setting up six casinos. The saw-off was announced later that year. Windsor would be the site of Ontario's casino experiment. A temporary casino would be established there in 1994, and a permanent facility built by 1996 or 1997.

Windsor casino enthusiasts were ecstatic. Civic officials in other hard-hit towns along the U.S. border, including Niagara Falls and Sault Ste. Marie, immediately began to agitate for casinos in their areas. To most urban dwellers at least, casino gambling seemed acceptable. Pro-casino telephone calls to the premier's office outnumbered complaints.

Steps were also taken to soothe competing interests. Horse-racers, who feared casinos might cut into their business, were told the government would set up teletheatres in selected cities where fans could sit, drink, place bets, and watch races on closed-circuit television. Rules for bingos and charity Monte Carlo nights were liberalized so that non-profit organizations, many of whom depended on small-scale gambling for revenue, wouldn't complain. Negotiations began immediately with Indian bands, who served notice of their intention to set up casinos on reserves.

The party itself, however, was taken by surprise. Former NDP president Janet Solberg later recalled speaking to an NDP women's caucus shortly after stories speculating on casino gambling had begun to appear in the press. "I remember one of the women asking, 'What about casinos?' and I said, 'Impossible.' What an idiot I was." Some New Democrats left the party in disgust, and one MPP quit the caucus. But these were dismissed by the government as old-fashioned.

In fact, the only spoilsports were police, some of whom warned, publicly and privately, that a casino across the river from Detroit would lead to more organized crime in Ontario. The government, pleased that it had finally hit upon something that won it public praise, paid no heed.

The proposed casino would bear the unique stamp of the Rae government—casual, slightly prissy, and run by U.S. big business. Initially, the government decreed that drinking would not be allowed at any gambling table and that smoking would be restricted. It later backtracked on the drinking. Unlike Winnipeg's casino, Windsor's would not require fancy dress; the cabinet deemed that élitist.

Most important, the government was determined not to follow the lead of the Manitoba Conservatives and operate the casino itself. Instead, it plunked squarely for private enterprise. Private money would build the casino; private money would operate it. The government would just sit back as the nominal owner and rake in the chips.

Initially, Consumer and Commercial Relations minister Marilyn Churley vowed the Windsor casino would not be a Las Vegas–style operation. But after visiting Las Vegas, government officials changed their minds. The best way to make the most money, they concluded, was to hand over operations to the biggest and glitziest operator. Eventually, a consortium of Las Vegas and Atlantic City gambling concerns, including Caesar's World, won the bid. Caesar's, as officials pointed out in a confidential memo, had once been associated with the mob. But that was in the 1960s and, to the NDP government, ancient history.

By the time the Windsor interim casino opened its doors to gamblers in 1994, the project had developed a life of its own. Extravagant predictions were made and circulated about the employment the casino would create, the economic spin-offs that would occur. One government-commissioned study predicted that seven casinos in Ontario would create 97,000 jobs and $1.4 billion in consumer spending.

More sober heads in government realized casino gambling was unlikely to solve either Windsor's or Ontario's economic problems. Initially, the Windsor casino proved lucrative for the provincial treasury. But, as critics had predicted, it provided few economic spin-offs to its host city.

So popular was a casino in recession-wracked Windsor, however, that no political party was willing to oppose the idea outright. In one visit to Windsor, Conservative leader Mike Harris publicly questioned the wisdom of the casino decision and was roundly condemned by civic boosters for his views. But, in this case at least, Harris probably had it right: As a piece of economic policy, the casino initiative was pathetic; it was no solution to recession, to unemployment, or to the specific problems of Windsor. But for the government, it was an idea. And that was a commodity in short supply.

113
The Casino
Economy II:
Pink Floyd
Meets the
Debt Wall

On the broader economic front, the government was getting more and more caught up in the problems of its own finances. In part, this was a function of Laughren's personality. Even in his own ministry, the treasurer did not like to be pushy. Indeed, some aides thought him not demanding enough. "If someone says this or that is too difficult to do, Floyd will generally say okay," said one. "He doesn't want problems. That's just his style." Rather, Laughren liked to operate through consensus. And the consensus among top Treasury bureaucrats was for restraint.

In part too, Laughren was instinctively conservative about money. He represented a working-class riding, Sudbury's Nickel Belt, which was also instinctively conservative. Moreover, he felt the government would be judged on how well it handled the public purse. "I can't think of anything that would sink us faster than letting the deficit get out of control," he said in late 1990, well before his first budget. In the fall of 1991, as the government was belatedly turning along a more conservative path, he made the same point. How well the NDP handled the deficit, he told reporters, "will be the test of this government." Inside government, it was recognized that Laughren was the hawk on the deficit. "Floyd sees his reputation on the line," said one aide. "He's been far more conservative on this than Rae, despite his reputation as Pink Floyd." To Sue Colley, senior aide to Frances Lankin, one of Laughren's main concerns as treasurer was "to maintain his dignity."

Rae, on the other hand, was initially less sure of the new direction. "I wonder if we are doing the right thing," he mused during an inner-cabinet meeting in December 1991 as the government forged ahead on its new restraint tack. "Rae was all over the place," said one aide, speaking of that period. "It would depend on how he felt on any particular day."

In public, though, Rae was a firm defender of the new harder line. His spirited public defence of fiscal orthodoxy bothered some in the government and party. "We spent enormous—and I was part of it—

enormous time and effort went into the communications packaging of expenditure control," said Janet Solberg, a senior aide in Rae's office during that period. "And I mean, this was the discourse of the neo-conservative landscape. Why adopt it?"

Laughren's second budget, on April 30, 1992, won some grudging respect from business and the financial press. The government raised taxes on senior citizens and most individuals but cut taxes for business. It announced training subsidies for business, and trimmed welfare spending. Fiscally, the government reversed its position of a year earlier. Rather than pump more money into the economy, it took out $1 billion in the form of spending cuts and tax hikes. However, continued high unemployment—and a further erosion of tax revenue—meant that the deficit figure remained almost untouched, at about $10 billion, for the coming year.

Inside government, Agnew and communications guru John Piper viewed the budget as a major public-relations coup. Rae showed his pleasure when Tom Enders, the former U.S. ambassador to Canada and by this time a New York investment banker, called his budget "miraculous." Still, there was little clarity as to what the government's overall economic strategy should be.

"It was hard to discern a strategy that lasted longer than a week in that place," recalled Rae aide Janet Solberg. "And it was often ass backwards. ... Strategy was often changing, and the primacy of different things was changing—equity or social justice, fiscal restraint, job creation. The six months I was there—and I reckon forever—these were the three posts of this government. And one would take primacy over another. Who knows how real that was? I'm not sure jobs ever took primacy."

One example of this confusion was the premier's first televised address. In December 1991, John Piper had decided the premier should appear on province-wide television. It would show he was in charge; it would allow the government's best communicator to bypass the media and give the NDP message directly to Ontarians. Rae readily agreed. The wheels were put into motion, and the government spent $62,000 on the effort. There was only one difficulty. No one knew what the government's message should be, what the great communicator should communicate. In the end, Rae gave an unmemorable address about the need to make tough choices. A poll taken after the speech calculated that, in spite of Rae's effort, 58 per cent of Ontarians had little or no confidence in the NDP government's ability to manage the economy.

As the economy continued to deteriorate over 1992, the government's uncertainty increased. That summer, Laughren invited a small group of Treasury officials and outside economists to dinner. These kinds of brainstorming sessions between government and selected outsiders were not uncommon. What struck one participant, however, was the general air of despair. "There was no energy on the government side; they had no ideas. There was a kind of tiredness. It wasn't just that they weren't going to tell us what they were going to do; it was that they had no ideas at all. I've never been at a meeting where officials seemed so defeated and the minister had so little to say."

115
The Casino
Economy II:
Pink Floyd
Meets the
Debt Wall

Almost by default, cut-backs became the only consistent thread of economic policy. Inside cabinet, this was beginning to raise hackles. Economic policy in 1992 was in the hands of a small group referred to derisively by female ministers as "the boys"—Rae, Laughren, deputy cabinet secretary Michael Mendelson, Treasury Board secretary Jay Kaufman, Agnew, and, by the end of 1992, deputy minister of Health Michael Decter. Other ministers weren't necessarily opposed to the policies of this group. They did not, however, appreciate the way in which crucial decisions were presented to cabinet as *faits accomplis*. This tension came to a head during a day-long cabinet meeting in the spring of 1992.

During the day, the premier and most of the men in cabinet had been arguing to push ahead with the restraint agenda. But the female ministers, plus Attorney General Howard Hampton, were digging in their heels. Frustrated, Rae told the dissidents that they just didn't understand. If only they could fully comprehend the gravity of the province's fiscal position, he said, they would surely agree with him. That made Housing minister Evelyn Gigantes angry. "Are you trying to say I'm dumb?" she asked Rae. History does not record the reply.

In the fall of 1992, the cabinet battled again over cut-backs. This time, the debate was whether the government should renege on its promise of a 2 per cent increase in transfer payments to municipalities, hospitals, and school boards. In the end, they compromised with a partial freeze.

To the fiscal conservatives of government, however, more had to be done. Laughren, frustrated by the constantly changing predictions about revenues and deficits from Treasury economists, asked for a worst-case scenario. The result, produced by Treasury Board secretary Jay Kaufman, was truly alarming: If absolutely nothing went right for the government and it did absolutely nothing, it could face a deficit in the coming year of $17 billion.

At the time, the assumptions behind the $17-billion figure were highly unrealistic; to most outside experts—even to the opposition Liberals—the figure seemed unduly high. However, it was the figure the government would choose to use. In the end, to the surprise of many, it would prove to be accurate.

Deputy Health minister Michael Decter—by then a key player in overall financial policy—and deputy treasurer Eleanor Clitheroe were dispatched to New York to sound out the province's bankers. The response they got when they hinted at the worst-case scenario was as expected. "It was a very theoretical conversation," recalled Decter. "A what-if. It became very clear that [a deficit] above 10 [billion dollars] was starting to be dodgy, above 12 was really dodgy, above 15 was—if I remember the comment of the bankers—completely uncharted territory." Returning to Toronto, Decter had what he called "a very tough talk with the premier.... Clitheroe and I were on one side, favouring hard things; others favoured letting the deficit run more."

By this time, the fiscal conservatives had new allies. Peter Warrian, a former student radical and the man who had given Bob Rae his entré into the union movement, had been hired as the Treasury's chief economist.

Warrian was a forty-nine-year-old former Catholic activist. In the early 1960s, he had studied for the priesthood in Baltimore, while involving himself in the U.S. civil-rights movement. Returning home to Canada to study economics, he entered student politics. In 1968, while Bob Rae was trying to rearrange the governing constitution of the University of Toronto, Warrian was president of the Canadian Union of Students (CUS). At the time, CUS was regarded as a radical organization. Warrian, unlike Rae, was regarded as a student radical.

Later Warrian worked for the unions—the Steelworkers, the Ontario Public Service Employees Union, and finally Steel again as executive director of the Canadian Steel Trade and Employment Congress (CSTEC).

Operated jointly by the Steelworkers and the steel employers, CSTEC was a practical attempt to deal with the tremendous restructuring going on in the industry. It focused on retraining, cooperation, and the development of new, flexible work patterns. "I like to work on the edge," Warrian explained later. "And the issues of labour are issues of economic restructuring. That's what the last ten years of my life have been about."

Warrian had been hired by Laughren mainly because the NDP government was worried about pending trade actions by the United States. These, it feared, could cripple the province's steel industry. In fact, the feared doomsday scenario for steel never materialized. So when Warrian arrived at his office on December 1, 1992, he had plenty of time to scroll through the province's financial predictions. What he saw disturbed him.

117
*The Casino
Economy II:
Pink Floyd
Meets the
Debt Wall*

On December 12, Warrian dashed off a memo to Laughren, warning of a looming debt crisis. The memo, entitled "Walking on the edge of the cliff," was turned back by Laughren's chief of staff, Simon Rosenblum, who saw it as alarmist. Later that month, with his two superiors, Eleanor Clitheroe and Jay Kaufman, both on holiday, Warrian was left in charge of the Treasury. On January 16, he wrote another, similar memo simply titled "What?" and made sure Laughren saw it. In the first week of February, updated financial figures from Ottawa predicting a significant fall in revenue for Ontario seemed to bear out Warrian's dire predictions.

"People couldn't speak," said one official later. "Treasury staff thought they were looking at the end of the world. Finally, Laughren said: 'We have to take this across the street.'"

Across the street, in the cabinet office, others were becoming alarmed. By this time, deputy cabinet secretary Michael Mendelson had switched sides on the deficit question. Two years earlier, he had been an enthusiastic proponent of boosting the deficit to counter recession. By early 1993, he had changed his mind; the recession was simply too serious for Keynesian economics to work. Inside government, Clitheroe, Warrian, Treasury Board secretary Jay Kaufman and Mendelson became known as "the Four Horsemen of the Fiscal Apocalypse."

In mid-February, the Four Horsemen were given a boost by the C.D. Howe Institute, a right-of-centre economic think tank. The institute had published an edited summary of a round-table discussion among business economists in which some participants had mused that Canadian governments, unless they got their fiscal houses in order, might hit a point at which no one would lend them money—what some would later call a "debt wall." Suddenly newspapers and television commentators were warning that Canada was on the edge of a debt crisis, one which had to be solved immediately.

In fact, as some participants in the C.D. Howe discussion acknowledged later, their language during the round-table discussion had been highly exaggerated. "It's not that one day that you wake up and the Germans say 'We won't buy your bonds,'" explained Bank of Nova Scotia chief economist Warren Jestin. Rather, it was that lenders might charge higher interest rates to those governments with large deficits. Irene Ip, one of the editors of the C.D. Howe report and an expert on government debt herself, said later she had never heard of a case in which an industrial country or province had hit a debt wall. In fact, she said, even the worst of third-world countries were usually able to find someone to lend them money. In short, even the participants in the C.D. Howe round-table were dissociating themselves from the dramatic notion of a debt wall.

Inside the NDP government, however, the debt-wall theory gained immediate credence. Most ministers and political staffers had no experience with international money markets and could be easily persuaded they were at the lip of the abyss. Moreover, to some New Democrats, the idea of a debt wall was perversely attractive. It fit in with their desire to see themselves as brave revolutionaries, threatened by an international conspiracy of financiers.

Others saw the debt in nationalist terms. While debt itself might not be bad, they said, Ontario's problem was that it owed most of its debt to foreigners. This, as Laughren argued, meant that interest payments on the debt were drained outside of the country.

In fact, most of the evidence contradicted the cabinet's belief. There was little evidence that international capital viewed the Ontario government as anything other than it was—a moderate, pro-business regime with an unemployment and fiscal problem. When interviewed, representatives of the Wall Street barons said that the world was awash with capital, that lenders were anxious to lend to stable jurisdictions such as Ontario, and that there was no debt wall.

As for the drain-to-foreigners argument, that was simply wrong. Treasury officials did not know the exact percentage of Ontario's $68-billion debt that was held outside the country. But they did know that it was less than 43 per cent, and almost certainly less than one-third.

Even the Ontario Treasury itself gave little credence to the debt wall. In a confidential memo prepared for Rae on the C.D. Howe Institute report, Treasury officials pointed out that Ontario had just floated a $3-billion bond issue that had been snapped up by international lenders and that domestic investors hold "much more" of Ontario's debt than foreigners.

None of this had the slightest effect on economic-policy makers. *119*
The Casino
Economy II:
Pink Floyd
Meets the
Debt Wall They had bought the debt-wall argument and were running with it. In mid-February, the Four Horsemen made a presentation to every member of the inner cabinet and every political staffer to persuade them of the danger of the debt wall. Simultaneously, Decter was working on Rae. In his "tough talk" with the premier, which dealt with Ontario Hydro as well as the government's debt, Decter argued that the government had a choice. If it allowed its debt to rise substantially, the interest costs would so eat into provincial revenue it could pay for nothing else. Even medicare would be threatened. Decter later acknowledged he made his argument "in the extreme way I put things in these kinds of debates." But it had impact. So, oddly enough, did a television journalist named Eric Malling.

The NDP prides itself on its critical suspicion of the capitalist media—a suspicion which is not entirely misplaced. To many party activists, inside and outside government, the media—particularly television—twist and distort events to coincide with the interests of the ruling class. This is why it is ironic that what ultimately convinced the NDP government's political apparatus of the need to curb the deficit was a television documentary, aired on CTV's public affairs program *W5* and hosted by Eric Malling.

Malling's documentary dealt with New Zealand, a nation of three million that was virtually unknown to most in the NDP government. His target was Canada's debt. In the documentary, he presented a compelling story, that of a nation whose debt had reached such levels that, by 1984, it was unable to borrow any more money. Faced with a cut-off of funds, the country's then Labour government had no choice except to slash social programs such as medicare. New Zealand, Malling reported, had become virtually bereft of public services.

In reality, the New Zealand story was far more complex than the gripping *W5* documentary suggested. Its situation in the mid-1980s was not, in anything except the most superficial manner, analogous to that of Ontario in the early 1990s. However, to the reinvigorated fiscal conservatives of the Rae government, Eric Malling was heaven-sent. New Zealand could be a metaphor for Ontario, a warning of what could happen to a social-democratic government that ran into the debt wall. The cabinet, caucus, and all NDP political aides were shown videotapes of the Malling documentary. At a March 11 meeting with labour leaders, Rae and Laughren were prevented from showing the New

Zealand tape only when Canadian Auto Workers president Buzz Hargrove objected strenuously.

Those in labour or the party who were sceptical of the debt-wall argument were dismissed as know-nothings unfamiliar with the hard realities of governing. Later, Janet Solberg would express her frustration with this attitude: "You cannot say to me that slashing the deficit by $2 billion or $3 billion more made a difference in the lives of Ontarians. If it resulted in their being laid off or taking lower wages? I think that's just crazy.... You don't pay it [the debt] off in bad times. You pay it off in good times.... I know we [the government] should have done differently. But I'm bewildered we didn't do it."

By the end of March, the cabinet was united in its fear. Ministers such as Frances Lankin who had been resistant to massive cut-backs were now convinced the province was just a few months away from hitting the debt wall, a wall which in fact never existed. Victim of its own naïvety and inexperience, the NDP cabinet had allowed itself to be guided by all the institutions it professed to distrust—the media, the right-wing think tanks, the bureaucratic number-crunchers. Caught up in the apocalyptic arithmetic, the government seemed to forget whatever political and economic common sense it had ever possessed. It was now ready to embark on the social contract.

8

With Friends Like These . . .

NOVEMBER 22, 1993: THE SCENE ON THE BASEMENT FLOOR
of Toronto's Sheraton Centre Hotel was chaotic. Inside the hotel ballroom, union delegates to the Ontario Federation of Labour's annual convention had just passed a sweeping resolution threatening to cut off all support to the provincial NDP and explicitly denouncing sixty-six sitting Ontario New Democratic MPPs—including veteran unionist and Labour minister Bob Mackenzie; Finance minister Floyd Laughren; and the man who until recently had been the darling of the labour establishment, Premier Bob Rae. Inside the ballroom to support the resolution were some of the top labour leaders of the province—OFL president Gord Wilson, CAW chief Buzz Hargrove, Ontario NDP president and OFL secretary-treasurer Julie Davis.

Across the hall, in another basement room of the Sheraton Centre, another equally raucous meeting was taking place. In this room were 450 union delegates who had left the ballroom rather than take part in a debate they knew they would lose. Most were from private-sector unions such as the Steelworkers. The leaders were also prominent Canadian unionists, headed by Steelworkers Canadian director Leo Gerard. Inside the big ballroom, approximately 1,000 people, delegates from most public-sector unions as well as the Canadian Auto Workers, were arguing that Bob Rae and his NDP government had become traitors to the labour movement. But to Gerard and those in the smaller room, it was their union colleagues across the hall who were flirting

121

with treason—treason against a party which, whatever its faults, was still labour's best friend.

In the middle, almost literally, was Julie Davis. Davis was a personal friend of both Rae, and his wife, Arlene; she had been a Rae supporter since he had tried for and won the Ontario leadership in 1982. As president of the Ontario NDP, she had—until recently—wielded considerable influence with the government.

But Davis was also a trade-unionist. She had worked her way up through the Canadian Union of Public Employees to her present position in the Ontario Federation of Labour, the umbrella organization for 800,000 of the province's unionized workers. The dispute now tearing apart organized labour, over whether to continue supporting the NDP, was personified in Davis. Should she stick with the premier she admired so much, the man who had finally brought the NDP—her NDP—to power in Ontario? Or should she go with her labour instincts?

Eventually, Davis would go with her instincts. Later that noisy afternoon, as the delegates from the two squabbling camps filed out of the hotel basement, she announced she planned to quit her post as party president. "It's sad we've come to this," Davis said. A few blocks away, at Queen's Park, Rae was unapologetic. "I look forward to working with all those people in the labour movement and in the broader public sector who have some respect for what we are trying to do," he told reporters.

The cause of all of this fuss, of the bitter, competing labour meetings and of Julie Davis's anguish, was a piece of legislation the government called its social contract. Rae was proud of his social contract. He insisted, to anyone who would listen, that it would become the model for progressive labour relations throughout the land. There were many in the editorial boardrooms of the daily press who agreed.

Ironically, Rae had achieved something else. His government had managed, in the space of just nine months, to do what no Liberal or Conservative regime had ever accomplished. It had driven a wedge between the NDP and the bulk of organized labour in Canada. And it had fostered a public split in the labour movement itself.

Relations between the CCF-NDP and organized labour had never been smooth. The party's official name at its founding in 1932 had been the Co-operative Commonwealth Federation (Farmer-Labour-Socialist). But the word "Labour" in the title referred not to unions but to the minuscule left-wing sects, such as the Independent Labour Party, which had come together to form the CCF. For almost a decade, the mainstream of organized labour in Canada refused to have anything to do with the CCF. The more conservative craft unions, represented by the Trades and Labor Congress, preferred to follow the tradition of American labour and throw their political support to whichever mainstream party promised them the best deal at election time—usually the Liberals. More radical unions were linked to the robust Communist Party. Not until 1938 did any union local directly affiliate with the CCF.

The party's real breakthrough came in 1943 when the Canadian Congress of Labour, representing new, fast-growing industrial unions such as the United Auto Workers and United Steelworkers of America, endorsed the CCF as labour's political arm. This was no accident, since prominent CCFers had been instrumental in organizing the new industrial unions.

Not everyone in the CCF was happy with the growing role of unions in the party. To the leadership, however, a formal alliance with labour was crucial if the CCF was to survive. The federal election of 1958, which swept the Diefenbaker Tories back into power and decimated the CCF, seemed to underscore the point. In 1961, Canadian organized labour—represented by the Canadian Labour Congress (an amalgamation of non-Communist craft and industrial unions)—and the CCF formed the NDP. To some New Democrats, such as former Ontario NDP leader Stephen Lewis, the unions were owed an eternal debt of gratitude; they had saved the party from extinction. Other CCFers were less thrilled. Labour's growing clout in the new party helped propel the CCF's last federal leader, Hazen Argue, to cross the floor to the Liberals in 1962.

Formally, the NDP—like the CCF before it—retained safeguards designed to limit the power of organized labour in the party. But, in reality, the labour leadership dominated. Labour's hierarchical and disciplined structure, its tendency to vote in a bloc, meant that anyone trying for a position of power within the NDP had to have the support of key labour leaders. In Ontario in 1990, this meant the leaders of the United Steelworkers of America and the Canadian Auto Workers.

Both unions had supported Rae's successful bid for the leadership of the Ontario NDP in 1982. Leo Gerard of the Steelworkers and the CAW's then president Bob White had been instrumental in trying to persuade Rae to run against Audrey McLaughlin for the federal leader's job in 1989. In the intraparty battles which constantly erupted inside the NDP—such as the fight over whether to support the Meech Lake constitutional accord—White and Gerard had loyally supported Rae and the rest of the New Democrat eastern establishment. For the unions, Rae's success in 1990 meant it was payback time.

Initially, however, labour's strategy was to go slow. Public-opinion polls show that unions are not universally popular in Canada. Union leaders understood it would be counter-productive for the public to see the Rae government as labour's puppet. As Gord Wilson, head of the Ontario Federation of Labour, explained shortly after the NDP victory, "Our role is to make sure he can survive."

What Wilson did want, however, was a role in governing. Shortly after the election, he met Rae and his principal secretary, David Agnew, to suggest a plan. The scheme, drawn up by union official John O'Grady, would have established joint labour–government working groups which would meet regularly and develop draft legislation. Government would have the final say. But labour would be involved in all policy development "in a way that is sustained, intensive, and at a high level."

Other labour leaders at that meeting dismissed Wilson's idea. Later Wilson would charge that Rae had deliberately ambushed him by priming critics to discredit his notion of labour and government co-management. Whatever the reason, any idea of giving labour a formal and privileged role inside the NDP government was almost immediately killed. Wilson would later call this the first, and perhaps most serious, mistake the government made.

Instead, the union leadership moved to win changes to the Ontario Labour Relations Act, the law which sets out the rules of engagement for employers and trade unions. The shift from a manufacturing to a service economy had hit unions hard. Unions are far harder to organize in pizza parlours than in steel plants. And in Canada, pizza was becoming economically more important than steel. Those unions trying to organize the new service industries were meeting with limited success. Changes to the labour relations act, union leaders figured, would make these organizing attempts easier.

Initially, labour's list of demands was modest. One of the long-time demands of labour and the NDP had been an anti-scab law, to prevent employers from hiring non-union workers during a strike. Quebec already had such a law. In 1990, as the OFL's Wilson explained, labour was not pushing for Ontario to follow suit immediately. While both

Labour minister Bob Mackenzie and Rae were on the record as favouring anti-scab laws, neither seemed in a hurry during those first few months to introduce such controversial legislation.

Labour's equanimity on anti-scab legislation was based on its past experience. In existing unionized industries, such as steel and auto, employers rarely hire strikebreakers to stay open during a labour dispute. Instead, they stockpile their finished products ahead of time. But, in the newer, service industries, this is not an option. The only way a pizza parlour can maintain cash flow during a strike is by having managers or non-union workers operate the ovens. It cannot stockpile a month's worth of pizzas.

The OFL's demands for changes to the Labour Relations Act presented to Mackenzie in the fall of 1990 were moderate. Most involved fairly technical changes designed to remove what labour saw as unfair barriers to its ability to organize. For the new government, however, the fall of 1990 was chaos. Cabinet proposals were coming from every ministry. Little was getting done. By the time the legislature recessed for Christmas, the labour relations act changes had still not made it to the cabinet order paper. "I ran into a buzz-saw with my cabinet colleagues," Mackenzie explained later.

By this time, labour had changed its mind. The sheer difficulty of getting even limited reforms through government had convinced the union leadership it should go for broke. "People thought you were only going to get one kick at the labour relations act so you should do it," said the OFL's secretary-treasurer Julie Davis. As well, there was some fear that the government might buckle under business pressure. Better for labour to get everything it wanted up front and all at once — before business had time to mobilize, before the government got cold feet. "We knew we would only get one chance," OFL president Wilson said later.

Early in 1991, the OFL presented a far more ambitious set of proposals to a government advisory panel of lawyers, drawn equally from business and labour. The labour-side lawyers on the panel accepted the proposals; the business-side lawyers did not. The new labour wish list — which by this time included a demand for an anti-scab law as well as proposals which would make it easier to organize — was passed on to Mackenzie.

Mackenzie was himself a long-time union member. Raised in Western Quebec, he had quit school to work at the E.B. Eddy paper mill in Hull. Later, he worked as merchant seaman, where, as he likes to tell friends, he met a Scandinavian who taught him about social democracy. Later, Mackenzie worked in a Windsor auto plant and ran campaigns for the NDP before landing a staff job with the Steelworkers. In 1975, he finally won a seat in the legislature as MPP for the working-class riding of Hamilton East.

But he had never forgotten his union roots. "I admit my bias," he said shortly after the being named Labour minister. "I quit school after Grade 7. The only education I got after that was through courses offered by the Auto Workers and Steelworkers. That's my background and I'm proud of it."

Although usually courteous, Mackenzie could exhibit a ferocious temper if he felt his union comrades were under attack. At one early cabinet meeting, for instance, Mackenzie had just finished delivering a passionate plea for aid to jobless Steelworkers in the hard-hit uranium-mining town of Elliot Lake, Suddenly Energy minister Jenny Carter spoke up. "Why bother?" said the Peterborough anti-nuclear activist. "They'll all be dead of cancer soon anyway." Mackenzie, according to one participant at the meeting, was so furious he literally lunged across the cabinet table at the hapless Carter. Luckily, it was a wide table.

Mackenzie was also practical. He knew that the withdrawal of labour support had helped skewer NDP provincial governments in British Columbia and Saskatchewan. "I don't want to make the same mistake [they] did and forget where we come from, who our supporters are," he said in 1991.

However, the rest of cabinet was not as sure about the proposed labour-law changes. For instance, labour wanted union organizers to have access to the names and addresses of employees, to enable them to make their pitch free from the intimidation of supervisors. To labour, this was a logical demand. After all, management had such a list for its anti-union propaganda. To deny labour equal access to that information during an organizing drive would be like denying the voters' list to opposition parties during an election campaign. Nonetheless, some cabinet members were uneasy about the provision, arguing that this would be an invasion of privacy.

In the spring of 1991, the OFL wish list was leaked to the press. Business was outraged. In spite of its rhetoric of consultation, business commentators said, the government was preparing to act as labour's handmaiden. Such language made the cabinet exceedingly nervous. Rae had already set the tone for government by insisting that he wanted

partnership with business, not confrontation. And Mackenzie had duti-
fully followed suit. "I've said many times the job should be minister *for*
labour, not minister *of* labour," Mackenzie had said after taking office.
"But I'm realistic enough to realize that even my hope of getting a
level playing field is going to dissipate more quickly if I'm seen as
nothing but a one-party advocate."

To the majority of ministers, this meant that any labour-law changes
could come only after extensive consultation with business. Privately,
however, Mackenzie was cool to the idea of consultation. His experience warned him that in the crucial field of labour–management relations, the interests of unions and employers were antithetical.

In late 1991, business launched one of the fiercest anti-government
campaigns ever witnessed in Ontario. The NDP cabinet was taken
unawares. Traditionally, business lobbying in Ontario is a sedate affair.
In 1989, for instance, when powerful business interests had wanted to
gut a proposed occupational health and safety bill, all that was required
was a discreet visit to then Liberal premier David Peterson. Peterson
obliged by demoting his Labour minister and removing parts of the bill
that business found distasteful. Everything was done behind closed
doors and with a minimum of fuss. But, with the NDP government, business was at a loss. It couldn't figure out how to get what it wanted from
the new government. So it turned to lobbying the public.

Business had scored a remarkable success with its pro–free trade
public lobby during the 1988 federal election campaign. In early 1991,
business firms came together in an *ad hoc* lobby effort to change parts
of the NDP's proposed wage-protection bill—and again met with
success. As well, business saw how effective the public lobby mounted
by insurers had been in derailing the NDP's scheme for public auto
insurance.

By late 1991, three high-powered business lobbies had been formed
to fight the labour-law amendments. Key among the business firms agitating against the proposals were non-union companies. Eaton's, the
department store chain which had successfuly fought unionization once
before, was asking its managers across the province to speak out and
organize local opposition to the bill. Through the Retail Council of
Canada, Eaton's was represented on the All Business Coalition, perhaps
the most strident of the three lobbies. A second, the More Jobs Coalition, aped the successful insurance-industry lobby (and even used the
same professional consulting firm, S.A. Murray) in taking a more

sophisticated approach. More Jobs, which included the Royal Bank and the newspaper giant Southam Inc., portrayed itself as the moderate voice of business interested only in saving jobs. Labour-law amendments, it argued, would decrease business confidence and destroy jobs. The third lobby, Project Economic Growth, had been organized by the giant retailer Dylex, and IBM Canada—both non-union. The best funded of the three, with almost $1 million to spend, it had hired the U.S. lobbyist Hill and Knowlton (best known for its media manipulation during the Gulf War) to make its case. Project Economic Growth included among its members Pepsico Inc. (fearful that its Kentucky Fried Chicken outlets might be unionized) and the Big Three auto companies. The car companies, while unionized themselves, worried that the proposed changes might disrupt their non-union suppliers. Confidential documents show that Project Economic Growth alone had budgeted $30,000 for "media management" and $312,000 to fight the bill through every stage of the legislature.

The cabinet had committed itself to labour-law changes. Nonetheless, it found the pressure difficult to take. One reason had to do with the media. The news media are prime examples of service industries. A newspaper, for instance, can't stockpile news. If hit by a strike, it either has to use non-union labour to keep operating or shut down and lose money. Major Ontario newspapers, which were heavily unionized, saw themselves as particularly vulnerable to the anti-scab provisions of the proposed law.

Throughout 1991 and 1992, newspaper owners became particularly strident in their opposition to the proposed changes. Southam Inc., the parent of several major Ontario dailies (including *The Ottawa Citizen*, *The Hamilton Spectator* and *The Windsor Star*)—and at the time partly owned by Canada's largest daily, *The Toronto Star*—had joined one of three business lobby groups agitating to have the bill killed. The Canadian Daily Newspaper Publishers' Association came out against the proposals, as did the smaller weekly newspapers.

A bitter, five-week strike at *The Toronto Star* in the summer of 1992, during which the paper was able to publish only because it used non-union labour, reminded owners of their vulnerability.

In 1992, the newspaper publishers' association organized a massive scare campaign. Advertisements were run in the daily press, warning that if the anti-scab law passed, factories would shut down, investors would flee, and public services would be in danger. The ads showed photographs of locked plants and mournful children. Unlikely scenarios were advanced; readers were warned, for instance, that the anti-scab law could allow a handful of striking janitors to shut down an entire school system.

Battered by the business opposition, the government's first response was to give way. About one-fifth of the OFL's original wish list was dropped even before the government began consulting with business; more was dropped later.

Throughout early 1992, the cabinet waffled back and forth as to just how much it should back down. Rae himself was apprehensive and wavering. Eventually, however, the business lobbies outsmarted themselves. They went too far. Media reports detailing the financial extent to which the business lobbies were prepared to go offended ministers and stiffened their spines. "They realized that Mackenzie wasn't just screwing up, that he was the victim of a multimillion-dollar campaign," explained one aide.

The scare campaign waged by the newspaper publishers was the final straw. "It got people mad," explained one senior aide later. "The lobbying became so intense it went to the point of ridiculousness. . . . At the end, they realized it was a campaign against the legitimacy of this government. . . . It got Rae's back up." The government refused to back down any more. On January 1, 1993, the labour-law amendments — including an anti-scab provision — became law.

Nonetheless, the two-year battle with business had left its mark on the government. Inside cabinet, there was a feeling that too much effort had been spent on something that had produced so few political rewards. As the OFL's Julie Davis acknowledged later, the labour-law changes — with the exception of the anti-scab provisions — were more important to union leaders than to the rank and file. "At the end, they [the cabinet] just wished it would go away," said Davis. "It was bringing them so much grief."

Moreover, there was a bitterness within government that labour had not been more supportive. Although the OFL did run a small advertising campaign favouring the changes, there had been no mass demonstrations, no clarion calls of solidarity from the unions.

"Labour didn't educate its own members," said Education minister Dave Cooke, an MPP in the union stronghold of Windsor. "Most of the calls I received against Bill 40 [the labour-law amendments] came from CAW members."

"It was as if they felt they didn't have to fight for it," said one government aide. "They could just sit back and wait for the government to deliver."

The final passage of the package of labour-law amendments marked a watershed. They had been conceived in the earliest days of government, when the NDP was still relatively feisty, willing to challenge the conventional wisdom of business and the right. By January 1, 1993, when the amendments became law, the Rae government had become fully converted to that same conventional wisdom. The arguments that the corporate lobbies had made in opposing the labour-law amendments—that at a time of recession anything that interferes with business confidence is counter-productive—were now being used by the government itself. Bill 40 would remain the anomaly. It would mark one of the few times the government didn't cave in to business.

As far as its relationship with organized labour was concerned, the NDP government had learned another bitter lesson: in politics, your friends take you for granted. The failure of labour to stand four-square with the government against one of the fiercest lobbying efforts in the province's history continued to rankle. Mackenzie would remember that the Canadian Union of Public Employees, the province's largest public-sector union, had refused even to contribute money to the OFL's advertising campaign in support of his labour-law amendments.

"We didn't provide the kind of support we should have when they were getting the shit kicked out of them over Bill 40," the OFL's Julie Davis acknowledged later. "In the light of that, it's not surprising that they would do what they did."

On March 30, 1993, Judy Darcy, the national president of the Canadian Union of Public Employees, received a telephone call from Floyd Laughren. Laughren had just emerged from a grim caucus meeting at a resort hotel in the small town of Niagara-on-the-Lake. The Rae government, he told Darcy, would announce it wanted to roll back the wages of the almost one million public servants in the province. And it wanted to do so through a series of negotiations it was calling a "social contract." Darcy was stunned. "Don't do it," she told the treasurer and fellow New Democrat. A forced wage roll-back that overrode the thousands of existing public-sector collective agreements in the province could drive a permanent wedge between the government and labour. "Too late," Laughren replied. "We've done it."

In fact, the decision to negotiate a social contract with public-sector unions had been taken a week earlier at a cabinet retreat near Picton, in the eastern part of the province. All in the NDP cabinet understood the momentous nature of their decision. To organized labour—and to the NDP—free collective bargaining was a sacred principle. Labour had bitterly opposed the federal government's imposition of wage-and-price controls in 1976 as well as its public-sector wage curbs, the so-called 6 and 5 policy, of 1982. In Ontario, the NDP had fought long and hard to give full collective-bargaining rights to public-sector unions. Now the province's first NDP government was planning to override these rights.

However, fear of the debt wall had convinced even the most ardent champions of labour that public-sector wages had to be rolled back. Labour minister Bob Mackenzie told his colleagues that he had never anticipated the day when he might have to agree to such measures, but that he was convinced the government had no choice. Frances Lankin, the minister with the closest ties to the public-sector unions, had reluctantly come to the same conclusion. The fiscal conservatives inside government—and CTV's Eric Malling—had done their work well.

Just a few months earlier, the cabinet had refused a suggestion from CUPE for a social contract in the health sector. Across Canada, governments had been shifting resources away from expensive large-scale hospitals to smaller, often cheaper community institutions such as clinics. In British Columbia, health-care workers, hospitals, and the government had been negotiating what they called a "social contract" to preserve jobs and wages. Leaders of CUPE, which represented Ontario health-care workers, thought a similar kind of deal might resolve a bargaining stalemate with Ontario's hospitals.

In 1992, CUPE approached the government and offered a deal: The union would accept a low wage increase in return for a range of job-security guarantees. Deputy Health minister Michael Decter and veteran Labour ministry conciliator Vic Pathe were charged with looking into the idea. They soon determined that this social contract, as CUPE called its idea, would need legislative change. But the Ontario Hospital Association, headed by Dennis Timbrell, a former Conservative cabinet minister, was strongly opposed to any measure which threatened the autonomy of hospitals. "Are you telling me just to bend over or should I be wearing a full-body condom?" Timbrell asked Decter.

Lankin, then Health minister, supported the CUPE proposal. But she was unwilling to bring it to cabinet for fear of interfering in collective bargaining. "She thought that being seen to move out of the traditional role of government, of being the honest broker, carried too high a price," recalled Decter later. "There wasn't the political will at the time. It bumped into the theology of intervening in collective bargaining."

Lankin explained her reluctance in slightly different words. "I do come from a background of respecting parties in collective bargaining. You might be on the side of the angels one time. Government could very easily not be on the side of the angels another time."

The ironies were rich. In 1992 the government had refused to legislate a limited social contract that labour wanted for fear of offending employers. A year later it would be legislating a major social contract with the support of most public-sector employers but over the bitter opposition of the labour unions the NDP claimed to represent.

By the fall of 1992, Laughren and his senior advisers in Treasury had come to the conclusion that the government had to cut public-sector compensation if it were to hold the provincial deficit to $10 billion. Initially, the idea met with scepticism inside government.

"I said no party attacks its own base of support," recalled Decter. "It seemed inconceivable to me that this government was going to do this. Therefore, I was kind of surprised when, about eight weeks later, it suddenly [happened]." Apparently, Decter had underestimated the effect of the selling job that he and others had done on the danger posed by the debt wall.

In early 1993, those anxious to cut public-service wage costs were given an inadvertent boost by Saskatchewan's NDP premier Roy Romanow. Saskatchewan had been going through its own desperate economic and fiscal problems. Romanow, a cautious man by nature, was alarmed by the size of his province's deficit and worried about his government's ability to float new bonds. On March 1, Romanow, Rae, and British Columbia's NDP premier Mike Harcourt met in Toronto. The trio emerged to denounce government debt and pledge themselves to deficit control. At a meeting with the executive of the Canadian Labour Congress the next day, Romanow continued his diatribe against debt. To Rae and the other fiscal conservatives in the Ontario government, the Romanow declaration helped legitimize their own attempts to control spending.

Meanwhile, the mechanism for cutting wages was beginning to take shape. Ironically, the person who first raised the idea of a social contract was CUPE president Judy Darcy. At a meeting on February 13 with

Rae and top government and labour leaders, Darcy broached her plan.

Her union, she pointed out, had suggested a social contract in the health area the previous year—wage restraint in return for real job protection. But the Rae government had been unwilling to buck the powerful hospitals then. British Columbia, on the other hand, had been able to work out an arrangement that satisified the government, the unions, and most hospitals. But the B.C. deal had taken time and careful negotiation.

"I'm not talking about a big umbrella deal," she told Rae. "But if you're prepared to try that again in health—and maybe in other sectors—we're willing to give it a try."

On March 11, Rae and Laughren met the labour leaders again. Present were Darcy and Sid Ryan of CUPE, Leo Gerard of the Steelworkers, Canadian Auto Workers chief Buzz Hargrove, Ontario Federation of Labour president Gord Wilson, and Ontario NDP president Julie Davis. The government ministers started off by trying to show labour leaders Eric Malling's documentary on New Zealand in an effort to put them in a restraint mood. The labour side, however, was already aware of the government's new obsession. "I don't want to see your goddamned New Zealand tape," said Hargrove. From there, the meeting moved on. The province, Rae said, faced a debt crisis; public-sector compensation accounted for a significant portion of the government's spending. He was going to have to do something. How could the unions help?

Again, Darcy raised the idea of a limited social contract. Not all labour leaders backed her. Hargrove made it clear he thought the idea was nuts. In the end, the meeting ended with nothing pinned down. To Wilson, it was clear that, whatever Rae was contemplating, it was not the kind of social contract Darcy wanted.

The idea of a social contract was not new. Over the previous two decades, European and Australian social-democratic governments had struck bargains with labour—bargains usually aimed at curbing inflation, whereby the unions gave up major wage demands in exchange for job creation. Some of these had worked; some had flopped. The 1993 B.C. health agreement was the closest thing to a Canadian social contract. And even that had almost failed. For, while the B.C. health unions agreed to a scheme that promised relatively generous terms to workers involved in restructuring, their employers—the hospitals—had been more difficult to draw in.

Meanwhile, some in the Canadian intellectual left had become critical of traditional collective bargaining. They argued that in a world where the aim was to enlarge the economic pie rather than just divide it, and where large factories were being replaced by small-scale workplaces, old-style, confrontational labour relations no longer worked. The new economy meant that workers were no longer strong enough to protect their own interests through old-style unions. Indeed, some old-style unions were terribly short-sighted. Instead, the state — and preferably a social-democratic state — had to intervene directly in the arena of labour relations. By creating new forms of labour relations — often involving corporatist partnerships with business and workers — a social-democratic government could supersede the limitations of collective bargaining.

Peter Warrian, former executive director of the Canadian Steel Trade and Employment Congress and the Rae government's new chief economist, was one intrigued by the idea of forging a social contract outside of the constraints of collective bargaining. So was Rae. The central theme behind the treatise he had written in opposition, "What We Owe Each Other," was that society works best when its constituent groups evolve a set of mutually agreeable bargains. During the constitutional talks of 1991 and 1992, Rae had pushed the idea of a social charter, a document which would made explicit the mutual obligations of state and civil society.

It was no surprise, then, that Rae seized on Judy Darcy's idea of a social contract. His government would not merely implement, as Laughren and Treasury officials were recommending, a public-service wage cut designed to solve a specific fiscal problem. Instead, the Rae government would produce something grander — a new vision, a new way of doing public business.

"We should not be pulling back from the social contract," Rae told his party later in 1993. "We have to extend it. And we have to extend the idea behind it. And we have to extend it across the province, and we have to extend it nationally."

On Sunday, March 21, the inner cabinet again met with labour leaders. Again nothing was resolved. But Rae seemed to have made up his mind. The next day, speaking to reporters, he signalled his intentions. The NDP government, he said, had raised its deficit in its first year to deal with recession. But now, the recession was over; recovery had set in. True, the unemployment rate in Ontario was still in the double digits. But it would come down. The government's task during this period of economic recovery was no longer to concentrate on anti-recession projects. Instead, its prime objective was to get its finances under control.

Would this affect public-sector workers? Rae's answer was that he had to represent bank presidents as well as union leaders. "I'm here to represent all the people." Finally, he finished with an apparent reference to a children's song he had once composed, a song called "We're in the Same Boat Now": "We're all in the same boat. We have to be practical—we're in the same boat economically and the same boat politically. . . . We've come through the recession. We've now got to build for a strong recovery."

The March 30 announcement that the government wanted a social contract to roll back public-sector compensation hit labour hard. Labour, despite its rhetoric, was not a house united. Many private-sector unionists thought their public-sector counterparts led a sheltered life, cushioned from the harsher realities of labour–management relations by anti-strike legislation and compulsory arbitration. To some in labour, the government's demands were not unreasonable. After all, the Steelworkers had made wage concessions to save jobs in Hamilton and Sault Ste. Marie. Why should public-sector workers be exempt?

As well, there were frictions between the unions affiliated to the Ontario Federation of Labour and the province's five teachers' unions. To many in the OFL affiliates, the teachers were spoiled—not real workers. They had become fat at the public teat during the previous twenty years and had never been confronted with the central reality of labour relations—sometimes you win; sometimes you lose. Even the teachers themselves were divided, between public and Catholic unions, high-school and elementary-school unions, unions for women and unions for men.

Between the major public-sector unions, the Ontario Public Service Employees' Union (OPSEU) and CUPE, there was open mistrust. To OPSEU, CUPE was a potential competitor trying to muscle in on its turf. To CUPE, the OPSEU negotiators were shifty. Each was sure the other would try to cut a separate deal with the government.

Then there was CUPE itself, probably the most decentralized union in Canada. No one was sure who spoke for CUPE. Some Ontario locals were affiliated with the Ontario section of the union, headed by Sid Ryan; some were affiliated directly with the national organization, headed by Judy Darcy. But neither Darcy nor Ryan had the kind of authority enjoyed by some other labour leaders to make unilateral decisions on behalf of their membership.

In addition, a growing rivalry had developed between the Steelworkers and the Canadian Auto Workers. Not only were they competing for members, but the two had developed different philosophies about politics and labour–management relations. The Steelworkers, with their experience in the government-sponsored bail-out of Sault Ste. Marie's Algoma Steel, were far more amenable to Rae's idea of labour–management partnership. The CAW saw this as a dead end. To the CAW leaders, partnership and worker ownership allowed workers to be caught up in the cost-cutting ethos of employers, an ethos which could ultimately mean only fewer jobs. Collective bargaining, the CAW argued, at least made it clear who was on which side.

The CAW's Hargrove had already earned Rae's enmity when, in late 1992, he levelled a public broadside at the deficit-busting government for adopting the language of the corporate right and failing to offer "a credible alternative around which to mobilize party and labour activists." To Hargrove and the CAW, the social contract not only concentrated on the wrong issue, public debt, but threatened the basis of class interest, which lies behind collective bargaining.

That a labour movement this fractious was able to unite at all over the social contract owed much to the inflexibility of the NDP government. For the unions knew they had no choice except to bargain. They enjoyed little public support and, in mid-recession, their members had no stomach for strike action. Some unions, such as OPSEU, even hoped to make non-wage gains.

Negotiations between the government and its reluctant unions began on April 5. Had the government offered any real inducements, labour leaders argued later, some unions could have struck a deal.

But it soon became apparent to the union side that the government had little to offer. The cabinet had decided to take $8 billion from the economy in the form of spending cuts and tax increases—the largest single cut-back made by any Canadian government up to that point. Even the deficit-conscious Mulroney Conservatives had never taken that much out of the Canadian economy.

Of this $8 billion, $2 billion in cut-backs had already been announced. That left $6 billion. Rae favoured a hefty tax hike, but others were unsure that business, or voters, would accept that. In the end, the

The young law student. By 1976, after a bout of depression and self-questioning in England, Bob Rae was back in Toronto eyeing a political career in the NDP.

Bob Rae under arrest. In September 1989, the NDP leader had defied the advice of his caucus mates to join an illegal anti-logging protest near the Northern Ontario town of Temagami.

The victorious 1990 NDP election team. Left to right: David Agnew, NDP provincial secretary Jill Marzetti, Julie Davis, David Reville, and Ross McClelland. Agnew, Reville and McClelland would end up becoming key advisors to the NDP premier. Davis, a labour leader, NDP president and personal friend of Rae, would eventually find her loyalties sorely tested.

September 6, 1990. Bob Rae and Arlene Perly Rae accept the cheers from a crowd of jubilant supporters as the NDP sweeps to victory for the first time in Ontario history.

A premier under attack. Bob Rae faces reporters as he announces the resignation from cabinet of health minister Evelyn Gigantes. It was another in a series of mini-crises which plagued the new government.

The NDP government caucus meets for the first time. A jubilant Bob Rae shakes hands with Frances Lankin while, over his shoulder, Bud Wildman grins delightedly. Three years later, Lankin would almost resign from cabinet over policy disputes.

NDP bad boy Peter Kormos takes a seat in the back benches after being fired from cabinet. The unrepentant Kormos would remain a burr in the side of the government.

Treasurer Floyd Laughren faces a hostile business audience as he tries to explain his first budget. The 1991 budget represented the NDP government's most serious attempt to fight recession. But under the pressure of business opposition, it quickly changed tack.

Northern development minister Shelley Martel battles for her political life before a legislative committee investigating her behaviour. The Martel affair continues to haunt the NDP government.

Chief government negotiators Peter Warrian (left) and Michael Decter listen attentively during the 1993 social contract talks. The social contract, an attempt to roll back public service wages, would end up alienating labour and splitting the union movement.

Ruth Grier faces the press. Behind the scenes, the feisty health minister would be locked in almost constant battle with Rae over whether to accede to the incessant demands of the multinational drug companies.

Maurice Strong (centre), his wife Hanne and an unidentified Brazilian contemplate the rain forest in 1992. Later, as head of Ontario Hydro, Strong would enter into discussions to have the electrical utility buy a tract of Central American jungle.

Two years into office, a glum Bob Rae surveys the political scene. Government scandals were continuing to accumulate, while the defeat of the Charlottetown Accord in October 1992 had been a personal blow. By this time, Rae was torn by doubts about his usefulness as a politician.

Premier Bob Rae performs his original composition "We're in the Same Boat Now" on the MuchMusic rock video channel.

premier was talked down, and a decision made to apportion the $6 billion in three roughly equal lots—$1.8 billion from tax hikes and other revenues; $2.4 billion from more spending cuts; $2 billion from the social contract. Laughren called this his "three-legged stool" strategy.

The symmetry of this metaphor, while perhaps aesthetically pleasing, made the social contract virtually impossible for labour. To get its $2 billion from the public service, the government would be under great pressure to override existing contracts and roll back the wages of almost one million people by 5 per cent.

It was on the issue of reopening existing contracts that labour united to draw the line. Had the government been flexible enough to allow existing contracts to work themselves out and negotiate a wage roll-back then, the unions might well have been agreeable. Certainly this was the tenor of the last-minute lobbying done by the OFL's Julie Davis, the Steelworkers' Leo Gerard, and others. But, in the end, the government decided it could not do this and still reach its $2-billion target for the year. And that target was set in stone.

As well, the other two legs of Laughren's stool offered labour little respite. On April 23, the government announced its $2.4 billion in spending cuts. This so-called expenditure-control plan cut deeply across the public sector. As Rae had promised, nothing was exempt, not even child-abuse programs. The employment effect of such massive cuts was obvious. By the government's own estimate, between 9,000 and 11,000 public-sector jobs would disappear.

A little under a month later, in his budget, Laughren revealed the third leg of the stool. Ontarians would face the largest tax hike in the province's history—more than $1 billion, mainly from increases in personal income tax. While a small corporate minimum tax was introduced, business was largely exempted from the tax increases. Again, this gave no joy to labour. In fact, to the rank and file of unionized labour, many of whom suddenly found themselves defined as wealthy by the NDP government, the tax hikes were the breaking-point.

Inside government, there had been some confusion as to how to proceed. Decter, whatever his original misgivings may have been, was now deeply involved in the project. He proposed that workers making less than $20,000 annually be exempted from the social contract and that everyone else face an across-the-board wage roll-back. Laughren, however, was uneasy about that idea. He wanted the low-income cut-off raised and the wage roll-back applied progressively—the higher the income, the greater the percentage cut to wages. Decter was outraged. Senior civil-service managers, he said, had already had their wages frozen for two years. A progressive cut would be unfair. "I can't support that," he told the treasurer. Besides, as he explained later, there were not enough high-income earners in the public service to provide the government with the $2 billion it wanted.

The whole debate was bumped up to cabinet. Lankin, by then Economic Development minister, was visibly upset. Among ministers, she seemed to be hardest hit by the contradiction between what the government was proposing and what the NDP had always said. Friends and former colleagues in the public-sector unions, such as Judy Darcy, were putting pressure on her. Julie Davis, the Ontario Federation of Labour's secretary-treasurer and one of Lankin's closest friends (the two shared a rented cottage on Lake Simcoe), was making labour's unhappiness with the social contract clear.

Under Lankin's prodding, the plan was revised: It would not take the form of a simple wage roll-back; rather, workers making more than $25,000 (eventually $30,000) would be required to take days off without pay. The government hoped the unions could buy what Rae aide Ross McClellan called this "leisure-for-wages tradeoff."

In reality, it was a lay-off. The government initially estimated each public servant would have to be laid off for about two and a half weeks to allow it to meet its $2-billion target. The "leisure-for-wages tradeoff" decision ended any notion of progessive wage roll-backs. For those over the cut-off limit, the layoffs—what became known as "Rae Days"—would be applied to all, regardless of income.

The negotiations themselves were bitter, marked by mutual recriminations of bad faith and dishonesty. Union leaders who had expected an NDP government to take their side against employers found that Rae had meant what he said: the government would be neutral. In fact, given the dynamic of the bargaining, some unionists felt they were being ganged-up on by employers and government, both of whom shared an interest in rolling back compensation.

At the same time, government negotiators felt they were being jerked around by the unions, that CUPE in particular was playing political games. "I've never seen lying on such a breathtaking scale," said one senior political aide later.

The government had insisted talks be wrapped up in two months.

Even with the best of faith on both sides, that deadline would have been hard to meet. For this was probably the most complicated set of labour negotiations in Canadian history, with hundreds of participants, ranging from doctors to garbage collectors, big-city teachers to small-town firefighters, and involving — in total — one-quarter of the provincial workforce.

Moreover, there was little good faith. To be a true social contract, a deal must offer each party something. To government, the trade-off was obvious; it was allowing public-service workers to keep their jobs in exchange for wage roll-backs. True, the social contract would require some lay-offs. But without it, Rae warned, between 20,000 and 40,000 public servants would have to be laid off; the social contract was in labour's best interests.

Labour's failure to appreciate these good intentions wounded the government. "That's why they felt so betrayed by the trade unions," said NDP stalwart Janet Solberg. Natural Resources minister Howard Hampton later explained it this way: "You enter into those [kinds of negotiations] hoping that the people you know in the labour movement, and that you've worked beside and fought with for many years, that there would be some understanding there. ... It wasn't there." To Frances Lankin, the apparent inability of her long-time labour friends to appreciate the crisis the government faced was puzzling; "It was really hard for me to understand how, if I had come — of all people — I had come to really believe that something had to be done at this point in time (and I did; I genuinely came to that conclusion), I felt that there had to be a way in which others, who were like me, and who think like me, who shared some of the experiences over the years, would also come to that."

However, the unions simply did not accept the government's premise. The trade-off — wage cuts for jobs — held only if the government were right that it had no choice except to shave $2 billion from public-sector compensation. But the $2-billion figure was arbitrary, inserted to permit the metaphor of the three-legged stool. Some unions argued the government could make one leg longer. Why not raise taxes more and cut, say $1-billion from public-sector compensation? Since the social-contract cuts were, in effect, a special tax on those who worked in the public sector, why not spread the pain around a bit?

Other unions pointed out that the government's entire deficit target was arbitrary. Why did it have to hold its 1993 deficit to $10 billion? Why not $11 billion or $12 billion? And was the government's worst-case scenario—that, without action such as the social contract, the deficit would hit $17 billion—accurate? Most independent economists said no, that probably a more accurate version of the worst-case deficit would be $14 billion or $15 billion.

To the general public, most of whom supported the social contract, this might appear as hair-splitting. Certainly, these kinds of objections were never accepted as valid by the government side. One senior political figure close to Rae would later dismiss the union arguments as a "sham ... designed to do nothing but blow up the process." But to an individual public-sector employee, a small change in any one of the government's assumptions could mean hundreds of dollars. To some it meant the difference between losing and keeping their jobs.

In the background, labour leaders struggled to keep the government and the public-sector unions from a final rupture. On the one hand, some such as Steelworkers chief Leo Gerard and Ontario Federation of Labour president Gord Wilson leaned on the public-sector unions to be reasonable. "You've got to come to the pump," Wilson told the public-sector leaders at one meeting in May. "The private sector's taken a shit-kicking; you can't goldbrick on this one."

On the other hand, Wilson and Julie Davis were lobbying Rae to bend on his fixation with the deficit and the three-legged stool. Wilson urged Rae to take labour's advice and raise taxes more instead of taking so much from the public sector. Davis, who in her role as NDP president saw Rae every two weeks, also urged him to compromise. Party officials warned the premier that angry members were abandoning the NDP. Even in the long-time NDP stronghold of Sudbury, party members were refusing to renew their memberships.

Rae listened to Davis, even debated her. But he didn't soften. "I'm not sure anybody on the inside—except Frances [Lankin]—appreciated what the fall-out would be," she said later.

Indeed, the government did miscalculate the difficulties. To Rae aide Ross McClellan, one of the government negotiators, the real challenge had been to get the unions to agree to talk. Once that had happened, he said, a deal was virtually certain. He was wrong. On June 3, one day before the government's self-imposed deadline, the unions walked out of the talks.

Rae was shaken and furious. To the unions, the government had abandoned its principles as a labour party. But to Rae and most of his cabinet, the public-sector unions were unreasonable ingrates. Just a few months earlier, the government had gone out on a political limb for the unions; in the face of great pressure, it had changed the Ontario Labour Relations Act to their liking. Where was the gratitude?

"People bang their fists and say 'I made you and now I'm going to break you,'" Rae said angrily. "I don't think that's consistent."

The government was faced with a terrible choice — to forge ahead, legislate the social contract, and risk labour's wrath; or to back down. Once again, the cabinet was split; loyalties were challenged.

Lankin debated with some of her closest friends and colleagues about whether to resign. On June 6, while driving from her home in Toronto's east end to a cabinet meeting, she made her decision: she would quit. But, on arriving at Queen's Park, as Lankin explained later, she was told something that changed her mind: Rae had been convinced over the weekend that there was no need to legislate.

The premier himself knew the danger involved in what his government was contemplating. A student of history, he was well aware of the fate of Ramsay MacDonald, British Labour prime minister at the eve of the Depression of the 1930s. MacDonald's ill-fated decision to give in to the demands of international bankers, abandon his party's principles, and join forces with the Conservative opposition split Labour and set back its fortunes for more than a decade.

"Rae had the ghost of Ramsay MacDonald looking over his fucking shoulder," an official close to the social-contract talks said later. "Don't forget, this is a real loner. He works these things out in his head. And he was faced with the conflict that MacDonald faced, between doing what he thought was right and splitting his party."

During that Sunday's lengthy cabinet meeting, Peter Warrian, who had replaced Michael Decter as chief negotiator for the social contract, argued that the government could get where it wanted without having to open existing contracts. Attrition, early retirement, short-term lay-offs, and voluntary leaves would be enough. Both Rae and Laughren were said to lean to this position. Lankin argued for a negotiated deal, a true social contract where the government would guarantee job security in exchange for wage concessions. But many, such as Housing minister Evelyn Gigantes, argued that the unions were merely protecting vested interests. The government's job, these ministers said, was to protect the most vulnerable. And if it took $2 billion from municipalities, hospitals, and schools without requiring that money to come from wages, these agencies would merely cut services to the vulnerable. Better to legislate a wage cut that would at least take money from those better able to afford sacrifice.

Still divided and undecided, the cabinet took the issue to the NDP caucus. Here labour got its biggest surprise.

Labour leaders are used to acting as a bloc. At NDP conventions, for instance, labour members usually meet the night before, decide on a strategy, and march in the next day to carry out that decision. It is a style of operation which involves discipline, solidarity, and deference to leadership. In the case of the social contract, labour leaders such as Gord Wilson figured they had an ace in the hole—the large number of NDP back-benchers who were trade-unionists. These MPPs, the leaders figured, would respond to the old loyalties. "We have leverage and we have it where it counts," Wilson told a group of union leaders early in May. "We have our MPPs and we can tell them to support us." At the end of June, Wilson, the CAW's Buzz Hargrove, Leo Gerard of the Steelworkers, and Canadian Labour Congress head Bob White held a press conference to denounce any attempt by the government to override existing contracts through legislation. It was message to the NDP back-benches.

What the labour leaders did not appreciate was that the loyalties of most labour MPPs had changed. They had new leaders now, accepted a different discipline and a new form of solidarity. What's more, the caucus of ordinary people had learned to become politicians—that is, to pay attention to what their constituents were saying. By and large, the majority of constituents thought public-sector workers needed to be brought down a peg.

To those who thought the caucus might want to go easy on the unions, the June 6 meeting with cabinet was a revelation. One participant called it "a dance of scorpions," as NDP back-benchers attacked the public-sector union leadership. When Lankin tried to advance pro-union arguments, she was booed. Back-benchers were outraged that CUPE's Sid Ryan had said Rae would be "toast" in the next election. And labour MPPs such as Norfolk's Norm Jamison were the toughest of all as they called for blood.

Rae himself said little. It was the caucus that decided the issue. The government wouldn't hold back and wait for existing contracts to expire. It would legislate a roll-back and it would do so right away.

Lankin seemed shaken. The next day, she met again with public-sector union leaders to talk about how to approach the government's decision. Again, the question of resignation was raised. Judy Darcy had already advised her to quit the cabinet.

"I really had to make a decision that day ... about whether I was resigning or not," Lankin said later. "Once I resigned, I had no ability to influence the contents of the legislation. I made the decision I would stay in."

Labour leaders themselves were taken aback by the hostilty of the NDP cabinet and caucus. They were even more shaken when the legislation was introduced. It was a crafty bill which allowed negotations to continue until the beginning of August but left virtually nothing to negotiate. Unions that agreed to enter the social contract voluntarily would be rewarded with access to an unemployment-insurance top-up fund. Those that did not agree would be denied access to this fund, and would be punished with a larger wage roll-back.

Even the satisfaction of direct refusal was denied. In a particularly Orwellian bit of doublespeak, the act permitted the government to declare an agreement reached in any sector of the public service even if no one except the government agreed. As well, the new law superseded all existing labour acts.

With the bill, a new phrase entered the language. The wage roll-backs were to take the form of compulsory unpaid days off—up to twelve days per worker per year. Soon public servants were referring to these as their "Rae Days."

The notoriety seemed to please the premier, who would often use the term himself. "Better a Rae Day than no days of work at all," he would say. Among Canadian politicians, only one other had seen his name enter the language in a similar way—R.B. Bennett, the Conservative prime minister of the 1930s. Decades later, the "Bennett Buggy" would remain a sad and sardonic symbol of government failure to deal with economic hard times.

Labour lawyers, including the firm that a young Bob Rae had articled with, were angry. Labour leaders were dismayed. An angry Stephen Lewis publicly castigated Rae's government. Julie Davis met Rae and pleaded with him not to interfere with existing collective agreements. "I was very upset and fairly emotional," she said later. "I don't think I was in tears, but I was pretty close to it." Labour's battle to amend the bill continued right until the last minute. Leo Gerard of the Steelworkers shuttled back and forth between government and labour, trying to work out a deal that would persuade the government not to open existing contracts. But to no avail.

At 1:00 a.m. the morning before the bill was to receive final reading, Davis—who by then was working on the federal NDP campaign—called Rae from the Yukon and woke him up. "It was a very difficult conversation," she said later. "And ultimately there was nothing more to say to each other.... It had been decided in cabinet and caucus, and they were going forward."

On July 7, the social contract bill passed the legislature with only three New Democrats opposed. Lankin had contemplated resigning over the issue. So had Culture minister Anne Swarbrick, according to her friends. But only Karen Haslam, a junior minister of Health, was offended enough to actually quit cabinet. Aides in the premier's office quickly tried to discredit her action by whispering that she had quit out of pique for being demoted in a cabinet shuffle four months earlier.

Labour's reaction nationally to the Ontario government's social contract was one of alarm. Most of the country's unionized workers live in Ontario. The Rae experience was bringing to a head a debate already raging within the labour leadership—just how close should labour be to the NDP? Already union locals in Ontario were breaking from the party. In Oshawa, the home of former federal NDP leader Ed Broadbent, the largest local of the Canadian Auto Workers had cut its ties to the party. Others were threatening to follow suit.

In an effort to contain the anger against the NDP, the CAW's leadership voted in August 1993 to dramatically reduce financial support to the Ontario party. Three months later, delegates to CUPE's national convention in Vancouver overruled their leaders and voted to break off support for the NDP—federally and provincially—anywhere in the country. The union's leadership recovered somewhat and subsequently persuaded delegates to give qualified support to the NDP outside of Ontario.

In May 1994, delegates to the biennial convention of the Canadian Labour Congress (CLC) agreed to set up a working group to re-examine labour's relationship to the NDP. It was a compromise resolution drafted specifically to avoid another bitter split over the Rae government. Significantly, the working group was asked to report in 1996, well after the next Ontario election.

Union anger with the NDP reflected a certain reality. At one level, the thirty-two-year-old relationship had been a flop. No matter what influence labour leaders won inside the party, the majority of the rank and file had stubbornly refused to vote NDP. And whenever NDP governments came to power—most notably in British Columbia under Dave Barrett in the 1970s and in Saskatchewan under Allan Blakeney in the 1980s—labour's interests had been sacrificed on the altar of the public good. To some, such as CLC head Bob White, labour should concentrate less on the NDP and more on forming broadly based coalitions with other social-action groups. To others, such as OFL president Gord Wilson, such ideas would lead to the abandonment of labour in politics. Without its own party, no matter how flawed, Canadian labour would find itself in the same position as the U.S. unions, forced to form tactical alliances with right-wing political parties over which they had no control.

At Queen's Park, however, the reaction of senior members of government was more sanguine. The premier and those around him comforted themselves with the same argument B.C.'s Barrett had used before his NDP government's humiliating defeat in 1975: the unions will have nowhere else to go; no matter how bad we are, any other party would be worse.

Not all were as enamoured of the way the social contract had been imposed. Michael Decter, the deputy minister who had led the first round of negotiations and who was soon to resign from government, was sceptical of the way the measure had been rammed down labour's throat: "Instead of having a full discussion with labour—maybe there was no way to do that—they had a sort of half-hearted series of meetings over six months and they didn't get anywhere, so they went and did it anyway. That's great. They [labour] are already mad; they just got more mad."

Sue Colley, Lankin's most senior adviser and an activist with close ties to the women's movement, quietly left the government, citing the social contract as one of her reasons.

The working out of the social contract proved to be remarkably complicated. In some sectors, workers ended up taking very few Rae Days. In others, workers were laid off—although the numbers involved remained a source of dispute between the government and the public-sector unions.

Meanwhile, some public agencies found themselves going through bizarre contortions in an effort to live up to the law. At the Guelph Correctional Centre, for instance, guards were being called in to work overtime, at time-and-a-half, in order to cover Rae Days. In some instances, guards were working overtime on their own Rae Days.

Metro Toronto had to pay almost $800,000 to hire replacements for child-care workers taking unpaid Rae Days. One Toronto nursing home got around the problem of being short-staffed by confining their elderly patients to bed for days at a time.

To Rae and others, however, the social contract was a major accomplishment. For the first time, the NDP government had won widespread public approval for its actions. For the first time, it had won sustained kudos from the editorial boards of the daily press. Most important, the government had been seen to actually do something. And, as Laughren and Rae explained to the caucus later, the NDP had shown the public it was not in anyone's pocket—that it didn't dance to labour's tune.

Unfortunately, it was Audrey McLaughlin and the federal NDP who paid the immediate price for this statement of principle. The social-contract negotiations occurred just as the country was preparing for a federal election. Disgusted by the actions of the NDP government at Queen's Park, scores of activists simply refused to work for the federal party, and thousands more decided to cast their votes elsewhere. That fall, in the midst of the federal election campaign, as support for the NDP plummeted in union strongholds across Ontario, Rae invited a few government people home to celebrate the success of the social contract. It was, as one guest observed later, an appropriately bizarre ending.

9

Taking Care of Business

IN LATE 1992, THE FEDERAL PARLIAMENT WAS IN AN uproar over drug prices. The Mulroney government had introduced Bill C-91, legislation to significantly increase patent protection for brand-name drugs produced by giant European and U.S.-based multinationals. The move was another body blow against Canada's twenty-three-year-old system of compulsory licensing, a system which—by permitting domestic manufacturers to produce cheaper, generic equivalents of brand-name drugs upon payment of a royalty to the original manufacturer—had saved Canadians billions of dollars.

At the centre of the drug controversy was an issue of principle. On the one hand, was the principle of private rights. The multinationals argued that a company, after pouring millions of dollars into research to create a drug, should have a period of exclusive patent rights—in effect a monopoly which would allow it to set the price for that drug. A new drug, they argued, was like any other invention. If the state could award exclusive patent rights to the inventor of a better mousetrap, why not do the same for the inventor of a drug?

On the other hand was the principle of social rights. Drugs have become such a health necessity, this camp argued, that society no longer can enjoy the luxury of granting exclusive monopoly rights to their producers. A new cancer-treatment drug, for instance, is not the same as a better mousetrap. Those who cannot afford to pay a monopolist's price for the better mousetrap may be inconvenienced, but those unable to pay for an anti-cancer drug may die.

In the case of drugs, therefore, social equity required the state to suspend some of the privileges usually granted to inventors. Since 1969 in Canada, this revision of patent rights had taken the form of permitting competition — allowing other firms to produce their own version of the new drug. The theory was that this competition would drive down drug prices. In most cases, it did.

In addition to points of principle, the drug debate involved practical issues. The drug multinationals were powerful firms with significant investments in both Ontario and Quebec; since 1969 they had warned successive Canadian governments that jurisdictions which did not bend to their wishes would be out of luck when the companies made investment decisions. From the other side, provincial governments had developed a vested interest in supporting compulsory licensing. All provinces had some sort of drug benefit plan, paid for in part or in full by government. By the mid-1980s, 23 per cent of all drugs purchased in Canada were paid for by these plans. The existence of generic alternatives to expensive brand-name drugs helped to keep the costs of these plans down.

For the federal NDP, the drug-patent issue was a natural. On one side were some of the world's largest, most profitable multinational firms. On the other were the generic-drug companies (mainly Canadian-owned), the sick, the elderly, the poor, and every provincial government except Quebec's. Ottawa had announced the patent-law changes in January 1992, ostensibly to bring Canada into line with new international standards being proposed under the General Agreement on Tariffs and Trade. By the end of the year, with the GATT proposals foundering, it had become clear that this was not the whole story, that Bill C-91 was tied in with Ottawa's efforts to be in on the North American Free Trade Agreement.

The drug multinationals wielded considerable power in Washington, and, through it, on the Ottawa Tory government. Brian Mulroney's government had already weakened Canada's compulsory licensing system once, in 1987, in order to win the Canada–U.S. Free Trade Agreement. Now, it seemed, it was getting ready to repeat history. To critics of the Mulroney government, the drug-patent issue was another blatant sell-out. If ever there was a black-and-white issue in politics, this seemed to be it.

In Ottawa, researchers for federal NDP health critic Jim Karpoff were in regular contact with the country's three NDP provincial governments. Here at least, the federal party thought it had powerful friends.

Certainly, the federal NDP could be forgiven for thinking that the Rae government was its strongest ally. Health minister Frances Lankin had publicly announced that Bill C-91 would cost the province's drug plan a stunning $1 billion over ten years in lost savings. To a province that was publicly fretting about its $10-billion deficit, this was not an inconsiderable sum.

More than that, the Rae government was New Democratic. Quebec's ruling Liberal government might be seduced by the honeyed words of the drug multinationals, their whispered promises of investment and research which somehow never entirely materialized. But not an NDP government. The NDP understood.

By the fall of 1992, however, the federal NDP caucus was beginning to get disturbing signals from Ontario. "It seemed to us that they [the Ontario government] were drawing back," said one federal NDP researcher involved in the drug issue. "We didn't get opposition from them. We just didn't get the kind of support we thought we should." The NDP government in British Columbia sent its Health minister, Elizabeth Cull, to testify against Bill C-91 at a parliamentary committee hearing. Ontario did not. Rae had been happy to appear before a parliamentary committee on the constitution. No Ontario minister, however, would come to Ottawa to argue for lower drug costs.

What the federal party did not know, was that, on October 20, 1992, the Rae cabinet had secretly capitulated. Partly in the hope of winning 150 new drug-company jobs in Metro Toronto, it had agreed to "accept the elimination of compulsory licensing." Nor did anyone outside of a small circle know Rae had been intimately involved in the negotiations, and that the premier had personally promised one firm, Eli Lilly Canada Inc., a two-year grace period for one of its more profitable drugs. Certainly, few knew that letters which appeared over the premier's signature, and which made significant concessions to Eli Lilly and other drug multinationals, had been drafted in part by the companies themselves.

Ontario Health ministry officials had been aware for some time that Ottawa was preparing another look at drug-patent protection. While the exact form and timing of Bill C-91 may have been unexpected, the issue was not. In October 1991, the ministry had prepared a 104-page confidential report outlining the major elements. The drug multinationals, the report noted, had never accepted compulsory licensing—not because the Canadian market was in itself important to them (Canada accounted for only 2 per cent of drugs sold worldwide), but because the drug companies were worried about precedent. If Canada were able to get away with allowing generics firms to copy brand-name drugs, other nations might follow suit. The brand-name multinationals might no longer be able to earn a rate of return double that of the average manufacturer.

The report noted the significant savings to the Ontario Drug Benefit Program from compulsory licensing. The $1.2-billion-a-year program provided free prescription drugs to people age sixty-five and over, and those on welfare. Ministry officials estimated that the mandatory use of generic drugs cut the program's costs by at least $80 million to $100 million a year.

Finally, the report dealt with the question of investment. The drug multinationals argued that better patent protection would encourage them to invest more in Canadian research and development. It is true, said the Health ministry report, that since 1987, when Ottawa first backed away from compulsory licensing, more drug research and development had taken place in Canada. However, 73 per cent of this R & D was clinical testing and other forms of applied research required to get a drug approved in Canada—in other words, research that would have taken place regardless of Patent Act changes. The hope that a more favourable patent climate would encourage foreign-owned companies to locate in Canada a significant portion of their basic R & D was, the report concluded, "the impossible dream."

In fact, the report noted dryly, statistics compiled by the Organization for Economic Cooperation and Development showed that nations with the highest level of foreign ownership in the drug industry (notably, Canada, Australia, and the developing world) had the lowest capacity for pharmaceutical innovation. It went on to conclude that Canadian-owned generic-drug companies, the largest of which were headquartered in Ontario, could well be a more significant source of future innovation than the foreign-owned brand-name firms.

Bureaucratic reports are rarely explicit. But the implicit conclusion of this report was that, in terms of both current drug prices and future innovative capacity, Ontario would do better to cast its lot in with compulsory licensing and Canadian-owned generics firms rather than with increased patent protection and the multinationals.

Consumed in a search for no-cost jobs, however, the government paid little attention to its own report. Instead, it listened to the arguments of the multinational drug lobby. The drug multinationals had long mounted one of the most sophisticated lobbies in the country. In Ontario, the assault took place on several fronts. First, there was the Pharmaceutical Manufacturers' Association of Canada, the trade group for the drug multinationals headed by former federal Liberal cabinet minister Judy Erola. Second, the drug firms hired specific lobbyists, such as Toronto consulting firm S.A. Murray. Third, major companies such as Eli Lilly Canada Inc. and Syntex Inc. (Canada) lobbied the premier and his office directly. The premier had made it clear from the beginning that his door was always open to business leaders. The drug multinationals were quick to take him up on the offer.

The multinationals wanted three things from Rae. First, they wanted the government to keep their products on what it called its "formulary," the list of drugs approved for use by the Ontario Drug Benefit Program. This program represented about 40 per cent of the Ontario pharmaceutical market. To drug manufacturers, having their products listed on the Ontario formulary could mean hundreds of millions of dollars in extra profits.

Under Frances Lankin, however, the Health ministry was looking closely at the formulary, trying to eliminate expensive drugs from the list if cheaper and equally effective versions already existed. This was called delisting, and the multinationals wanted to ensure that it didn't affect their top-selling products.

Second, the drug companies wanted user fees to be introduced into the drug benefit program. The reasoning here was simple. User fees would mean more money going into the drug system; they would also mean less pressure to remove brand-name products from the formulary. Finally, the drug companies wanted Bill C-91 passed into law. They wanted Ontario to ease up on its opposition to patent extension.

Throughout 1992, one of the point firms in the multinational assault on Ontario was Eli Lilly. The previous year, the U.S. multinational's Canadian subsidiary, Eli Lilly Canada Inc., had ranked as the most profitable company in Canada, with a stunning 107 per cent return on shareholders' equity.

In 1991, Eli Lilly had announced it wanted to rationalize its operations worldwide, including the company's plant in the Toronto suburb of Scarborough. Eli Lilly Canada president Nelson Sims made it clear publicly that continued investment in the Scarborough plant was contingent on successful passage of Bill C-91.

There was more, however. As a confidential government memo details, Sims told Rae that Scarborough investment was also contingent on his receiving a guarantee that Ceclor, an Eli Lilly product, would remain on the government's drug formulary for five years. And he wanted guarantees that the government would be quick to add new Eli Lilly products to the formulary as they were developed. In a letter to Rae dated January 22, 1992, Sims warned Rae that the government's failure to comply would "most certainly negate [Eli Lilly's planned] investment in Ontario."

Rae took the drug company lobbying most seriously. "The drug companies were in there [the premier's office] all the time," recalled Sue Colley, at the time executive assistant to the Health minister. Initially, David Agnew, Rae's trusted principal secretary, was charged with handling the drug executives. In 1992, Rae and Agnew journeyed to the United States one weekend to talk to those in the drug company head offices.

The strategy of the drug companies was simple and effective. The Canadian subsidiaries presented themselves to the government as allies with a common interest—jobs and investment for Ontario. The sceptics who had to be convinced, they told Rae, were their own U.S. head offices. For only at head office were the final investment decisions made.

To help in this battle, the subsidiaries said, the government should draft letters to the parent firms. The subsidiaries would suggest the content of the letters. Then the premier would sign them.

By midsummer of 1992, Rae and his aides had been fully drawn into the game. What they forgot was that the definitions of friend and foe, as presented by the drug branch plants, were not entirely accurate. In fact, the branch plants and their head offices had the overriding common interest. The government had put itself into a bargaining situation in which its ostensible partners were on the side of its adversaries. It was a dynamic guaranteed to wring concessions from the NDP government. And it did. Even deputy Health minister Michael Decter, no enemy of the drug companies, was alarmed by the extent to which Rae was willing to concede points to the multinationals.

In a confidential memo to Rae that summer, Decter reminded the premier that Eli Lilly was the most profitable firm in the country, earning 107 per cent return on shareholders' equity. "At 107 per cent-plus, it must be that our marketplace in Ontario is not entirely unfavourable to the pharmaceutical industry," he noted wryly.

Decter's warning had little effect. To the premier, the multinational drug firms were precisely the kind of high-technology companies that he wanted to keep in Ontario. More important, business attacks on the NDP government for its labour-law reforms were worrying Rae.

"A lot of it was smoke," said one aide later. "But the head offices did get all of their information [about Ontario] from *The Wall Street Journal....* We were on the defensive. If anyone said they were moving out of the province, it would be front-page news."

Moreover, caught up in the midst of complicated constitutional negotiations, Rae seemed convinced of his ability to drive a hard bargain. Indeed, the drug companies had hit the NDP government at one of its most vulnerable spots, its vanity. Because of their experience with the labour movement, Rae and some of those around him thought of themselves as shrewd, hard-nosed negotiators. Compared with the drug multinationals, however, they were babies.

Negotiations with Eli Lilly over drug listing in the provincial formulary continued. The company's second-most important product in Ontario was Ceclor, a grape-flavoured antibiotic often prescribed for children. Government documents show that in 1993 alone, the government-funded Ontario Drug Benefit Program spent more than $8 million on the product. To Eli Lilly, therefore, it was most important that Ceclor remain listed on the drug benefit plan formulary.

However, it was debatable whether there was any medical reason to keep Ceclor on the formulary. There were plenty of medically equivalent antibiotics—or anti-infectives, as they are often called—available in Ontario. Many were cheaper than Ceclor. The Health ministry's Drug Quality and Therapeutic Committee had wanted to delist Ceclor for years. Ministry estimates suggested that, based on 1993 figures, the government could save $4 million to $5 million annually by striking Ceclor from the drug formulary. In fact, Saskatchewan's NDP government had already moved to cut Ceclor from its formulary.

In 1992, however, Rae was less concerned about saving money for the province's drug program than in securing jobs for Scarborough. On September 25, a letter drafted jointly by Eli Lilly and government officials, and addressed to Eli Lilly president Sims, was presented to Rae for his signature. As confidential government documents point out,

Sims had wanted, in return for upgrading the Scarborough plant, a guarantee that Ceclor would remain listed on the formulary of the drug benefit plan for five years. To Lankin, this was too long. However, she figured it would take her ministry officials a lengthy period of time to review Ceclor fully.

In his letter, Rae guaranteed two years' grace. "I believe I can offer you positive reassurances," he wrote. "The review of anti-infectives [of which Ceclor is one] will be completed at the earliest in early 1994. From there, as you know, the recommendations must be considered by the Ministry, Cabinet Committee, Cabinet and then promulgated. Any changes in the formulary, therefore, would be implemented at the end of 1994."

As for Eli Lilly's worries about getting new, expensive drugs on the formulary, Rae was blunt. In the past, health and cost issues alone had decided which drugs the province would subsidize. But the NDP was changing this; it was now willing to bargain access to the formulary in exchange for investment *promises* by the multinationals: "The Drug Reform process is specifically considering ... the role which investment and economic development considerations should play in the Formulary approval process," Rae's letter read. "You have my personal assurance of my own interest in this matter. Research and development is [*sic*] critical to the future of Ontario and I am committed to encouraging it [*sic*]. Other jurisdictions understand these links and so do we."

In case Eli Lilly didn't get the point, Rae repeated it. "I can assure you," he wrote, "that decisions about Drug Program benefits are not, and will not, be made on the basis of drug cost containment alone."

The desire to do business with the drug multinationals spilled over into the government's handling of Bill C-91. Initially, the Rae government had been firm in its opposition to drug-patent extension. By the fall of 1992, all of this had changed. David Agnew had long argued that Ontario should stick to its own area of jurisdiction. Drug-patent law was in Ottawa's bailiwick and, for better or worse, Canadians had democratically elected the Mulroney government. Why fight a battle you can only lose? To Agnew, Lankin, Housing minister Dave Cooke, and many others in cabinet, it made more sense to get whatever concessions Ontario could from the drug companies.

"Did we continue to wave the banner on something that we were absolutely assured of losing within the next week, when it would also be held up publicly, probably, that investment decisions were going to be quote unquote cancelled because of the NDP government?" said Lankin later. "We're judged differently as an NDP government. Stuff sticks to us around scaring away business investment."

For Dave Cooke, the issue was equally practical. "The bottom line was the legislation was going through. There was a practical question of whether or not we [would] continue to oppose, and lose, and turn off the drug companies to such an extent that we had no opportunities for investment in Ontario."

On October 8, on a joint recommendation from Lankin and Industry minister Ed Philip, the cabinet's committee on economic and labour policy decided it would accept the elimination of compulsory licensing under Bill C-91 while still pushing for amendments to it. "With additional patent protection," the committee said in a confidential report to the full cabinet, "Ontario expects the industry to proceed with investments in the province and co-operate on drug programs reform." All that remained was the final coup-de-grâce. That happened on October 20, when cabinet formally adopted the no-opposition position.

While the drug companies were aware of the government's change of heart, no public announcement was ever made. In fact, not even all of the ministers seemed to know. Seventeen months later, Ruth Grier—by this time Health minister—would insist that she had no idea the cabinet of which she was a part had ever backtracked on this particular proposal: "I was really surprised after I became Health minister when seniors said to me 'Why didn't Ontario oppose C-91?'—because I believe we did oppose C-91."

A minor kerfuffle occurred on October 28, when Lankin, in a speech to the Ontario Hospital Association, said Bill C-91 would cost the government's drug program $1 billion over ten years. In fact, her figure was conservative. By her ministry's reckoning, Bill C-91 would cost the government $1 billion, and other drug consumers, including companies with private drug plans, another $1 billion.

The drug multinationals were furious that the NDP seemed to be reneging on its deal and enlisted the help of federal Industry minister Mike Wilson to counter Lankin's figure. Two days after the Lankin speech, the government held a high-level meeting with the drug companies to soothe their ruffled feelings.

On December 7, Rae, Wilson, and Sims announced Eli Lilly's decision to invest $170 million over five years in its Scarborough operation—including a $50-million expansion of its plant and a North

American mandate for certain kinds of drug production. The expansion, Eli Lilly said then, would create 150 new jobs.

To one cabinet minister involved in the discussion, the Eli Lilly decision had nothing to do with Bill C-91: "The issue there had nothing to do with that legislation. The issue was around stuff going on in the drug formulary, what drugs are being listed or not listed.... It was in that context they made their final decision to announce what they were going to announce anyway." Sims, however, was blunt about the *quid pro quo*. "If Bill C-91 was to derail, clearly Eli Lilly would have to re-evaluate its business plans," he said.

Rae was conciliatory. "We don't want to be so opposed to Bill C-91 that we turn away investment," he told reporters. He didn't mention that his government was no longer opposed to Bill C-91. Nor did he mention the deal he had struck on Ceclor. "It's great to be here on a good day with a good announcement," the premier said.

Three days later, over the last-ditch protests of Audrey McLaughlin and her NDP, Bill C-91 passed the federal Commons. Federal New Democrats were bitterly resigned to being left in the lurch by their Ontario comrades. "We sensed we couldn't expect anything," recalled one. "The [Ontario] government was clearly on the run ... [but] if they had really wanted to declare war on the drug companies in terms of price, they would have had every justification. They certainly had the information to back it up."

There was an ironic postscript to the Eli Lilly caper. In March 1994, the company's head office decided it would not, in fact, expand manufacturing capacity at its Scarborough plant. The promised 150 jobs, a spokesman said then, were never considered as part of the expansion *per se*. Rather, they were jobs that Eli Lilly hoped to create if and when business improved. The company still planned to invest the $170 million it had promised, the spokesman said then—but it was no longer sure what form this investment would take.

These were not the only dealings between the NDP government and the drug multinationals. Throughout the fall of 1992, the government had been negotiating with the British giant Burroughs Wellcome Inc. Burroughs Wellcome manufactures the AIDS drug Retrovir, a brand-name azidothymidine, commonly known as AZT. Since 1991, Burroughs Wellcome and the Canadian generic-drug firm Apotex Inc. had been locked in lawsuits over who owned the AZT patent.

In May 1992, Apotex received Ottawa's permission to sell its version

of AZT, Apo-Zidovudine, in Canada. It announced it would do so at
somewhere between 30 and 50 per cent off the brand-name price. Burroughs Wellcome responded by threatening to sue any druggist or hospital who sold the cheaper generic. It also threatened legal action against the Ontario government if it purchased Apotex's generic AZT for use in its Special Drugs Program (a program for those suffering from certain catastrophic illnesses, including AIDS, who required expensive medication).

For Ontario, the savings involved in using the Apotex product could have been significant. The government spent about $5.7 million on AZT in its Special Drugs Program. Replacement of the Burroughs Wellcome drug with Apotex's generic AZT could save the government close to $3 million a year. However, there was the threat of suit.

Here opinions were divided. Some Health ministry lawyers advised that Burroughs Wellcome could not win a suit against the government. Other counsel argued that since the province actually purchased AZT (through Sunnybrook Hospital) for use in AIDS treatment, it could be held liable in any suit. Health minister Frances Lankin preferred caution and, in a press release announcing the government's capitulation to the drug multinational, said: "We have been given clear legal advice. We must respect the [Burroughs Wellcome] patent."

Factors other than legal considerations were in play too. Rae, according to those around him, seemed captivated by the arguments the drug multinationals were making about the sanctity of intellectual property. As well, Burroughs Wellcome managed to appeal to the AIDS establishment. In December 1992, it agreed to donate 25 per cent of the money it made from its Ontario sales of AZT to AIDS-related programs—for a period of three years. The total amount of the donation would be between $1.5 million and $3.75 million. The deal pleased Sunnybrook Hospital (which was promised a chunk of the money), as well as AIDS activists. Prominent AIDS physician Phil Berger praised the government for being "able to swing a deal that is in the best interests of the patients."

The deal pleased the government, which got good press even though it had caved in. It pleased Burroughs Wellcome. The fact that Ontario had given up close to $3 million a year in perpetuity in exchange for a one-time shot of between $1.5 million and $3.75 million did not seem to disturb this general consensus.

Oddly, economic considerations and jobs seemed to play no part in this drug decision. Burroughs Wellcome had twenty-nine workers in Ontario. Apotex employed about 1,400. By mid-1993, Apotex was planning to manufacture not only its generic AZT in Ontario, but also the ingredients involved, the so-called fine chemicals.

In the summer of 1993, another issue came to a head, this time with the U.S.-owned firm Syntex Inc. (Canada). California-based Syntex was contemplating a global restructuring of its operations and had dangled before the NDP government the possibility of locating one of its so-called mother plants in Ontario. But it had a price. Rhinalar, a Syntex prescription nose spray, was listed on the formulary of the province's drug benefit program. Pharmascience Inc., a small, Canadian-owned firm in Montreal, was about to introduce a cheaper, generic competitor, Rhinaris-F. Syntex wanted to make sure that nothing could get on to the Ontario formulary that might cut into Rhinalar's market share.

On May 21, Rae and Health minister Ruth Grier met with Melvin Booth, president of Syntex Pharmaceuticals Pacific, the parent firm, and Michael Ball, president of the Canadian subsidiary. Following that meeting, Susan Fenton of Syntex's Canadian operation and Chuck Rachlis of the premier's office worked together to produce a letter for Rae's signature that could be sent to the drug company's head office. Rachlis would fax a draft version of the Rae letter to Syntex Canada; Fenton would fax back with proposals to strengthen the wording in her company's favour. Most of her suggestions were incorporated into the final version of the letter.

Again it was the same game. The Canadian subsidiary and the government would team up to persuade the parent to invest in Ontario. Again, the government made the same false assumption — that Syntex Inc. (Canada) and its U.S. parent were somehow on different sides.

In the end, Rae made an extraordinary concession. He agreed that "there will be no contemplation of listing the competitor to Rhinalar as an interchangeable product [on the drug-benefit formulary] *at least until the conclusion of litigation.*"

At the time, this pledge might have seemed unimportant to Rae. In June 1993, there was no competitor to Rhinalar available in Canada; Pharmascience did not win federal approval to bring out Rhinaris-F until later that year. Nor was Syntex suing Pharmascience at the time of Rae's writing. Nonetheless, the Rae letter represented a signal victory for the drug multinationals. The brand-name giants were almost always involved in litigation with their generic competitors, litigation that

could go on for years. Should Syntex have decided to sue Pharmascience, the cheaper generic version of Rhinalar could be kept off the
formulary indefinitely.

More important, the Rae letter set a new precedent. If the Ontario
government had agreed to do this for one drug multinational, surely it
would have to do the same for others. Rae's pledge to Syntex over a
simple nose spray had opened the door even wider.

In the fall of 1993, Merck Frosst Canada Inc. came waltzing through
that door. Merck Frosst produced the country's top-selling pharmaceutical product, a heart medication called Vasotec. In 1993, according to
Health ministry officials, Vasotec sales in Ontario alone were estimated
at $52 million—$36 million of that paid for by the provincial drug
benefit program. Vasotec was one of the drugs retroactively given extra
patent protection by Ottawa's Bill C-91. In September, Apotex had
received federal permission to produce a generic version of Vasotec.
According to Health ministry figures, listing the Apotex generic would
save the province about $9 million a year.

Economic considerations also favoured the generic firm. In March
1993, Apotex had announced a $285-million expansion that would,
over three years, employ 650 additional workers. Part of the expansion
was to produce generic drugs for the export to the United States. The
Ontario government, apparently recognizing the strategic value of supporting a domestic firm trying to export, had invested $1 million of
public money to help the Canadian company along.

However, as government officials warned Rae, the Apotex expansion was contingent on its being able to list its generic version of
Vasotec in the drug benefit formulary. Such a listing, according to the
government's own estimates, would be worth $35 million to $40
million annually to Apotex and, as one internal memo to Rae put it,
would be "critical to the success of Apotex's investment projects."

Merck Frosst, on the other hand, employed only 125 people in
Ontario in sales and distribution. It had no production or research facil-
ities in the province, except for a small joint venture with Connaught
Laboratories, employing fifteen workers to produce hepatitis-A vaccine.

Still, the multinational was determined not to lose any share of the
lucrative Canadian heart-drug market. To that end, it had threatened
legal action against any provincial government which dared to list the
generic. By early 1994, the threat had worked in Manitoba but failed in
Quebec and Alberta.

In January 1994, Merck Frosst Canada Inc. president Michael Tarnow wrote Rae to say he was disturbed by news that Ontario might list the Apotex version of Vasotec on its drug formulary. Merck Frosst, Tarnow went on, was in a legal tussle with Apotex over patent rights to the drug. He reminded the premier that Ontario had already set a precedent by refusing to list the generic version of AZT while similar litigation was underway. To list the Apotex product before all lawsuits had been conluded would be "clearly inconsistent with previous decisions." As well, it would cost Merck Frosst $5 million a month. Then came the carrot. "We are currently reviewing, with the intention to accelerate, several proposals that *could* substantially increase Merck Frosst's presence in your province." No details were given of these "proposals" except that, if they did proceed, they would be worth more than $1.5 million.

Finally, Tarnow showed the stick: "You will appreciate that our investment activities are affected by our revenues. Actions such as that being considered by the Health Ministry could not only impact on our ability to invest, but could also be seen nationally as well as internationally as an indication of a change in your government's protection of intellectual property.... We feel that your government would want to avoid ... not only possible embarrassment but also potential liability.... In conclusion, I am asking you to personally intervene...."

Lawyers for the Health ministry and the attorney general argued that the multinational would have no case if it tried to sue the province for listing a federally-approved generic drug on its formulary. In fact, the cabinet was warned, Ontario might be sued successfully by Apotex if the government did bend to Merck Frosst. Nonetheless, the Tarnow letter seemed to have considerable influence with Rae.

On February 16, 1994, the issue went to cabinet. On one side was Health minister Ruth Grier, arguing to list the cheaper generic. On the other were Rae and Economic Development minister Frances Lankin. The premier was vehement in his defence of Merck Frosst. He praised the drug company as a worthy economic partner for the NDP government; he cited the importance of patent law and the necessity for Canada to adhere to internationally accepted rules. Cabinet secretary David Agnew privately supported Grier. But he had seen his boss in this mood before and chose to keep quiet. So did virtually every other minister. Only two spoke up. Citizenship minister Elaine Ziemba said she agreed with Rae that a decision to list the generic might upset senior citizens used to Vasotec (apparently no reason was given by either Rae or Ziemba for the bizarre assertion that users would be able to differentiate between two identical and chemically equivalent drugs). Attorney General Marion Boyd spoke up only to say that her lawyers had told her Merck Frosst did not have a case.

In the end, the cabinet agreed to put off a decision. It was an expensive move. For every day the government delayed placing Apotex's generic version of the heart drug on its formulary, the province lost $25,000.

On March 9, the cabinet met again. By this time, the dynamics had shifted. Lankin had met a day earlier with representatives of the generics firm, Apotex. She had also been convinced that Merck Frosst would have no case if it tried to sue the province for listing the generic competitor. Rae still held out, at one point accusing Grier of acting as an advocate for the generic-drug companies.

However, Lankin's change of heart seemed to settle the matter. The cabinet would defy at least one multinational drug company. The generic form of Vasotec would be listed in the Ontario formulary. Grier was ecstatic.

As news of the NDP government's susceptibility to corporate blackmail became widespread, drug-company demands became ludicrous. In one instance, a multinational with operations in Mississauga came to see a political aide. "These people were really vague," said the aide later. "I couldn't understand what they wanted. So eventually, I just said: 'What do you want?' It came out they wanted $1 million or $2 million just to show head office they could do it, that they were heavy hitters."

That particular branch plant was unable to return to head office with the required trophy. Rae's government might be easy. But even it had its limits.

In spite of its desire to please, the NDP government was not much trusted by business. Some business people had been hostile from the start. One group, connected to the right-wing National Citizens' Coalition, had erected a huge billboard in downtown Toronto soon after the NDP election with giant mug-shots of Marx, Stalin, and Bob Rae. In the summer of 1991, another group, organized by a pair of young Toronto businessmen, staged two large anti-NDP demonstrations in Queen's Park (one featuring rock icon Rompin' Ronnie Hawkins) to protest the

$10-billion budgetary deficit. Publicly, two of the province's most vocal business groups—the Canadian Federation of Independent Business and the Ontario Chamber of Commerce—took every opportunity to slam the government.

To Rae and Laughren, this hostile business reaction was unfair and dishonest. The treasurer, after his brief fling with Keynesianism in 1991, had quickly retreated into fiscal orthodoxy. Rae argued that he spent more time seeing business leaders than anyone else. Yet still they got no respect.

In late 1993, Laughren expressed his frustration this way: "I look at how the business community and the right wing feel about it. Holy mackerel. They are still ferocious about the level of our deficits, the labour reform bill and employment equity and pay equity. They don't see that we've done anything other than cater to our constituency. I once had a meeting with the financial community. It was a dinner meeting, and after dinner, one fellow said to me: `You know, all I'm waiting for is when I hear you and the premier make a speech that doesn't sound as if it was designed for a union hall.' I got very angry. It was really outrageous. That feeling is still out there in the business community that that's where we're at—despite the social contract, despite our expenditure controls. Gee, it's not even fair."

The NDP government's decision to play ball with business had been made immediately after the 1990 election. All knew the sorry history of Dave Barrett's NDP government in British Columbia. Barrett had angered powerful business interests almost immediately after coming to power in 1972; business had united behind the reinvigorated Social Credit Party to help oust Barrett in 1975.

More important, the so-called partnership approach appealed to Rae's own instincts. What defined social democracy, he had written in his opposition treatise, "What We Owe Each Other," were values—particularly the value of helping one another, of solidarity. It was why Rae could define socialism as love. What a social-democratic government should do, therefore, was create institutions that would allow people to work together and express their common humanity. In practical terms, this meant government working with business. For were not business people human too?

Finally, many in the new government felt their victory had been unearned, that the NDP had won power not because a majority, or even a plurality, of Ontarians favoured social democracy, but through a series

of flukes — dissatisfaction with the Peterson Liberals, the vagaries of
three-way vote splits, and the temper of the times.

For some New Democrats, the party's 1990 campaign methods, and in particular the scathing attacks on Peterson's personal integrity, had caused a crisis of conscience. "It was all lies," NDP strategist Gerry Caplan said later. "I am embarrassed to have been part of it." Even David Reville, the former MPP who had embraced the dirty-tricks strategy during the 1990 campaign, expressed a twinge of regret afterwards. "We'd been flogging detailed policy shit for years. No one ever gave a shit. So this time we said, `Let's go right to the heart — say the Liberals are captives of the special interests.' I didn't believe that. I don't believe that."

All of this played into the psychology of the new government. In Canada, political parties are often able to form a majority government with only a plurality of the popular vote. Yet for the Rae government, the fact that only 38 per cent of Ontarians had voted NDP seemed particularly nettlesome. Although it held a solid majority in the legislature, the new government seemed unsure of its own legitimacy. At a fundamental level it believed it did not deserve to be in power and therefore had no right to impose NDP policies on business, or indeed, on anyone else.

Rae himself set the cautious tone the night of his 1990 election victory. "Public trust must be earned," he told his supporters. One of the NDP government's self-imposed tasks would be to prove to the province, and to itself, that it had the right to govern. In practical terms this meant proving it was not a pie-in-the-sky socialist government but one that could work with private business.

The new government got straight to work. In October 1990, Ontario, Ottawa, and the Canadian Auto Workers signed a generous deal with Varity Corp., successor to the troubled farm-machinery giant Massey-Ferguson. The deal permitted Varity, on payment of $50 million, to move out of Ontario and escape prior commitments to employ Canadians. It also cancelled the $200-million debt which Varity would have otherwise owed Ottawa and Ontario.

In opposition, Rae had been a persistent critic of governments which permitted private corporations to welsh on their obligations to the public treasury. But now he was more forgiving. "We live in a real world," he told reporters. "It was the best we could do."

A few weeks later, business got another positive signal from the NDP government. In November 1990, Rae announced he was letting foreign-owned British Gas buy Consumers' Gas, a private company that delivered natural gas to most of the province. In doing so, Rae was backing away from both the NDP's long-held opposition to foreign ownership of crucial industries and a decades-old party policy calling for public ownership of the natural-gas distribution system. "I'm not going to advocate a solution because it's the ideologically correct thing to do," Rae said after that British Gas decision.

Business understood and applauded the symbolism of both Varity and British Gas. Some spokesmen said the decision showed the new government was being sensible. Rae and others at the top were thrilled by the unaccustomed praise. They confided to other New Democrats outside the government that they felt they had made a breakthrough, that it was possible for an NDP government to get business on-side.

By May 1991, the honeymoon had turned abruptly sour. Laughren's first budget and the news of a $10-billion deficit—as well as the inability of the government to explain where that deficit had come from—played right into the business stereotype. The NDP, business commentators said, really was a party of spendthrifts.

More important, newspaper reports had revealed that the government was preparing to make wholesale changes to the province's labour relations act, the law which governs how employees and employers interact. To the government, this seemed only fair. It would do some things, such as British Gas, for business; it would do others, such as the labour-law changes, for the unions.

To business, however, these matters were not equivalent. Being nice to foreign investors might be laudable. But labour law speaks to the heart of capitalist enterprise, sets the ground rules for the most important relationship in any firm. To business, the labour-law proposals confirmed what many had always suspected—that, in spite of Rae's conciliatory talk, the NDP was still in the pocket of the unions.

At the same time, businesses were unsettled by another legislative proposal. In this case, the NDP was attempting to come through on a promise to help those thrown out of work when their employer goes bankrupt. In Ontario, corporate bankruptcies had left workers not only without jobs but also without wages they were legally owed. Meanwhile, some owners of bankrupt firms appeared to get off scot free, running their companies into the ground, welshing on debts to creditors and workers, and then using personal assets to start all over again.

Rae had spoken many times in opposition on the inequity of this situation. His Labour minister, Bob Mackenzie, was determined to change it. To this end, Mackenzie introduced a law requiring employers to put aside a certain sum each year into a new, government-run, wage-protection fund. In the event of bankruptcy, workers owed back wages and severance would get first call on this fund.

By itself, the wage-protection fund idea was hardly radical. Even the federal Conservative government had come up with a similar proposal. What angered business were the government's ancillary proposals, such as one which would increase the personal liability of corporate directors—even those who no longer served on the company's board. To Mackenzie and his aides, the proposed law was a sensible way to deal with a small number of firms who had been using loopholes in the bankruptcy law to stiff their employees. But the bill's net was so widely cast that it drew in reputable as well as disreputable firms—even incorporated charities.

Under previous Liberal and Conservative governments, a few strategic telephone calls from well-connected business executives would have sufficed to derail the Mackenzie scheme. But, with the new government, there were no automatic pipelines between business and the cabinet. Business executives didn't play golf with ministers, didn't run into them at the Rotary Club. When the head of a large corporation did call a minister during those first few months, he was likely to be fobbed off onto a junior aide—just like any other Ontarian. To business, the NDP was like an alien presence, an entity from another planet. In the months following the NDP victory of 1990, businesses scrambled to find consultants, government-relations firms—anyone—who knew something about this strange party. Graham Murray, a former NDP researcher, who was running his own consulting firm, was ecstatic. Other New Democrats found their services suddenly in demand from lobbyists such as Hill and Knowlton or S.A. Murray. In one example of desperation, firms paid to hear Larry Grossman, a former provincial Conservative leader, give his insights into the NDP.

The great irony of this was that Rae's government wanted nothing more than to talk to business. But, in the early days of 1990 and 1991, it simply did not know how. Business people, like athletes, occupied their own clubby world, one where the rules of behaviour were unspoken. Few in the NDP knew anything of that world.

In 1990, a senior aide to Treasurer Floyd Laughren confessed privately that he had no idea how to talk to the business people that his job required him to meet. Nor was the premier himself adept at the jock talk and forced *bonhomie* that serves to lubricate the relationship between senior male business executives and their political pals.

Certainly Rae tried. Early on, Arden Haynes, the chairman of Imperial Oil, set up a dinner party for Rae to meet about ten top business people. Every three months, the premier and Laughren would meet with the Ontario Business Advisory Council, a group of about forty of the most powerful chief executive officers in the province who headed companies such as Inco Ltd., Ford Motor Co., the Toronto-Dominion Bank. The CEOs would promote a common agenda, such as the need for fiscal probity, or the villainous nature of the proposed labour-law changes. Rae and Laughren would listen, stiffly.

"They were not pleasant encounters," recalled Lynn Spink, who, as Rae's executive assistant, accompanied him everywhere. "He [Rae] felt the pressure. It was always crafted and scripted. The business side had obviously worked out ahead of time the message of the season. In the room, he was polite; he took part in the conversation; he listened. But afterwards, you could tell he felt the pressure. He didn't look forward to going. Sometimes, it felt like an assault."

Over time, Rae got more used to business people. But rarely did he relax. On a 1992 flight to Tokyo, for instance, Rae found himself trapped in the first-class section with a group of Canadian businessmen who insisted on hectoring him about his government's faults — its deficit, its labour law, its friendship with unions. Eventually, Rae escaped to the economy-class section. As he told a reporter, the businessmen were driving him nuts; he couldn't even read the book he had brought.

Still, the meetings with the Ontario Business Advisory Council and other groups had an effect. "He learned about the economy," said Spink. "He found it wasn't as easy to dismiss the business arguments." And, she said, there was a more subtle but important influence.

"Over time, he got more used to the other world. They [the NDP government] all did.... They got used to living in a world where people never eat in cafeterias or ride on buses ... that's part of it. And that other world is used to being a part of government." Increasingly, Rae began to speak about himself as the premier "for all the people." To Spink, the phrase was telling and disturbing: "When he said 'all the people,' he didn't mean the factory workers who vote Reform. He didn't really mean all the people. He meant business and all of those interest groups that he used to oppose. For someone who used to value language ... this was a real degradation of language."

For Rae, however, his gradual rapprochement with business seemed a signal accomplishment. By 1993, NDP strategists were told that they could count on tacit business support in any upcoming election because chief executive officers thought Rae smarter than either his Liberal or his Conservative opponent. Some business people were happy to laud the premier. Walter Curlook, for instance, the vice-chairman of Inco Ltd. and a man who had tangled in the past with former NDP radicals such as Floyd Laughren, had nothing but praise for the premier. Curlook, who served on an advisory group called the Premier's Council on Economic Renewal, had this to say about Rae: "He was more pragmatic and more focused than I expected. I didn't realize he was so strongly focused on industrial recovery in Ontario.... Bob Rae is hardworking and intelligent; he has a high mental capacity.... He's provided stimulus, focus. He does that unabashedly. You can talk to him about new things. You can put any label on him—NDP or anything. But in industrial-development terms, he is a strong proponent."

While Rae was making headway in the corporate world, other ministers remained confused about their approach to business. They knew they didn't approve; but they couldn't quite remember why.

In large part, this confusion stemmed from the NDP's ambivalence on the issue of class. To a classic socialist party, business and labour are inexorably opposed simply because that's the way the world works; that's the logic of a capitalist economy. Indeed, the CCF had originally spelled this out in its 1933 Regina Manifesto.

By the 1980s, the NDP no longer had a clear critique of either the economy or class. The anti-business rhetoric which would lard NDP speeches during the party's time in opposition was based on moral rather than economic grounds: Big business was bad; it was unfair; it ripped off the people the NDP called "ordinary Canadians." The party's rhetoric about business was like the language of the picket line during a particularly vicious strike.

Such demonism was easy to maintain when few in the NDP knew any business people. But, once in government, many New Democrats were surprised to discover that business people were human and, like anyone else, potentially likeable. Indeed, to some NDP political aides, business people, with their decisive ways, were natural allies against a common enemy—the Ontario bureaucracy.

For most in the new government, the NDP's primitive and Manichean prejudices could prove no match for the seductive blandishments of the real world. In opposition, they had been secure in their own smugness, convinced that their enemies were either ill intentioned or wrong. What they had neglected was that capitalism has its own logic; things happen for reasons. Presented with this logic, by reasonable people without horns, the NDP government had few comebacks. It couldn't challenge the economic logic of business with one of its own because it had none of its own. On the ideological front, most ministers quickly capitulated.

Rae, however, was different. He did have a theory of government. He accepted the liberal-democratic notion that, at base, all classes have common interests. In effect, he had become attracted to the notion of what political scientists call "corporatism," a view of the world in which government's role is to forge accommodations with and among powerful interest groups such as business and labour. Rae called these accommodations "partnerships."

Soon, everything the government did was being described in the language of partnerships: Labour and business became the "economic partners," while municipalities and other lower levels of public administration which depended on provincial grants became "transfer partners." Nothing was to be done unilaterally; all was to be done "in consultation" with the appropriate "partners."

In September 1991, the government capitulated to its insurance-industry partners by killing plans for public auto insurance. By December, it was time to help the auto partners. Ontario had a strict pension law which required companies to prefund their benefits—that is, have money on hand in the event of, for instance, a plant shutdown which would create severance-pay obligations.

General Motors, the world's largest auto manufacturer, was in contravention of that law. Government officials figured it owed between $500 million and $700 million to the province's Pension Benefits Guarantee Fund. For obvious reasons, GM didn't want to pay.

Negotiations dragged on for months until, finally, GM Canada president George Peapples asked to meet Rae. Officials briefed the premier beforehand to make sure he understood what was at stake. "There's no way we're going to be the Alabama of Canada," the premier retorted.

But at the meeting, after hearing Peapples's case, Rae was converted. Pointing to one of his aides, the premier told the GM head, "He'll get you everything you need."

"It happened so quickly that Peapples didn't realize at first he had won," a government insider said later. In the end, the cabinet changed its pension regulations to allow GM and other major manufacturers to put off funding their pension-benefits packages until actually required.

By early 1992, the new line was solidified. At a caucus retreat, former federal secretary Gerry Caplan gave an impassioned speech about the meaning of being a New Democrat. Caplan was allied with the NDP's powerful Lewis clan. As such, he represented a body of opinion that was becoming increasingly uncomfortable with the government's pro-business stance. Rae, however, ignored Caplan's remarks and spent most of his time at that retreat talking about the need for business confidence.

Inside the cabinet, some were uneasy about kowtowing to business. In part, this stemmed from anger at the fierce business lobby against labour-law reforms. Some ministers had become convinced it was useless to try to appease business, that corporations would always be hostile to the NDP.

But such opposition to the government's business agenda remained confused and inchoate. The left in cabinet was virtually silent. Labour minister Bob Mackenzie, the old Steelworker firebrand, had used up all his energy pushing through the labour-law changes. Laughren, the one-time Sudbury Red, was overwhelmed by his worries about the deficit. Sudbury MPP Shelley Martel had been badly damaged politically by a controversy over the confidentiality of medical records. Even before this, she had said little in cabinet. By 1992, she was almost invisible.

To New Democats outside government, the role of Frances Lankin semed mysterious. One of the government's most competent ministers, Lankin was seen by labour and women's groups as their champion. But why, some asked, did she acquiesce so easily to the business agenda? Friends said that Lankin was working from within, that she chose her battles carefully. Critics said she was ambitious. Lankin herself would often say she felt the government had no choice. As well, she had confided to associates, she had come to realize that much of what she had said in opposition was ill considered.

A fourth, interesting explanation comes from a woman who worked with Lankin. She said that, despite her public poise, Lankin was insecure—particularly in the area of economic policy. In the end, said this former aide, and in spite of her record as a strong feminist, Lankin deferred to men she thought were smarter.

What overwhelmed the cabinet, however, was a deep sense of futility. Few would have called themselves Marxists. But the majority seemed to have accepted the most pessimistic and determinist elements of Marxism—that, in the end, the state has few degrees of freedom, that all real decisions are made in the boardrooms of giant firms, that there are few choices for government. At a time when their federal cousins were campaigning on the theme that there is a choice, the Ontario NDP government had quietly come to the opposite view.

To Laughren, the government's decision to embrace large elements of the conservative agenda was not an attempt to please business (although this might be a fortunate side-effect) but the result of being in a situation where there were no choices. Housing minister Evelyn Gigantes, expressed the government's sense of its own impotence this way: "I don't believe, and I did not before we came to government, that national governments can isolate national entities, national publics, from international capitalism. . . . I don't think the Americans could pull off any more what happened in the Roosevelt era. I just don't think that there are national governments that have the kind of control of economic forces that permits that any more. . . . And when I've been challenged by people who say, 'Well, you know as a government you simply have to carry out policy at the provincial level that recognizes certain principles of justice and fairness and economic equality,' I say, 'But you can't take on international capitalism in Ontario. It's not possible to do that.' At the national level, there are limited powers to struggle with these economic forces. Even a national government in the States doesn't have an easy time of coping with those forces, with the best intent in the world. So it's really unrealistic and silly to think that—and I say silly—to think that a provincial government is going to be able to do what national governments find extremely difficult."

However, this gloomy prognosis did not mean to Gigantes, and others, that government was entirely useless—merely that it could act only in concert with the forces of private enterprise. That meant creating—as the Tories and Liberals had always argued—a climate of fiscal stability and openness to investment that would attract private firms.

Summer 1991: Six provincial bureaucrats and David de Launay, executive assistant to Northern Development minister Shelley Martel, were hiding in a van, on a back street in the small Northern Ontario town of Kapuskasing. Unionized workers were angry that the government seemed unwilling to bail out their employer, a paper mill owned by the U.S. giant Kimberly-Clark. So they had set up a roadblock on the highway to the airport. "Here we were, the NDP government, blockaded by a bunch of mill workers," de Launay said later.

Eventually, the Queen's Park group was rescued, in a manoeuvre reminiscent of the fall of Saigon. A helicopter swooped over the roadblock, picked them up in a hospital parking lot, and ferried them back over the roadblock to the airport, There, before any angry millworkers could catch up to them, they were bundled onto a small plane. In the annals of NDP industrial policy, it was not a stellar moment.

Later, Rae would point to a trinity of bail-outs—Kapuskasing, Sault Ste. Marie's Algoma Steel, and Toronto's de Havilland Aircraft division of Boeing of Canada—as examples of partnership in action, situations in which business, government, and labour could act together to obtain results. In these instances, he was right. The de Havilland deal involved Ottawa and the Ontario government putting up $500 million to keep the struggling company alive. Ontario became a minority shareholder in the company and the jobs of 3,700 workers were, for a while at least, protected.

In the case of Kapuskasing, government action helped save slightly fewer than half of 1,450 jobs at the Spruce Falls Power and Paper Co. Ltd. mill, the town's main employer. Of the three bail-outs, however, Algoma emerged as the real success story.

By 1990, the troubled Sault Ste. Marie steel plant had run into serious problems. It was old and unprofitable. Like all Canadian steel plants, it was being hammered every which way—by U.S. trade harassment when it tried to export, by the recession. The company's 5,000 workers were warned that Algoma might go under. Its death would have dealt a major blow to Sault Ste. Marie, a northern city perched at the point where Lake Huron meets Lake Superior.

In an effort to salvage something, the company, the Steelworkers (representing the bulk of the 5,000 employees), the NDP government, and Algoma's creditors entered a complex series of negotiations.

Later, government insiders would credit the Steelworkers for pulling off the deal. The international union already had some experience in situations of this sort and had flown in experts from the United States to help it along. But Rae's government deserved praise too, for plugging along in a venture that its critics said could only lead to spectacular failure.

The NDP government was under its own internal pressure though. The Steelworkers were important in the party, and Leo Gerard—Canadian director of the union and a Rae loyalist—figured he was owed. In particular, Gerard had gritted his teeth in 1991, when the government allowed Ontario Hydro to back out of a uranium contract that had been keeping the mining town of Elliot Lake—and the jobs of 1,000 Steelworkers—alive. Algoma was payback time.

"Leo felt he'd been hosed in Elliot Lake," said one knowledgeable insider. "He had put the party ahead of his workers. Now he wanted his own back."

In the final deal, announced in early 1992, Ontario agreed to put up $110 million in loan guarantees and an unspecified amount in other forms of restructuring aid. Algoma's workforce agreed to a 14.5 per cent wage cut in return for ownership of 60 per cent of the company. The workforce would be cut by a third, to about 3,500, over four years.

Within two years, Algoma was booming, its stock trading at 300 times the 1992 price. Conventional wisdom had been turned on its ear; a government-sponsored bail-out had worked. For the Rae government, Algoma would represent an unequivocal high point in its handling of the Ontario economy.

Later, Rae would return to Algoma, Kapuskasing, and de Havilland as examples of economic partnership in action. However, what looked in hindsight as a coordinated application of this principle was at the time nothing of the sort. De Havilland, Algoma, and Kapuskasing were specific crises to which the new government had to respond. All were major employers in their communities; all were in danger of going under. All involved important unions. Far from being an integrated plan, the government's response was *ad hoc* and chaotic. That it could work out in the end owed a great deal to luck.

Nothing exemplifies this more than the story around Kapuskasing. The town had been a vassal of Kimberly-Clark since the 1920s when the paper giant, in combination with the Times Inc., publisher of *The New York Times*, built a mill to supply newsprint to that publication. By 1991, Kimberly-Clark was getting out of the newsprint business. Company chairman Darwin Smith offered to give the Kapuskasing mill to the employees—but only if Ontario Hydro agreed to buy a nearby hydro-electric generating station from Kimberly-Clark for $134 million. It was clear the employees' purchasing group would need millions of dollars in capital improvements as well as a private-sector partner to keep the mill alive.

For months, the Ontario government, Kimberly-Clark, an employee purchasing group, the mill's unions, and a Quebec paper company called Tembec carried on negotiations. The talks were Byzantine. "Each had its own agenda," said one official involved. "Even the people I thought were friends, weren't friends in this." Northern Development minister Shelley Martel was handling the negotiations for the government. But, given the resistance of Hydro and the lukewarm attitude of Kapuskasing's main union, the Canadian Paperworkers (now known as the Communications, Energy and Paperworkers), she had little support in cabinet.

Under pressure from the Steelworkers, the government had already committed itself to bailing out Algoma Steel in Sault Ste. Marie. Under the pressure of Toronto politics and the Canadian Auto Workers, it was already committed to bailing out the de Havilland aircraft plant in Toronto. Who cared about Kapuskasing? At the end, according to her then press aide, Kathleen O'Hara, Martel refused to even visit the town.

On June 27, 1991, Rae met with Martel and a small group of advisers. Martel wanted to do a deal with Kimberly-Clark but wasn't willing to push too hard. "What does Floyd think?" Rae asked. He was told; Laughren was opposed to spending the money. "Better not do it then," said Rae. The issue seemed dead.

Over the summer, however, lobbying from inside government slowly persuaded Rae and Laughren to change their minds. Laughren was told the NDP could lose seats in Northern Ontario if the government failed to help out, that the Kapuskasing issue was taken seriously throughout the region. Rae became more interested once he heard Laughren was interested. Meanwhile, one of Martel's aides persuaded Steelworkers chief Leo Gerard to pressure the recalcitrant Paperworkers union. In mid-July, spooked by a newspaper story that talks had failed and on the advice of David Agnew, Rae took over the Kapuskasing negotiations from Martel. On July 14, he telephoned Kimberly-Clark's Darwin Smith in Wisconsin.

"I went to the morning meeting at 8:15 the next day," said one aide later. "Everyone was there—people from the premier's office, the cabinet office, Shelley's people. And Bob was telling them all about his negotiations with Smith. He was engaged, involved. I knew it was in the bag."

With the premier's direct involvement, Kapuskasing had become a matter of prestige for the government. There would have to be a deal. Eventually, there was. It was virtually the same deal that Martel had negotiated with Kimberly-Clark two months earlier and that had been turned down by cabinet. But, now that it was Rae's deal, it was accepted — and lauded — as a major success, an example of partnership in action.

Fall 1993: New Democratic constituency assistants, the aides who help MPPs in their home ridings, had gathered in a Toronto hotel to receive a pep talk. The party was on an election footing, the aides were told. And an election meant war. The enemies of the NDP were legion. But none, the aides were told, were more insidious than the media and, in particular, *The Toronto Sun* (or, as caucus chair Steve Owens called it that day, "The Toronto Scum").

Rae had already made much the same point in the legislature a few days earlier, when he dismissed *The Toronto Star*, the country's largest daily (and one which usually does support the Liberals editorially) as "the Liberal Star." In another meeting with NDP aides, the premier had warned of a media "conspiracy" against the NDP. Throughout the government, the message was being drummed in: Media moguls were out to sink Ontario's first social-democratic government; the monsters were on the march.

That the media and a sitting government in its third year were at loggerheads was not unusual. That the NDP was suspicious of media which rarely, if ever, supported the party editorially was also not surprising. What was odd was that a government committed to mending fences with business should find it so hard to make peace with that section of the corporate world which controlled the press, radio, and television. What was particularly odd was that Rae himself not only was skilled in the use of media but counted some of the most influential media managers as friends or acquaintances.

Toronto Star editor John Honderich, for instance, had been a friend since Rae was a federal MP. Honderich's wife, Katherine Govier, and Rae's wife, Arlene Perly Rae, remained close. Rae also played tennis with Brian Segal, publisher of *Maclean's* magazine. The two had met through lawyer Lenny Wise when Rae, Wise, and their families had shared a cottage in Muskoka. Rae was also a regular in a media personalities' informal tennis tournament in which Honderich, among others, participated.

Moreover, while the three Toronto dailies had hammered the government editorially on many issues, and particularly on its labour-law reforms, the press was not uniformly negative. *The Toronto Star*, for instance, had lauded the government's social contract editorially. Even the odd *Globe and Mail* editorial had been condescendingly polite.

Rae's relationship with *The Toronto Star* was instructive. The *Star* had the largest circulation of any daily newspaper in Canada. Not only did it take a proprietary interest in the Ontario government, it was widely available throughout most of the province. In the world of Ontario politics, it was an influential newspaper.

Editorially, the *Star* was not unsympathetic to Rae's NDP. Not only was its editor a personal friend of the premier but the traditionally Liberal paper had come within a hair's breadth of endorsing the NDP editorially in 1990—in large part because Honderich had recognized that Rae was the kind of liberal the *Star* liked. "It was a very, very close call," said Honderich later. "[A] lot of the ideas that he was espousing were things that we supported. There was a great deal in common. Our sense was that the Liberals hadn't done that bad a job in three years, although there were a lot of concerns. The way Peterson ran his campaign cast even more doubts. I guess it was clear at that time that the economy and management of the economy were the really deciding issues. And we were a little nervous about some of what Bob was saying.... That was the final deciding issue that tipped it to stay with the provincial Liberals."

Soon after the election, Honderich's friendship with Rae developed strains. The *Star* editor had expected the kind of relationship he had enjoyed with David Peterson, that the premier would feel free to call and engage in private conversation about issues of the day. But it never worked out. "The fact we were friends perhaps made it more difficult for him," said Honderich later.

The relationship suffered another setback when, in late 1991, the *Star* invited the premier to meet its publisher, senior editors, and editorial board for lunch. Newspapers' editorial boards like to meet face to face with political leaders. They like to feel included. Even if the premier or prime minister reveals little beyond his public statements, the fact that he is willing to appear in the flesh, to have his measure taken, seems to count a great deal. So it was with the *Star*. A luncheon with the new premier was a matter of some import, and the newspaper took it seriously.

To the premier's office, the proposed luncheon seemed just another demand on the time of a very busy man. To the *Star*, however, it was symbol of great significance—a chance for each side to acknowledge the importance and role of the other. The fact that it took weeks to negotiate a luncheon date irked the *Star* side. But what finally outraged Honderich was a call from the premier's office in September 1991. Rae, the premier's spokesperson said, would be happy to lunch with the *Star*. But, in return, it was understood that the newspaper would write a feature article on Tony Silipo, Rae's minister in charge of Management Board.

Honderich fired off a stiff letter to Rae. "[A] senior member of your staff informed my secretary that the lunch would only take place if a profile of Tony Silipo was done. As you can well imagine, this newspaper does not work that way. If that is the basis on which this luncheon is to take place, then we will have to bow out now." Six days later, the premier replied in handwritten note. "Dear John," he wrote. "Relax.... I think the idea about Silipo was simply that we're doing something interesting on public sector bargaining ... and you might want to talk to him. Warm regards, Bob."

Honderich would later say he found the idea of a *quid pro quo*—one lunch with the premier in exchange for one feature article on a cabinet minister—deeply offensive. To Rae, who may well have felt offended by individual editorials, columns, and news stories in the *Star*, it seemed a minor fuss. The luncheon eventually occurred, but the relationship continued to deteriorate.

In June 1992, the Newspaper Guild, representing the bulk of *Star* employees, struck the newspaper. The government's response was quick. On the one hand, Rae privately offered Honderich government help in settling the dispute and assigned the government's top labour mediator, Vic Pathe, to help sort out the issues. On the other hand, Rae and his cabinet were quick to show their support for the striking workers. The government cancelled all *Star* advertising and subscriptions for the duration of the strike.

It was a move greatly appreciated by the strikers and certainly consistent with the labour principles of the NDP. But Honderich was "surprised." And he was angered when the premier's office sent a fax to his office informing him personally that Rae and his family had cancelled their home subscription to the *Star*. To Honderich, this seemed to be rubbing it in. "I was most distressed," he said later. That incident, he said, did affect his friendship with Rae.

Later that summer, the *Star* took part in a vitriolic advertising campaign waged by the Canadian Daily Newspaper Publishers' Association against the government's proposed labour relations bill. Honderich could argue that advertising is separate from the newspaper's editorial stance (editorially, the *Star* conducted a similar but more reasoned campaign against the labour relations bill). But to many in government, such distinctions were moot. To them, the *Star*'s involvement in the publishers' propaganda campaign, in combination with a series of attacks from the newspaper's columnists (some from the left, some from the right), demonstrated it was out to crucify the NDP.

By 1993, even Rae saw "the Liberal *Star*" as part of the conspiracy against his government. What he seemed unable to appreciate—perhaps because of his strained relationship with Honderich—was how much the Liberal *Star* and the neo-liberal NDP government now had in common.

From early on, the NDP's strategy towards business had been to engage it in partnership. In the end, the results were decidedly mixed. Algoma, de Havilland, and Kapuskasing stood out as signal successes—specific cases where the government had used its clout to work with business and labour to salvage jobs. That this trio of successful bail-outs stood out so starkly against the NDP economic landscape was in itself significant, however. In most other cases, the partnership approach produced little. In the case of the multinational drug companies, the government was decidedly hosed.

To Rae, business presented a personal conundrum. Intellectually, he was determined to work with business people. He saw this as not just a question of practicality, but as the only principled way in which an NDP government could operate. But, emotionally, his reactions to business were those of the perpetual outsider. Business was yet another group that eluded and excluded him. It was like being back in his first year at the University of Toronto, an expatriate in his own country; it was just as it had been in 1982 when the golden boy from Ottawa had inherited an in-bred and hostile NDP caucus. Rae might never feel comfortable with business people—just as he had never been comfortable with his own caucus or indeed anywhere. However, he was determined to do what he had done before: dazzle them with his mind, prove that he was as smart or smarter. Business leaders might never accept Rae as one of their own, but he was determined that they would learn to respect him.

In the end, perhaps, it was this combination of pride and pique which accounted for the way in which Rae approached business. On the one hand, there were his relations with the business people who ran the Ontario media, relations which, given the circumstances, should have been relatively easy but which seemed to founder in a sea of suspicion and mutual hurt feelings. On the other hand, he could be almost naïve with some of the world's most cut-throat multinationals as he attempted to prove that he was as skilful, tough-minded, and decisive as any corporate chieftain.

In his meetings with Nelson Sims of Eli Lilly or Darwin Smith of Kimberly-Clark or George Peapples of General Motors, the premier seemed to try to present himself as corporate Bob Rae, the CEO of Ontario, a man willing to wheel and deal. In some cases, such as the negotiations over Kapuskasing, the result benefited the province. In others, such as his dealings with the drug companies, the results were disastrous. In almost all, the NDP government—in spite of the oft-acknowledged brilliance of CEO Rae—was out-classed by its corporate adversaries.

Did Rae ever earn the respect from business he seemed to want? For Inco executive Walter Curlook, the answer was yes. "If he were in my riding, I'd vote for him," said Curlook, a man who had never voted NDP in his life. Yet for some business people, Rae's determination to cooperate with private enterprise seemed to have won him only their mild contempt. Returning from a trade mission with the premier to the Middle East in early 1994, Ontario Chamber of Commerce president Pat Palmer referred to Rae as "our mascot for Ontario." It was a revealing phrase, one that the head of a major business group would have been unlikely to use in reference to a Liberal or Tory premier. The NDP might still mean pretty bad news for business. But at least "mascot" Rae had been tamed.

10

A Nation's Greatness

RUTH GRIER WAS IN A HURRY. IT WAS THE END OF JULY 1993, and she was scheduled to go on holiday in four days. Fuelled by the controversy over the government's social contract, the legislature had been grinding on all summer, long past its usual end-of-June cut-off date. Grier had been Health minister for only a few months. Earlier that year, over her objections, Rae had shifted the fifty-seven-year-old MPP from Environment, for which Grier had developed a passionate attachment, to the minefields of Health. Like all ministers, she had found her last months consumed by the social-contract talks. In Grier's case, her ministry was charged with negotiating a roll-back in public medicare funding to the province's 23,000 doctors. Now, at last, the talks seemed to be over and she could take a break. She would even be able to go on a belated summer holiday in Wales with her husband, Terry. When she was told that officials in her ministry and the Ontario Medical Association had worked out a deal, she was glad to approve it.

Unfortunately, as Grier would acknowledge later, she okayed the 1993 Interim Agreement on Economic Arrangements without reading most of it. The substance of the government–OMA social-contract deal was contained not in the short, eleven-page main text but in five appendices and thirteen schedules attached to the agreement. One of these, Appendix I, was a secret protocol that had not been made public.

Grier did not see any of these schedules or appendices before signing. "I didn't see the final draft wording before I left," she explained later. "I don't think I saw the wording in the actual schedules." She would remain unaware of some of the contents of the deal for several months.

The OMA–Health deal was the doctors' version of the social contract, the government's attempt to slash $2 billion a year from the public-sector payroll. Initially, doctors had been incensed at being included in the social-contract talks along with teachers and trash collectors. Like teachers and trash collectors, doctors received the bulk of their income from tax revenues—through the Ontario Health Insurance Plan, the province's version of medicare. But doctors did not see themselves as ordinary public servants; they wanted their own talks. By midsummer, they and judges (who also objected to being lumped in with the *hoi polloi*) had been hived off from the main social-contract negotiations. Instead, the OMA bargained head to head with the Ministry of Health's Negotiations Secretariat.

In every other social-contract negotiation that summer, the government had been adamant. It wanted money. Backed by legislation that allowed it to overturn any existing agreement or contract, it was determined to get it. Traditional NDP allies such as the Ontario Public Service Employees Union were livid as the Ministry of Finance's chief economist Peter Warrian and his Social Contract Secretariat frogmarched them through the talks to a preordained end.

In the collegial atmosphere of the Ministry of Health, however, talks went more smoothly. True, the doctors would have to give up money—about $130 million that year—but, in return, the ministry negotiators agreed to concessions the doctors had been demanding for twenty-five years.

The reason for this extraordinary generosity lay in the political circumstances of the social-contract talks. Negotiations elsewhere were not going smoothly. In the hospital sector, it was evident that the employers, through the Ontario Hospital Association, were balking and would have to be legislated into submission. The government was desperate for a voluntary deal—particularly with the doctors.

For doctors were different. The government could impose a settlement on other public-sector workers with virtual impunity. But grumpy doctors could cause enormous political trouble. The word to the Health ministry from the premier's office was: Do whatever it takes; get a deal.

"This was a negotiated social contract," Grier said later. "It was not an imposed one by legislation as was the rest of the social contract. . . .

Doctors have always had a unique role in Ontario's health-care system."

Three elements of the deal stood out. First, the ministry agreed to continue subsidizing the doctors' malpractice insurance fund, operated by the Canadian Medical Protective Association, to the tune of about $37 million a year—this even though the fund held a surplus of $600 million. When ministry officials were asked later why they had conceded this perk, they shrugged and answered that it was "an emotional issue" for the doctors.

Second, the ministry negotiators agreed to indemnify the OMA in the event of lawsuits involving out-of-province doctors. This was the secret protocol, Appendix I, and it was highly unusual. Under another, public section of the interim agreement, the government had agreed to limit the right of out-of-province doctors to practise in Ontario. In Appendix I, the OMA won assurances that if it were sued over this restriction, the government would pick up the tab. Later, those on the OMA side would say it was the government which wanted this aspect of the deal kept under wraps, for fear of setting a precedent.

So successful was the government at hiding Appendix I that neither Grier nor the Health ministry's own lawyers were made aware of it until long after the deal had been signed. In the opinion of the lawyers, the government had inadvertently agreed to something almost unprecedented—to pay the OMA's legal costs "should the OMA sue the government."

Finally, ministry negotiators made an extraordinary concession. For almost a quarter of a century, doctors had been asking for the right to incorporate. Incorporation, if properly carried out, can save a professional a considerable sum in taxes. Successive Conservative and Liberal governments had turned the doctors down. But now, under the NDP, the Health ministry had suddenly caved in. It even agreed to pass the appropriate legislation into law within a specific period of time.

For a government to allow its legislative timetable to be dictated by an outside party was almost unheard of. "It was part of their [the doctors'] insistence," explained Grier later. "It was very important to them that there be some timetable."

What's more, the ministry negotiators agreed to consider allowing not only doctors but all health professionals—such as dentists, nurses, physiotherapists—to incorporate. Just why the ministry conceded this when it was negotiating only with doctors, and not with the other professionals, was a mystery. Officials later explained they wanted to make the other health professionals, at the time involved in the main social-contract talks with the more hard-nosed Warrian, feel a little less put-upon. Grier did not know of this measure until months afterward. She would later explain it as an effort to demonstrate that the issue of physician incorporation could not be dealt with in isolation.

All of this would have made some sense if the Health ministry had had any idea what these concessions would cost. But it hadn't. Neither, when she okayed the deal before flying off to Wales, did Ruth Grier. The government, she explained later, had to offer incorporation: "Otherwise the doctors would not have agreed."

Not until much later did the figures come in. By April 1994, Finance officials calculated that permitting doctors alone to incorporate would cost the Treasury between $30 and $35 million a year, and probably more. If all health professionals were permitted to incorporate, the cost in lost income-tax revenues to the province alone could be double that. Altogether, the NDP government had handed the doctors concessions potentially worth at least $67 million a year, in perpetuity, to win three years of social-contract cut-backs worth a total of $390 million. (Once Grier realized the enormity of the government's gaffe, she and her staff began to plot ways to go back on the incorporation aspect of the deal. By then it was too late. The OMA would be able to wave the written promise in the face of any future government.)

What's more, the bonus to doctors would be financed in part at the expense of the sick. As part of its deal with the OMA, the government agreed to cut $20-million worth of medical services from the list of procedures covered by medicare. Doctors could still perform these services (the final list included routine circumcision and some kinds of *in vitro* fertilization) but they would be paid for by patients rather than by the province.

For doctors, this was a double bonus. First, they were shifting some of the burden of the social contract on to users, a privilege denied other public-sector workers (trash collectors, for instance, were not permitted to protect their salaries by insisting that municipalities charge householders user fees to pick up certain kinds of garbage). Second, in so far as physicians still performed these so-called delisted services, they would be outside of the regulatory limits of medicare — that is, doctors could charge whatever fees they chose; any income received would not be counted for purposes of social-contract roll-backs.

Coming to power had brought the NDP face to face with the vexing question of health-care costs. Medicare costs were rising across Canada. In Ontario, about one-third of the provincial budget was spent on health. In 1990–91, that figure had been rising at about 11 per cent a year.

While in opposition, Rae's New Democrats had never come to grips with the issue of health costs. On the face of it, this was odd, since much of the path-breaking work in the area was being carried on by active New Democrats, such as Toronto physician Michael Rachlis (a cousin of Rae senior aide Chuck Rachlis) and Hamilton health economist Jonathan Lomas.

However, in opposition, the NDP found it easier and more politically satisfying to take a scatter-shot approach. On the one hand, they castigated the Liberal government over long hospital waiting-lists, demanding more resources for the institutional sector. On the other hand, they criticized the government for its reliance on institutional medicine, calling for more community clinics, local control, openness to non-traditional forms of health such as midwifery, and an emphasis on prevention.

In fact, the Peterson Liberals—under Health minister Elinor Caplan and her deputy Martin Barkin—had been developing the kind of integrated approach recommended by NDP activists such as Michael Rachlis and Lomas. The reformers argued that health care was a commodity like no other, one in which the supplier (the doctor) determined how often the system was used rather than the consumer (the patient). After the first visit, it was invariably the doctor who determined how often the patient would return, how many specialists he would see, or what diagnostic tests he would take. Each of these procedures meant income for the medical profession and a cost to the taxpayer. That doctors acted in this perfectly understandable fashion seemed to be borne out by the data: Every time the government squeezed physicians' fees, doctors responded by seeing more patients. Medicare costs continued to rise.

Better and cheaper medicine could be provided, the reformers said, by altering the system in three ways. One was to get doctors to agree not to use expensive medical procedures proven to be worthless. The second was to encourage, where applicable, the treatment of patients outside of expensive hospitals. But the most important reform needed was a change to the prevalent fee-for-service system whereby doctors are paid every time they see a patient. Other kinds of payment systems—either putting doctors on salary or providing them with a budget based on the size of their regular patient roster—could provide different incentives and reduce the tendency of physicians to overuse the system.

All of these recommendations were politically difficult since they involved challenging the power of doctors and hospitals. But the Liberals had tried. Since facing down a physicians' strike in 1986, Peterson had been tough with the doctors. Annual fee negotiations with the OMA had produced little joy for physicians. At the same time, the Liberals had been working on ideas for non-institutional long-term care, hospital rationalization, and even so-called hospital-in-the-home services.

However, the Liberals never had the nerve to challenge doctors over the central issue of fee-for-service medicine. As a result, doctors made up for low fee increases received from government by seeing more patients. Health costs continued to skyrocket.

On coming to power, the NDP decided not to get tougher with the doctors. Quite the contrary. The New Democrats knew what powerful political adversaries doctors could be. They knew that doctors could, through the medical equivalent of slowdown, create and publicize health crises—line-ups for heart surgery or shortages of cancer treatment. They knew that opposition parties could use such so-called crises to great effect—just as they themselves had.

As well, the NDP knew that the internal politics of the Ontario Medical Association had created a unique situation. Usually, the OMA is governed by hard-line doctors still angry that state medicare even exists. By 1990, a new, moderate group had captured the OMA executive, a group willing to cooperate with a cooperative government. What this group wanted—*de facto* unionization, compulsory dues check-off, and bipartite management of the health system—seemed to fit right in with NDP ideology.

The doctors had been unable to make a deal with the Liberals. If the NDP could succeed where their predecessors had failed, strategists figured, the new government could win on several fronts. It could show it was willing to work with a group not usually sympathetic to the NDP; it could demonstrate partnership in action; it could win five years of peace with the politically troublesome doctors. If physicians could be persuaded to make cost-saving changes in the way they did business, it might even save money.

No doubt some of these advantages were relayed to the new

government by Brian Harling, former provincial party secretary, who
in 1990 was working for the OMA. In early 1991, the government
assembled its team — former MPP Ross McClellan, by this time a senior
adviser to Rae; bureaucrats Jay Kaufman and Jim Thomas; Michael
Decter, a Montreal consultant and former Manitoba bureaucrat.

The OMA had hired one of the top NDP labour law firms in Toronto.
As members of the organization's brass would boast later, the OMA
cleaned the government's clock. By April 1991, a deal had been
reached. The OMA agreed that doctors' gross incomes would be limited
after reaching $400,000 annually (a concession that affected only 700
of 23,000 physicians). The government agreed to put fee disputes to
binding arbitration; give the OMA the kind of trade-union perks it
wanted; and, most important, set up a joint management committee —
composed entirely of doctors and health bureaucrats — to oversee
medicare. The joint management committee meant that doctors would
be intimately involved in any decisions about curbing medical costs.

The OMA deal was announced as a great victory by Rae. In some
sense it was. Any political problems with doctors had been put off. As
well, the rate of increase of health-care costs dramatically slowed after
the agreement. On the cost front at least, partnership with the doctors
did seem to produce results.

What the government did not seem to appreciate, however, was that
by means of this deal it had given the doctors, through their trade union,
a veto over almost $4-billion worth of government's annual spending.
Under the 1991 deal, the government and the OMA, through their joint
management committee, would oversee the $3.5-billion pool used to
pay fee-for-service doctors. It was an extraordinary concession. A government which would have balked at giving teachers a veto over education spending or trash collectors one over environmental spending had
no compunction about giving this kind of power to the doctors.

In practical terms, the 1991 deal meant the government could never
attack the crux of the health problem — the manner in which doctors
are paid. For, as Ruth Grier would later find out, much to her chagrin,
any attempt to shift money in the fee-for-service pool towards alternative forms of payment (such as hiring doctors on salary) was subject to
an OMA veto. Unable to attack the central cause of rising health costs,
government would be forced to cut medical services.

To Michael Rachlis, the decision to give doctors this kind of control
over the health system was the NDP government's gravest mistake, one

which other provincial governments faced with equally nettlesome physicians were only too eager to copy. By 1994, five other provinces had followed Ontario's lead and set up doctor–government joint management committees to oversee health spending.

"They really blew the health stuff," Rachlis said in 1994, speaking bitterly of the NDP government he had helped elect. "Even as a one-term government, they could have left a legacy. Well, they actually have left a legacy—the destruction of medicare in Canada."

Over its term, the government would take the initiative in a few significant areas—it was the first government in Canada to fund midwifery from medicare; it agreed to fund non-hospital abortion clinics; it raised the status of non-medical health practitioners such as occupational therapists. Significantly, most of these were areas in which the NDP in opposition, or at least activist groups associated with the party, were committed and had laid the groundwork. Equally significant was the fact that these reforms cost relatively little. In some cases (the area of long-term care was one example), the new government took work that had been almost completed by the outgoing Liberals, scrapped it, redid it, and came up one or two years later with policies remarkably similar.

More than anything else, the 1991 doctors' deal set the pattern for the way the NDP government would handle health issues. Two concerns would override all others—cost-cutting and smooth relations with doctors and the hospitals. For, as government communications aides would warn, unhappy doctors and hospitals could turn voters against the NDP.

Doctors were not the only sacred cows. The NDP government was also reluctant to challenge hospitals—even when it knew they were squandering public money. This became particularly evident when, in 1993, the Health ministry conducted a confidential, internal audit of its Special Drugs Program. The program represented a relatively minor part of the $8-billion hospital budget. The way it was handled, however, was indicative.

Started in 1986, the Special Drugs Program was designed to help those Ontarians who required unusually expensive drugs to combat catastrophic diseases—in particular, kidney disease. Money was allocated to designated hospitals across the province. The hospitals, in turn, were to provide the drugs, free of charge, to outpatients with specific conditions such as AIDS, transplants, or kidney failure. Over five years, however, costs had escalated exponentially—from $2.7 million in 1986 to $42 million by 1991.

The 1993 audit report was scathing. Neither the hospitals nor the ministry, it said, checked the prices they paid for special drugs against the prices they had contracted to pay. Nor, with a few exceptions, did hospitals try to arrange volume discounts. Instead, they paid whatever was billed, no questions asked. In one case, a drug supplier overcharged the government by $87,000—a mistake which was not found until the auditors went through the books.

This casual approach to money extended to other areas. In early 1991, the auditors reported, the ministry had hurriedly advanced $40 million to hospitals for the Special Drugs Program, simply to use up its surplus before the end of the fiscal year. Few conditions were placed on the $40 million and, according to the report, the hospitals "spent the advances on drugs more than required [*sic*] and other administrative expenses irrelevant to special drugs."

Over time, the report said, the problem of the "questionable" use of funds by some of the hospitals in the program continued. Sunnybrook Hospital, for instance, hired ten staff members to distribute AIDS drugs such as AZT to other hospitals. Sunnybrook charged the government $700,000 a year in adminstrative expenses for this service. According to the auditors, however, the number of employees required for the operation should have been not ten but one—a shipping clerk. Sunny-brook's administrative expenses, they concluded, were "excessive and unjustifiable."

Most hospitals, the audit found, had no restrictions on the amount of special drugs they could purchase—and few controls on who received them. They just kept buying—at government expense—until their storerooms were full. In 1992, for instance, Sunnybrook Hospital spent more than $2 million to purchase five years' worth of an expensive AIDs drug which, by the time of the auditor's report a few months later, was considered out-of-date.

As well, some hospitals charged patients dispensing fees of $10 to $12.50 per prescription for the special drugs, even though it was the government's policy to distribute them free of charge. The reason? The government had never specifically told the hospitals not to. Hospitals kept any surplus money they received under the program—surpluses which at the end of 1992 were worth $6 million. Then they would ask the government for more.

In some cases, the hospitals would, in effect, bill the government twice. One unnamed hospital received $1 million as an advance to purchase drugs. When it actually bought drugs, however, it didn't use this advance; rather, it billed the government again. This particular hospital then applied for and received another $600,000 advance from the government to add to the $1 million already in its possession.

In September 1993, the Health ministry warned hospitals that funding for special drugs would be cut by 25 per cent, to about $32 million. If the hospitals didn't meet this lower target, the ministry warned, the government might have to "cease providing 100 per cent reimbursement" for catastrophic drugs. The memo was soon leaked to opposition Liberal leader Lyn McLeod who, in the legislature, accused the government of planning to charge user fees to AIDS and kidney patients.

The ministry received hundreds of angry letters. Not wanting to incur the wrath of what it called the organized "disease groups," the government quietly backed off from that threat. While it did crack down on some of the abuse of special drug funds by hospitals, it did not solve all of the problems identified in the audit.

By the end of the 1993–94 fiscal year, the amount spent on special drugs had not fallen to $32 million; it had risen to $45 million.

Throughout much of the NDP period, the key figure in Health was Michael Decter. A former cabinet secretary under Manitoba New Democratic premier Howard Pawley, Decter was part of a new generation of NDP bureaucrats. Fiscally conservative, tough-minded, and adept, he had cut his teeth in the Manitoba NDP government's planning secretariat of the early 1970s. The planning secretariat, known colloquially as the Red Secretariat, was a group of politically motivated civil servants charged with keeping then premier Ed Schreyer's government on an appropriate NDP course. Fresh from Harvard, Decter was seen as the boy genius of the group.

However, Schreyer's defeat in 1977 at the hands of Conservative Sterling Lyon threw the Red Secretariat into crisis. Some quit; some were fired. Decter, as acting head, stayed to work with Lyon, thereby earning himself notoriety within the small world of the NDP. To some, he had become an informer, the man in the hood, whose job was to finger NDP sympathizers in the civil service. Old friends shunned him. A group of NDP civil servants and academics who met every Sunday for a friendly game of soccer refused to let him play any more.

To Decter, he was just doing his job—getting along with whatever government the people had chosen to elect. Years later, he still seemed bitter about those days, insisting that, contrary to the charges of his critics, he had used his influence to ensure that fellow bureaucrats on the Red Secretariat didn't lose their jobs. As proof, he would point out that only "about two" were fired.

Whatever his status within the Manitoba left, Decter's skills remained in demand with New Democratic governments. In 1981, the newly elected Pawley hired him as cabinet secretary, Manitoba's top civil servant. Decter stayed until 1986 before joining the lucrative world of private consulting. In 1990, Martin Barkin, then deputy minister of Health, recruited Decter to lead the negotiations with the OMA. And that brought Decter to the full attention of Rae.

In some ways, Decter was the person Rae might have been. One had chosen elected politics as a path to power. The other had realized early on, as he put it, that a senior civil servant has "a lot more to do with how the thing work[s]" than does an elected politician. Both were quick studies, stubborn to the point of arrogance, and in the end convinced they were right. Both were essentially conservative.

Unlike Rae, Decter was comfortable in small groups. Like Rae, he could get angry if crossed. But whereas an angry Rae tended to be petulant, Decter would explode. He evoked strong reactions. Decter's tantrums could reduce senior Health ministry bureaucrats to jelly. "He was a classic hard-nosed boss from the jackboot school," said one official who worked closely with him. "His command of most topics was superficial. But he was able to fudge his way through meetings in a way that inspired great confidence among people like [Health minister] Frances [Lankin]."

Other colleagues, even those critical of Decter, tended to admire him. "He's as tough as any private-sector businessman and with an agenda of his own," said one senior Ontario civil servant. Sue Colley, whose role as chief political aide to Health minister Frances Lankin brought her often into conflict with Decter, called him the government's most effective deputy. "Decter is a most interesting man to watch in a meeting," said Colley. "He'll let everybody else talk, and then he sums it all up in a charming way. He's very charming. He knows how to run a meeting. He knows the terms. He knows the jokes. He knows who is important. He knows who to refer to. This is a skill a lot of people have. But, in government, nobody had it. . . . So Decter, very very quickly on coming into government, became *numero uno* right off the bat."

In particular, Decter was *numero uno* with Rae. The premier valued his advice, admired his performance in the Health portfolio, and offered him more. In late 1992, according to Decter, Rae asked him to replace Peter Barnes as cabinet secretary, the top civil-service job. Decter declined, and Rae appointed David Agnew, his chief political aide, to the job instead. Later, Rae asked Decter to replace Eleanor Clitheroe as deputy minister of Finance; again, Decter says, he declined.

By late 1992, Decter was one of a select group of ministers advising the cabinet on their budgetary and economic policy. When Rae decided to impose a social contract on public-sector workers in early 1993, he turned once again to Decter to handle the job.

In Health, sparks flew almost immediately between Decter and his minister, the moody, mercurial Frances Lankin. Decter was the fiscal conservative with the premier's imprimateur. Lankin and her political staff favoured a more aggressive, reformist agenda. Decter tended to side with employers in the health sector, Lankin with the unions. Decter wanted user fees introduced in the provincial drug benefit program; Lankin initially did not. But more than that, aides say, there was a serious personality clash.

"Michael couldn't work with strong people," said one who watched the clashes. "And Frances wasn't confident about her intellectual ability or her ability to handle economic matters. Decter would push all the wrong buttons—male, arrogant, intellectual. When she felt threatened, she got haughty and arrogant herself."

Both Decter and Lankin downplayed any personality clash. "I have enormous regard for [Lankin] and I think it's a two-way street," Decter said later. "[We were] very tough back and forth. That's how Frances and I always were. Lots of respect and a willingness to have a no-holds-barred discussion, to take extreme views."

"It worked," Lankin said later, speaking of her relationship with Decter. "Michael was big picture; I was detail. In some ways, our roles were reversed. He was principle and direction, and I was more pragmatic."

Lankin's frank appraisal was probably the more accurate one. For, on the biggest issues, the two were in sync—particularly in areas they mutually agreed to ignore. In terms of key reforms, such as shifting from institutional to non-institutional care or devising more sensible methods of payment for physicians, the NDP government was virtually silent. Pilot projects contemplated by the Liberals, such as the hospital-in-the-home, a way to bring acute-care services to the patient rather than vice versa, were continued but not expanded. Plans to encourage alternatives to fee-for-service medicine were downplayed.

"There was a lack of political will," said one Lankin aide. "Decter opposed taking on the doctors and hospitals at the same time; Frances wouldn't push it." Indeed, only after both Decter and Lankin had vacated the Health ministry did the government begin to resume tentative moves, started by the Liberals, to provide alternatives to fee-for-service medicine. In early 1994, for example, Grier announced the province would put more money towards the training of nurse-practitioners, who, in many areas, are as competent as physicians but get paid less.

For the most part, however, New Democrats who had been promoting reform measures felt excluded by the NDP regime. One telling example was a dinner meeting, organized in early 1993 by the Health ministry. Those present included some well-known figures in provincial health reform—Toronto doctor Michael Rachlis; Hamilton health economist Jonathan Lomas; and Robert McMurtry, dean of medicine from the University of Western Ontario. The dinner was to be hosted by Decter. However, he failed to appear. "He phoned once, after we'd all been there half an hour, and said he would be late," recalled Rachlis. "Then he never showed up—or phoned again. He certainly never called to apologize." To Rachlis, this was indicative of a certain arrogance, an unwillingness to take advice from others who might know something. "Most of us felt we had no role," said Rachlis later. "It still grabs me sometimes. I supported the party all my life, spent all of my adult life preparing for this moment, and now feel I have no useful role to play because the guy in charge of the health sector is Michael Decter."

To lay the entire responsibility for NDP government health policy at the feet of Michael Decter is, depending on how one views that policy, either unfair or overly complimentary. Certainly, however, Decter was instrumental in setting the pattern. As Lankin said, he was the big-picture man. By the time he bowed out of government in November 1993 (Health minister Ruth Grier's going-away present to him was a silver nutcracker, the symbolism of which remains unclear), that pattern was firmly in place: cut spending while trying to placate doctors and the politically powerful hospitals. Unfortunately, that put $12 billion of a $17.5-billion budget virtually out of bounds.

To this end, the government started by looking elsewhere for its cuts.

Reforms were undertaken in the $1.2-billion-a-year Ontario Drug Benefit Program, which provides free prescription drugs to welfare recipients and those age sixty-five and over. Some attempts were made to strike drugs deemed too expensive or not particularly useful from the formulary, the list of pharmaceuticals approved for use in the program. Here, the government ran into another powerful pressure group, the drug companies.

For more savings, the government would have to turn to health-care users. Patients would have to bear the brunt. Under the terms of the 1993 social contract agreement with the OMA, the government had removed some medical services, including certain kinds of *in vitro* fertilization, from the list of procedures paid for by medicare. Later, payments to Ontarians who required emergency treatment outside of Canada were slashed to such a degree that the province fell afoul of the Canada Health Act, the federal medicare law that CCFers and New Democrats had fought so long to win. However, the bitterest battle was waged over a plan to hit the elderly and poor by introducing user fees in the Ontario Drug Benefit Program.

The four-year battle over drug user fees illustrates the contradictions which had overtaken the NDP government. It was a clash of principle and of personalities. Most indicative was the nature of the terrain. By refusing to grapple seriously with powerful social groups, such as doctors, the government was left bickering over how much it could take from those patients with the least power. Ultimately, the only thing which stopped the government from introducing user fees was the crassest of political reasons—its fear of losing votes. This was not the Ontario NDP government's finest hour.

The dispute initially pitted Lankin and her staff against Decter and the premier. Decter, Rae, Treasury Board deputy minister Jay Kaufman, and some of the premier's top advisers wanted a means test for seniors. All except the poorest would be charged user fees, or co-payments, for their drugs. With the money saved here, this camp argued, the government might eventually be able to expand the drug benefit system to include the working poor. Why should a retired bank president get free drugs when a waitress working at minimum wage could not?

On the other side, Lankin's staff argued that drug user fees would be the thin edge of the wedge. Not only would the NDP be contradicting a central plank of party policy; it would be opening the door to user fees in other areas of medicare. The NDP, they pointed out, had always supported universal social programs, available to anyone, regardless of income. The argument that social programs should be targeted only to those most in need was the siren call of the right; it was the argument the federal Tories had used (over the objection of the federal NDP) to eliminate baby bonuses. Former federal leader Ed Broadbent had put it well: Programs targeted only to the poor lose the political support of the middle classes. Once that support is gone, the programs can be eliminated. The Mulroney Tories had shown how this could be accomplished. Did Ontario's NDP government really want to follow in this path?

For Rae and many in cabinet, the answer was yes. Throughout late 1991 and early 1992, the user-fee battle raged. By the spring of 1992, it seemed that Lankin had won. Drug user fees were not included in that year's spring budget.

But it was just a reprieve. By early 1993, user fees were on the agenda again. Fear of hitting a so-called debt wall had driven the government to make the decision. By this time, however, personnel within cabinet had changed. Lankin had been shifted to the Industry ministry; Ruth Grier had replaced her in Health. In cabinet, Grier argued against drug user fees. Lankin, however, had become more ambivalent. To some of Lankin's supporters, it seemed she had been captured by her new Industry portfolio and the arguments of the multinational drug firms, which, by this time, were lobbying her mercilessly. To her critics, she was simply being opportunistic.

Lankin herself later insisted that she had always been consistent on the drug-user-fee issue. Philosophically, she said, she was not opposed to user fees for seniors — as long as it was part of a total drug-reform package. If she opposed user fees at any time, she said, it was because she felt such a comprehensive drug-reform package was not ready. "In the context of total reform, I was willing to look at co-payments," she said.

In his budget of May 1993, Finance minister Floyd Laughren publicly signalled the government's intention to impose user fees. That June, Grier released a comprehensive reform plan. Universal free drug coverage for seniors and welfare recipients would end. Both groups would be expected to pay user fees. At the same time, drug coverage would be expanded to cover the working poor, those with family incomes under $25,000 a year. To pay for this expansion, and produce about $100 million for the Treasury's battle against the deficit, user fees would be introduced. Very poor old people, those making less than $14,000 a year (or $22,000 for a couple), would be expected to pay up to $250 a year in drug user fees. Any senior with an income higher than this would have to pay up to $750 a year.

As a piece of social policy, the drug reform plan was ambitious but shallow. The government wanted too much: it wanted to save money from the program for its deficit battle; it wanted to preserve its compassion credentials by expanding the program. Mathematically, the two contradictory aims could work only if the government adopted a particularly severe definition of "needy." For example, under the government plans, a seventy-year-old widow earning $15,000 a year — a figure well under the poverty line — would be deemed well-off, and subject to drug user fees.

More important, the reform plan was confused. The party which had for so long argued that health care was a right of citizenship, independent of income, was now preparing to back away from whatever elements of universality existed in a state drug benefit program. In accepting drug user fees, the NDP had implicitly conceded the point being argued by thinkers of the new right, the same arguments being used by those who want to dismantle universal medicare: It is up to individuals to look after their own welfare; the state should step in only to help those who cannot help themselves.

Inside government, officials were struggling over how to sell what they expected to be a roundly unpopular move. "Seniors' organizations and their allies will focus on erosion of a 'universal' program. . . . Special Drugs Program recipients [such as AIDS victims] will decry the government's lack of compassion," warned one internal memo. Ministers were told they would have to counter these expected criticisms. But no one knew how. All officials could recommend was that the government conduct polls. Maybe these would generate some ideas. Perhaps, one internal memo suggested, the government could engage in more consultations with seniors, welfare recipients, and "disease groups."

Meanwhile, Grier was beginning to tire of being pushed around. The new Health minister did not approve of user fees and, according to associates, resented being put into the position of having to implement unpopular decisions that had been taken for fiscal rather than health reasons. In the summer of 1993, she released the government's drug proposals for public discussion. The result could have been anticipated.

The government was berated by seniors' groups, the trade unions, and the extraparliamentary NDP.

What's more, the NDP caucus was in a feisty mood. Back-bench MPPs had become increasingly frustrated at having to explain cabinet decisions over which they had no control. Like most governments, the NDP ministry had paid little attention to its back-benchers. Government decisions were brought to the caucus before being announced publicly, but usually as a formality.

In the fall of 1993, however, the NDP government decided to give its caucus virtual veto power over any government action. The reason was straight politics. By 1993, the NDP was in full pre-election mode. One way to keep seats, the government figured, was to adopt the radical idea of paying attention to its own MPPs. If enough voters told enough New Democrat MPPs they didn't want something done, the government would not do it.

In November, the drug proposals went to the NDP caucus. They were torn apart by MPPs who, all through the summer and fall, had been taking a walloping from the seniors' lobby. Lankin argued for user fees, saying that the government would look foolish if it backtracked on a decision it had already made publicly. But, in the end, only Rae and a few diehards were left supporting co-payments. Even Decter, pleading political reality, had gone over to the other side. Finally, Rae gave way.

Only temporarily, however. Within four months, the issue of drug user fees had been resurrected. Once again, the reason was money. The fiscal situation was still deteriorating, Laughren said. He needed cuts. In late March 1994, the entire drug-reform package that had been killed the previous fall, including user fees, was on the table again. This time, Lankin was arguing strongly for user fees, as were Laughren and Rae. On the other side, were Health minister Ruth Grier, Community and Social Services minister Tony Silipo, and Education minister Dave Cooke.

Ultimately, the anti–user fee camp won again. Ultimately, the deciding reason was—as before—politics. To go ahead with user fees would be to risk getting killed by both the seniors' lobby and the unions. Again, reluctantly, Rae had to back off.

The NDP has long prided itself on being the party of compassion, the only organized political voice willing to speak for the poor and the dispossessed. In opposition, Rae and others would speak eloquently of the plight of those on welfare. Welfare recipients, the NDP argued, were shabbily treated—left on the margins of society, with little money and little chance to escape the trap of social assistance. Those who argued that too much was being spent on welfare, the NDP said, were out of touch: Most welfare recipients are children; most live below the poverty line. In particular, the NDP criticized governments which tried to draw moral distinctions among those on welfare. "There are not deserving and undeserving poor," said Ontario NDP welfare critic Richard Allen in June 1990. "There are only people in crisis and need."

Rae himself had long criticized those who would make moral judgments about poverty. In his Oxford Bachelor of Philosophy dissertation, he attacked Beatrice and Sidney Webb, two of the intellectual founders of the British Labour Party, on just this point. Writing in the early twentieth century, the Webbs had argued that welfare recipients and the state were tied together in bonds of mutual obligation: The state has an obligation to help the destitute; but the destitute in return have an obligation to use this aid for "moral improvement." Those who failed to improve themselves morally, the Webbs said, were "hardened vagrants" and deserved little help. To a twenty-two-year-old Bob Rae, this attempt to separate the deserving and undeserving poor was wrongheaded; it carried the "earnest tone of the Victorian governess."

In opposition, Rae and his caucus had enthusiastically supported a 1988 report which proposed to overhaul the Ontario welfare system. Set up by the Liberals in 1986, the Social Assistance Review Committee (SARC) made 274 specific recommendations. Most could be lumped into one of three categories: rationalize the welfare system to get rid of jurisdictional confusion; give recipients more money to bring them above the poverty line; change the system so those on welfare would be better able to find work. The SARC report also destroyed several stereotypes. It found that most welfare recipients were not bums unwilling to work but people unable to do so—children, single mothers without child care, and the disabled. It pointed out that most receiving social assistance did not linger on the dole but got off welfare as soon as they could—often within three months. It found welfare rates to be far from generous; in fact, most recipients lived below the poverty line.

In opposition, the NDP praised SARC, attacking the Liberals only for not moving fast enough on the report's recommendations. After taking power, the NDP promised to rectify this and implement the SARC proposals. "A nation's greatness is measured in what it does for the least fortunate," Rae said at the swearing-in ceremony for his government. A few days later, he was more explicit, noting that "everybody knows that the next thing on the agenda is a reform of welfare legislation." Six weeks later, Community and Social Services minister Zanana Akande told the legislature that the government was committed to the SARC reforms and would put them into place as soon as possible. As a first step, she boosted welfare rates.

However, the new government had not taken into account two developments. First, the recession was pushing more and more people onto welfare. By February 1991, welfare costs in Metro Toronto had risen by 83 per cent. Second, Ottawa had drastically cut back on the amount it was willing to pay for welfare. Welfare was a shared federal-provincial program. In 1990, the Conservative federal government had capped the amount of money going to welfare programs in Ontario, British Columbia, and Alberta.

Gradually, the NDP government began to back away from some of its costlier promises. Akande acknowledged that the NDP would not be able to eliminate food banks. Rae himself began to talk less about the need to reform welfare in favour of the poor and more about the need to reform welfare financing in the interest of taxpayers. Taxpayers have to be given a break, the premier told the Association of Municipalities of Ontario in April 1991. "Something must be done." Still, Ontario welfare rates were high compared with those of other provinces. By 1992, the government could boast it had implemented many of the SARC recommendations. Even so, the bulk of welfare recipients in Ontario still lived below the poverty line.

However, 1992 also marked the real break-point in the government's attitude towards social assistance. Having discovered, late in life, the virtue of spending restraint, the NDP government began to look at its old assumptions about welfare reform with a different eye. Carleton University professor Allan Moscovitch had been appointed to head a panel suggesting ways for the government to push ahead on welfare reform. Moscovitch's first set of recommendations, delivered in 1991, had been accepted. Community and Social Services minister Marion Boyd had promised to implement his second set of recommendations, released in 1992.

But some in government—particularly Rae adviser Ross McClellan—were not happy with Moscovitch's second report. "We expected something different," explained one senior political aide. "He didn't take into account the recession and mass unemployment. We wanted something better and more social-democratic—geared more to train-ing and an active labour market." In particular, the government did not want to spend a great deal of money. It wanted welfare reform that would be linked more directly to its overall economic strategy, which was to retrain the unemployed for jobs which might eventually exist.

Meanwhile, Rae himself had begun to develop different thoughts about welfare. As a university student, he seemed to have accepted the social-democratic analsyis of poverty—that it was a structural, social phenomenon which required state action to solve. But under the pres-sure of government, Rae appeared to revert to an earlier, more basic view, one that emphasized the individual's responsibility for his own life. According to Rae's long-time friend Lenny Wise, Rae's parents had always preached the virtue of self-reliance—to such an extent that their son was reluctant to ask them for help.

Indeed, Rae's father, Saul, was a kind of Horatio Alger figure himself. An immigrant's son from a broken home who, as a child, had sung vaudeville to help keep his family in food, Saul Rae—through sheer perseverance—had worked his way into the country's diplo-matic and political élite. Bob Rae, according to his friends, could never forget that.

In a rambling speech to business students in early 1993, the premier talked of the need for a new welfare system, one that would give the poor an incentive to work. "Welfare isn't working," he told the students. His government was committed to changing the system, not because of "some neo-conservative enthusiasm" but as part of an effort to forge a new public philosophy based on a "common agenda." Asked if he would penalize welfare recipients who did not actively seek retraining, the premier answered he had long been thinking about these very problems. "Simply paying people to sit at home is not smart," he said. "It makes little sense simply transferring money to people so they can sit at home."

That April, at a weekend government session devoted to cost-cutting, Rae expanded on his ideas for welfare reform. Welfare recipients should bear their fair share of cut-backs, he told ministers, aides, and senior officials. The fiscal problems facing the province were so great that no one could escape. All had a responsibility to unite behind the common agenda of deficit control; that meant rolling back welfare rates.

Some of his listeners were horrified. Consumer and Commercial Relations minister Marilyn Churley, who had been a single mother on welfare, argued passionately against the premier. "If we can cut back on the poorest and most vulnerable, what do we stand for?" asked Churley, before leaving the room in tears. Later, she would note that the country's social safety net "saved my daughter and me." Senior Rae aide Ross McClellan, a former social-worker, made the same argument. "Bob's view was that if we're going to cut, everybody's going to suffer and that means social-assistance recipients," said one official who watched the wrangle. "Ross's view was: 'If you touch them we don't have any right to be here. . . .' Ross fundamentally wouldn't let them do it. He took the whole group on, including the premier, and turned them around on it. It took him probably half a day."

The premier may have temporarily conceded the battle over social-assistance rates, but he continued to develop his new thoughts on the philosophy behind welfare—thoughts very much in line with those of other liberal politicians. In New Brunswick, Liberal premier Frank McKenna was talking explicitly of workfare. In the United States, Democratic president Bill Clinton had proposed a two-year cut-off for those on social assistance; if, after that period of time, a welfare recipient still hadn't got a job, tough luck.

In his 1990 opposition treatise, "What We Owe Each Other," Rae had dismissed such right-wing "neo-liberal" ideas. He had talked instead of the responsibility society owes to those who are less fortunate. But, by 1994, Rae was talking explicitly of the responsibility the less fortunate owe society. "[Welfare recipients] need to be available for training and education," he told a CBC Radio interviewer. "I like to call it mutual responsibility." Society, he went on, owes all of its members a basic living. "And in return, we all owe each other the willingness to work."

While Rae's specific welfare proposals were not as Draconian as Clinton's, the language was startlingly similar. Nowhere in the CBC interview, for instance, did he address the fundamental problem behind rising welfare costs—the lack of jobs. It was left to Saskatchewan NDP premier Roy Romanow, who followed Rae on the same radio program, to raise the obvious question: "Education and training for what?"

By the spring of 1994, the elements of the Ontario NDP's proposed new welfare strategy were in place. It had two key thrusts: the first was to encourage welfare recipients to become retrained through a system of financial incentives; the second was to expand social benefits for children so as to cover not only welfare families but the working poor.

As such, this could be the first step towards a provincial guaranteed annual income. Gone, however, was the emphasis, made in the 1988 SARC proposals, of raising the income of welfare recipients to bring them above the poverty line; this was deemed just too expensive.

As initially devised, the NDP welfare scheme would have three parts: adults who qualified for social assistance would receive a basic sum called an adult benefit. Those who agreed to be retrained would get an extra training supplement. Children of poor families, whether their parents were in the workforce or on welfare, would receive a child benefit.

What were not decided, however, were the sums involved. This was crucial. The amount of money Queen's Park was willing to put into welfare reform would determine the level of compulsion, the degree to which welfare was becoming, if not workfare, at least "trainingfare." Would the basic adult benefit be equivalent to the amount an adult already received on welfare? Or would it be scaled back, to encourage him to enroll in a training course? Similarly, would the education supplement merely cover the cost of being retrained—tuition, materials, transportation—or would it include something extra, as an incentive? The answers to these kinds of questions would determine whether the NDP was embarking on precisely the kind of two-tier system it had once so fiercely criticized, a system that distinguished between the deserving poor (in this case, people willing to be retrained) and the undeserving (those who, in Rae's words, just "sit at home").

Similarly, how would the government pay for expanding child benefits to the working poor? Would it do so by cutting back the basic adult benefit for those on social assistance? Welfare recipients already lived below the poverty line. Any cut-backs would run into the same kind of objections from inside the NDP already expressed privately by Marilyn Churley and Ross McClellan. Yet any expansion of welfare costs would skewer attempts to curb the deficit.

By January 1994, Finance minister Floyd Laughren knew that revenues for the coming year would be $1.6 billion lower than he had anticipated. Word began to leak out that the government might have to gut its ambitious welfare reforms for lack of cash. However, the final announcement was delayed until after the federal budget.

On February 22, federal Finance minister Paul Martin announced that Ottawa planned to continue, for at least two years, its policy of curbing transfer payments to the provinces. On March 2, an outraged Rae—citing Martin's refusal to fund more of the province's welfare bill—announced Ontario had no choice except to scale back its planned social-assistance reform.

The reasons had much to do with politics. Laughren's grim revenue predictions had shattered the government's re-election strategy. As Laughren and Rae had explained to back-benchers in the fall of 1993, this strategy had consisted of two stages. First, through the social contract and the budget cut-backs of 1993, it might be able to convince the majority of voters (most of whom are not NDP supporters) that the government could get tough with unions and that it could manage the province's finances. Then it could use 1994 to win back its traditional base—through the announcement of progressive measures such as welfare reform.

With revenues down, however, the government faced an unenviable choice. It could go ahead with reform anyway and let its deficit rise above $10 billion, thus undoing whatever reputation it had gained for fiscal sobriety. Or it could scale back plans for welfare reforms, thereby risking the further alienation of its base.

The government's answer was to scale back reform and blame Ottawa. Rae's so-called Fair Share campaign, which he had been articulating in one form or another since 1991, went into full gear.

The bulk of the work on "Fair Share" had been done by Rae's old university chum Jeff Rose, the deputy minister of Intergovernmental Affairs. Rose, an intellectual, former union boss, and collector of fine glassware, was well regarded by Rae for his strategic abilities. "Fair Share" did seem to have possibilities. The gist of it was this: In the past, Ontario had been well off and did not mind paying a bit more towards the rest of the country. Now, recession had hit Ontario relatively harder than any other region of Canada. As Rae had said during the 1991–92 constitutional debate, Ontario could no longer afford to be the big guy at the end of the bar who bought everyone a round. Now it was time for Ontario to get its fair share.

The province's main complaint lay with Ottawa's decision to cut back on its share of welfare payments to the country's three richest provinces. Under the Canada Assistance Plan, Ottawa had been committed to picking up half of the welfare bill in every province. In 1990, the federal Conservative government announced it would allow its share of welfare payments to increase by no more than 5 per cent per year for the country's three richest provinces—Alberta, British Columbia, and Ontario.

That 5 per cent increase barely covered the growth in population. It certainly did not begin to meet the needs of provincial welfare systems when, in 1990, social-assistance rolls began to explode. By 1993, Ottawa's share of Ontario's welfare costs had dropped to 29 per cent. In speech after speech that fall, Rae pointed to what he saw as the essential unfairness. Why should federal tax dollars (the bulk of which come from Ontario) pay 50 per cent of the costs of Quebec's welfare system but only 29 per cent of Ontario's? The federal government, he said, was merely off-loading its debt problems onto the provinces—particularly onto Ontario.

The premier's complaint, particularly his deliberate comparisons with Quebec, struck a chord. Whether he was justified was another question. Though the recession had hit Ontario relatively hard, other provinces—including Quebec—were still far worse off. If Ottawa did indeed face a serious fiscal problem (and Rae seemed to acknowledge that it did), it made some sense—in NDP terms—for the three richer provinces to ante up more. The NDP had, after all, always favoured progressive tax systems in which the rich pay proportionally more than the poor.

As for the question of off-loading debt, the premier was on even shakier ground; for, just as Ottawa was cutting back on the provinces to solve its debt problems, so the province was cutting back on municipal governments to solve its own.

To blame Paul Martin for Ontario's decision to scale back welfare reform was not entirely warranted. Martin's budget did predict future cut-backs to the provinces. But it did not announce any new immediate cuts in transfers. Instead, it just continued with the curbs already put in place by the Tories.

It is possible that the NDP's entire welfare reform was contingent on wishful thinking, on the hope that the federal Conservatives would be defeated and that whoever replaced them would give Ontario more money. But it is unlikely. The Rae government was not that daft. What seems more likely is that, at the end, the NDP government was spooked at the cost. Faced with a choice between serious welfare reform and the deficit, it chose, as always, the deficit.

By March 1994, deficit worries had once again overwhelmed the Finance ministry. Without more cuts, Laughren told his colleagues, he had no hope of meeting his deficit target. Bureaucrats were told to prepare plans to slash transfer payments by 2 to 3 per cent for hospitals, schools, and municipalities. The cut-backs would probably lead to lay-offs in the public sector; but this could not be helped.

The cabinet, led by Lankin and Education minister Dave Cooke, balked at cutting transfer payments. After the social-contract cuts, this would be just too much. Instead, ministers agreed to consider cutting welfare rates. Inside the cabinet, Lankin, Rae, and Laughren were the most vocal in arguing that welfare-rate cuts should at least be considered. (Lankin would later tell associates that she privately opposed cuts but chose not to argue that position in cabinet.) Rae pointed out that international bankers would like to see the government control its so-called open-ended expenditures, such as welfare and the drug benefit program.

From the other side, Cooke, Grier, and Silipo argued strenuously against fighting the deficit on the backs of the poor. They were boosted by internal polls which demonstrated that voters no longer viewed the NDP as compassionate. Welfare and labour activists who had gotten wind of the idea also made their opposition known to the government.

The message got through. "I guess we can't do it," Rae finally told his cabinet. Nonetheless, he gave up the idea of welfare cuts only reluctantly. On April 5, at a meeting of the inner cabinet, Rae raised the topic again. The government, he said, had to bite the fiscal bullet; it really should take a look again at both drug user fees for seniors and cutting back welfare rates. Finally, Cooke spoke up. "Bob," he said gently. "We decided those issues two weeks ago."

On May 5, 1994, Finance minister Floyd Laughren rose in the Legislature to deliver his government's fourth budget. It was an unmemorable document, one expressing the stalemate in which the government had found itself. There would be no welfare or child care reform; the government was afraid to spend the money. There would be no cuts to the Ontario Drug Benefit Program or to welfare rates; the government was afraid of alienating its base. There would be no further attempts to scale back the deficit by raising taxes or slashing spending; the government faced an election within fifteen months.

However, the most striking aspect of this, Laughren's last serious budget, had to do with tax reform. What was striking was that the phrase "tax reform" was never mentioned.

For years, tax reform had been central to the NDP. Laughren himself had entered politics, in large part, because he wanted to make the tax system fairer. One of his first actions as Treasurer had been to establish a $9 million Fair Tax Commission to look into reform. Now, three-and-a-half years later, the government had nothing to say on the subject. The reasons, Laughren conceded, had to do with political reality. Not only was tax reform complicated, it created political enemies. "A major reform of the tax system at this point would require shifting some existing taxes on to new taxes," he said. "And we decided there should be no new taxes at this time."

More than any other single issue, tax reform had been at the heart of the NDP reform agenda, both federally and provincially. The party had long argued that the tax system favoured large corporations and the rich. When the NDP talked of fairness, it meant tax fairness. It argued that a fairer tax system, one which hit the rich and the corporations more heavily, could provide government with the extra revenue needed to carry out other elements of the party's program.

In 1972, federal NDP leader David Lewis had touched a national chord with his attack on what he called "corporate welfare bums," big companies which used legal loopholes to avoid paying any tax. For Laughren in particular, tax reform was pivotal. As an economics instructor, he had been radicalized by the critique of Canadian tax policy contained in the 1967 Carter royal commission on taxation. A drive to reform the inequities of the tax system was one of his main reasons for joining the NDP. His concerns seemed to be shared by Rae. In 1982, for instance, Rae called for increases in corporate taxation and an end to tax loopholes.

In 1989, Laughren released a full-scale critique of the tax system. The key elements were eightfold. First, Ontario should, like Quebec, operate its own personal-income-tax regime rather than piggyback on that of Ottawa. This would allow it to create a more progressive income tax system, one which hit the rich harder than the poor.

Second, the province should take over the bulk of school funding from municipalities. This would mean that education was funded not through the property tax, which hit the poor proportionally harder than the rich, but through the more progressive income tax.

Laughren also called for a tax on wealth, similar to that levied in some European countries. He wanted a minimum corporate levy to hit those companies which, by taking advantage of loopholes, pay no taxes. He proposed to tax speculative profits made through real estate sales.

Once in government, Laughren set up a commission to look into tax reform. His Fair Tax Commission ran into trouble almost immediately.

To ensure that the commission would adhere to notions of partnership, the government had drawn in representatives from diametrically opposed camps. On the one side were those calling for radical tax reform, including labour, some academics, and some tax experts. On the other were those opposed to reform, including business, other academics, and other tax experts. Eight working groups were set up to look into specific areas. But, in many groups, the two sides could find no common ground.

The result was a flurry of minority reports from the working groups, the labour-reform side supporting minimum corporate taxes, speculation taxes, and wealth taxes; the business-conservative side opposing.

Added to this was another dispute between experts and so-called popular groups. In an effort to be inclusive, the NDP had appointed what it called ordinary folks—including women, aboriginals, non-whites, and poor people—to working groups. The experts felt these popular groups knew too little about tax policy to be useful; the popular groups thought the experts élitist. This split reached a crescendo when the seventeen-member working group looking into a land-speculation tax issued thirteen minority reports—business people, reformers, experts, academics, and the popular groups, all going their separate ways.

Determined to bring some order to the chaos, the Commission's executive director Hugh Mackenzie (a former Rae aide) and Commission chair Monica Townson laboured to produce a report that the government might realistically use. Some of the NDP's more controversial notions—including a provincial wealth tax and land-speculation tax—were abandoned along the way. The wealth tax was deemed impossible to implement in one province alone; capital, the commission decided, would simply shift elsewhere.

"I remember being frustrated when they came to me about the wealth-tax stuff," said Laughren later. "Because I wanted to do a wealth-tax thing. Gee, if there's one area that needs to be addressed, it's that."

More significantly, and over the objection of some of its members, the commission also decided not to recommend any major increase in corporate taxes.

In late 1993, the commission issued a massive 1,114-page report. Of the 135 recommendations, two categories were particularly important. First, the commission recommended that Ontario overhaul the personal income tax system. Some of these recommendations (such as the elimination of a tax deduction for a dependent spouse) were bound to be controversial. However, none could be carried out unless Ontario either got agreement from Ottawa or broke away and set up its own personal-income-tax system. Since neither condition could reasonably be met until well after the next provincial election, this set of proposals was politically safe: The government could run on a credible tax-reform platform but not have to face the inevitable flak which would result from actually implementing these ideas.

The second set of proposals had to do with the property tax. Here the commission called for education to be at least 90 per cent funded by the province, with money coming from income taxes rather than the regressive property tax. Politically, this too was an auspicious suggestion. The NDP could campaign in the next election on a promise to reduce property taxes. The other half of the equation, the inevitable rise in income taxes required to make up for any property tax cut, would not have to be dealt with until afterward.

As for corporate tax reform, the commission said little. The majority of commissioners accepted the business argument that if Ontario's corporate taxes got too far out of line with those in neighbouring states or provinces, firms would flee. As commission vice-chair Neil Brooks noted, in a dissent to the report, the commission had failed to test the hypothesis that corporate tax levels are significant factors in business-location decisions. Whatever the truth of the argument, the commission's decision to stay away from corporate taxes soothed business.

Indeed, the one fundamentally different kind of business tax that Laughren managed to win was his corporate minimum tax, introduced in the spring of 1993. The amount of money involved was minor. However, Laughren could, and did, argue that he had set a precedent. "To me that's important, to get it established, to get the base up there and get it running," he said later.

In the end, NDP tax reform—a policy which for more than a decade had been at the heart of its drive for fairness in the economy—was remarkably modest. In opposition, the party had a vigorous and apparently well-considered tax agenda. Once in government, it discovered real and practical problems.

Moreover, to many NDP supporters in the middle-income range, Laughren's tax hikes—the largest in Ontario history—overwhelmed any notion of fairness. Factory workers making overtime suddenly found themselves included in the class of the wealthy, those expected to pay an extra surtax. They didn't like it. John Beneteau, a Windsor auto worker and, until 1993 an NDP supporter, put it succinctly: "I was told by the NDP we'd tax the upper class. And now I'm the upper class."

Perhaps tax reform can be counted as a near-success. It was pursued with more vigour than health reform and with less confusion than welfare reform. Yet, in all three cases, the proposals which ultimately emerged were pale imitations — or even reversals — of the kinds of changes the NDP had long advocated. "A nation's greatness is measured in what it does for the least fortunate," Rae had said on taking office in 1990. The poor, the sick, the old, the unemployed, and others who saw themselves as belonging to the "least fortunate" could be forgiven for wondering what had happened along the way.

11

Same Boat Now

ON CHRISTMAS EVE 1993, THE PREMIER OF ONTARIO WENT
into his office, sat down at his word processor, and tapped out a letter.
The big, pink sandstone legislative building was virtually empty that
evening. Most of the MPPs, political aides, government bureaucrats, and
reporters who work in the building had made it an early night. Rae
himself was facing a hurried Christmas. He and his wife, Arlene, were
scheduled to make a whirlwind tour of the Middle East, where Rae
hoped to drum up business for Ontario as well as satisfy his curiosity
about one of the flashpoints of international politics.

But first there was a letter to be written to Mike Roth, head of publishing for Sony Music. Rae is a competent pianist; he is even a member
of the Musicians' Union. The premier had met Roth once at a music-
related function; and Rae had written this song that maybe, just maybe,
Sony would like to record. Music was, after all, in the blood. The
premier's uncle, Jackie Rae, was well known in the business. A successful songwriter, Jackie Rae has had his work perfomed by Andy
Williams, Eddy Arnold, and Engelbert Humperdinck.

Since the 1970s, Bob Rae too had been trying his hand at song-
writing. And, while he had not had the success of his uncle, he was
proud of his efforts, particularly a children's song he had written in the
1980s. As a bemused Jim Coyle, provincial columnist for *The Ottawa
Citizen*, noted, the NDP had once paid $6,000 to have a black children's
gospel choir sing back-up while Rae performed this song to a room full

of puzzled party stalwarts. And in 1990, Rae had been thrilled when
Toronto musician Ken Whitely agreed to perform the song at Roy Thomson Hall. Rae, then leader of the opposition, had his office issue a press release on that occasion, inviting Queen's Park reporters to hear what it called, tongue-partly-in-cheek, an "international debut." In short, Rae thought his song worthy of some promotion.

"I think it might have a wider audience," he wrote in his Christmas Eve missive to Sony's Roth. "I'd appreciate your unvarnished opinion."

The song the premier of Ontario was trying to peddle to Sony Music was called "We're in the Same Boat Now". Later, Rae would sing it on CBC Radio's *As It Happens*, CBC Television's *Midday*, and the television rock channel *MuchMusic*. It started like this:

> Some folks come here yesterday
> Some folks come from far away
> Whether yesterday or far away
> We're in the same boat now.

(Chorus)
> Go to the schoolyard and look around
> Faces are yellow, black, white and brown
> Come by car
> Come by train
> Come by plane
> We're in the same boat now.

Some New Democrats, such as former Rae press aide Rob Mitchell, thought the song sappy. Presumably Roth too was unimpressed. After putting up with a barrage of political songs and recordings from would-be impressarios, unleashed when news of Rae's offering became public, he sent the premier a polite but terse rejection. Ironically, Mitchell was by this time working for Roth. It fell to him to draft the rejection notice.

For the media and much of the public, the episode seemed a weird joke. But, for Rae, it was deadly serious. To the premier, his song reflected both a profound truth and a hope—that people could overcome their differences in order to work together in the spirit of solidarity. In fact, "We're in the Same Boat Now" was probably the most succinct version of Rae's own political philosophy, of what he thought it meant to be a New Democrat. When, as premier, Rae talked about his "equity agenda," the sentiments behind "Same Boat Now" were at the back of his mind.

However, many in his party had been developing another, more aggressive idea about equity and social justice. This other view, influenced by developments both in the United States and among Canadian aboriginal groups, rejected as simplistic and patronizing the liberal notion that people of goodwill could overcome social problems by working together—the very notion behind "Same Boat Now." In the United States, this had been carried to an extreme. A growing number of black activists were calling for voluntary segregation: blacks should patronize stores owned by blacks, borrow money only from other blacks, attend all-black schools, and in university enroll in black-only courses on Afro-American culture. Their argument was that, in an inherently racist society, blacks could find freedom only through their own, separate institutions.

Meanwhile, in Canada, Native peoples were agitating for the right to self-government—to withdraw from mainstream society and act as sovereign nations within the country. The Native argument was based in part on legal and historical grounds; Canadian treaties recognized Native peoples as sovereign nations. But it was also based in part on the more compelling logic of despair. Native communities and cultures had been left devastated by more than a century of subordination to the Canadian state; self-government might be their only chance to survive.

Behind both of these developments was a resurgence of interest in race as one of the defining characteristics in any society. Even the women's movement was affected. White, middle-class women, the new minority activists argued, could not hope to fully understand what were called "women of colour." This debate surfaced in 1992 when June Callwood, a white, middle-class feminist, was forced off the board of a Toronto women's hostel she had helped to found. Callwood's sin, her opponents charged, was a failure to be properly sympathetic to the plight of non-white women.

Decades of liberalism had taught that race didn't matter, that those who thought it did (usually those of the majority race) were racist. But the new racialism confounded liberals, for it came at the behest of the racial minorities themselves. Rae, for instance, would have made short shrift of anyone who suggested a Toronto high school for whites only or a Toronto credit union to be patronized mainly by whites. Yet his ministers were silent when a task force, including representatives from the

NDP government, recommended creation of "black-focused" schools in Toronto. In 1993, the government did fund a credit union for what it called "Caribbean Canadian Africans."

The new interest in the politics of race came at the same time that the NDP was going through one of its periodic crises. The party's failure in the 1960s and 1970s to attract the majority of union votes and become a British-style class-based labour party had been a profound disappointment. Partly to make up for this, partly because of the CCF's social-gospel history, partly because of the type of individual who was attracted to social democracy, many in the NDP began to agitate for coalitions with cause-oriented social movements.

If there were a just cause—from South African democracy, to rights for women, to acid rain—these New Democrats felt the party should embrace it. Within the party, this caused increasing tensions—pro-choice women versus anti-abortionists, anti-nuclear activists versus unionized atomic plant workers, environmentalists versus loggers. But it also reinvigorated the NDP, drawing in activists from cause-oriented groups prepared to work for a party which they felt supported their aims.

The most influential of these groups was the women's movement. Women activists pushed the NDP to take strong positions supporting non-profit daycare, pay equity (paying men and women equally for work of equal value), and employment equity (hiring and promoting men and women equally). The battle to get the party to agree to support the idea of state-funded abortion clinics was a tough one—pitting women activists against a party establishment unwilling to veer too far from the majority public mood. It too was eventually won.

Non-whites had never been well represented in the NDP—to such an extent that when, after its election, the new government began looking for members of racial minorities to act as political aides, it did not have, in the words of Janet Solberg, "a lot of people to turn to."

Rae's attitude towards all of these developments was puzzling. With some cause groups, particularly the women's movement, he could be inordinately cautious. In their book on the Ontario NDP, *Giving Away a Miracle*, George Ehring and Wayne Roberts spell out the difficulties the women's movement had in persuading Rae to support abortion clinics.

Yet, in other areas, Rae could be daring. In opposition, for instance, he educated himself in the area of employment equity, and even presented a private member's bill to the legislature on this issue. As premier, his 1992 constitutional proposals on Native self-government would have — if accepted — revolutionized the country, permitting aboriginal people, even in the country's largest cities, to establish new political institutions separate from mainstream society.

In 1983, Rae — arguing the sanctity of the law — refused to support an illegal abortion clinic opened by Dr. Henry Morgentaler in Toronto. Yet, in 1989, he was willing to be arrested at an illegal blockade near the Northern Ontario town of Temagami, in support of environmentalists and a local Indian band opposed to logging. During the 1992 constitutional debate, the premier supported Native self-government proposals with singular passion. And yet he had little sympathy for women's groups, including Native women's groups, which argued that the constitutional proposals would harm them.

A common thread running though Rae's approach to social movements was an affinity for abstraction. One who worked closely with the premier called him "a fiscal conservative with the ideals of an undergraduate." The more distant the cause, the more unequivocal was Rae's support.

In 1990, after a trip to remote, impoverished Indian communities along the Hudson and James Bay coasts, Rae wrote eloquently about what he saw as remnants of colonialism: "The meaning of the phrase 'self-government' suddenly became very clear, and its historic parallels with the demands of other colonized people around the world are immediate and visceral.... It is impossible to escape the conclusion that what we are talking about here is racism.... Canadians ... share with every 'settler culture' the compelling need to accept the claim, the rights, the history, the personality, yes, the nationhood of those who were here before European settlement."

Once a cause became more concrete, however, Rae's quixotic enthusiasms were tempered. His more ambivalent attitude to the women's movement, for instance, seemed to stem in part from his having to deal head on with its leaders. Key activists in that movement, such as Judy Rebick, former head of the National Action Committee on the Status of Women, were constantly challenging Rae inside the NDP.

Similarly, the rights of gays and lesbians were fine in the abstract or when they were limited. In 1990, the government moved quickly to grant most employment benefits to same-sex partners of its own civil servants. But for Rae and many around him, same-sex rights became less appealing when activists made the politically difficult argument that homosexual couples should be eligible to adopt children. Not until

early 1994 was Rae convinced to come around to this position. However, his caucus remained badly split—agreeing to introduce the
country's most comprehensive homosexual spousal rights bill by a
margin of only one vote. Even then, opposition to the measure inside
the caucus forced the government to permit a free vote, one in which
back-bench MPPs would be allowed to say aye or nay as their conscience (and the demands of their constituents) demanded. In the end,
Ontario's same-sex bill, which would have given homosexual couples
the same status in provincial law as heterosexual common-law couples,
was defeated.

One area in which Rae's government seemed to remain steadfast—its
commitment to Native self-government—may be explained in large
part by distance. Discontent over this policy, such as disputes between
Natives and non-Natives over fishing rights, tended to occur well outside
of Toronto. Many in the Toronto-centred NDP government dismissed
such complaints about the government's Native agenda as the racist
whining of red-necked northern whites. Whether the premier explicitly
endorsed this view is unclear. But its existence may have permitted him
to maintain, for some time, a romantic view of Native governments.

In other areas, Rae found specific applications of NDP social
activism at odds with his own same-boat-now instincts of fairness. In
1993, the NDP government's Anti-Racism Secretariat quietly funnelled
funds towards groups protesting what they called "racial stereotypes in
the theatre"—such as the musical *Show Boat* or the Broadway hit *Miss
Saigon*. Yet Rae himself attended *Miss Saigon*, slipping in through a
side door in order to avoid pickets.

The result of all of this was that much of the government's so-called
equity agenda remained confused, buffeted by competing forces of guilt
and muddled thinking, punctuated by bursts of strong activism, and
subject always to the chilling influence of fiscal conservatism. Where
ministers themselves were strong advocates, the direction was clearest.
But even here, the equity agenda could be derailed if it interfered with
the overriding goal of deficit control.

This was particularly true in the area of women's issues, where ministers such as Marion Boyd had come to government with a clear feminist agenda. In 1991, the government announced it would spend an extra
$20.3 million to fund campaigns against sexual assault and wife abuse.
In 1991, it vowed—in spite of the premier's reluctance—to devote
$105 million to non-profit child-care centres. It funded midwives from

medicare. Perhaps most important, it put paid to a decade of argument within the NDP and agreed to fully fund non-hospital abortion clinics.

On the issue of pay equity, however, the government was more skittish. The previous Liberal government, under the prodding of its accord with the NDP, had introduced one of the most far-reaching pay equity laws in North America, one which required employers to pay men and women equally not only for doing the same job but for doing different jobs of equal value. For instance, under pay equity a firm cannot pay secretaries (mainly female) less than stock-room employees (mainly male) if both are deemed to do work of comparable worth to the employer.

However, the Liberal's 1987 law had not covered some of the province's lowest-paid workers, those such as nurses and child-care attendants who worked in the so-called female ghetto. During the 1990 election campaign, the NDP vowed to rectify this. In December 1991, Labour minister Bob Mackenzie introduced a bill to extend pay equity to 420,000 of these women by 1995. Less than a year later, he quietly pulled back. Spooked by the rising deficit and fearful of the cost of pay equity in the public sector (expected to reach $1 billion annually within six years), the government had extended the deadline to 1998. It also weakened the original bill in other significant ways, removing for some employers all deadlines for compliance.

Traditional NDP allies were outraged. The non-profit child-care lobby and the Ontario Nurses Association castigated the weakened pay equity bill as "shocking" and "fundamentally misdirected." Even Julie Davis, at the time NDP president, appeared before a legislative committee on behalf of organized labour to criticize the government bill as "a possible step back."

The centre-piece of the government's equity agenda, however, was to be employment equity. Employment equity legislation, or what the Americans call "affirmative action," is designed to encourage employers to hire and promote groups thought to be disadvantaged. Usually, this outcome is achieved through quotas. Employers are required to hire and promote members of disadvantaged groups until their workplace comes into some kind of sexual and racial balance. In practice, this can mean that certain occupations which historically have been the preserve of white men—such as firefighters and police officers—become barred to this group until such a balance is reached. Critics, not always inaccurately, refer to employment equity as reverse discrimination.

To the NDP, employment equity would meet the needs not only of women but of racial minorities who felt discrimination in the job market. In opposition, the party had accused the Liberals of moving too slowly on the issue. Rae had even introduced his own private member's bill on employment equity.

In fact, work on employment equity had been started by the previous Liberal government and was well under way. Literally cartons of material had been accumulated. But when the new government took power, all this was abandoned. Citizenship minister Elaine Ziemba's staff, on the advice of employment equity advocacy groups, declared all work done by the previous government racist. Instead, a highly respected Montreal civil-rights lawyer, Juanita Westmoreland-Traoré was hired as employment equity commissioner to draw up an employment equity bill. "The NDP wanted employment equity to be its own," said one official working in the area. "Juanita said, 'We don't consider past work; there has to be a fresh start.' It was as if everything done in the past was flawed."

Eventually, four so-called disadvantaged groups were identified— women, racial minorities, the disabled, and aboriginals. The process, however, soon bogged down. To the frustration of cabinet, Ziemba's ministry seemed incapable of coming up with a workable plan, one that would put into place an employment equity law without causing a massive backlash in the province. "Elaine was nuts and berries," said one Citizenship official.

The first effort, a discussion paper produced in the summer of 1991, was deemed too confrontational in tone. "It was sophomoric and polemical," recalled one senior government figure later. "Bob wanted something that could draw together a consensus."

Part of the problem seemed to lie in the new Employment Equity Commission. The commission had been set up by Rae specifically to advance the cause of disadvantaged groups, including racial minorities. Most staff members hired were from the four disadvantaged groups. But soon it was torn itself by racial animosity. Julie Mason, former director of communications for the federal NDP, worked for about one year at the commission. She later called it the most racist workplace she had ever experienced.

"I've never seen anything like it," Mason said. "It was absolutely vicious.... The blacks hated the Indians; the Indians were the most antisemitic; everyone hated the lesbians and gays.... There was a real pecking order. At the bottom were people with disabilities. Next to the bottom were white women. There were no white men, not until they had to bring in John DeMarco [a senior bureaucrat in Citizenship] to fix up the mess."

In mid-1992, following a racially tinged riot on Toronto's downtown Yonge Street, the government rushed ahead to introduce its employment equity bill to the legislature. However, the conflicts between Rae's vision and that of Ziemba and Westmoreland-Traoré had not been sorted out; employment equity was not yet ready. As a result, the bill was a most peculiar piece of work. Aside from setting out the government's intention to improve the lot of the four target groups, it was absolutely empty. The guts of the bill — how employment equity would work, to which employers it would apply — were to be filled in by regulation.

Just what those regulations would be was the subject of great debates within government. On the one hand, there was Rae, calling for caution. On the other, there were Ziemba and Westmoreland-Traoré, backed by advocates for racial minorities, women's groups, and the disabled, taking a more radical stand. One crucial battleground had to do with unions.

Most union contracts include seniority clauses. In the case of lay-offs, for example, those who have worked the shortest period of time in any given job category are let go first; those with the most seniority have the most job security. To many employment equity advocates, seniority clauses only perpetuated the fundamental inequalities of the workplace. Women, the disabled, and members of racial minorities were always last hired and first fired.

However, to union leaders — many of whom actively supported employment equity — any interference with seniority rights was fraught with danger. Michael Lewis, an official with the Steelworkers Union and an influential figure in the NDP, warned the government bluntly. "He said he was worried there would be violence if we went ahead with it," said one government insider. Westmoreland-Traoré, however, was equally adamant on the other side. "Juanita wanted to jump all over seniority in hob-nailed boots," said Julie Mason.

In desperation, a group within the premier's office and cabinet office decided to wrest control of employment equity from Westmoreland-Traoré. However, allies of the employment equity commissioner got wind of the plot. Soon, Rae was flooded with complaints from advocacy groups for visible minorities, who organized an "appreciation night" for Westmoreland-Traoré. Already caught up in growing controversy over his government's handling of another case involving a high-profile black appointed by the NDP—the Carlton Masters scandal—Rae kept her in her position. Instead, the employment equity issue was quietly taken away from Ziemba and Westmoreland-Traoré. A group of senior deputy ministers reporting directly to Rae's office was told to come up with a workable set of employment equity rules.

Government ministers pointed out that employment equity would benefit the vast majority of workers, that more than 60 per cent of Ontarians belonged to one or another of the targeted groups. This was true only because women, one of the target groups, accounted for more than half of the population.

Women's groups were active in the fight for employment equity. But, for most white women, the issue did not seem to catch fire in the same way that abortion rights or pay equity, or even child care, had. To some, it was out-of-date. To others, it had little relevance in time when jobs of any kind were scarce.

Many women seemed to share, with men, a suspicion of hiring quotas. In part, this was because such quotas did not seem to work. As one long-time NDP women's activist put it, thirty years of affirmative action in the United States had not much improved the lot of American blacks.

Added to this was another contradiction. Many women are mothers. Those with white, able-bodied male children had to face the possibility that an employment equity law, unlike pay equity or abortion access legislation, might discriminate against their offspring. It was one thing to argue that men and women should have an equal chance to be fire-fighters. It was another to support quotas (or "numerical goals," as the government called them) which might well bar their sons from having even a crack at a firefighter's job.

Still other women, such as Julie Mason, changed their mind after having seen the way the Employment Equity Commission worked." I had come into [the commission] as a supporter of employment equity," Mason said. "But now I think the legislation is unworkable. And I think the principle is unworkable.... I had the real feeling we were trying to legislate attitudes, and you just can't do that. You can't legislate the number of people in an environment. It's not workable. I used to work with Alan Borovoy [in the Canadian Civil Liberties Association] and I guess, after the complete chaos of the [employment equity law] process, I agree with him now. You can legislate against discriminatory barriers that stop people from being hired or getting ahead. But you can't do what we were trying to do."

Meanwhile, the feared backlash had already begun. Many white able-bodied males saw the proposed law as an attempt to establish hiring and promotion quotas, which—all government protestations to the contrary—it was. To some working-class men, employment equity was the final betrayal by the NDP. Mutterings of discontent could be heard from union rank-and-file members and long-time New Democrats in cities such as Sudbury.

The male working-class backlash reached a head in 1993 when the Oshawa local of the Canadian Auto Workers, the union's largest, voted to disaffiliate from the NDP. Many reasons were given, including dissatisfaction with government economic policy. But fear of employment equity played a major role. The response of both the government and the CAW leadership was to dismiss the Oshawa disaffiliation as a kind of conspiracy cooked up by agents of the Reform Party—a critique which begged the question.

At the same time, the government was failing to satisfy those pushing for employment equity. Caught between its desire to appeal to what it called these "non-traditional groups" without offending either business or the general ideological consensus, the government pleased no one.

The final regulations covered all government agencies. But in order to mute business opposition, only private firms with more than fifty employees were covered. These firms would be required to draw up plans to ensure that racially, sexually, and in terms of able-bodied versus disabled, their workforces mirrored the community around them.

However, enforcement provisions were weak. The law did not require employers to match their plans against specific numerical standards. And though employers had to come up with acceptable plans within three years, they faced no time limit when it came to implementing those plans. The maximum penalty for a firm that contravened the law was also relatively small—$50,000.

Employment equity activists were outraged. "To have an employment equity bill that does nothing is worse than having no bill at all," wrote Avvy Go of the Women's Coalition for Employment Equity. Judy Rebick, former head of the National Action Committee on the Status of Women, called the NDP bill "smoke and mirrors." In spite of the difficulties that the unions themselves were having with their own members over employment equity, labour leaders from the Canadian Auto Workers, the Canadian Union of Public Employees, and the Ontario Federation of Labour came forward to denounce the NDP bill as too weak.

When the bill finally passed its last legislative hurdle in December

1993, Ziemba boasted it was the toughest in North America. The applause, nonetheless, was muted.

The government also decided to pursue employment equity more actively in its own bailiwick. In the summer of 1993, the cabinet quietly approved what it called a "positive measures program" to boost the number of women, non-whites, aboriginals, and disabled people within the civil service.

Just what "positive measures" meant became clear that November when the government's Management Board ran an advertisement for an information technologies director. White able-bodied men, the advertisment made clear, need not bother even applying; the job was open only to women, non-whites, aboriginals, and the disabled. The public and media reaction was furious. After a few days of stonewalling, the government backed down and withdrew the ad. But the suspicions over employment equity had again been heightened.

In May 1992, Toronto experienced an evening of mayhem and looting. The city had gone through such experiences before, but this one sent a shiver down the collective spines of all the élites. For initially, at least, it looked like a race riot.

The day of May 4 had started as a march to protest the acquittal, in Los Angeles, of four white police officers who had severely beaten black motorist Rodney King. By nightfall, however, a crowd of youths was swarming through downtown Toronto, breaking windows and looting stores. By the time order was restored, the city was in shock.

Newspapers and television were quick to point out that youths of all colours were involved in the mêlée, not just blacks. But to the provincial government, the Yonge Street riot was a wake-up call. Action had to be taken immediately to ameliorate the conditions of the Toronto black community—or else this might happen again. Rae asked former NDP leader Stephen Lewis to head up a task force into the riot and report within a month.

Lewis's report did not produce startlingly new ideas. What it did do though was pull together and express, in a powerful form, themes that had been circulating through minority cause groups. As such, it became the most influential document on race relations within the government.

A key aspect of the thirty-seven-page report, written in the form of a letter from Lewis to Rae, was the author's insistence on a hierarchy of those who are victims of racism. The "primary target" of racism, he wrote, were blacks: "While it is obviously true that every visible minority community experiences the indignities and wounds of systematic discrimination throughout Southern Ontario, it is the Black community which is the focus," Lewis went on. "It is Blacks who are being shot, it is Black youth that is unemployed in excessive numbers, it is Black students who are being inappropriately streamed in schools, it is Black kids who are disproportionately dropping out, it is housing communities with large concentrations of Black residents where the sense of vulnerability and disadvantage is most acute, it is Black employees, professional and non-professional, on whom the doors of upward equity slam shut. Just as the soothing balm of 'multiculturalism' cannot mask racism, so racism cannot mask its primary target. It is important, I believe to acknowledge not only that racism is pervasive, but that at different times in different places it violates certain minority communities more than others."

Previous governments had insisted that any attempt to discriminate against anybody on the basis of race was a violation of civil liberties. The thrust of the Lewis report was this liberal approach to racism was not enough, that the government had to move quickly to alleviate systemic racism against black Ontarians.

Seven of Lewis's twenty-two recommendations dealt with the police and criminal justice systems, nine with education. But to Lewis, one recommendation which could "really make a difference" was the expansion of the Ontario Anti-Racism Secretariat. The secretariat should be given more money and influence to become "the driving force behind a policy which seeks to eliminate intolerance and discrimination from the public life of Ontario." In particular, it should develop "an unprecedented community development plan which incorporates the many proposals and ideas that never seem to be examined by others."

What were these ideas never examined by others? Here, Lewis made no specific recommendations. He did, however, refer sympathetically to ideas advanced by members of the black community for what he called "ethno-specific services." In particular, he noted some black activists had argued for black-only health services, black-only welfare services, black-only cultural agencies, black-only financial institutions, black-only job programs.

The NDP government had already moved to strengthen its race policies. The former Race Relations Directorate, a department within the Ministry of Citizenship, had been transformed into the Anti-Racism

Secretariat. The change was significant in two ways. First, in bureau-cratic terms, the new secretariat had more clout than the old direc-torate. Second, the new secretariat's mandate was to be far more aggressive. The original directorate had concerned itself largely with mediating in specific instances where races clashed. Under assistant deputy minister Anne-Marie Stewart, a former Toronto school superin-tendent, the new secretariat's aim was to actively fight racism—mainly through public education.

More important, for the first time, it was given the authority to fund specific minority groups engaged in anti-racism. As such, it became more responsive to the aims of client minority groups. Just as the Labour ministry tended to work for unions and the Industry ministry for business, so the Anti-Racism Secretariat became, in a fundamental sense, the property of minority cause groups.

In specific terms, blacks were to be its most important client group. Taking its lead from the Lewis report, the secretariat directed the bulk of its money towards black community organizations, mainly in Toronto. In part, as officials explained, this was done because black organizations were more fragile and fragmented than those of other groups.

Other minority groups were uneasy about differentiating among kinds of racism. Karen Mock, national director of the League for Human Rights for B'nai Brith Canada, worried that focusing on the plight of one minority could transform anti-racism into racial chauvin-ism. In particular, Mock was concerned about the growth of anti-semitism within the anti-racism movement, a development she said predated the NDP government.

Still, B'nai Brith supported the Lewis report's recommendation that Queen's Park concentrate on racism against blacks. "Any racism is inexcusable," said Mock. "In terms of the black community, it was so great that that little kerfuffle they called a riot [the 1992 Yonge Street riot] could turn into something else.... It's not to say that antisemitism is not an issue. But the black community at large has it worse."

To Mock, the Anti-Racism Secretariat was, in fact, an improvement. Its staff, she said, was more tied into the minority communities. While it might focus on blacks, it did give money to Jewish groups to fund their anti-hate campaigns. The secretariat, she said, was not as prone to anti-white racial chauvinism as its predecessor, the Race Relations Directorate.

Within Citizenship, members of racial minorities themselves were disturbed by the way in which anti-racism could transform itself into a new kind of racism. According to some, the ministry itself had been plagued by racial infighting. "It used to be that whenever a white person came in, he was called a racist," said one black official.

As well, some were uneasy about the NDP's decision to concentrate so narrowly on race. "It's too narrow and sterile a thing to live and breathe," said one black activist working closely with the secretariat. "Because this race thing doesn't seem to allow for any other aspects of analysis. It's an unreal construct, sterile.... Unless you bring some sort of political analysis—some sort of class analysis—into your analysis to do this work, you have difficulties. When races are competing with each other purely on the basis of race, you can lose sight of the fact that in society all racial minorities are marginalized."

Racial tension heightened in 1993 during the controversy over *Show Boat*. The 1920s musical, which had orginally featured American black Communist Paul Robeson in the starring role, was scheduled to kick off a new theatre in the Toronto suburb of North York. Some Toronto blacks argued that *Show Boat* presented a patronizing and inherently racist view of black people and thus should not be shown. Groups such as the Jamaican Canadian Association and the Black Action Defence Committee, as well as some black artists, joined together to form the Coalition to Stop *Show Boat*.

Opinion in the Toronto black community was not unanimous, however. Some prominent black figures, including pianist Oscar Peterson and singer Salome Bey supported *Show Boat*. Non-black opinion was split too. The Ontario Council of Agencies Serving Immigrants opposed *Show Boat*, as did some Reform Jewish groups. Quickly, however, the anti–*Show Boat* protests took on an antisemitic tinge. Black activists began to make much of the fact that the show's producer, Garth Drabinsky, as well as North York's mayor, Mel Lastman, were Jewish.

Within the government, the *Show Boat* controversy added to tensions over race. Inside Ziemba's Citizenship ministry there was still a tendency to treat any critic as racist. The logic was simple: Any white who had risen to a position of authority within government had done so within a social context that was systemically racist; thus, unless that white explicitly admitted his own racism and adopted an acceptable anti-racist position, he was a racist.

White bureaucrats within Citizenship were encouraged, in scenes reminiscent of Maoist self-criticism sessions, to admit publicly to their inherent racism. In one instance, a black Citizenship bureaucrat challenged a female white colleague in a public meeting. If she were really a committed anti-racist, the black said, the white civil servant would quit her job and give it to a woman of colour. The fact that she did not indicated that she was a racist.

The strategy of silencing critics by labelling them racist was said to be particularly evident in the Employment Equity Commission. White NDP aides from other areas of government who disagreed with the commission routinely found themselves labelled racist. Julie Mason, a long-time NDP feminist, activist, and federal party official, finally quit the commission after a particularly bitter meeting in which she was accused of being racist, anti-homosexual, and paternalistic. Her crimes, said Mason, included telling an aboriginal woman working for her to rewrite a speech (racism) and suggesting that a lesbian who seemed upset should go home and have a cup of tea (paternalism; homophobia). Mason later recalled her time at the commission as "the worst year of my life."

When the *Show Boat* controversy arose, the Anti-Racism Secretariat was gung-ho to support those groups opposed to the musical. In particular, it wanted to fund anti–*Show Boat* demonstrations. Secretariat head Anne-Marie Stewart argued that the stereotypes of black people produced in the 1920s were simply unsuitable for a city with a growing race problem, as Toronto was in 1993.

But Rae did not want to be in the middle of a race battle. For that reason, the premier's office decreed that the government would not take any position on *Show Boat*—for or against. The Anti-Racism Secretariat was told, in no uncertain terms, not to involve itself in anti–*Show Boat* demonstrations. Stewart was even told not bring up *Show Boat* when speaking publicly.

The response inside Citizenship was to accuse the premier's office of racism.

As the *Show Boat* controversy heated up, the Anti-Racism Secretariat had to content itself with playing a more subterranean role. Instead of supporting anti–*Show Boat* demonstrations directly, it quietly, and without informing the premier's office, funnelled $200,000 into various groups that were part of the Coalition to Stop *Show Boat*.

One grant worth at least $60,000 went to York University fine art professor Jeff Henry to set up a nine-month project to help young people understand racism in the performing arts. Henry was also head of the Coalition to Stop *Show Boat*.

To officials inside Citizenship, the secret *Show Boat* grants were seen as a way to get around Rae's timidity. To Henry, on the other hand, the entire government—including the Anti-Racism Secretariat—had been a disappointment. Indeed, Henry denied that his grant was used to promote anti–*Show Boat* demonstrations. The *Show Boat* issue, he said, had been raised in only one of many workshops held to look at racism in the arts. The timing was coincidental; the *Show Boat* controversy had merely made him aware of the number of negative racial images in the media. That, he said, was why he approached the Anti-Racism Secretariat for money: "One didn't tie in with another. If the government saw it that way, that's their short-sightedness."

Short-sighted or not, that was the view inside Citizenship. When only 135 demonstrators turned up on the musical's opening night, the mood in the ministry was one of profound disappointment.

The government moved to implement some of Lewis's other recommendations too. A few days before he issued his report, the government had announced a special summer-jobs program for black youth. The government agreed to fund a Caribbean Canadian African credit union (which, it insisted, was not just for blacks). A commission made up of representatives of all levels of government, including the province, recommended establishment of "black-focus" high schools in Toronto.

Separate from all other racial minorities were the aboriginal people. Here, Rae had moved firmly and quickly. "The new government is committed to negotiating self-government agreements that will have real meaning, in this term of office," he pledged at his swearing-in.

The government quickly set up what it called a political relationship with Indian bands, or First Nations. In effect, the political relationship was a recognition of the inherent sovereignty of the aboriginal groups. It meant that they and the province would deal with one another government to government rather than government to client.

In practical terms, this was a signal that the NDP government was willing to grant to Indian reserves the right to operate their own versions of provincial programs. This devolution could take many forms. Soon after it announced its casino plans for Windsor, the government began negotiations with Indian bands to look into setting up Native casinos and gaming authorities.

Even in the aboriginal area though, the reality fell far short of Rae's first enthusiatic rhetoric. In its first three and a half years, the

government was able to complete only one land-claim or self-government negotiation.

"We raised expectations too high but never delivered," said one dis-
illusioned NDP official who had worked on the aboriginal agenda. "We
signed the political accord and took the high road in the Charlottetown
Accord ... but we delivered very little on the ground." A very senior
government figure would later characterize the government's native
agenda as "one step forward, two steps back." The political accord, he
said, had created an unintended result—it allowed the more pressing
native problems to be lost in a miasma of constant consultations and
negotiations. Some native bands, he said, were simply overwhelmed by
government demands for consultation. "We kept faxing them: 'What
do you think of this? Do you have an opinion on that?' A lot didn't have
the capacity to handle it."

At times, the NDP equity agenda seemed to be a parody of itself. In
1993, the government had consolidated funds from other programs to
dedicate $300 million towards what it called Jobs Ontario Community
Action (JOCA). In most ways, JOCA was an old-style program, designed
to fund worthwhile community projects such as hockey rinks, particularly in ridings where the government needed political support.

There were differences, though. First, JOCA was supposed to
support projects that encouraged Ontarians to prepare for the globally
competitive world of the twenty-first century. Second, JOCA projects
were supposed to be sensitive to the "non-traditional" groups—
women, aboriginals, visible minorities, the disabled, old people, youth,
and francophones.

The difficulties of marrying these different elements surfaced
when the town of Tecumseh, in southwestern Ontario, applied for
$1.2 million to build a new skating rink.

Inside the government, the Tecumseh skating rink proposal had to be
vetted by the various ministries with a hand in JOCA—including Citizenship, Tourism and Recreation, and Economic Development. Would
a rink in Tecumseh aid the economic restructuring of Ontario and
prepare the province for global competition? Opinions among officials
were mixed. But some were able to argue that skating would permit
Tecumseh residents to briefly take their minds away from the worry of
unemployment and joblessness. Surely, the mental invigoration encouraged by skating in a brand-new rink would prepare these Ontarians at
least for the harsh gales of global competition.

But what about non-traditional skaters, the Citizenship officials asked. Would there be a sufficient number of disabled people who would use the rink? And aboriginals? How did it fit in with the aboriginal agenda? One official noted that there was not an "abundance of aboriginals" in Tecumseh. But others pointed out that there were aboriginal communities elsewhere in southwestern Ontario. Perhaps the rink should go in one of these.

A feasibility study had been done three and a half years earlier, but it was not clear that this was good enough any more. In the summer of 1993, boosters of the Tecumseh rink produced another feasibility study. "We're hoping to service females and others," explained Leo Lassard, one of the organizers of the Tecumseh effort. "It won't just be for hockey.... We've sent letters to all groups ... including aboriginal ones." A Tourism ministry official later said that Tecumseh had managed to "cover all the bases" in this regard.

In April 1994, several months after Tecumseh had submitted its second request, the rink was approved by the government. The town would get its $1.2 million.

The government's difficulties with employment equity, pay equity, and JOCA were bad enough. Where the NDP's equity agenda truly became tied in knots, however, was the Carlton Masters affair.

Rae had never taken to Joan Sutton Straus, the former *Toronto Star* love columnist appointed by the Liberals as Ontario's agent general in New York. Moreover, he felt the symbolic aspects of the prestigious New York job could be put to better use. In 1991, he appointed Bank of Montreal vice-president Carlton Masters, a black, to replace Sutton Straus.

By the summer of 1992, disquieting rumours were starting to filter back to Toronto. On August 5, according to a sworn affidavit later filed by Masters in a court action against the government, the agent general was told that allegations of sexual harassment had been made against him, that a formal investigation would be launched, and that until the matter was resolved he would be suspended from his post with pay.

For the NDP government, the politics of the situation were most delicate — a black man accused of sexually harassing women, most of them white. The feminist and race elements of its equity agenda threatened to collide.

A procedure did exist in the public service for investigating allegations of sexual harassment internally. Instead, however, the government chose to hire Toronto lawyer Mary Eberts to do an independent investigation.

Just how thorough or fair was the investigation later became a matter of dispute. In his affidavit, Masters argued that he was never told the identity of his accusers, nor given a chance to respond to all allegations made. Government officials, for the most part, refused to discuss the case. What does seem beyond dispute is that an investigation was done and a report received by the premier. Six weeks later, Masters resigned. Initially, Rae steadfastly refused to release the report. But, in early 1993, after Masters held a press conference to, as he put it "clear my name," Rae made the report public.

The report concluded that Masters had indeed broken government policy by harassing five women. Masters disputed the findings and, in particular, the manner in which the investigation had been carried out. In his sworn affidavit, Masters recounted his version of the events following the initial allegation of sexual harassment. As a record (admittedly one-sided) of Rae's role in the fiasco, it makes fascinating reading.

By late September, Masters said, he had become truly alarmed by the direction the investigation was taking and had decided to hold a press conference to attack the process. But a public dust-up was the last thing the government wanted. According to Masters, NDP president Julie Davis telephoned him—at Rae's request—to ask him to cancel the press conference. Masters did so.

By late October, the government had the final report of the outside investigators in hand. But still, it wanted to avoid controversy. Citing privacy concerns, Rae refused either to release the report to the legislature or to say publicly what he was going to do with his agent general. Zanana Akande, the only black member of the NDP caucus, warned Rae that Toronto blacks were threatening to hold a press conference attacking the government; the premier, according to Masters's affidavit, told her, "Carl will be okay, don't worry."

On November 6, Masters's affidavit continued, Rae finally contacted his agent general directly. The scenario described by Masters reads like something from a John le Carré novel. Rae, Masters said, asked him to fly to Toronto. But rather than meet at Queen's Park, where the two might be spotted together, Masters was told to reserve a hotel room on Toronto's airport strip. On November 7, Masters checked into the Howard Johnson Hotel and called Rae. Soon, the premier arrived at the hotel room. According to Masters's reconstruction of the conversation, Rae said he had read the investigator's report and that it was "shabby" and "inconclusive." He then told Masters that they both shared a common burden—both worked for the NDP. However, Rae went on, Masters had a second burden: he was a black man. Rae said that the negative publicity around the issue meant that Masters could not return to New York as agent general.

"I was advised by the premier . . . that I had two choices," Masters said. "I could sue the government, which would take a very long time, or I could continue to work within the government." According to Masters, Rae then offered him a job, with no loss in rank or salary, as the premier's adviser in Finance. David Agnew, Rae said, would handle the details.

That night a party in Masters's honour was held in Toronto. At that party, according to Masters, NDP president Julie Davis said Rae had told her: "Carl has been vindicated. . . . Please spread the word."

Over the next two weeks, however, the government was shaken by two mini-scandals—both involving allegations of sex-related harassment. On November 13, Tourism minister Peter North resigned over allegations he had attempted to trade a job for sexual favours. On November 20, Rae's communication adviser, John Piper, resigned after allegations he had tried to smear a woman involved in another ministerial sex scandal. According to Masters's affidavit, the government's enthusiasm for giving him a senior post seemed to cool rapidly after the Piper and North scandals. Cabinet secretary David Agnew, for instance, seemed suddenly unavailable whenever Masters's lawyer called.

Still Rae seemed to want to avoid a public battle with the black community. According to Masters, Akande was told by Rae on November 24 to "tell Carl to calm down, everything is okay." Three days later, however, Masters said he received a new ultimatum from the government. He was to apologize to all the women he had allegedly harassed. And his senior adviser job had turned into what he called "a junior position at Queen's Park." The government also insisted that it alone would issue a press release outlining the resolution of the situation and that Masters would have to keep silent. He could accept all of these condition or be fired. Master refused and, on December 4, quit.

Rae's only public comment came in the spring of 1993, at which time he denied ever asking Julie Davis to deliver any messages to anyone about Masters. Otherwise he remained tight-lipped, saying only that the matter was before the courts.

Whatever the merits of the original harassment allegations, by 1993 the Masters affair had thrown the government's race-relations agenda into turmoil. To many in the black community, it seemed as if the premier had sacrificed Masters for purely political reasons—his reluctance to face another sexual-harassment scandal in the wake of the North and Piper affairs. Community groups such as the Black Business and Professional Association lauded Masters and criticized the government. Akande, a former minister and the NDP caucus's lone black, pointedly compared Masters to Martin Luther King Jr. The implication was not lost on Toronto blacks; King's enemies had tried to destroy the U.S. civil-rights leader by spreading allegations that he had had affairs with white women. Masters, Akande seemed to be saying, had been destroyed by a stereotype as old as slavery—a stereotype in this instance wielded by Bob Rae's equity-conscious NDP government.

In the late fall of 1992, Premier Bob Rae met with a group of his government's senior bureaucrats. He had just come through the bitter disappointment of the constitutional referendum. Rae had spent two intense years trying to come up with a compromise to break apart the country's constitutional logjam, only to see the fruit of his efforts—the Charlottetown Accord—repudiated across the country. Ontario had voted for the deal, but only by the slimmest of margins, and then only because of Metro Toronto. Everywhere else in the province, the accord had been solidly voted down.

"I took a risk," Rae told the bureaucrats, speaking of the accord. "And I consulted to death. But I'm not encouraging any more consultation. It's expensive and undemocratic." One participant recalled later that there were tears in the premier's eyes.

To many in his government, including Finance minister Floyd Laughren and senior aide Ross McClellan, the constitution had been a colossal waste of time, a cul-de-sac that had drawn Rae away from important issues such as the economy. "It really cost us to have the premier otherwise engaged during that first crucial year," said one aide later. But for Rae, it was a calling.

He had been fascinated by constitutions since his time as an undergraduate, when he helped design one for the University of Toronto. Constitutions, he argued later, are not merely abstractions filled with windy language but practical documents with practical results.

During the 1987–90 Meech Lake constitutional talks, Rae had been a study in frustration. He could not abide the fact that the province's then premier, Liberal David Peterson, was representing Ontario in a matter of such national importance. During the final fruitless negotiations over Meech in the summer of 1990, Rae haunted the old Ottawa train station where the prime minister and premiers were meeting, hoping that someone would ask his advice. No one did.

Within a few short months, however, he was premier, and the constitutional debate was heating up again. Rae hesitated briefly, unsure of whether he should devote his young government's energies to the constitution. But within three months of taking office, in a speech to the legislature, he served notice he was plunging in.

Plunge he did—into a debate that interested few of his cabinet colleagues. Howard Hampton, the attorney general at the time and one who had little patience for the constitutional debate, would later refer to Rae as "reclusive" during this period. "For a while there, he was really hard to reach," recalled Hampton. "It seemed like he was almost possessed."

Initially, there were four strands to Rae's constitutional policy. The first was a deeply held view—which he had articulated ever since his days as a University of Toronto undergraduate—that Canada must include Quebec. If that meant decentralizing the federation to accommodate Quebec nationalism, then so be it. The second was his passion for what he called a "social charter." The social charter would be a kind of social and economic bill of rights written right into the constitution, spelling out the obligations of the federal government to all citizens and provinces. As such, it would compensate for the weakening of national institutions which would almost certainly result from meeting Quebec's demands for a new division of constitutional powers. The third was Native self-government. Rae was determined that any constitutional document he signed would have to recognize, in a practical way, aboriginal government. Fourth was process: Rae argued that some sort of constituent assembly should be convened to discuss the constitution and take it out of the back rooms. Constitution making was to be inclusive.

The constitutional position of Rae's party, however, was full of contradictions. On the one hand, it espoused the right of Quebec to determine its own future, a right which—given the dynamics of federal-provincial relations—was sure to lead to decentralization. On the other, the NDP had long supported strong central governments and national social programs.

New Democrats supported the notion of Native self-government. At the same time, most in the Ontario party supported individual freedoms

guaranteed by the Charter of Rights and Freedoms, and bitterly
opposed granting any government, Native or otherwise, the power to override this charter. Women's groups in particular saw the charter as a hard-won instrument which guaranteed their rights. All of these elements were in delicate balance. As long as he could keep them there, Rae could count on support from his party.

By late 1991, however, the balancing act was becoming more difficult. Aboriginal leaders were adamant that Native governments not be bound by the Charter of Rights. Rae supported them. Other premiers were cool to the idea of a constituent assembly. Rae was backing off that too.

Most important, however, Rae began to water down his idea of a social charter. Many, including Saskatchewan NDP premier Roy Romanow, had long been suspicious of such charters, arguing they granted too much political power to unelected judges. Faced with opposition from Romanow, Quebec premier Robert Bourassa, and others, Rae began to talk of his social charter as a political commitment rather than a judicially enforceable set of principles. The problem with that, however, was that an unenforceable charter was no longer a counterweight to the very real decentralization demanded by Quebec.

By the time a final deal had been hammered out in August 1992, Rae's position had undergone a metamorphosis. The idea of a constituent assembly had evaporated. Instead there would be a high-pressure, winner-take-all referendum. The social charter was, to all intents and purposes, gone — weakened to the point of non-existence. Rae had agreed to an equal and elected Senate, an idea which just months earlier he had refused to countenance.

Native self-government rights, as demanded by the aboriginal groups, were still there. In fact, Rae had written much of this section himself. Significantly, the new Native governments would have the power to override some civil liberties, including — according to the Native Women's Association of Canada — those of Indian females. Some federal powers would be decentralized to appease Quebec. But such decentralization, Rae argued, could also benefit Ontario, which itself was not getting a square deal from Confederation.

Partly from necessity, partly from conviction, largely at the prompting of his old friend Jeff Rose, the deputy minister of Intergovernmental Affairs, Rae had latched onto an Ontario-first theme not heard in the province since the days of former premier Mitch Hepburn. Later, this would become known as Rae's Fair Share campaign. It was a theme he would pursue with increasing enthusiasm as his government sank in the polls.

The final Charlottetown Accord expressed some of the same contradictions which had dogged the Ontario NDP government's entire equity agenda. The attempts to create new rights for Quebeckers and Native people made other groups—particularly women—feel threatened. Many NDP members were dismayed by what they saw as a willingness to erode national social programs. Judy Rebick, then head of the National Action Committee on the Status of Women and herself an active New Democrat, waged a public battle against the deal. (Rae responded by dismissing NAC as an interest group.)

Perhaps more than anything, New Democrats—and, as it turned out, most Canadians—resented the high-pressure salesmanship, the apocalyptic language of the accord's supporters, who warned of everything from economic collapse to national destruction if their side, the Yes side, failed. The premier's own remarks on the last day of the campaign suggested frustration. "You know trust is a two-way street," he told *The Toronto Star*. "We [the politicians] are trusting people in this referendum with exercising their sound judgement."

In Toronto, senior government aides worked overtime trying to bring out canvassers and organizers for the Yes side. The NDP cabinet and the bulk of his caucus threw their weight behind Rae. But most New Democrat rank-and-file members, like those of the other major parties, preferred to sit on their hands.

The Charlottetown Accord had been in large part Bob Rae's creation. But ironically, the failed deal did not measure well against even Rae's own standards. It did not put Canadians in the "same boat now." Quite the reverse. Charlottetown would have put Quebec even more into its own distinct-society boat; aboriginals, retreating to the homelands of the reserves, would have been in theirs. The federal government, which the original Fathers of Confederation had hoped would express the commonality of Canada, would have been relegated to a smaller vessel, and the provinces permitted greater manoeuvring room in theirs.

The metaphor which Rae himself used to describe the Charlottetown vision was Canada as a "meeting-place." He could have called it a mooring spot, a place where disparate peoples tie up occasionally to exchange hellos before resuming their separate voyages.

12

No Sex Please, We're New Democrats

IN LATE 1993, PETER DONEGAN, A MARKET RESEARCH consultant working for the NDP government, came up with some unsettling results. Donegan specialized in what he called "psychographic" techniques—burrowing beneath the skin to get at subconscious and often unarticulated thoughts. He had done yeoman work for the NDP in the 1990 election campaign. Using focus groups—small groups of individuals who are interviewed intensively as to their views—he had divined the province's deep dissatisfaction with David Peterson, a dissatisfaction not reflected in ordinary public-opinion polls. Donegan had done this by asking participants in his focus groups to draw pictures that expressed their opinions of the Liberal premier. The fact that they insisted on portraying Peterson as, for instance, a devil with a pitchfork, seemed to suggest a lurking disaffection. The NDP used Donegan's insights to wage a sustained, personal, and—as some acknowledged later—unwarranted attack on Peterson's integrity to win the election.

Donegan's 1993 focus-group results, however, did not bode well for Rae's government. In one case, he had asked participants to choose from among a group of pictures the one that most reminded them of the NDP government. Most had chosen one featuring a man in a suit, in a tree, with his back to the viewer. The connotations seemed clear—the NDP was out of touch, aloof, élitist. Other focus groups, which looked at, for instance, NDP government health-care reforms, revealed that participants saw these as shams, designed to reduce services at the public's expense. Murray Weppler, Rae's new communications adviser, warned his colleagues that the NDP's stock-in-trade image as the party of compassion was in serious jeopardy.

Even more disturbing, however, was the persistence of another image. Asked to comment on government integrity, focus-group participants continued to harken back to a 1991 mini-scandal, one involving Northern Development minister Shelley Martel. What stuck in their minds was that Martel had lied, and then taken a lie-detector test to prove she had lied. Donegan's conclusion, according to those familiar with his analysis, was that the Martel case was the turning-point. "At that point it was lost," said one New Democrat involved in the government.

To even call the Martel case a mini-scandal is an exaggeration. Indeed most of the so-called scandals which embroiled the Rae government in its first three and a half years were hardly worthy of the title. Compared with the cases of insider trading which had rocked the Conservative government in the 1950s during Ontario's version of the great pipeline row, Rae's scandals were trifles. Compared even with the routine scandals of Ottawa—where Brian Mulroney's Tory MPs were being charged and convicted in record numbers for various tawdry improprieties—the events in Ontario were picayune.

Indeed, most were absurd—the minister who was fired for appearing, fully clothed, as a male pin-up; the minister who quit after he was alleged to have had a sexual affair in which no one had sex; the minister who took a lie-detector test to prove she was lying. None involved corruption, the exchange of money for favours, or the abuse of office. Most, if recounted to someone unaware of what was going on in Ontario, would have seemed like a series of jokes—something created by the fertile imaginations behind the CBC Radio's satirical *Double Exposure* perhaps, or maybe a wacky *SCTV* sketch.

For a while, the NDP government took solace in the fact that its scandals were goofy rather than venal. When his government was compared to *The Beverly Hillbillies*, Rae responded by noting that *Hillbillies* had enjoyed an unusually long run on television. But, by 1993, it was becoming clear that goofiness could be as politically lethal as venality. Episodes such as the Martel affair seemed only to reinforce the popular image that the NDP was utterly incompetent.

The gist of the Shelley Martel scandal was disarmingly simple. The government's 1991 agreement with the Ontario Medical Association had put limits on medicare payments going to the small minority of the province's doctors earning $400,000 a year or more. This had particularly irked highly paid specialists in Martel's home city of Sudbury; by year's end, the Sudbury doctors were involved in a running war with the NDP government.

On December 5, 1991, at a mining convention cocktail party in Thunder Bay, Martel was bearded by a local Tory councillor named Evelyn Dodds. Dodds told the minister that the NDP government was treating physicians shamefully. The name of a Jean-Pierre Donahue, a dermatologist critical of the government in Martel's home city of Sudbury, came up. What was said exactly after that is open to some question. Dodds would later claim that Martel had said she had seen the file on Donahue and that the government was thinking of laying charges against him. Martel never denied this; her champions would say later that the fiery twenty-eight-year-old minister had merely lost her temper when confronted with the name of a man causing grief for the government in her home town.

The essence of the controversy, however, was that Martel was not supposed to have access to confidential Health ministry files on Ontario doctors. By law, only the Minister of Health was privy to such information. Even if Martel did have access to Health ministry files, she was bound not to reveal their contents. Rae's government had already lost one Health minister, Evelyn Gigantes, because she inadvertently revealed confidential health information about an Ontario patient to the legislature. Potentially, Martel's argument with Dodds was a firing offence.

None of this came home, however, until the next day when Martel, by this time in Kenora, received an urgent message from her executive assistant, Mary Lou Murray. Dodds had made her conversation with the minister public; Martel was accused of using confidential medical information to lead a witch hunt against a doctor critical of her government.

The minister was visibly shaken by the news. "She was just ghostly," said press aide Kathleen O'Hara later. "I put her into bed, put a damp cloth on her head and wastebasket by her bed. She knew she had fucked up big time."

The next day O'Hara and Martel drove to Atikokan. Martel, lying in the back seat of the car, talked despondently of resigning. She bounced back sufficiently to attend a public event, after which they returned to Thunder Bay with Attorney General Howard Hampton. Among other things, Martel was worried whether Donahue would sue her for slander.

As O'Hara later recalled, throughout the drive the minister seemed determined to resign.

"I'd said don't panic," recalled O'Hara. "Howie tried to cheer her up. He said 'I'll be gone in a few months too.'—Bob [Rae] didn't like Howie. But Shelley wanted to resign. She said, 'I'm too burned out; I should resign; I've made too many mistakes.'"

On Sunday Martel returned to Toronto. By this time, the government had hired lawyer Julian Porter to advise Martel. Porter's advice, according to O'Hara, was that Martel should say she had "popped off" and stick to the story. The premier's office devised a press strategy to do just that.

From that flowed what became known as Martel's mantra. To all questions she said only that she had been tired the day of the Dodds argument and that any of her statements about Donahue had "no basis in fact and were unfounded." As a legal defence against a potential slander suit, the mantra was useful. Politically, however, it was disastrous. Almost immediately, the press interpreted Martel's statement to mean that she had told an untruth about Donahue—that is, she had lied. Asked if it were true she had lied, Martel would only repeat the mantra.

Martel's aides soon recognized the danger. "I told [David] Agnew that what she was saying was incredible," said O'Hara, "that she had to say something more. He said that if she says anything else, it might implicate someone else." What Agnew presumably meant was that the government had no intention of allowing this health scandal to touch Health minister Frances Lankin.

Within a week, the Martel affair had become a full-fledged political scandal and was being handled directly from the premier's office by assistant principal secretary Melody Morrison. The government had already seen two ministers, Zanana Akande and Evelyn Gigantes, forced to resign. Rae worried that another hasty resignation would make his cabinet look particularly incompetent.

Moreover, Martel was popular in the caucus and the party. And then there was her father, Elie. The former MPP and NDP firebrand had never particularly liked Rae. According to those familiar with the affair, Elie Martel warned whoever would listen that his daughter was not to be sacrificed.

Initially, however, Shelley Martel herself was still prepared to go. She set up a meeting with Rae to discuss her resignation. However, according to Rae's executive assistant, Lynn Spink, by this time the decision had already been made. "There was concern about the effect on the caucus. They were afraid to demoralize it further," said Spink.

The decision stiffened Martel's resolve. Within a few days of the Dodds *contretemps*, her closest advisers were telling her to resign to save her political skin. "But by that time she thought that would be a betrayal," said O'Hara. "Once she had decided not to resign, she couldn't be budged." Another aide put the responsibility for that decision, and Martel's subsequent political disgrace, on Rae and her father. "Elie and Bob talked her out of resigning. I think Bob destroyed Shelly. Her father and Bob destroyed her."

Meanwhile, Rae was having second thoughts. Some of his advisers were warning that the only way to shut off the escalating controversy was to have Martel quit. After a few months in the back-benches, when things had cooled down, she could be brought back into cabinet. At one point the premier was convinced and said he would drop Martel. But he changed his mind again.

The opposition parties were delighted. The NDP had always been so sanctimonious when the Liberals or Tories were in power. Now it was payback time. The two opposition parties demanded a full inquiry by a legislative committee, one which would give Liberal and Tory MPPs exceptionally broad powers. Unless the government agreed, the opposition parties said, they would force the legislature to sit over Christmas. But Rae was scheduled to go to Florida for the Christmas break. "Arlene [Perly Rae] was insistent," explained one aide. The government agreed to all opposition demands; Rae went to Florida.

On the eve of the hearings, Martel once again offered to resign. However, Rae and Morrison insisted that she soldier on. She should have ignored them. For Martel, the inquiry was a nightmare. Dominated by the opposition parties, it went on for two months, spent $400,000, and discovered almost nothing. Martel was cleared of revealing confidential health information. More important to the government, Health minister Lankin emerged unscathed.

Politically, however, Martel was destroyed. Rarely did she waver from her mantra. At one point she even agreed to privately undergo a lie detector test to prove that her remarks about Donahue were unfounded. That was bad enough. What was worse, fellow New Democrat MPP Peter Kormos, acting as a well-meaning champion of Martel's interests, decided to make the results of that test public.

On March 6, 1992, someone pulled the fire alarm at Queen's Park. The legislature's denizens, including reporters, were cleared from the building. By the time they returned, an anonymous hand had placed brown envelopes in reporters' mail slots, each containing results of the Martel polygraph test. By the next day, the story had ricocheted around the province: a minister in the NDP government had taken a lie-detector test to prove she had lied. What had begun as an issue about confidentiality ended as farce, one in which Martel and the Rae government seemed to be conspiring against themselves.

Before her unfortunate encounter with Evelyn Dodds, Martel had been one of the bright stars in Rae's cabinet, a popular minister often touted as a future NDP leader. By the end of March 1992, she was reviled even in her own party. Around Queen's Park the phrase "to Martel" was being being used as a synonym for fibbing. While Martel probably did not lie (at least not in the sense of deliberately setting out to mislead) all that the general public would remember was that she had—and that she had taken a lie detector test to prove it. Thanks to four months of political ineptness on the government's part, the NDP's reputation for integrity was seriously wounded. If Peter Donegan's focus groups could be believed, it remained that way two years later.

Integrity in government had been one of the mainstays of the NDP when they came to power in 1990. Part of this had to do with the party's analysis of its election win. The Liberals had lost, New Democrat strategists concluded, mainly because the voters no longer believed in David Peterson's integrity. For the NDP to win again, therefore, integrity had to be a hallmark of its time in office.

More than that, the New Democrats believed in their own virtue. Other governments might be corrupt, other ministries might be torn by scandal, but not an NDP government. Confident of this, the premier introduced, as one of his first acts, the toughest conflict-of-interest guidelines in the province's history, guidelines requiring ministers to divest themselves of absolutely all business interests.

Within a few months, he was forced to water these guidelines down. Even New Democrats, it seemed, owned assets such as rental condominiums, stores, and self-directed Registered Retirement Savings Plans. Adjustments to the toughest conflict-of-interest guidelines in provincial history were quietly made, as Rae put it, to prevent "hardships for many members."

Moral integrity was to be emphasized as well. Almost immediately after taking office, Rae kicked Toronto MPP Tony Rizzo out of the NDP caucus for running afoul of the Ontario Labour Relations Board a year earlier. In March 1991, Rae came face to face with Peter Kormos.

Kormos, an MPP from the working-class town of Welland, was already a controversial figure at Queen's Park. Popular in the NDP, he combined a demagogue's flair with an in-your-face attitude. Kormos had been put in cabinet by Rae to bring public auto insurance to the province. But Kormos couldn't resist shoving it to his fellow ministers, most of whom he would dismiss privately as sanctimonious yes-men captive to whichever trends of political correctness happened to be in fashion.

In particular, Kormos got on badly with some of the women in cabinet—Frances Lankin, Anne Swarbrick, and Evelyn Gigantes. Some female New Democrats found him abusive. Some, including Shelley Martel, initially found him charming. Around Queen's Park he cultivated his reputation as a wild man. Consequently, rumours abounded—Kormos in a bar; Kormos in a car; Kormos in all manner of exotic combinations. All of this came to a head in March 1991 when Kormos, as part of his ongoing guerrilla warfare against the rest of cabinet, posed as a *Toronto Sun* "Sunshine Boy."

The *Sun* is an unabashedly right-wing tabloid—anti-NDP, anti-feminist, anti-Rae. The fact that it was read by the very working-class people the NDP claimed to represent infuriated the Rae government. More than anything, New Democrats were irked by the tabloid's daily "Sunshine Girl" feature—a full-colour photo of a shapely and scantily clad woman. To answer critics who found the "Sunshine Girl" feature sexist, the *Sun* would—tongue-in-cheek—occasionally run photos of good-looking men. These it called its "Sunshine Boys."

As a beefcake shot, Kormos's "Sunshine Boy" photo was tame. It was in black and white; it was at the back of the paper; he had on all of his clothes. But he knew it would infuriate his cabinet colleagues, and he was right. They wanted Kormos's head.

Kormos was already in the midst of controversy over well-known past indiscretions. Rae was anxious to avoid more. After several days, on Sunday March 17, he decided to ask for Kormos's resignation from cabinet and called the minister in.

Rae did not enjoy face-to-face confrontations, and he was not looking forward to this meeting. As his car approached Queen's Park that Sunday, Rae spotted Kormos about to enter the building. "Drive around the block," he ordered. The driver complied. By the time the premier arrived at the east door of the legislative building, no one was in sight. The premier shot up to his office to prepare for his fifteen-minute meeting with Kormos.

Kormos refused to resign. The next day, Rae fired him.

Kormos remained popular in the NDP, particularly when, later that year, he openly opposed the cabinet's decision to scrap public auto insurance. The Welland MPP, his sidekick, Wentworth East MPP Mark Morrow, and maverick Anglican priest Dennis Drainville would form an unlikely ginger group within the NDP caucus—never organized or powerful enough to influence the government, but always there on the sidelines smirking, the burrs beneath Rae's saddle.

More important, Kormos's punishment seemed far out of proportion to his crime. He had not broken the premier's conflict-of-interest guidelines; not been revealed as incompetent; he had not even caused a public row. The opposition had not demanded his resignation. As the government wore on, Rae found himself defending ministers who were on far dicier ground—one whose staff had intervened in a traffic case (in apparent contravention of Rae's guidelines), another who appeared to be entirely ignorant of a sex-abuse scandal in his ministry. And of course there was Shelley Martel. Because Kormos had not really done anything wrong, his firing set a standard for ministerial behaviour that could never be met. More than any other so-called scandal, the Kormos incident revealed Rae's inconsistency.

For a while, Rae tried to avoid that inconsistency. In April 1991, Evelyn Gigantes quit cabinet after revealing privileged health information publicly. In June of the same year, Shelley Martel and Anne Swarbrick offered to resign after it was revealed they had intervened, contrary to the premier's guidelines, in a quasi-judicial proceeding. They were saved only by Liberal leader Bob Nixon, who advised Rae that the crime was too minor for such a punishment.

Soon, the government realized it did not have the luxury of firing every minister who got into a scrape. There were too many. In April 1991, Rae had defended Solicitor General Mike Farnan, whose aides had written to a justice of the peace over a traffic matter—apparently in violation of the premier's guidelines. (Rae would drop Farnan at the next cabinet shuffle.)

In October 1991, Community and Social Services minister Zanana Akande quit cabinet after being hauled before the province's rent-review board on charges of rent-gouging. In late 1991 came Martel.

Finally, in February 1992, Energy minister Will Ferguson resigned after allegations were made that he had, some nineteen years earlier, helped a sixteen-year-old prisoner named Judi Harris escape from a girls' reform school. At the time, former inmates were alleging that staff at the school (not Ferguson) had sexually abused girls in the 1970s.

Ferguson was eventually acquitted of all charges. But his troubles led into what, for Rae, turned out to be the most distressing of his government's scandals — the John Piper affair.

One of the most important people in any political leader's office is the person in charge of communications — sometimes referred to as the "spin doctor." Governments can do any amount of good work, but if the voters aren't aware, the effort is for naught. Some spin-doctoring is devious — propaganda and manipulation of information. But much is more straightforward: trying to present a clear and focused message free of jargon and gobbledegook, making sure that good news announcements are not lost in a welter of background noise. To many New Democrats, such as Janet Solberg, the Rae government had been fatally hampered by a failure to communicate the good things it had done.

In fact, the government's problems went far deeper than communications. The confusion of messages presented to the public probably accurately reflected the NDP's own confusion about what it should be doing. But Solberg's critique had some truth: When the government did do something right, it often neglected to tell anyone.

Rae's first communications aide had been Norm Simon, a long-time New Democrat. In mid-1991, however, Simon went back to Ontario Hydro. To replace him, Rae called on John Piper, a boisterous, boyish-looking man working with the lobbyist Hill and Knowlton.

Later Piper would be described as one of Rae's good friends. In fact, it was probably Piper's wife, Anita Shilton, who was the closer friend. Shilton had previously been married to D'Arcy Martin, Rae's old comrade from the Commission on University Government at the University of Toronto. When Rae had returned from Europe in 1974, dazed and depressed, he had stayed with Martin and Shilton.

Shilton and Rae remained friendly after she married Piper. Indeed, one friend of Piper and Shilton described them as "the truly political couple. They hung around with all the right people." By 1992, Shilton was a senior official at the Premier's Council on Health. Since late 1991, John Piper had been the premier's communications wizard.

Piper quickly impressed those around him. "He came along and told us how, by March 1992, we were going to have signs all over Ontario with electronic lights that said how many jobs are being created, going round and round," recalled Sue Colley, who until 1993 was Frances Lankin's chief of staff. "He was good at big ideas—big, bold image things," said another aide. "He wanted to address everything with an ad. I remember once he called a bunch of us in and said, 'Selling government is like selling boots. When you think of boots, you think of Brand A. We want it so that when people think of government, they think of the NDP.'"

In spite of Piper's energy, the government still seemed unable to convince the public it was in charge of events. "I really think John has a lot of vision," Colley said later. "He's exciting in terms of his conceptual thinking—one of those creative people that comes in and gets you going. . . . But he didn't get anyone else going, in my view. . . . Piper had his ideas but they never jelled."

As the government lurched from one crisis to another, Piper began to operate increasingly on his own. In late 1992, Will Ferguson approached Piper. The twenty-year-old reform-school incident was killing him politically. It was based on the word of Judi Harris, a woman who had been in and out of trouble with the law since she was a child. Ferguson even had a copy of Harris's criminal record. Maybe it could be passed on to a reporter sympathetic to his plight. He had already been interviewed by one reporter who seemed to understand the situation. Why not give Harris's criminal record to that reporter— *The Toronto Sun*'s Anne Dawson.

On November 17, 1992, Piper asked Dawson to come to his office. He had something for her, he said, holding out a piece of paper—Judi Harris's record. Dawson folded her arms and refused to accept the paper. Harris's criminal record had already been widely reported. But Piper had inadvertently presented her with a far better story: a top aide to the premier was trying to smear a woman who had raised serious allegations against an NDP minister.

Dawson spent a day checking the story. It ran in the *Sun* on Friday, November 20, as Rae was winging his way back from Japan.

Politically, the Piper story was a disaster. Not only had a top government official been involved in trying to discredit a citizen making an allegation against that government, but the citizen in question was a woman. And not just a woman, but one of a group of women who claimed they had been sexually abused as children by officials at a provincially run reform school.

Piper was immediately called in by the premier's office and told he would have to resign. Rae himself was notified when his plane touched down in Vancouver. By the time the premier reached Toronto, David Agnew was at the airport to greet him, and a strategy had been established. The strategy was simple: cut Piper loose.

Not only would Piper go but so would his wife, Rae's old friend Anita Shilton. Plans had already been under way to eliminate her job through a bureaucratic reorganization. Moreover, she was complaining publicly about the way the government was treating her husband. That, according to one aide, was her real sin.

By early 1993, both Piper and Shilton were out of work and — according to fellow New Democrats — unhappy about the way they had been treated. "Anita is extremely bitter about what happened," said Janet Solberg. "I don't know if that was deliberate with Bob. He's just bad about those things. Give him a personal problem, a personal scenario, and his reactions are usually wrong — kind of dumb, ungenerous or inflexible." Rae's old university chum Lenny Wise was equally glum about the Shilton experience. "Bob ain't got many friends left," he said.

Some who knew Piper's style of operation weren't surprised by what had happened. "He always played close to the edge," said one. "He just never got caught before." Piper himself, in an emotional press conference during which he broke down in tears, acknowledged that he had made a big mistake.

Others in government said the Piper affair had a more systemic cause, that it flowed from what one of Rae's aides called the "dysfunctional" nature of the premier's office: "It's no surprise to me that John got into trouble. Because it's such an isolating kind of place in that office. I mean, people just do things and never check.... It's like — and I don't mean this literally — but it felt like they were saying 'Bob pays you a lot of money; do your job; and don't come and bother the rest of us.'"

The Piper affair may have been felt most deeply by the premier; the Martel affair may have been the one the public recalled. But probably the most bizzare incident of the NDP government's time in office was the Peter North no-sex sex scandal.

North had been appointed to cabinet as Tourism minister in part because he was one of the few business people in the caucus. (Ironically, under Rae's stringent conflict-of-interest guidelines, North had to get rid of his small carpentry business when he joined the cabinet.) North was not considered one of the heavyweights of government. But then tourism was not high on the NDP's agenda.

All went along placidly until November 1992. *The Toronto Star* had run a story in which a woman alleged that North had offered her a job in exchange for sexual favours. Police investigated and found no substance to the allegation. But, by the time the police had turned in their report, a second woman had hand-delivered a letter to both the premier's office and the *Star*. In this letter, Michele McLean, a former waiter at Toronto's Loose Moose Tap & Grill, alleged that North had offered her, too, a job in exchange for sex. McLean had broken off the affair, she wrote, only because North had been making "unreasonable sexual demands."

With Rae in Japan, the premier's office panicked. North was told to quit cabinet while police investigated this second charge. Again, they found no evidence of wrongdoing. As more came out, however, the North affair began to appear more satiric than satyric. McLean said that she and the Tourism minister had never actually had sex—just lay in bed, fully clothed, petting. His "unreasonable sexual demands," she said, referred to his unwillingness to use a condom during these encounters. "I had an affair with Peter North," McLean told the press. "I didn't say I had a sexual affair. People automatically assume 'affair' and 'sex' go hand-in-hand."

The denouement came several months later. North, who had not been invited to rejoin the cabinet after he was cleared by police, decided he'd had enough of being a New Democrat. On August 26, 1993, he held a press conference to announce he was quitting the NDP to join the Tories. Unfortunately, he had forgotten to check with the Conservatives first. Tory leader Mike Harris regretfully announced there was no room in his caucus for the former New Democrat. North had to sit as an independent.

Peter North had been the first Ontario cabinet minister forced to resign for alleged involvement in a sex scandal in which no one had sex. By the end of 1993, he had become the first government MPP to cross the floor only to find no other party wanted him. It seemed a fitting end to three and half years of goof-ups.

13

Mo of the Jungle: On and Off the Privatization Bandwagon

SEPTEMBER 1992: ANOTHER CRISIS SEEMED IN THE MAKING
for the NDP government—this time over Ontario Hydro. Since its creation in 1906 by the legendary Adam Beck, the provincially owned utility had been one of the pillars of strength in Ontario. Although nominally under government control, Hydro had operated almost as a law unto itself, a fiefdom. It was, after all, the largest public utility in North America and one of the largest companies in the world.

From Beck on, Hydro's powerful chieftains had tended to regard their political masters politely, but with a touch of world-weary disdain. Politicians, after all, were merely transitory. Governments might come and go. Hydro remained. It had its rituals, its own peculiar perks of office. Every Christmas, for instance, it had been the custom of the Hydro board of directors to gather solemnly for a small celebration. A glass of sherry perhaps, and a nibble of chocolate. The chocolates were Hydro's own, made especially for the utility, each embossed with the utility's corporate emblem.

By late 1992, however, Hydro was in serious straits. The recession had slashed the demand for power. At the same time, the massive Darlington nuclear station east of Toronto had finally come on line, increasing the utility's generating capacity. Darlington, begun by the former Conservative government in 1981, had been a disaster—fraught with delays and cost-overruns. When it finally came on-stream ten years later, its cost was $14 billion, more than twice the original estimate.

Hydro had borrowed heavily to pay for Darlington, Pickering, and the province's other nuclear plants. By 1992, it found itself with a massive $36-billion debt.

The utility's response had been to jack up rates. By 1992, rates were 30 per cent higher than they had been two years earlier when the NDP had come to power. Senior citizens were flooding Energy minister Brian Charlton's office with calls, saying they could no longer afford to pay their electricity bills. The province's manufacturers, led by the powerful Association of Major Power Consumers in Ontario—a lobby for the major resource companies—were in an uproar. Rising power costs meant they were losing any competitive edge they had ever possessed. That meant, they warned the government, more job losses.

To make matters worse, Hydro chairman Marc Eliesen—Rae's personal appointment—had just quit in a huff. He had announced in August 1992 that he was heading off to British Columbia. The government needed a replacement who could keep the confidence of business and sort out the mess at Hydro without alarming the vocal environmental lobby. But who?

Rae turned to Stephen Lewis for advice. Rae and Lewis had never been fast friends and, within a few months, they would fall out over the premier's social contract. However, in the fall of 1992, they were still close enough that Rae could look to his predecessor for help.

Lewis did have a suggestion. As Canada's former ambassador to the United Nations, Lewis had worked with just the kind of person he thought Hydro needed—a fixer with impeccable business, government, and environmental credentials who had a reputation for getting things done. The two, the former ambassador and the globe-trotting fixer, had become friends, occasionally dining at each other's homes. The fixer's name was Maurice Strong. When Lewis suggested Rae hire Strong to run Ontario Hydro, the premier thought it a capital idea.

If Maurice Strong were American, someone would have made a movie about him. His background was almost too romantic. Born to a working-class family in Oak Lake, Manitoba, during the Depression of the 1930s, he quit school at age fourteen and literally ran away to sea, working freighters in the Pacific and into Hudson's Bay until, at the age of seventeen, he discovered the world of business. By age thirty, Strong had his own company; by thirty-five, he was running one of Canada's largest conglomerates; by forty-three, *The New Yorker* magazine was lauding him as the man upon whom "the survival of civilization in something like its present form might depend."

What defined Strong's style was the elaborate network of friends, partners, and acquaintances he created—a network that wound through the business, political, and intelligence communities of three continents. In particular, Strong's life was interwoven with New York banking, U.S. oil interests, Canadian big business, and the Liberal party. As journalist Elaine Dewar points out in an intriguing *Saturday Night* magazine feature piece on Strong, the same names kept appearing in his life: the Texas Company, the Rockefellers, the Loebs, the Bronfmans, Power Corp., and the Paul Martins—both senior and junior. In Ottawa, one of the influential Liberal mandarins Strong kept up with was Saul Rae, Bob's father.

Physically, Strong was unprepossessing, a slightly paunchy, balding sixty-three-year-old with a squeaky voice and a toothbrush moustache. His public manner was modest but reassuring—like that of a small-town prairie bank manager. Indeed, Strong was reminiscent of George Smiley, the self-effacing master spy of John le Carré's novels, described by his creator as being both eminently forgettable and slightly out-of-date.

Like Smiley, Strong had the knack of always turning up at the right moment. When the Cold War started, the RCMP used the mineral exploration office in which Strong worked to spy on suspected Communists in the Canada–U.S.S.R. Friendship Association next door (the Friendship Association's wartime treasurer would later become one of Strong's business partners). "I wasn't a spy," Strong told journalist Dewar later. "I was too young."

A few years later, as anti-colonial movements heated up in Africa and the Middle East, Strong was there too, working for U.S. oil interests embroiled in the region's politics. By the early 1960s, Strong was running Power Corp., an influential Montreal-based conglomerate with close ties to the ruling Liberal party. One of the bright young men he hired was Paul Martin Jr., the future federal Finance minister.

In 1968, at the behest of the Liberals, Strong created the Canadian International Development Agency—a federal government-aid organization designed, in part, to persuade the new, poor countries of francophone Africa not to support Quebec independence. A year later, he was asked to head the United Nation's first international conference on the environment in Stockholm.

By the 1970s, Strong had been picked by Prime Minister Pierre Trudeau to head Petro-Canada, the new state-owned oil company which the NDP of David Lewis (Stephen's father) had demanded as their price for keeping the minority Liberals in power. In November 1976, as Mao Tse-tung's widow and the rest of the so-called Gang of Four were about to be arrested in Beijing, a company linked to Strong was flying antiquities, gold, furniture, and jewellery out of China.

By the early 1980s, Strong was back in Ottawa heading up the Liberal government's newest idea for state-sponsored industrial growth, the Canada Development Investment Corp. By the mid-1980s, he was working for the United Nations in concert with Stephen Lewis, sorting out the complex politics of Africa and the Middle East so as to get aid to starving Ethiopians. Meanwhile, he was involving himself in an American real estate firm known as AZL Resources Inc., which itself was connected to Saudi Arabian arms dealer and Middle East political wheeler-dealer Adnan Kashoggi.

Strong and his second wife, Hanne, were also in the forefront of the New Age movement. Their money helped survivalists build a new verison of Noah's Ark, in preparation for the second deluge. Strong's AZL sold land in Colorado's San Luis Valley to fellow New Age enthusiasts such as Shirley MacLaine. Many of these New Agers later turned against Maurice and Hanne when another Strong-related company proposed to pump out the water that sustained this valley and pipe it to Denver.

By 1992, the environment was the issue. The head of the gala U.N. Earth Summit in Rio de Janeiro that year—a summit which garnered acres of media publicity but accomplished little else—was Maurice Strong.

To Rae, Strong represented the dedicated and skilful public servants of Pearsonian Liberalism—of Saul Rae's time. Indeed, as a child, young Bobby Rae had been virtually dandled on Maurice Strong's knee. As the premier pointed out proudly, Strong had often been a visitor at Saul Rae's during that period.

Rae was adamant that Strong was to be hired. This caused some trouble for Energy minister Brian Charlton, who had already engaged a head-hunting firm at a cost of $100,000 to find a new Hydro head. But the sham was allowed to come to a conclusion. On October 29, 1992, Rae announced Strong was his choice as chairman of Ontario Hydro.

As Elaine Dewar has pointed out, Strong's signature throughout his business life had been the "mingling of public and private in the cause of public policy." The new chairman brought that characteristic approach to Hydro. Within weeks of being appointed, he was musing publicly about privatizing parts of the giant utility. Charlton was not amused; the day Strong's remarks were published, Charlton denied that privatization was under consideration by the government. The seed had been planted.

249
*Mo of the
Jungle: On
and Off the
Privatization
Bandwagon*

More than any other single institution, Ontario Hydro embodied the contradictory Red Tory political culture of Ontario—a socialized industry created by a Conservative government. Since its formation in 1906, at the behest of manufacturers anxious to break the power of the private electricity companies, the utility had received the whole-hearted support of the province's business class. They found its mandate—to provide power at cost—a glorious slogan.

By the time Strong took over, Hydro was the largest publicly owned utility in North America. While opposition politicians (and even government ministers) had always grumbled at Hydro's regal ways, no one in a position of authority had ever seriously contemplated dismantling it. Hydro was the province's flagship.

The Tories had long used it as a kind of industrial development corporation. Hydro had kept the entire Ontario-based Canadian nuclear industry alive. Hydro nuclear and heavy-water plants kept workers employed in regions of the province that would have otherwise withered. Inflated Hydro contracts subsidized the uranium mines of Elliot Lake, keeping both owners and workers happy.

The Liberals, during David Peterson's short reign, had been advised to use Hydro as an industrial-development engine to encourage high-technology firms. At first, the NDP government was no different.

Rae appointed Marc Eliesen, one of his most influential bureaucrats, to the position of Hydro chair in 1991 in order to bring the utility under firm political control. The Hydro board of directors was stacked with environmentalists and New Democrats to act as a counterweight to old Tory and Liberal appointments. Eliesen, former research director for the federal NDP and former chair of the board of directors of Manitoba Hydro under Howard Pawley, was ordered to bring the utility to heel.

To that end, Hydro under Eliesen helped to bail out both Elliot Lake and the northern pulp town of Kapuskasing. Hydro involved itself in the government's Native agenda by scaling back hydro-electric projects in the North. It supported the government's environmental agenda through a vigorous campaign to encourage energy conservation. It became more amenable to buying power from small-scale private generators, the latest darlings of the environmental movement.

The relationship between Eliesen and Rae soon soured. Among senior bureaucrats, Eliesen was seen as greedy. Among political aides, he gained the reputation of being imperious. At one point, for instance, he telephoned Energy minister Brian Charlton to berate him for the way he had answered a Hydro question in the legislature. "Marc was not an easy person to deal with," Charlton would acknowledge later. "But I didn't have as many problems as, I think, my predecessor did or as, I think, the premier did."

For his part, according to friends, Eliesen was increasingly angered by what he saw as the government's refusal to stand by him. In the legislature, Eliesen's $400,000 salary became an issue as opposition politicians accused Rae of rewarding political cronies. The fact that Eliesen, a New Democrat, had been brought into the Ontario civil service by the Liberals seemed not to matter. Nor did the fact that Eliesen's predecessor had been paid an even higher salary, $540,000. Indeed, when Rae was asked about Eliesen's salary, he noted pointedly that it was more than he made as premier. Eventually, Eliesen offered to have his salary cut to $260,000. To the Hydro chairman's annoyance, Rae accepted.

There were disputes on other levels too. Eliesen argued that the government had become overly obsessed with its deficit. Rae, on the other hand, increasingly worried about Hydro's finances, was said to be demanding staff cuts at the utility. The Hydro chairman later told friends that Rae had called for "blood on the floor."

Money seemed to be front and centre—money and pride. The opposition barrage continued as Liberal MPPs attacked Eliesen's pension arrangements and perks. After one such foray against Hydro's bonusing practices, in which Eliesen felt the government had left him dangling, the chairman quietly made other plans. In August 1992, he announced he was quitting to become head of B.C. Hydro.

Eliesen's successor, Maurice Strong, was equally, if not more, imperious. In taking the Hydro job, he was required to put himself at arm's length from business affairs that might create a conflict-of-interest. But Strong was a man of many interests. According to Charlton, he had taken the Hydro job on the condition that he be permitted to continue jetting around the world to minister to those he continued to hold. The Hydro chair's peripatetic habits, Charlton said, were never a problem for him as Energy minister.

251
*Mo of the
Jungle: On
and Off the
Privatization
Bandwagon*

However, neither Charlton nor Bud Wildman (who replaced Charlton as Energy minister in early 1993) was ever quite sure what Strong was doing. Energy ministry staff were convinced that Strong was operating on his own, rather than the government's, agenda. No one was sure what this agenda was. The Hydro chair travelled the world at will. Not even the premier was sure where to find him.

One anecdote is telling. In May 1994, Wildman was annoyed and embarrassed to find that, without notifying the government, Strong had begun negotiations to purchase a 12,500 hectare rain forest in Costa Rica. Opposition MPPs pointed out that Strong had investments in Costa Rica and questioned why a crown corporation that was $36 billion in debt needed a rain forest. The newspapers had a field day with, as one *Toronto Star* headline writer called him, "Mo of the Jungle."

Strong, however, was unrepentant. Jungle acquisition was an idea worth looking into, he insisted, one in line with the most modern principles of sustainable development. After all, trees in Central America could absorb the carbon dioxide that Hydro and other world polluters produced. Critics, he said, were focusing "primarily on the petty, the peripheral, and the parochial." Ministers such as Frances Lankin who were dubious about the jungle scheme were speaking "impulsively." Soon, some of Strong's powerful friends in business and politics were telephoning opposition MPPs such as Liberal Sean Conway, advising them to lay off. The story quickly died.

In terms of the NDP government, Strong did possess something Eliesen never enjoyed—Rae's unqualified support. When Strong announced he would lay off 4,500 Hydro workers, the premier praised him for being "courageous." While Rae had never been comfortable with the idea of Eliesen making $400,000 a year, he saw nothing wrong with Strong's $425,000 a year salary. Indeed, when reporters questioned the sum, the premier seemed personally offended that anyone could question the worth of such a man.

When, soon after being appointed, Strong started talking about privatizing Hydro, Rae didn't think it necessarily such a bad idea. At one level, this might have seemed odd. For, in opposition, Rae had presented himself as a fierce opponent of privatization. Speaking to a 1986 conference in Washington, the NDP leader had slammed then premier David Peterson for selling off one of the province's more minor Crown corporations. Privatization, Rae said, was "a symptom of a diseased economic order ... a casino economy" in which governments sell off "the family silver ... while the company itself is often left to decay or shut down in a process euphemistically called rationalization." Privatization, he went on, was a fundamental element of what he called neoliberalism.

"Proponents of neo-liberalism are attracted to right-wing economic ideas but disapprove of its [the right's] social ideas," Rae told his audience. "How many times have you heard the common refrain 'I'm a conservative on economic issues but progressive on social issues.' This idea, that you can separate economic and social life is bizarre in itself, but again it would be naïve for anyone to underestimate the potential popularity and danger of this approach. ...

"We will lose if we give all the economic arguments to the right by climbing on the privatization band-wagon."

Before entering NDP politics, however, Rae had been far more ambivalent about public ownership. In his Oxford thesis, for instance, Rae criticized those who saw all state intervention as socialist. "This is mistaken," he wrote, "because it blurs important distinctions about *why* the state has decided to interfere, what kind of policy it is imposing, and in whose general interest this intervention is being carried out." Public ownership, he went on, "is often simply a means for the propertied classes to use the state as an ally in the exploitation of wealth."

In short, with public enterprise, as with almost everything else, there were two Bob Raes. One Bob Rae took a case-by-case approach to the issue: How would public ownership work in a specific situation? Whom would it benefit? Whom would it hurt? The other, the New Democratic Bob Rae, took a more global approach, seeing public ownership as a concept worth preserving, one of the few remaining manifestations of a set of social values and ideas that were under constant attack from the right.

In opposition, it was the New Democratic Bob Rae who dominated. In government, the more basic Bob Rae had re-emerged. When Maurice Strong began to make practical arguments about why it might be a good idea to sell off parts of the province's oldest Crown enterprise, the more basic Bob Rae listened intently.

Even before Strong's appointment, the NDP government had already made its first tentative moves towards privatizing public enterprise. In this case, it was highways. The government wanted to build new highways. But it didn't want to spend any of its own money. Other Ontario

governments had flirted with the idea of toll roads but had pulled back *253*
Mo of the
Jungle: On
and Off the
Privatization
Bandwagon for fear of public opposition. The NDP government, however, decided to go one step farther: it would privatize new highways.

As explained by Transportation ministry officials, the plan would work this way: Queen's Park would find a private-sector consortium (a "partner," in NDP government lingo) willing to put up the capital needed to build a highway. In return for building and operating the highway, the consortium would be allowed to charge tolls. The arrangement would last for a period of thirty years. By that time, it was assumed, the road would require rebuilding, and the government could start all over again.

In February 1993, the government announced it would enter into agreements with companies to finance and build an expressway north of Toronto. As a way to get around the political problem of large deficits, the scheme seemed ingenious. New highways would be built, but none of the billions of dollars borrowed to build them would appear, officially at least, on the government's books. As a piece of economic policy, however, the scheme had serious problems.

First, the government would, in practical terms, always be liable for the money borrowed. Any loan default by the private-sector partners could put some of the province's major transportation routes at risk. No government would be able to allow that. Keeping the capital costs of new roads officially off the government's books might fool the general public, but it wouldn't fool the people who count in so far as deficits are concerned—the creditors and bond-rating agencies. They would soon come to recognize that monies borrowed by private contractors to build Ontario highways were, to all intents and purposes, contingent liabilities of the province.

Second, no matter who officially borrowed the money to build the new highways, the same people would ultimately pay—the users. These users (including consumers who bought products transported along the new highways) would have to pay more than if the highways were publicly operated. Tolls paid to a public authority have to cover the cost of building and maintaining a road. Tolls paid to a private consortium must cover not just these costs but the operator's profit, a not-inconsiderable sum.

Through its private-highway scheme, the NDP government had threatened higher costs for drivers and consumers—without actually addressing the fiscal problem of debts and deficits it had set out to solve.

By April 1994, the government had realized the obvious downsides involved in privatizing highways and quietly backed off. But the flurry of interest in privatization that the highway scheme represented had already taken hold. It was first blood. If the NDP could privatize highways, why not something else? Why not Hydro?

Those who favoured privatizing Hydro never contemplated selling off the entire utility. As Energy minister Bud Wildman later commented, no one would have wanted it. For Hydro was saddled with expensive but under-utilized nuclear generating plants that were responsible for the bulk of its $36-billion debt. Rather, privatization enthusiasts favoured splitting Hydro into three parts. The nuclear plants, plus the bulk of the Hydro debt, would be kept by the government. The transmission grid, the wires and transformers, would remain a public monopoly. But the non-nuclear generating plants would be sold. The publicly owned transmission grid would then buy power from anyone willing to supply it.

By early 1993, with Strong still musing about privatizing parts of Hydro, Energy minister Brian Charlton had become less categorical in his denials. "We're looking at everything and anything," Charlton told *The Toronto Star*. "If you don't consider every option, you are subject to criticism."

Inside government, the crisis in Hydro had become a major issue. At the centre was fear of what would come to be called the "debt spiral." It went something like this: as Hydro raised rates to cover its debt, industries and consumers would cut back energy consumption even more. Indeed, some industries and cities were already warning that they would produce their own power, using natural gas, rather than buy electricity from Hydro. If demand fell, Hydro would be even more hard-pressed to pay its debt and have to raise rates even more—and the spiral would continue.

Two camps had formed around the debt-spiral issue. Michael Decter, then deputy Health minister, would later refer to them as the "bail-it-out camp" and the "cut-it-loose camp." The former—including deputy cabinet secretary Michael Mendelson, Treasury Board secretary Jay Kaufman, and deputy minister of Energy George Davies, wanted to keep Hydro as a government monopoly and have the province take over the bulk of the utility's $36-billion debt. Since the province already guaranteed Hydro's borrowing, they argued, what would be the difference? Socializing Hydro's debt and cutting off the limited competition from independent power generators, this camp said, would give the public enterprise a chance.

On the other side were Decter and deputy minister of Finance Eleanor Clitheroe (she would later move to a senior position at Hydro). The cut-it-loose camp argued that Hydro's monopoly should be abolished, more competition permitted, and shares in the utility sold— perhaps to municipal utilities, perhaps elsewhere.

The fiscal conservatives in this camp were also joined by some environmental conservatives outside government, particularly those associated with an anti-nuclear group called Energy Probe. For environmentalists had long argued that small-scale generating plants—the so-called non-utility generators (NUGs)—were far less disruptive than the traditional nuclear behemoths of Hydro. If Hydro were broken up and its monopoly on generation truly broken, Energy Probe argued, private NUGs could have a real chance.

The debt-wall scare that swept the NDP cabinet in early 1993 put an end to any notion of the province helping out Hydro. Decter warned the premier that bailing out Hydro would mean "in the extreme way I put things in these kinds of debates, that that was the end of medicare. The way I put it to the premier was: If there's only room in the lifeboat for either medicare or Hydro, I know which one I'm for.... There's certainly no particular logic to the government continuing to own a Hydro utility in an increasingly competitive energy world."

Meanwhile, at the utility, Strong carried on with his characteristic management style. His usual method in other ventures had been to rearrange the business into an array of interlocking companies and then bring trusted associates on board to run them. Strong himself would then continue his peripatetic existence—jetting back and forth to his headquarters in Geneva, his ranch in Colorado, and to other interests around the world, returning from time to time to make major decisions.

At the height of the 1993 social-contract talks, for instance, the government's chief negotiator, Michael Decter, needed urgently to talk to the Hydro chairman. Strong was nowhere to be found; he was, Decter was told, incommunicado somewhere in Europe. In frustration, Decter finally turned to Rae. Did the premier have any advice on how to get hold of his Hydro chairman? Rae's wry response was not that helpful. "My advice, Mike," he told Decter, "is to go to the nearest hub airport and wait. He'll probably be through."

In March 1993, Strong announced he was laying off 4,500 employees. Within a year, Strong would have laid off 2,000 more workers. By April, Hydro had reorganized itself into three distinct operating units. Analysts inside and outside the utility saw the move as a prelude to privatization.

By the fall of 1993, Rae himself seemed to be hinting at privatization. In a speech to a conference on technology, he lauded Strong as a modern-day Adam Beck, the man who had brought public power to Ontario in 1906. Public ownership may have been appropriate for Hydro then, Rae said, but in changed times, Hydro must change — and Strong was the man to make such change happen. In a newspaper interview, Rae signalled that his government would not be bound by NDP public-ownership policies in its dealings with Hydro. Instead, the premier said, he would approach Hydro reform in a "non-ideological way."

However, according to Michael Decter, the premier seemed reluctant to privatize any part of Hydro before the next provincial election. Politically, Rae knew he would run into serious trouble — from the public sector unions and from his own party. "I don't think Bob came to any conclusion," recalled Wildman later.

Elsewhere in cabinet, opposition to privatizing Hydro was hardening. Both Energy minister Bud Wildman and Finance minister Floyd Laughren were opposed to the idea. In Wildman's Energy ministry, officials and aides began to plot ways to derail Maurice Strong.

At the same time, the pressures for immediate privatization were lessening. Strong's Draconian staff-cutting measures had worked. They had alleviated the cost pressure on Hydro. A 20 per cent hike in the price of natural gas had soured the appetite of municipalities and large firms to produce their own, gas-fired, electrical power. So the danger from that side had retreated too.

In early 1994, Wildman informed Hydro there was no appetite in cabinet for privatizing Hydro. "At no point was there a serious consideration to privatize it," he would say later. In February, Rae himself made his strongest public statement to date on the issue. "I do not think that a wholesale or fire sale of assets of this magnificent public institution is in the public interest," the premier told a conference of business people. "I don't think it makes sense." Just what the premier meant by "fire sale," however, he refused to say.

Later, Charlton would argue that privatization — in the sense of selling major Hydro assets to private operators — had never been seriously contemplated. He acknowledged that the government was thinking of permitting more "partnerships" with private industry in the generation of electricty. "We were not interested in privatizing the basic capacity. We had no problem in considering a more flexible approach. . . . We had to find some of that flexibility through partnership."

To others in government though, it had been a near miss. Strong himself, according to aides, had come eventually to realize the near political impossibility of an NDP government privatizing Hydro during its last year of office. Nonetheless, the stage had been set. Privatization of Ontario Hydro had been put on the political agenda. The once unthinkable had been thought. An NDP government had come close to buying the idea. Indeed, as one government figure opposed to privatizing Hydro put it: "Who knows? We still might do it."

More important though, Strong had laid the foundation. Whichever party won the next election would inherit a utility in which the groundwork for privatization had already been done.

14

That Was Then;
This Is Now

IN EARLY 1994, NELSON RIIS, ONE OF THE FEW REMAINING
federal New Democrat MPs still sitting in Ottawa, suggested that his
party consider changing its name. Unpopular provincial New Democratic governments, he said, had tarnished the federal NDP's reputation
with voters. A new name might solve the problem.

As a strategy for political renewal, Riis's idea was roughly equivalent
to suggesting that federal New Democrats wear false noses. Nonetheless, it did reveal the depth of the identity crisis within the NDP. In the
past, New Democrats may not have won many elections. However, they
always knew who they were.

Bob Rae's government had shaken that self-image. New Democrats
had always seen themselves as different from members of other political parties—more committed, more principled, more virtuous. But, in
Ontario, they saw a government willing to jettison party policies, seemingly with abandon. They saw a government that stepped on labour,
catered to business, contemplated slashing welfare for the poor, and
toyed with imposing health user fees on the old. They saw a government
that acted and sounded much like a Conservative or Liberal regime—
that insisted on the primacy of the private sector, that put deficit reduction ahead of job creation. They saw a government unwilling to stand up
to the élites—one that made cozy deals with doctors while scaling back
the wages of nurses, one willing to cut back services paid for by
medicare even as it was making secret concessions to multinational

drug companies that would ensure their continued high profits. They saw a government that had come to power promising to stop the mad practice of filling prime land with garbage and that ended up approving the largest dump site in North America. And on, and on.

"Let's not kid ourselves," Rae told Ontario New Democrats six months after taking office. "This is a different kind of event. We've become a different kind of party."

Indeed, it had. And for many New Democrats, the change was traumatic. Shortly after the débâcle of the 1993 federal election, Janet Solberg, one of the most prominent figures in the Ontario party, candidly expressed her frustrations. Rae's government, she said, had done many good things—fulfilled many of its election promises. But the major reversals, such as the retreat from public auto insurance or the imposition of the social contract, left party activists feeling fundamentally betrayed. What was more important, she said, was that this sense of betrayal was felt not just by a few party militants but by voters who in the past had voted NDP.

"There's a whole group of people out there who also feel betrayed by this government," she said. "It's not just because of the flip-flops. You go out canvassing and you hear it.... It's because they're just like any other government ... because Bob Rae talks like all the others.... His style as a socialist premier has let people down the most. And not just the activists. I think you can't get elected [by saying] that you're going to be different and come out talking the same. And what I mean by talking the same is: deficit, deficit, deficit. Cut-backs. Control expenditures.... I mean this is the discourse of the neo-conservative landscape. Why adopt it? To me it's hidden so much of the good things we've done."

Another influential New Democrat, a charter member of the party establishment, was far more bitter. He didn't want to openly attack Rae, he said, for fear of escalating the divisive debate inside the NDP, a debate that would ultimately be futile because, until the next Ontario election at least, "Bob is firmly in control." But a party that embraced the ideas of Bob Rae, he said, was a party that had no place for him.

"It's as if everything I've ever fought for was under siege. If Bob Rae wins the next provincial election, he has the right to dictate a new direction of social democracy to the federal party. He'll be able to say, 'I was right and I'm making over the party in the image that I think works.' People like me will be sidelined if Bob wins."

To government stalwarts, however, such remarks were naïve and misplaced. There was no point in comparing the government's action with its opposition promises, because government and opposition were two entirely different worlds. The term which, for opposition and government MPPs alike, had become the slogan of the NDP government said it all: "That was then; this is now."

Ironically, it was Rae himself who had made the most elegant critique of that-was-then-this-is-now politics. During a televised leaders' debate in the 1990 election campaign, Rae had been asked about the growing credibility problem faced by politicians. "I think it comes from politicians who say one thing when they're running for office and another thing when they hold office," he answered. Then, facing the camera, he outlined a credibility test voters should apply to any politician: "What are people's records? What have they said in the past? Whose interests are they defending? Is this something they've said before, or is it just something they're saying now?"

Using those criteria, the Bob Rae of opposition would have damned the Bob Rae of government. To the premier's defenders, however, all that this meant was that Rae himself had been captive of what, by 1994, was being dismissed as the "opposition mentality." They argued that a party in power does not have the luxury of consistency, that things change.

Indeed, to many in the Rae government, the experience of power demonstrated just how bankrupt the party had been in opposition— how misguided, naïve, and just plain wrong. As Rae aide Ross McClellan put it: "We're not going back to the NDP of the period 1930 to 1990." It was both a shrewd observation and a promise.

Shortly after the government backtracked on public auto insurance, a senior aide to the premier tried to explain that the NDP was transforming itself as a necessary reaction to events in the real world. Yes, we're breaking our promises, he said. But in these circumstances so would any NDP government. "Do you really think that if Audrey McLaughlin in Ottawa won, she'd scrap the free-trade agreement? Of course, she wouldn't."

To some, experience in government permitted the NDP to break away from a blind reliance on party dogma. That was what Frances Lankin seemed to be suggesting as she tried to explain her own transformation.

"As a party activist ... there were a number of parts of party policy that I would absorb and then state as fact and analysis, which didn't necessarily stem from any ... deep understanding of the issue," she said. "That's not true of all issues.... I feel this experience has at least made me more disciplined ... [caused me] to ask a lot more questions and understand a lot more.... I don't want to leave the impression . . . that I've seen the light and others are misguided. It's not that. It's an experience in which . . . I insist on more information . . . than I did in the past."

For Ruth Grier, such a movement away from traditional NDP positions was only natural. "Those that have known their true values and principles and have moved as the times changed . . . have developed and survived," she said. "Those that have said, 'This is where we started from in the 1930s; nothing changes,' haven't."

New Democrats uneasy about what the government was doing, usually had one of four explanations: inexperience, the recession, Rae himself, or the centralized structure of the party. Each had some truth to it. The government was raw. Of seventy-four MPPs elected in 1990, fully four-fifths were newcomers to the legislature. Even the twenty-six-member cabinet contained twelve neophytes.

"This is the first time the province had a government of real people," said party president Julie Davis. "They're not doctors and lawyers and high-priced executives, but they're real people. And so they've made mistakes, like real people will.... No one has made any gains for themselves out of some of the silly things that have gone on in the last three years [such as] Shelley Martel's major *faux pas* ... [but] there's not been any kind of forgiveness, either inside the party or from the public and media."

By far the most popular explanation within government for its actions, however, was the recession. To those on the left, the experience only confirmed their suspicion that, faced with the immense power of late-twentieth-century capitalism, governments had become largely irrelevant. As Housing minister Evelyn Gigantes put it: "You can't take on international capitalism in Ontario." For Finance minister Floyd Laughren, the government's increasingly conservative economic policy was not something it had set out to do. Rather it was something it had to do. "There's no choice," he said. "I really believe that. You can make the argument that we should have challenged the financial community and challenged our borrowing capacity and all that kind of stuff ... but I really think that [we could not have]."

To those more to the right inside government, the challenge of the recession also forced the NDP to become realistic. Michael Decter called it making the "hard choices." And by 1993, the spin artists of government were trying to turn necessity into political virtue. The cutbacks, the tax increases, the harsh measures taken against traditional

NDP constituencies would show that the party was finally able to "manage the economy," to "run the store," and make "tough decisions." As a political strategy, this had not worked for the federal Conservatives in 1993. But maybe it would work for the Ontario NDP.

The recession, and the consequent plunge in government tax revenues could not, however, be held entirely responsible for the government's actions. The decision, after the abortive 1991 budget, to keep the province's annual deficit below $10 billion was based more on politics than on economics. Even after four years of the most punishing slump to hit the Ontario economy since the 1930s, the province's debt-servicing charges were still, relatively speaking, far below those of almost every other government in Canada. The fact that the government chose to hold the line at $10 billion rather than $8 billion or $12 billion stemmed more from a desire to prove its fiscal mettle politically than from the real constraints of the international capital market.

Similarly, actions which flowed from the government's fiscal stance were not the result of some form of economic predestination. During the social-contract talks, for instance, Rae would say the government had only two choices: lop off 40,000 jobs or roll back civil-service wages.

That wasn't quite true. In fact, the government had other choices. It could have, for instance, started social-contract negotiations a year earlier as the province's largest union had suggested, and thereby increased the likelihood of a negotiated deal acceptable to all parties. But it didn't. It didn't, in large part, because it did not wish to alienate the province's powerful hospitals.

As well, the government could have negotiated a social-contract deal that did not override existing union contracts. The labour movement pressed for that strenuously, as did the government's own social-contract negotiators. But the government chose not to do that—in part, because it had already inflamed public opinion with dire, and false, warnings that the province was about to hit a debt wall; in part, because it was politically more convenient to cater to the voters' general animosity towards public-sector workers; in part, out of pique at being criticized by the unions.

Nor did the recession, and the province's incessant search for cash, explain other actions. Why, if the province was in such need of revenues, did Rae invariably champion multinational brand-name drug companies against the cheaper generics firms? Whenever the province did side with the multinationals, it raised the costs of its own Ontario

Drug Benefit Program. When costs for this program rose, Rae's response was to press for so-called co-payments by its users—the poor and old.

In effect, Rae's drug policy ended up benefiting the brand-name pharmaceutical companies at the expense of consumers. The premier's aides justified this approach by saying that the government wanted to attract investment and jobs. But, in the case of drugs, Rae always seemed to prefer multinational investment and jobs to those provided by the Canadian-owned generics firms. Why?

This in turn leads to the third explanation for the Ontario NDP government—that all of its actions were the result of Bob Rae. In this view, Rae is portrayed as some kind of Svengali, able to hypnotize otherwise sensible cabinet ministers and bend them to his will. Not everyone bought the idea. "I really refuse to put it all at Bob's feet," said Janet Solberg. "I think that's so unfair."

Indeed, the blame-Bob theory did allow other ministers too easy an out. The government's hard-line fiscal policy was more the creation of Floyd Laughren than of Bob Rae. Frances Lankin, the former union activist, may have tried to ameliorate the effect of the social contract, but, ultimately, she agreed with the need for it, as did veteran unionist Bob Mackenzie.

In fact, the only cabinet resignation over a matter of principle was Karen Haslam's. For the remainder of ministers and, after September 1993, for the NDP caucus, responsibility for government actions was truly shared.

Still Rae was the government's First Minister. To the public and the party, he represented and articulated the NDP regime. Inside government, he used both his position as premier and his intellectual skills to set the tone. There were many arguments in cabinet, some of which the premier lost. But, in the most important areas, those he really cared about, his key ministers usually did defer. For inside the cabinet—as in the party itself—there was the sneaking suspicion that maybe Rae really was smarter than anyone else.

Over time, perhaps without consciously realizing it, Rae was able to begin the transformation of his party. He did not do so in a vacuum. There was an international depression. Ontario did face serious structural and fiscal problems. As well, social-democratic parties around the world—in New Zealand, France, Britain—had already moved to the right.

Rae could argue he was merely being pragmatic. Taking power, holding it, appealing to a broader constituency — was this not what the NDP had been trying to do federally and provincially for twenty-five years? Was this not what New Democratic leaders such as Stephen Lewis and Ed Broadbent had been aiming at?

However, Rae transformed the NDP far more radically than a Stephen Lewis would have ever imagined. "The only difference between the NDP and the Liberals is that the NDP is a labour party," Sue Colley, long-time aide to Frances Lankin, said once. Others might have been kinder to the NDP (or the Liberals). But in essence, Colley's analysis was shrewd one. The NDP had been created by merging the labour movement with a twenty-eight-year-old populist, and predominantly Western, party. Rae's social contract was a direct challenge to organized labour. By attacking collective bargaining, it struck right at the heart of everything trade unions do.

To Janet Solberg, whose father, David Lewis, had been instrumental in creating the CCF–union coalition that became the NDP, the split with labour was disastrous: "That's the most grievous injury of all. That makes my father turn in his grave, I'm sure. It is inconceivable to me that we can have a democratic-socialist party without trade-union support."

The reverberations were felt throughout the country. By early 1994, there was a growing feeling among union leaders that labour would have to re-evaluate its relationship to the NDP nationally. To some, this re-evaluation would probably have to wait until Ontario's voters had delivered their verdict — one way or another — on the Rae government.

By breaking with the bulk of the union leadership — with Canadian Labour Congress head Bob White, with the Ontario Federation of Labour, with his own party president, Julie Davis — Rae had set the NDP adrift in uncharted waters. There had been fights before between provincial NDP governments and organized labour. But none had been as fundamental as this. Rae had taken a bold risk. He had gambled that, by demonstrating its fiscal toughness, by showing its independence from labour, by behaving like a mainstream party, the NDP could win the affection of the mainstream voter.

In the past, the NDP had tried to challenge what it thought of as the conventional politics of the old-line parties. Rae's instincts seemed to lead him in a different direction. In the long run, he appeared to be saying, the NDP would succeed by being on the cutting edge of convention, rather than challenging it. To that end, Rae prided himself on running a tighter fiscal policy than Brian Mulroney, on understanding the need for training and welfare reform before Bill Clinton, on setting up government–business partnerships that won the respect of federal Liberal Finance minister Paul Martin.

What was interesting about these standards of comparison is that they were set by former enemies. Increasingly, the Rae government began to feel alienated from its old allies. Following the 1991 retreat from public auto insurance, the government came under increasing attack from the party itself. Rae could always bring the party around — with a stirring speech and an appropriate amount of behind-the-scenes arm-twisting. But the strains were clearly growing.

Inside government, labour and party critics were accused of having an "opposition mentality," of not being with it. By the end, Rae and those around him felt more appreciated by business than by their own party. At least, they felt, business understood what had to be done. Former NDP president Janet Solberg compared the relationship between party and government to a particularly nasty divorce.

"[The government says] we've never supported them, never been supportive enough," she said. "We don't understand the terrible situation they're in economically, fiscally. All we do is criticize and carp. All we do is impugn their integrity. They're as good socialists as we are . . . that kind of stuff. They feel terribly betrayed. It's really like a divorce. That's what it feels like. It feels like both sides just don't communicate with each other very effectively, the party and the government. Both feel so bitter and betrayed that it's almost beyond useful communication."

To some New Democrats, however, the Rae experience was merely an example of the party's chickens coming home to roost. This is the view articulated by George Ehring and Wayne Roberts in their book on the Ontario NDP, *Giving Away a Miracle*. The two, both associated with the party's left wing, take issue with what they call the anti-democratic aspects of the NDP that had, they say, long predated 1990: "Once a visionary political movement," they write, "the NDP has become a party dominated by grey administrators with polls in their heads but no fire in their bellies."

In particular, Roberts and Ehring point to the NDP's 1971 expulsion of its Waffle faction as an action which eliminated vital left-wing energy and ideas. Sue Colley agreed. To her, the NDP was "intellectually decapitated in 1971 . . . by the Waffle purge."

What this critique ignores, however, is that many who ended up critical of the government — including leftists such as Colley herself —

were brought into the government. University of Toronto economist Mel Watkins, one of the founders of the Waffle, was even offered a job in the Finance ministry, a job that failed to materialize only because the government and his employer couldn't reach an accommodation in time. Canadian Auto Workers chief Bob White was offered a job, which he turned down. So was Stephen Lewis.

Former Trotskyists and Maoists were scattered throughout the government—often in senior positions. Simon Rosenblum, Laughren's chief of staff, was well known inside the NDP as a gadfly and vocal member of the party's left caucus. Laughren himself was on the party's left wing.

Labour too had its beachhead in the government: Frances Lankin, with close ties to the public-sector unions; Ross McClellan, who was supposed to represent the Ontario Federation of Labour in the premier's office; Bob Mackenzie, the life-long unionist; Anne Swarbrick, with her ties to Toronto labour. So too, the NDP's women's movement was well-represented in government—Marion Boyd, the women's rights activist, Lankin and Swarbrick, Evelyn Gigantes, the feisty Ruth Grier.

Indeed, if anything characterized the government, it was its intellectual eclecticism—from the left-wing meta-economics of Riel Miller in Treasury, to the heretical labour-relations theories of one-time student radical Peter Warrian, to the sensible-shoes Manitoba bureaucratese of Michael Decter. The Rae government was open to advice from many. It chose, however, to follow that of only a few.

The problem was not a lack of ideas. It was that few of these ideas were well-developed and none was taken seriously. This was particularly true in the economic field. Chuck Rachlis, Rae's economic policy adviser and head of NDP research in opposition, was characteristically blunt: "There was not much coherent thinking [in opposition]. No one thought we'd ever win, so it wasn't a priority."

Thus, when the NDP came to power in 1990, it did so with an elaborate and often internally contradictory platform that none of the principal players really believed in. Under the real strain of governing, it was easy to be knocked off course. Kathleen O'Hara, a former aide to Shelley Martel, compared the experience to child birth: "Going into government is like going into labour. If you haven't practised breathing, if your principles aren't completely ingrained so that they are a natural reflex, once the pressure starts, you lose it."

In the end, though, the explanation for the Ontario NDP government keeps coming back to Rae. The underlying conditions—weaknesses within the party, economic forces from outside—virtually determined that the NDP could not remain as it had been after winning power in Ontario. But it was Rae, more than anyone, who set the new directions his party would travel. Without the guidance of any deeply felt political beliefs, the government was steered by Rae's own moral compass, by his instinct of what was both possible and desirable.

Through the experience of the Ontario government, the sketchy outlines of the party that Rae was beginning to reinvent emerged. It would not be particularly interventionist. It would be fiscally conservative and rely on the private sector for economic growth. It would be a corporatist party, one that would try to forge partnerships among labour, business, and government. It would concentrate on training rather than job creation, assuming—like the Liberals—that the latter was best left to private business.

In some ways Rae's reinvented NDP would be like the group of neo-liberal Democrats who had gathered around Bill Clinton before he became U.S. president (a group which, ironically, referred to itself as the new Democrats). In some ways, it would be like Jean Chrétien's federal Liberal party—fiscally conservative, although perhaps not as bold.

Like the Liberals and Conservatives, the new NDP would talk of governing for all. But, in practice, it would ultimately cater to those with economic and political power. For to do otherwise would be the worst sin of all—it would be impractical.

However, what the reinvented party would keep from the old NDP—if the Rae experience was any guide—would be its prickliness, a whiff of self-righteousness. Like the old New Democrats, the new New Democrats would believe wholeheartedly in the purity of their intentions, a belief which would make them particularly hostile to criticism.

All of this would occur only if Rae managed to convince a sizeable portion of Ontario voters that governing had changed the NDP—that it was, indeed, a mainstream, progressive-conservative party capable of running the province in the accustomed manner; that it was free of undue union influence; that it was concerned about social issues such as poverty, but not so concerned as to be disruptive to the broad majority. To Janet Solberg, a second Rae victory in Ontario would seal the future for the NDP.

"If we get re-elected, it's Bob's party," she said. "Then he was right. His new economic model for the '90s—which is different from the neo-conservatives' because it believes in public investment, because it believes in equity and because it believes in training—then I guess the electorate passes judgment and I guess this brand of socialism is working. If he gets creamed, and it's hard to see how we could turn things around ... then I guess it's going to take several generations to make the party credible again."

This was the double-bind that the NDP, federally as well as provincially, found itself in. If Rae were to win a second term in Ontario, the NDP would no longer be the NDP. But if, after abandoning so much of his party's platform, he were to lose, the NDP would end up with nothing from the experiment—neither credibility as a left-wing party, nor power.

For many New Democrats, this posed an agonizing dilemma. Would it be better for the party and the future of democratic socialism in Canada if Rae's government were to win a second term? Or would it be better if it lost? When asked that question, even former party president Solberg was at a loss. "I don't know," she said after some thought. "I don't know the answer to that question." For one of the NDP's fiercest and most loyal partisans, it was a remarkable answer.

"How's it going to be?" she went on. "The Liberals or Tories get elected to government. How's it going to be if they bring in an anti-labour piece of legislation? We're going to stand up and criticize so that they can talk to us about the social contract? How's it going to be if they cut back social programs? Are we going to stand up and yell at them about homeless people and starving people, and they're going to remind us of the cut-backs we made?"

To Canadians outside the game of politics that may have been the greatest loss of all. No matter what else happened, the NDP had changed irrevocably. And it would be missed, even by those who never considered voting New Democrat.

For the NDP, in spite of all its faults, its quixotic posturing, and its smugness, did act as a kind of political conscience from the near left. It was the party that could be counted on to stand up for what it thought was right—even when to do so was difficult or politically unpopular.

In 1970, a small band of federal New Democrats stood against overwhelming public opinion to oppose imposition of the War Measures Act. In British Columbia, Dave Barrett's New Democrats crashed after only three years in power. But they left an institution which endured, and which no other B.C. government has had the nerve to terminate—

public auto insurance. In Saskatchewan, a New Democratic government withstood a punishing doctors' strike to bring in medicare.

By comparison, the Rae government seemed sadly weak. It caved in on auto insurance; its health strategy consisted of attempts (often unsuccessful) to bribe both the province's doctors and the multinational drug firms. Even its so-called equity agenda—already beset by the government's deficit obsession—foundered on its own contradictions. Loyal New Democrats, including those such as Stephen Lewis who had become open critics of Rae, would routinely point to what they saw as the good things the government had done—increased minimum wages, expanded pay equity, effected the bail-outs of towns such as Kapuskasing. But they did so with little enthusiasm.

For most people, the Ontario NDP government's most memorable legacies would be anti-union legislation, a casino, and a field of broken dreams. To a country desperate for choices and hoping for a new way out of adversity, its lesson was that there are no choices. "It destroyed hope," said Judy Darcy, the national president of the Canadian Union of Public Employees.

This was perhaps the real tragedy of the Rae experience. By its actions and words, the Ontario NDP government dashed the hopes of all those who fought for and believed in an alternative to the orthodoxy of the Liberals and Conservatives, the banks, the Business Council on National Issues, and the editorial board of *The Globe and Mail*. In effect, the Rae government said to the country: It's pointless to argue with the dominant ideology; acquiesce and get it over with; you have no choice.

The NDP had always claimed that winning power in Ontario would have a demonstrable effect on national politics. It may have been correct. In 1990, the New Democrats were the only serious political force remaining on the left wing of Canada's political landscape. When they abandoned that terrain they did not just leave it empty. They sowed the ground with salt.

Notes

PREFACE

"We were young and vulnerable together." Michael Ignatieff to author, Oct. 13, 1993.

CHAPTER 1

"It's time the party showed Rae the plank...jump." Thomas Walkom, "Rae's not entirely to blame," *Toronto Star*, Oct. 27, 1993.

From Windsor, defeated New Democrat MP Steven Langdon...quit. Geoffrey Scotton, "Anger at Ontario government blamed for rout of federal NDP," *Financial Post,* Oct. 26, 1993.

"The people of Ontario...resign." Mel Swart press conference, Toronto, Oct. 29, 1993.

"The reality is...defeated." Walkom, Oct. 27, 1993.

In Newfoundland...social contract. Interview with Dick Proctor, Jan. 31, 1994.

"The effect extended...done." Ibid.

His social contract...Canada. Rae to Ontario NDP Provincial Council, June 19, 1993.

"It will certainly...scale." Interview with Julie Davis, Oct. 29, 1993.

"I was excited...down." Interview with Dick Proctor, Jan. 31, 1994.

"Nobody cares...country." Interview with Janet Solberg, Nov. 11, 1993.

"capitalist stooge." See Desmond Morton, "Public sector unions lead flight from NDP," *Toronto Star*, Nov. 19, 1993; Desmond Morton, "Bob Rae's conservative progressivism," *Toronto Star*, Nov. 22, 1990.

"We will never...1990." Quoted in "The Course of Politics: 1993-1995, Feature Interview: Ross McClellan," *GPC Ontario Quarterly* (Government Policy Consultants, Sept. 1993), p. 32.

CHAPTER 2

Lenny Wise calls it his "obsessiveness." Unless otherwise indicated, all statements attributed to Lenny Wise in this chapter are from an interview with the author, Oct. 27, 1993.

...during a tour of the Fort Albany nursing station...The author was present.

Former press aide Rob Mitchell...stuff like that." Interview with Rob Mitchell, Dec. 15, 1993.

"Someone once said Bob was only comfortable...at ease." Interviews with Lynn Spink, Dec. 3, 1993; Mar. 18, 1994.

"As a kid...do." Jeffrey Simpson, "The making of a social democrat," *Saturday Night*, Jan. 1981, p. 20.

"Caucus members would...him." Interview with Rob Mitchell, Dec. 15, 1993.

"When my father was...fake." Interview with Anne Creighton, June 22, 1993.

Robert Keith Rae...Much of the material on Rae's early background is drawn from the following: Interview with Lenny Wise, Oct. 27, 1993; Interview with Jonathan Guss, Jan. 26, 1994; Judy Steed, "Premier Bob," *Toronto Star*, Sept. 29, 1990; Ken Waxman, "Socialist in spats," *Financial Post Magazine,* Oct. 1980, pp. 31-34; "Bob Rae: Working hard for for working people," *Solidarity,* Summer 1983, pp. 19-22; Simpson, Jan. 1981, pp. 19-24; Canada, Department of External Affairs, "Diplomatic Appointments," No. 65, June 25, 1976.

"...the Mammy Yokum...107." Unless otherwise indicated, all statements attributed to Jonathan Guss in this chapter are from an interview with the author, Jan. 26, 1994.

Grace, Saul and Jackie...Little Raes of Sunshine. Ken Waxman, "This songwriter's life began at 40," *Canadian Composer*, April 1978, pp. 26-46.

Years later, Esther Myers.... dying. Unless otherwise indicated, all statements attributed to Esther Myers are from an interview with the author, Nov. 4, 1993.

"As a child...not terribly athletic." Paul Kaihla, "The road to premiership," *Maclean's*, Sept. 14, 1992, p. 25.

John dismissed...nuts. Steed, Sept. 29, 1990.

Not until he was 17...Jew. Interview with Lenny Wise, Oct. 27, 1993; Michael Posner, "Desperately seeking Bob," *Toronto,* Dec. 1990, p. 37.

"I was always...different." Simpson, Jan.1981, p. 20.

Rae helped his friends...affairs. Jeffrey Rose and Michael Ignatieff, eds., *Religion and International Affairs* (Toronto: Anansi, 1968), p. iii.

Rae "is fiercely ambitious." Kaihla, Sept. 14, 1992, p. 25.

Indeed, Rae scored second to last...College. *The Varsity*, Mar. 8, 1968.

"...compromised intellectuals seem...phenomenon." *The Varsity*, Feb. 16, 1968.

"the kind of radical...with." Waxman, Oct. 1980, p. 33.

"...campaign contribution cheque from...Bissell." Interview with Lenny Wise, Oct. 27, 1993.

"This...direct conflict with his father." Simpson, Jan. 1981, p. 20.

Reviewing a book...inadequate. *The Varsity*, Nov. 17, 1967.

"There was no redeeming...principles." Bob Rae, "Pierre Elliot [*sic*] Trudeau: purveyor of the just as it is society," *The Varsity*, Oct. 18, 1968.

that was Rae's last year...Much of the material on Rae's time in England is drawn from an interview by the author with Rae on Jan. 31, 1990; an interview with Esther Myers, Nov. 4, 1993; an interview with Jonathan Guss, Jan. 26, 1994.

For his Bachelor of Philosophy degree...Webbs. Robert Rae, "The Social and Political Thought of Sidney and Beatrice Webb" (Thesis submitted for the degree of Bachelor of Philosophy at the University of Oxford, May 1971). I am grateful to Bob Shenton of Queen's University for providing me with a copy of Rae's thesis. Excerpts quoted in this chapter are from pp. 3, 6, 7-8, 11-12, 20-23, 36, 56, 14-15, 66, 70, 84-92.

the elitism of the Webbs...him. Steed, Sept. 29, 1990.

"I wanted to break . . . box." Ibid.

"I felt a kind of depression . . . week." Simpson, Jan. 1981, p. 20.

For about two years . . . degree. See Waxman, Oct. 1980; Steed, Sept. 29, 1990.

"I was feeling lost . . . screwdriver." Thomas Walkom, "Rae seeks a new path to practical politics," *Toronto Star*, Feb. 5, 1990.

he recalled meeting a Mrs. Blair . . . her. Ibid.

Rae managed to pick up an old piano . . . songs. Interview with Lenny Wise, Oct. 27, 1993.

One evening in 1975 or 1976 . . . general counsel. Interview with Bob Parkins, Mar. 2, 1994; Interview with Peter Warrian, Jan. 26, 1994. Oddly enough, the party where this world-historic event—the introduction of Bob Rae to his destiny—seems to have occurred was at the author's home.

"I'd been an organizer . . . before." Interview with Richard Johnston, Aug. 4, 1993.

"He engenders a lot of personal antagonism . . . minutes." Interview with Janet Solberg, Nov. 11. 1993.

Attacks on his Liberal background . . . involved." Simpson, Jan. 1981, p. 22.

"I don't remember . . . become." Interview with Stephen Lewis, Jan. 8, 1994.

But John Gilbert was impressed . . . choice. Interview with Richard Johnston, Aug. 4, 1993.

To make the point clearer . . . Rae. Interview with Lenny Wise, Oct. 27, 1993.

. . . he and his principal aide . . . three university economics courses between them. Charlotte Gray, "The Private Bob Rae," *Chatelaine*, May 1991, p. 111.

Perly . . . joined the NDP before Rae. Carol McDowell, "Don't put your faith in a handsome prince," *Toronto Sun*, Nov. 23, 1989.

"I used to worry . . . skirts." Susan Kastner, "I'm always me: Arlene," *Toronto Star*, Nov. 11, 1990.

"one of those people . . . years." Waxman, Oct. 1980, p. 32.

"The grey old spinster . . . NDP." Rae, Oct. 18, 1968.

CHAPTER 3

"We've been there . . . result." Bob Rae at La Rotonda, Sept. 6, 1990.

"all who believe . . . institutions." See Michael Cross, ed., *The Decline and Fall of a Good Idea: CCF-NDP Manifestos, 1932 to 1969* (Toronto: New Hogtown Press, 1974), pp. 19-20.

The Ontario CCF . . . similar lines. See J.T. Morley, *Secular Socialists: The CCF-NDP in Ontario, a Biography* (Montreal: McGill-Queen's University Press, 1984), pp. 39-41.

By 1934 . . . leadership. Ibid., p. 40.

Riding on wartime disillusionment . . . seats. Ibid., pp. 54-57.

MacDonald was by no means . . . development. See Donald MacDonald, *The Happy Warrior* (Markham: Fitzhenry and Whiteside, 1988), pp. 29-31.

In a carefully engineered coup . . . Lewis. See Desmond Morton, *The New Democrats 1961-1986: The Politics of Change* (Toronto: Copp Clark, Pitman, 1986), pp. 86-91, 108-109.

In 1968, Stephen Lewis was dispatched . . . 1971. Cameron Smith, *Unfinished Journey: The Lewis Family* (Toronto: Summerhill, 1989), p. 414.

. . . brandishing a .22 calibre automatic rifle . . . *Toronto Star*, June 9, 1975.

. . . the Wafflers were hardly extreme. For the Waffle Manifesto, see Cross, ed., *The Decline and Fall* . . .

. . . blistering attack on the Waffle. See Smith, *Unfinished Journey*, pp. 431-440;

George Ehring and Wayne Roberts, *Giving Away a Miracle: Lost Dreams, Broken Promises and the Ontario NDP* (Oakville: Mosaic, 1993), pp. 52-54; Morton, *The New Democrats* . . . , p. 133.

"People firmly believed . . . government." Unless otherwise indicated, all statements attributed to David Reville in this chapter are from an interview with the author, July 5, 1993.

Lewis, who was deemed to have erred . . . moderate. . . . Morton, *The New Democrats* . . . , p. 183.

"decent, utterly uncharismatic . . . membership." Ibid.

In 1981 over dinner . . . government. Speirs, who is an excellent cook, had been asked to host the dinner by Lewis and Landsberg (Speirs to author, Apr. 20, 1994).

"head and shoulders above the others." Interview with Janet Solberg, Nov. 11, 1993.

. . . Toronto MPP David Warner . . . Al Jolson imitations. Interview with Rob Mitchell, Dec. 15, 1993; author's conversation with David Warner, Jan. 26, 1994.

In 1989, after one particularly raucous evening . . . steps. Interview with David Reville, Apr. 20, 1994.

Wildman would say later . . . leader. Interview with Bud Wildman, May 4, 1994.

Even Floyd Laughren . . . like his leader. Interview with Floyd Laughren, Oct. 12, 1993.

"Bob never enjoyed . . . him." Interview with Rob Mitchell, Dec. 15, 1993.

"I became a New Democrat . . . mentally ill." Beth Gorham, "Illness made MPP what he is," *London Free Press*, July 13, 1989.

Rae liked the idea of coalition. Rosemary Speirs, *Out of the Blue: The Fall of the Tory Dynasty in Ontario* (Toronto: Macmillan, 1986), p. 136.

Rae stayed on the fence . . . moment. Interview with Richard Johnston, Aug. 4, 1993.

Much later, Rae would brag . . . Liberals. On June 19, 1993, Rae told his party's Provincial Council: "I'm proud, for example, of the fact that in 1985, there were a lot of people who said you shouldn't do it; it's much too risky. We said goodbye to 42 years of Tory rule and we brought in reform with the Liberals."

"Bob came out . . . really low." Charlotte Gray, "The Private Bob Rae," *Chatelaine*, May 1991, p. 112

Floyd Laughren was preparing to leave . . . so. Interview with Floyd Laughren, Oct. 12, 1993.

"It was just absolute craziness. . . . craziness." Unless otherwise indicated, all statements attributed to Lenny Wise in this chapter are from an interview with the author, Oct. 27, 1993.

"I lost three years out of my life." Judy Steed, "Premier Bob," *Toronto Star*, Sept. 29, 1990.

"You're racist." Interview with Rob Mitchell, Dec. 15, 1993.

"jackboot" of colonialism. Bob Rae, "Canada should support Lithuania," *Toronto Star*, May 4, 1990.

Agnew warned . . . he would be trashed. Interview with Rob Mitchell, Dec. 15, 1993.

Wildman and Ruth Grier . . . leadership. Interview with Floyd Laughren, Oct. 12, 1993.

"I thought we were posturing . . . it." Interview with Richard Johnston, Aug. 4, 1993.

CHAPTER 4

"I am very, very proud . . . unexpected." Ontario, Premier's Office, "Speech Given by Premier Bob Rae at the swearing-in ceremony at Convocation Hall, University of Toronto, Oct. 1, 1990."

"I thought we'd keep enough members...more." Interview with Richard Johnston, Aug. 4, 1993.

the party had gone to great lengths...willing to run. Rae to Ontario NDP Convention, Mar. 3, 1991.

In the rural riding of Lambton....winning. Interview with Ellen MacKinnon, Apr. 25, 1994.

Kimble Sutherland...Labatt Park. Interview with Kimble Sutherland, Apr. 26, 1994.

Norm Simon, still known...as Nooky. Interview with Lenny Wise, Oct. 27, 1993.

While he did offer Lewis a job...office. Interview with Lynn Spink, Mar. 18, 1994.

Bob White...turned down a job...office. Interview with Bob White, Apr. 28, 1994.

Agnew's father...years. See, for example, Judy Steed, "The ex-hippie is a power broker," *Toronto Star*, Nov. 18, 1990.

power struggle...Sears. Interview with Rob Mitchell, Dec. 15, 1993.

"David is just as controlling...sleeve." Unless otherwise indicated, all statements attributed to Janet Solberg in this chapter are from an interview with the author, Nov. 11, 1993.

...when Rae proposed he be arrested...it. Interview with Rob Mitchell, Dec. 15, 1993.

Rae is colour blind. Ibid.

To Lynn Spink...impediments. Interview with Lynn Spink, Dec. 3, 1993.

"I told him I'd spent a month...week." Interview with Kathleen O'Hara, Nov. 15, 1993.

"I told Ross McClellan...hang there and rot." Interview with Gord Wilson, Apr. 6, 1994.

Following Rae's victory...fit in. Interview with Sue Colley, Dec. 8, 1993.

"with quill pens." Rae to students, University of Toronto Faculty of Management, Feb. 9, 1993.

Meetings of the Policy and Priorities Board...10:00 p.m. Interview with Dave Cooke, Mar. 31, 1994.

"There was a real need...bureaucrat." Ibid.

"I've always believed...had." Ibid.

"No, I don't feel close...issues." Interview with Howard Hampton, Dec. 15, 1993.

"Their hope was...gang." Ibid.

Lenny Wise remembered...book. Interview with Lenny Wise, Oct. 27, 1993.

"You have to have....level of trust we had. Interview with Howard Hampton, Dec. 15, 1993.

Finally Hogan quit. For the Hogan controversy, see Tracy Tyler, "There's more trouble in Hampton's Ministry," *Toronto Star*, Feb. 29, 1992.

"The NDP took legislative power...power." Interview with Sue Colley, Dec. 8, 1993.

"It's not clear who the buck stops with...discussion." Interview with Michael Decter, Nov. 21, 1993.

...hop over his back fence...talking. Interview with Lenny Wise, Oct. 27, 1993.

...gourmet cooking club...conversation. Interview with Jonathan Guss, Jan. 26, 1994.

Grier, a committed environmentalist...too. See Thomas Walkom, "Environment Minister Ruth Grier is trying to implement a real NDP policy on garbage," *Toronto Star*, Apr. 6, 1991.

...not one but three new landfill sites...America. See Thomas Walkom, "And now folks, the old disappearing promises trick," *Toronto Star*, Nov. 18, 1993.

...tough new regulations to limit the amount of chlorine...weakened. Jim Wilkes,

"Province tells pulp mills to phase out chlorine use,"*Toronto Star*, Feb. 3, 1993; Rick Hallechuk, "Views mixed on proposal to cut chlorine," *Toronto Star*, Feb. 4, 1993; Peter Small, "Pulp industry facing tougher pollution rules," *Toronto Star*, Nov. 26, 1993.

Publicly, Grier put on a good face . . . later. Interview with Ruth Grier, Mar. 16, 1994.

She had told Rae . . . moved. Interview with Frances Lankin, Apr. 12, 1994.

. . . Floyd Laughren . . . pitfalls of her new ministry. Interview with Floyd Laughren, Oct. 12, 1993.

"We are not wackos from outer space." Rae to *New York Times* quoted in Slinger, "Premier quick to deny rumour he's a space wacko," *Toronto Star*, Oct. 7, 1990.

"My brain has not . . . alien forces." William Walker, 'Embattled Rae takes to the road to preach deficit-cutting gospel," *Toronto Star*, May 17, 1993.

CHAPTER 5

. . . Rae spelled out both . . . in blood. See Richard Mackie, "Rae accuses Liberals of giving in to industry on car insurance plan," *Globe and Mail*, Aug. 7, 1990; Matt Maychak, "NDP Agenda: Taxes, deficit to fund reform," *Toronto Star*, Sept. 5, 1990.

"the public does not like change." Allan Blakeney and Sandford Borins, *Political Management in Canada* (Toronto: McGraw-Hill, 1992), pp. 49, 188.

". . . screw it up a bit." Interview with George Cooke, Apr. 25, 1994.

"I had guys in the industry . . . paranoid." Interview with Peter Kormos, Apr. 28, 1994.

"I was the minister . . . office." Ibid.

"In the six months . . . once." Ibid. In fact, Rae did speak to Kormos once — the day he asked him to resign.

. . . it would take three years . . . properly. Interview with Brian Charlton, Apr. 15, 1994.

Public insurance in Ontario . . . 10,000 jobs. State Farm Insurance, "Job losses another cost of government auto insurance" (Press release, Aug. 13, 1991).

As Andrew Rogacki . . . years. Interview with Andrew Rogacki, Aug. 19, 1991.

Anonymous denunciations . . . past. Elaine Carey, " 'Why should I be miserable or unhappy?' unrepentant Kormos asks," *Toronto Star*, Mar. 23, 1991; Thomas Walkom, "Rae should take care tackling Kormos," *Toronto Star*, Mar. 16, 1991. The controversies included the fact that Kormos had once worked at a bookstore which sold, among other things, pornographic magazines; that as a student he had been fined for failing to file income tax returns; that in 1982 he had been fined $25 for obstructing police; and that in 1988 he had been cited for contempt of court (the charge was withdrawn when he apologized).

Rae fired him from cabinet. See Chapter 12 below.

"In the context . . . symbolic." Interview with Brian Charlton, Apr. 15, 1994.

"Ross said . . . right." Interview with Janet Solberg, Nov. 11, 1993.

"That was lower . . . liked." Interview with Brian Charlton, Apr. 15, 1994.

"I had watched . . . election." Interview with Evelyn Gigantes, Dec. 9, 1993.

George Cooke warned his clients to go slow . . . vulnerable. Interview with George Cooke, Apr. 25, 1994.

"It certainly led me to ask . . . answers." Unless otherwise indicated, all statements attributed to Julie Davis in this chapter are from an interview with the author, Oct. 29, 1993.

At one meeting . . . top priority. Interview with Julie Davis, Oct. 29, 1993; Interview with Gord Wilson, Apr. 6, 1994.

5,000 ordinary, polite...work. George Brett, "5,000 protest insurance plan," *Toronto Star*, Aug. 16, 1991. Cooke had his pink ladies demonstrate at the more central City Hall square rather than Queen's Park in order to gain more public attention.

"But as I thought about it...ahead." Interview with Howard Hampton, Dec. 15, 1993.

"It was a very vigorous debate...down." Interview with Dick Proctor, Jan. 31, 1994.

"[David Peterson] finished...thing." Frances Russell, "Rae let nation down by dropping insurance scheme," *Winnipeg Free Press*, Sept. 11, 1991.

"This is escape from power...supporters." Interview with Peter Kormos, Sept. 6, 1991.

CHAPTER 6

"In opposition, the NDP had fought...even lotteries...Depression." See comments by Ian Deans, Floyd Laughren, and Mike Farnan in Legislative Assembly of Ontario, *Official Report of Debates* (June 8, 1971), pp. 2510-11; (May 29, 1990), pp. 1375-79; (May 30, 1990), pp. 1427-30. See also Dennis Drainville, "A New Democrat's Case Against Casino Gambling" (h.p.,1992).

"The casino economy...economy." Bob Rae, "Speech to Ontario NDP Provincial Council," Dec. 7, 1986.

An NDP government...enterprise. Darcy Henton, "Greed in 'casino economy' rips off workers, Rae says," *Toronto Star*, Nov. 27, 1986.

"The casino...values." Bob Rae, "What We Owe Each Other" (Jan. 10, 1990), p. 16.

"a lot of mob involvement." Ontario Casino Project, Windsor Casino Complex Selection Committee and Review Panel, "Notes of a Meeting, Tuesday, July 20, 1993," p. 7. The mob reference was to Caesar's, one of three partners in the consortium which eventually won the bid to operate the Windsor casino. For Caesar's former links to organized crime, see also David Johnston, *Temples of Chance: How America Inc. Bought out Murder Inc. to Win Control of the Casino Business* (New York: Doubleday, 1992), p. 124. Caesar's was also fined a total of more than $1 million in 1991 and 1993 by the New Jersey Casino Control Commission after it "inappropriately paid cash rebates or incentive payments" to gamblers. See Donna Laframboise, "Windsor casino partner fined twice in the U.S.," *Toronto Star*, Dec. 10, 1993.

The casino plan...off guard. Thomas Walkom, "NDP studies plan for six casinos," *Toronto Star*, Mar. 19, 1992; Thomas Walkom, "NDP cabinet okays casinos," *Toronto Star*, Apr. 22, 1992.

the chief of police in Peel...Ontario. Thomas Walkom, "A top cop fears gambling on casinos," *Toronto Star*, Feb. 6, 1993.

"My dad was 100 per cent...involved." Unless otherwise indicated, all statements attributed to Floyd Laughren in this chapter are from an interview with the author, Oct. 12, 1993. When sworn into cabinet, Laughren was called Treasurer and his ministry the Treasury. In 1993, the name was changed to Ministry of Finance and Laughren's title to Minister of Finance. Throughout this book, both versions are used interchangeably.

a tax system heavily biased...wealthy. See Linda McQuaig, *Behind Closed Doors* (Toronto: Penguin, 1987), pp. 123-182.

B.C.'s first NDP premier...government. Lorne J. Kavic and G.B Nixon, *The 1200 Days: A shattered dream; Dave Barrett and the NDP in B.C., 1972-75* (Coquitlam: Kaen, 1978), p. 226.

"We know things are bad...do." Unless otherwise indicated, all statements attributed to Julie Davis in this chapter are from an interview with the author, Oct. 29, 1993.

Walter Curlook, chairman...nationalize. Interview with Walter Curlook, Jan. 7, 1994.

the Canada-U.S. deal signalled trouble...Windsor. See "Auto industry layoffs in Canada," *Toronto Star*, Jan. 26, 1990; "Plant shutdowns in Ontario," *Toronto Star*, Jan. 28, 1990; Patricia Lush et al. "165,000 factory jobs vanished in past year, Statscan report says," *Globe and Mail*, June 9, 1990.

But as the Polish economist...contradictions. Michael Kalecki, "Political Aspects of Full Employment," in E.K. Hunt and J.G. Schwartz, eds., *A Critique of Economic Theory* (Harmondsworth: Penguin, 1972), pp. 420-430.

The Bank of Canada's anti-inflationary...mushroom. See Arthur Donner, "Ottawa created situation for the dollar's collapse," *Toronto Star*, Mar. 5, 1990.

"Tinkerbelle economics...recession." Canada, House of Commons, *Debates* (Nov. 13, 1981), pp. 12752-7; Thomas Walkom, "Budget," *Globe and Mail,* Nov. 14, 1981.

"The government can...intervene." Quoted in Thomas Walkom, "Why Ontario must shame feds," *Toronto Star*, Apr. 13, 1991.

"The alternative to neo-conservatism....labour." James Laxer, "Which party can reverse neo-conservative agenda," *Toronto Star*, Dec. 18, 1988.

As Laxer wrote bitterly...Keynesian. James Laxer, "One obsession replaces another for believer Rae," *Toronto Star*, July 13, 1993.

Within the major unions...gains. See, for example, John O'Grady, "Beyond the Wagner Act, What Then?" in Daniel Drache, ed., *Getting on Track: Social Democratic Strategies for Ontario* (Montreal: McGill-Queen's University Press, 1992), pp. 153-169; Sam Gindin and David Robertson, "Alternatives to Competitiveness," ibid., pp. 32-48.

"There was not much coherent thinking...rest." Interview with Chuck Rachlis, Mar. 9, 1994.

"It was like a graduate seminar...terms." Unless otherwise indicated, all statements attributed to Mel Watkins in this chapter are from an interview with the author, Aug. 4, 1993.

In their 1989 thinkfest...capitalism. Dr. Isabella Bakker (compiler), "Economic Policy Review: Issues for Discussion and Debate" (Ontario NDP Caucus Planning and Priorities Committee, Economic Policy Review, August 1989).

Rae remained interested...going. Interview with Floyd Laughren, Oct. 12, 1993.

"Once again, the sources and character...credibly." Riel Miller, "Preliminary First Draft, Economic Policy Statement" (prepared for the Economic Subcommittee of the Planning and Priorities Committee of the ONDP Caucus, Mar. 14, 1990), pp. 6-7, 11, 14.

Indeed, the document...say. Georgette Gagnon and Dan Rath, *Not Without Cause: David Peterson's Fall from Grace* (Toronto: HarperCollins, 1991), p. 313. Gagnon and Rath say it took four days to write the document. NDP insiders say it took only two.

CHAPTER 7

"We had a choice...recession." Ontario Treasury, *1991 Budget* (Apr. 29, 1991), p. 3.

"It is nothing...activity." William Thorsell, "Bob Rae takes his first big step and shoots himself in the foot," *Globe and Mail*, May 4, 1991.

Newspaper tycoon Conrad Black...chain. Tony Van Alphen, "Conrad Black to shun an NDP-led Ontario," *Toronto Star*, June 21, 1991; Daniel Girard et al. "Black buys 23 per cent of Southam in deal with Torstar," *Toronto Star*, Nov. 9, 1992.

...Kim Campbell harkened...Ontario. Patrick Doyle, "Campbell calls Rae two-faced," *Toronto Star*, Aug. 11, 1993.

Foreign investment . . . into Canada. Statistics Canada, *Canada's Balance of International Payments* (Catalogue 67-001, fourth quarter 1991), p. 66.

According to the Conference Board . . . country. Shawn McCarthy, "Ottawa think tank comes under fire for praising NDP," *Toronto Star*, June 28, 1991.

An analysis of the province's finances . . . nothing. Thomas Walkom, "This budget could end up satisfying no one at all," *Toronto Star*, Apr. 30, 1991.

interest charges on Ontario's debt . . . received. Thomas Walkom, "Where does PM get off knocking our Floyd," *Toronto Star*, May 4, 1991.

"burden you are placing . . . grandchildren." Ibid.

"The Treasury people . . . recession. Interview with Howard Hampton, Dec. 15, 1993.

But for Laughren, the advice from Treasury . . . risk. Interview with Floyd Laughren, Oct. 12, 1993.

"It was so appalling . . . financing." Unless otherwise indicated, all statements attributed to Floyd Laughren in this chapter are from an interview with the author, Oct. 12, 1993.

"What I need is a busload of Steelworkers . . . world." Interview with Lynn Spink, Dec. 3, 1993.

Mendelson continued to promote . . . higher. Interview with Michael Decter, Nov. 21, 1993.

"It was clear . . . it." Interview with Mel Watkins, Aug. 4, 1993.

The result was the worst of all worlds . . . beer. See Walkom, Apr. 30, 1991; Thomas Walkom, "Why Ontario must shame feds," *Toronto Star*, Apr. 13, 1991.

"The one thing . . . high." Rae on Global Television's "Focus Ontario," Oct. 31, 1992 (transcript courtesy of Robert Fisher).

The NDP government boosted . . . Action. See Ontario Treasury, *Budget* (Apr. 30, 1992); Ontario Treasury, *Budget* (May 19, 1993}.

Rae had articulated . . . training. Rae to Ontario NDP convention, Mar. 3, 1993.

"Not yet . . . mandate." Laughren to reporters at Queen's Park, Sept. 10, 1991.

. . . the NDP produced its industrial strategy . . . competitive fundamentals. For the NDP industrial strategy, see Ontario Ministry of Industry, Trade and Technology, "An Industrial Policy Framework for Ontario," July 1992. For the Liberal industrial strategy, see Ontario Premier's Council, *Competing in the New Global Economy*, Report of the Premier's Council. vol. I (Toronto: Queen's Printer, n.d.), pp. 19-24.

The newspapers carried letters . . . on. See, for instance, Andrea Tomonko, "How much education does one need," *Toronto Star*, Jan. 22, 1994; Thomas Walkom, "Civil servants are real people with real problems," *Toronto Star*, June 21, 1993.

But the bold hope . . . markets. "Ontario settles for smaller venture fund," *Globe and Mail*, Nov. 19, 1993; James Daw, "Fund for start-ups unveiled," *Toronto Star*, Nov. 19, 1993.

"After that, nobody . . . again." Unless otherwise indicated, all statements attributed to Sue Colley in this chapter are from an interview with the author, Dec. 8, 1993.

Governments of all political stripes . . . control. Unless otherwise indicated, all statements attributed to Janet Solberg in this chapter are from an interview with the author, Nov. 11, 1993.

"A couple of us . . . casinos." Interview with Dave Cooke, Mar. 31, 1994.

More cautious voices . . . casinos. Interview with Marilyn Churley, Apr. 28, 1994.

In fact, the only spoilsports . . . Ontario. Lynda Hurst, "Ontario betting on casinos,"

Toronto Star, May 19, 1992; Thomas Walkom, "A top cop fears gambling on casinos," *Toronto Star*, Feb. 6, 1993.

Caesar's had once . . . mob. See notes to Chapter 6, above.

One government-commissioned study . . . spending. William Walker, "Toronto prime site as casino study sees windfall," *Toronto Star*, Aug. 14, 1993.

Profits and taxes . . . annually. Moira Welsh, "Casino in Windsor faces long odds, critics say," *Toronto Star*, July 7, 1993.

"I can't think of anything . . . control." Laughren to reporters, Nov. 9, 1990.

"will be the test of this government." Laughren to reporters, Oct. 1, 1991.

Rae showed his pleasure . . . miraculous. Interview with Lynn Spink, Mar. 18, 1994.

the government spent $62,000 . . . effort. It would have spent $112,000 but, after a public outcry, the government persuaded the private television station CFTO to donate the $50,000 worth of broadcast time for which the premier's office had already contracted. See "NDP spent $62,000 to stage Rae's talk on curbing costs," *Toronto Star*, Mar. 3, 1992.

A poll taken . . . economy. Angus Reid Group, "National Angus Reid/Southam News Poll, Ontario Provincial Party Standings," Feb. 14, 1992.

"Are you trying . . . dumb?" Gigantes's recollection of the incident is most diplomatic. "I remember the discussion. It was a discussion about . . . whether we were all at the same place when we looked at the question of how much is enough to borrow. . . . And there have been times, I think it would be fair to say, [when] Bob was unsure about whether we were all at the same point in terms of our view about the significance of those questions." Interview with Evelyn Gigantes, Dec. 9, 1993.

the assumptions behind . . . high. Martin Mittelstaedt, "Deficit overstated, Liberal MPP says," *Globe and Mail*, Apr. 13, 1993.

"It was a very theoretical . . . uncharted territory." Unless otherwise indicated, all statements attributed to Michael Decter in this chapter are from an interview with the author, Nov. 21, 1993.

"I like to work on the edge . . . about." Interview with Peter Warrian, Jan. 26, 1994.

By early 1993, he had changed his mind. Interview with Michael Decter, Nov. 21, 1993.

The institute had published . . . debt wall. See "Debt Crisis Looms, study warns," *Globe and Mail*, Feb. 16, 1993; "Debt Crisis may drive lenders away, economists fear, " *Toronto Star*, Feb. 16, 1993; Thomas Walkom, "Debt crisis? What debt crisis?" *Toronto Star*, Mar. 27, 1993.

. . . representatives of the Wall Street barons . . . no debt wall. See, for instance, Douglas Goold, "Foreigners aren't running for cover," *Globe and Mail*, Apr. 26, 1993.

As for the drain to foreigners argument . . . one-third. Thomas Walkom, "Ontario's debt crisis is more fiction than fact," *Toronto Star*, Apr. 19, 1993.

In a confidential memo. . . . foreigners. Ministry of Finance, "Current Issue," Feb. 16, 1993.

In reality, the New Zealand story . . . 1990s. See Thomas Walkom, "One hour tape is real horror show for NDP," *Toronto Star*, Mar. 29, 1993; Martin Holland and Jonathan Boston, eds., *The Fourth Labour Government: Politics and Policy in New Zealand*, 2nd ed. (Oxford: Oxford University Press, 1990); Brian Easton, ed., *The Making of Rogernomics* (Auckland: Auckland University Press, 1986); Simon Walker, ed., *Rogernomics: Shaping New Zealand's Economy* (Auckland: New Zealand Centre for Independent Studies, 1989).

At a March 11 meeting . . . strenuously. See Chapter 8, below.

"It's sad we've come ... trying to do." Leslie Papp, "Organized labor split over rift with NDP," *Toronto Star*, Nov. 23, 1993; Rae to reporters, Nov. 22, 1993. I am grateful to Derek Ferguson for providing me with a copy of Rae's remarks.

He insisted ... labour relations throughout the land. Rae to Ontario NDP Provincial Council, June 19, 1993.

There were many ... who agreed. See, for example, "Working together to save jobs," *Toronto Star*, Sept. 6, 1993.

The party's real breakthrough ... unions. Keith Archer, "Canadian Unions and The NDP: The failure of collective action" (Duke University PhD thesis, 1985), p. 165.

Labour's growing clout ... in 1962. Desmond Morton, *The New Democrats 1961-1986: The Politics of Change* (Toronto: Copp Clark, Pitman, 1986), p. 32.

the unions were owed ... extinction. Thomas Walkom, "Stephen Lewis is one critic Rae can't ignore," *Toronto Star*, June 12, 1993.

Leo Gerard ... federal leader's job in 1989. Judy Steed, "Blakeney, Quebec NDP chief urge Rae to run for leadership," *Toronto Star*, Sept. 29, 1989.

Public opinion polls ... Canada. A 1987 poll, for instance, showed that 30 per cent of Canadians feared big labour while only 15 per cent feared big business. Alan Whitehorn, *Canadian Socialism: Essays on the CCF-NDP* (Toronto: Oxford University Press, 1992), p. 15.

"Our role ... survive." Thomas Walkom, "Why Rae won't be labor's handmaiden," *Toronto Star*, Oct. 6, 1990.

The scheme ... intensive and at a high level. Ontario Federation of Labour, "Structuring the Labour Movement's Participation in the Policy Process" (1990).

Later Wilson would charge ... made. Interview with Gordon Wilson, Apr. 6, 1994.

Changes to the labour relations act ... easier. John O'Grady, "Beyond the Wagner Act, What Then?" in Daniel Drache, ed., *Getting on Track: Social Democratic Strategies for Ontario* (Montreal; McGill-Queen's University Press, 1992), pp. 162-164.

In 1990 ... labour was not pushing ... immediately. Interview with Gordon Wilson, Oct. 3, 1990.

While both Rae ... anti-scab laws. Thomas Walkom, "Strike has Rae between rock and hard place," *Toronto Star*, Oct. 13, 1990.

"I ran into a buzz saw ... colleagues." Thomas Walkom, "Business and NDP head for showdown," *Toronto Star*, May 11, 1991.

"People thought you were only going to get one kick ... it." Unless otherwise indicated, statements attributed to Julie Davis in this chapter are from an interview with the author, Oct. 29, 1993.

"We knew ... one chance." Walkom, May 11, 1991.

"I admit my bias ... proud of it." Interview with Bob Mackenzie, Oct. 3, 1990.

"I don't want to ... supporters are." Walkom, May 11, 1991.

"I've said many times ... advocate." Walkom, Oct. 6, 1990.

The third lobby ... legislature. Thomas Walkom, "Business teams up to fight Rae's labor reforms," *Toronto Star*, Feb. 22, 1992.

Battered by business opposition ... later. Thomas Walkom, "NDP buckles to business pressure on labour reforms," *Toronto Star,* Nov. 6, 1991.

"Labour didn't educate ... CAW members." Interview with Dave Cooke, Mar. 31, 1994.

On March 30 ... "We've done it." Interviews with Judy Darcy, June 30, 1993; Apr. 27, 1994.

"Are you telling me to bend over . . . condom." Interview with Michael Decter, Nov. 21, 1993.

"She thought that . . . theology of collective bargaining." Interview with Michael Decter Nov. 21, 1993.

"I do come from a background . . . another time." Interview with Frances Lankin, Apr. 8, 1994.

By the fall of 1992 . . . $10 billion. Interview with Floyd Laughren, Oct. 12, 1993.

"I said no party attacks . . . [happened]." Interview with Michael Decter, Nov. 21, 1993.

"I'm not talking . . . give it a try." Interviews with Judy Darcy, May 12, 1993, Apr. 27, 1994.

On March 11 . . . wanted. Interviews with Julie Davis, Oct. 29, 1993; and Gordon Wilson, Apr. 6, 1994.

. . . some in the Canadian intellectual left . . . bargaining. See John O'Grady, "Beyond the Wagner Act, What Then?" in Drache, ed., *Getting on Track,* pp. 153-169; John Richards, "Collective Bargaining is not enough: the case for a new social contract," in Simon Rosenblum and Peter Findlay, eds., *Debating Canada's Future: Views from the Left* (Toronto: Lorimer, 1991), pp. 75-88.

"We should not be pulling back . . . nationally." Rae to Ontario NDP Provincial Council, June 19, 1993.

The next day, speaking to reporters . . . recovery. Rae to reporters at Queen's Park, Mar. 22, 1993.

The CAW saw this as a dead end . . . side. See Sam Gindin and David Robertson, "Alternatives to Competitiveness," in Drache, ed., *Getting on Track*, pp. 32-48. Both Gindin and Robertson were senior officials in the CAW.

"a credible alternative . . . activists." Buzz Hargrove, "President's Report to CAW Council," Dec. 11, 1992.

Certainly, this was the tenor . . . others. Interview with Gordon Wilson, Apr. 6, 1994.

between 9,000 and 11,000 . . . jobs . . . would disappear. Ontario Ministry of Finance, "Ontario's Expenditure Control Plan," Apr. 1993, p. 4.

Ontarians would face . . . increases. Ontario Ministry of Finance, *Ontario Budget 1993* (May 19, 1993). The rest of the $1.8 billion revenue leg came from non-tax measures.

Besides, as he explained later . . . wanted. Interview with Michael Decter, Nov. 21, 1993.

"That's why they felt so betrayed . . . unions." Interview with Janet Solberg, Nov. 11, 1993.

"You enter into . . . there." Interview with Howard Hampton, Dec. 15, 1993.

"It was really hard . . . that." Interview with Frances Lankin, Apr. 8, 1994.

You've got to come to the pump . . . public sector. Interview with Gordon Wilson, May 7, 1993.

"People bang their fists . . . consistent." William Walker, "$2 billion will be cut, Rae vows," *Toronto Star*, June 5, 1993.

Lankin debated . . . legislate. Interview with Frances Lankin, Apr. 8, 1994.

MacDonald's ill-fated decision . . . decade. See Ben Pimlott, *Labour and the Left in the 1930s* (Cambridge: Cambridge University Press, 1977), pp. 11-15.

During that Sunday's . . . surprise. Thomas Walkom, "Lankin's near-defection put NDP on thin ice," *Toronto Star*, July 7, 1993.

"We have our MPPs . . . us." Interview with Gordon Wilson, May 7, 1993.

Judy Darcy had . . . quit the cabinet. Interview with Judy Darcy, Apr. 27, 1994.

"I really had to make a decision... in." Interview with Frances Lankin, Apr. 8, 1994.

"Better a Rae Day... all." Bob Rae, "The hard reality of governing," *Toronto Star*, Nov. 25, 1993.

An angry Stephen Lewis... government. Walkom, June 12, 1993.

Leo Gerard... contracts. Interview with Gordon Wilson, Apr. 6, 1994.

with only three New Democrats opposed. The three were Karen Haslam, Peter Kormos, and Hamilton MPP Mark Morrow. Anti-casino maverick Dennis Drainville, who had already quit the NDP caucus to sit as an independent, also voted against the bill. Drainville later quit the Legislature.

Three months later... Ontario. Virginia Galt, "NDP given second chance, but CUPE cuts off Ontario," *Globe and Mail*, Nov. 19, 1993.

In May 1994... the Canadian Labour Congress... relationship to the NDP. Tony Van Alphen, "Labor to review links to NDP after emotional vote," *Toronto Star*, May 19, 1994.

"Instead of having... mad." Interview with Michael Decter, Nov. 21, 1993. Decter said he quit the government not over the social contract but because he had become too publicly identified with the NDP government, to such an extent that he could no longer do his job.

Sue Colley... one of her reasons. Interview with Sue Colley, Dec. 8, 1993.

In others, workers were laid off... unions. See Leslie Papp, "Laid-off workers in social contract limbo," *Toronto Star*, Jan. 12, 1994; Canadian Union of Public Employees, Ontario Division, "Job Loss Survey," Jan. 31, 1994; Thomas Walkom, "The people knocoked over in the social contract's wake," *Toronto Star*, Nov. 27, 1993.

At the Guelph Correctional Centre... Days. James Rusk, "Rae days covered by overtime shifts," *Globe and Mail*, Mar. 2, 1994.

Metro Toronto... bed. Metro Toronto Community Services, "Impact of Unfunded Social Contract Costs in Children's Services," Feb. 23, 1994; Walkom, Nov. 27, 1993.

CHAPTER 9

By the mid-'80s... plans. Heinz Redwood, *The Pharmaceutical Industry — Trends, Problems, Achievements*, (London: Oldwickes, 1988), p. 254.

On the other... except Quebec's. Quebec, as home to about 40 per cent of brand-name drug manufacturing in Canada, seemed particularly susceptible to lobbying from the multinationals.

Brian Mulroney's government... Agreement. Linda McQuaig, *The Quick and the Dead: Brian Mulroney, Big Business and the Seduction of Canada* (Toronto: Penguin, 1991), pp. 132-142.

Now, it seemed... history. Stevie Cameron, "How the drug-makers influence the policy-makers," *Globe and Mail*, Nov. 30, 1992.

Bill C-91 would cost... $1 billion... savings. Lisa Priest, "New drug law will hike costs by $1-B, Lankin says," *Toronto Star*, Oct 29, 1992.

Partly in the hope... licensing. Ontario Ministry of Industry, "Premier's Briefing Note," Dec. 3, 1992. This was the exact phrasing used in the cabinet decision.

In October 1991... multinationals. Randall White, "Intellectual Property Rights and the Canadian Pharmaceutical Industry in Ontario: Background on the debate in 1991," (report prepared for the Ontario Ministry of Health, Oct. 1991), p. 13, 24,

15-16, 48, 50, 65; Statistics Canada figures show that in 1987, after-tax profit as a percentage of income was 10 per cent for the brand-name drug companies compared to 4.4 per cent for all manufacturers.

'This program for old... market.' White, Oct. 1991, p. 29.

Eli Lilly... 107 per cent return on shareholder's equity. Financial Post, *Financial Post 500*, 1992, p. 128.

Nelson Sims made it clear... C-91. William Walker, "U.S. drug firm expands facilities in Scarborough," *Toronto Star*, Dec. 8, 1992.

"The drug companies... time." Interview with Sue Colley, Dec. 8, 1993.

Initially, David Agnew... offices. Interview with Lynn Spink, Dec. 3, 1992.

"At 107 plus per cent... industry." Decter to Rae re Eli Lilly Canada Inc., May 29, 1992.

"I believe I... 1994;" "[The] Drug Reform... alone." Rae to Sims, Sept. 25, 1992.

"Did we continue... investment." Interview with Francis Lankin, Apr. 8, 1994.

"The bottom line... Ontario." Interview with Dave Cooke, Mar. 31, 1994.

"With additional patent... reform". Ontario Cabinet Committee on Economic and Labour Policy, "Report," Oct. 8, 1992.

'While the drug companies... made.' In a letter to Rae, Nicholas Leluk, executive director of the Canadian Drug Manufacturers Association, the lobbyist for the generics, blasted the premier for giving "credibility to the cause of the multi-national pharmaceutical industry." Leluk to Rae, Dec. 16, 1992.

"I was really surprised... C-91." Interview with Ruth Grier, Mar. 16, 1993.

"If Bill C-91 was to derail... announcement." Walker, Dec. 8, 1992.

In March 1994... out. Thomas Walkom, "Has the NDP sold its soul for a bouncing cheque?" *Toronto Star*, Apr. 7, 1994; Art Chamberlain, "Lilly vows 'good news' in job plan halt," *Toronto Star*,, Apr. 8, 1994.

Since 1991, Burroughs... patent. Paul Taylor, "UK firm's AZT patent challenged," *Globe and Mail*, Jan. 22, 1991.

Burroughs Wellcome responded... program. Rossana Tamburri, "Drug firm threatens legal action," *Globe and Mail*, June 25, 1992.

"We have been given... patent. Paul Taylor, "Province, firm sign AIDS-drug deal," *Globe and Mail*, Dec. 12, 1992.

Prominent AIDS physician... patients." Paul Taylor, "Province, firm sign AIDS-drug deal," *Globe and Mail*, Dec. 12, 1992. Ironically, by 1993, new research had cast doubts on the usefulness of AZT as an early treatment for AIDS.

Burroughs Wellcome had 29 workers... 1,400. This information was received from the Canadian head offices of Burroughs Wellcome and Apotex, June 1, 1994.

Pharmascience Inc... Rhinaris-F. Interviews with David Goodman, Feb. 2, 1994, and Jeff Courtney, Mar. 1, 1994, both of Pharmascience. Interview with Julie Tam of the Canadian Drug Manufacturers' Association, Feb. 21, 1994.

"there will be contemplation... litigation." Rae to Melvin D. Booth and Michael Ball, June 9, 1993. My emphasis.

Vasotec was one... Bill C-91. Stephen Schondelmeyer, "The cost of Bill C-91: an economic impact analysis of the elimination of compulsory licensing of pharmaceuticals in Canada," University of Minnesota, College of Pharmacy, Nov. 27, 1992, p. 7.

A small joint venture... vaccine. Ministry of Health, "Press Release," Dec. 6, 1993.

"clearly inconsistent with... intervene." Tarnow to Rae, Jan 11, 1994; my emphasis.

"I look at... fair." Interview with Floyd Laughren, Oct. 12, 1993.

What defined social democracy . . . love. Bob Rae, "What We Owe Each Other" (Jan. 10. 1990), p. 12; Thomas Walkom, "Rae preaches caution not revolution," *Toronto Star*, Nov. 17, 1990.

"It was all lies . . . it." Georgette Gagnon and Dan Rath, *Not Without Cause: David Peterson's Fall from Grace* (Toronto: HarperCollins, 1991), p. 272.

"We'd been flogging . . . that." Interview with David Reville, July 5, 1993.

"We live in . . . do." Rae press conference, Oct. 18, 1990. For details on the Varity deal, see James Daw, "Varity pays $50 million to leave," *Toronto Star*, Oct. 19, 1990.

In doing so . . . distribution system. Donald MacDonald, *The Happy Warrior: Political Memoirs* (Markham: Fitzhenry and Whiteside, 1988), p. 100.

"I'm not going to advocate . . . do." Rae press conference, Nov. 7, 1990.

"They were not pleasant . . . assault." Interview with Lynn Spink, Nov. 3, 1993.

On a 1992 flight . . . brought. Rae to author, May 8, 1992.

"He learned about . . . language." Interview with Lynn Spink, Dec. 3, 1993.

"He was more pragmatic . . . proponent." Interview with Walter Curlook, Jan. 7, 1994.

cabinet changed its pension regulations . . . required. Derek Ferguson, "Ontario promises GM to relax pension laws," *Toronto Star*, Dec. 18, 1991.

To Laughren, the government's . . . choices. Interview with Floyd Laughren, Oct. 12, 1993.

"I don't believe . . . difficult." Interview with Evelyn Gigantes, Dec. 9, 1993.

Summer 1991 . . . moment. Interview with David de Launay, Sept. 3, 1991.

The de Havilland deal . . . protected. Dana Flavelle, "De Havilland deal locked up," *Toronto Star*, Jan. 23, 1992.

In the final deal . . . four years. Matt Maychak, "Last-minute Algoma deal rescues 5,000 jobs," *Toronto Star*, Feb. 29, 1992.

Within two years . . . 1992 price. Alistair Dow, "Algoma stock a wild success story," *Toronto Star*, Mar. 19, 1994.

At the end . . . town. Interview with Kathleen O'Hara, Nov. 15, 1993.

. . . the premier had warned . . . conspiracy against the NDP. William Walker, "How Ontario government plans to blow its own horn," *Toronto Star*, Dec. 4, 1993.

"It was a very, very close call . . . saying." Unless otherwise indicated, all statements attributed to John Honderich in this chapter are from an interview with the author, Dec. 17, 1993.

"[A] senior member . . . now." Honderich to Rae, Oct. 1, 1991.

"Dear John . . . Bob." Rae to Honderich, Oct. 7, 1991.

"If he were . . . him." Interview with Walter Curlook, Jan. 7, 1994.

"our mascot for Ontario." Kelly Toughill, "Former business foes laud 'our mascot' Rae," *Toronto Star*, Jan. 13, 1994.

CHAPTER 10

"I didn't see . . . schedules." Interview with Ruth Grier, March 16, 1994. For publicly available details on the OMA social contract, see the agreement itself entitled "1993 Interim Agreement on Economic Arrangements," Aug. 1, 1993; Lisa Priest, "The OMA contract pill wasn't all bitter," *Toronto Star*, Aug. 19, 1993; Thomas Walkom, "New medicare cuts are poor medicine for health care," *Toronto Star*, Dec. 7, 1993.

"This was a negotiated . . . system." Interview with Ruth Grier, Mar. 16, 1994.

This was the secret protocol. Appendix I is formally titled "Indemnification agreement between the government of Ontario and Ontario Medical Association,"

Aug. 1, 1993. Grier, in her Mar. 1994 interview with the author, said she was unaware that the protocol had never been publicly released.

"It was part of their insistence...timetable." Interview with Ruth Grier, Mar. 16, 1994. The agreement required the government to submit the issue of incorporation to an arm's length advisory body and, within six months of receipt of a report from that body, pass and give royal assent to a bill permitting incorporation of physicians.

She would later explain...isolation. Interview with Ruth Grier, Mar. 16, 1994.

"the doctors would not have agreed." Ibid.

Finance officials calculated...year. See Ministry of Finance, "Effect of Incorporation on 1994 Combined Federal/Provincial Income Tax and EHT," Jan. 20, 1994. The finance ministry's initial conservative calculations as to the cost of incorporation were later doubled. By April, Finance figured the move could cost the federal and provincial levels of government together between $65 million and $75 million annually.

Better and cheaper medicine...For a discussion of health reform see Michael Rachlis and Carol Kushner, *Second Opinion: What's Wrong with Canada's Health-Care System* (Toronto: Collins, 1989).

On the cost front...results. Kelly Toughill, "NDP health care cuts exceed expectations," *Toronto Star*, Mar. 6, 1993.

For as Ruth Grier...OMA veto. Interview with Ruth Grier, Mar. 16, 1994.

"They really blew the health stuff...Canada." Interview with Michael Rachlis, Apr. 5, 1994.

In some cases...identical. Thomas Walkom, "Second coming of long-term care plan," *Toronto Star*, Nov. 2, 1991.

The 1993 audit was scathing. See Ministry of Health, Special Drugs Program, "Audit Report," Jan 31. 1993; Derek Ferguson, "NDP studies user fees for special costly drugs," *Toronto Star*, Nov. 3, 1993

As proof..."about two" were fired. Unless otherwise indicated, all statements attributed to Michael Decter in this chapter are from an interview with the author, Nov. 21, 1993.

"the government's most effective deputy...bat." Interview with Sue Colley, Dec. 8, 1993.

"It worked...pragmatic." Interview with Frances Lankin, Apr. 12, 1994.

"He phoned once...Decter." Interview with Michael Rachlis, July 7, 1993.

"In the context...co-payments." Interview with Frances Lankin, Apr. 8, 1994.

Even Decter, pleading political reality...side. Interview with Michael Decter, Nov. 21, 1993.

"There are not deserving...need." New Democrats, "Communiqué," June 7, 1990.

In his Oxford Bachelor of Philosophy...governess. Robert Rae, "The social and political thought of Sidney and Beatrice Webb" (University of Oxford Bachelor of Philosophy Thesis, 1971), pp. 7-8, 10.

The SARC report...line. See Ontario Ministry of Community and Social Services, *Transitions*, Report of the Social Assistance Review Committee (Toronto: Queen's Printer, 1988); Lois Sweet, "Welfare reform stalled," *Toronto Star*, Apr. 29, 1990; Matt Maychak, "Give 'working poor' more money to meet basic needs, report urges," *Toronto Star*, Sept. 6, 1988.

"A nation's greatness...fortunate." Ontario Premier's Office, "Speech given by Premier Bob Rae at the Swearing-in Ceremony at Convocation Hall, University of Toronto," Oct. 1, 1990.

"everybody knows that...legislation." Derek Ferguson, "Welfare reform tops agenda, Rae says," *Toronto Star*, Oct. 16, 1990.

Six weeks later....rates. Ontario Ministry of Community and Social Services, "Statement by the Honorable Zanana Akande, Minster of Community and Social Services, on Addressing Poverty in Ontario," Nov. 29, 1990.

By February 1991...Alberta. Susan Reid and Jane Armstrong, "Ontario vows to ease welfare burden on cities," *Toronto Star*, Feb. 23, 1991; Rosemary Speirs, "Ontario's poor will pay the cost as budget freeze hits welfare plan," *Toronto Star*, Feb. 24, 1990.

Akande acknowledged...food banks. Maureen Murray, "Anti-poverty rally calls on Rae to stand by promises to poor," *Toronto Star*, Apr. 11, 1991.

"Something must be done." Bruce Campion-Smith, "Welfare overhaul needed, Rae says," *Toronto Star*, Apr. 25, 1991.

Even so...poverty line. Bob Cox, "PM-Welfare Rates," CP newswire, Nov. 19, 1991.

Moscovitch's first set...1992. Richard Mackie "Changes urged in welfare system," *Globe and Mail*, June 10, 1992.

Rae's parents had always preached...help. Interview with Lenny Wise, Oct. 27, 1993.

"Welfare isn't working...home." Rae to students at the University of Toronto Faculty of Management, Feb. 9, 1993.

"saved my daughter and me." Interview with Marilyn Churley, Apr. 28, 1994.

"[Welfare recipients] need...what." Rae and Romanow on CBC Radio's "Sunday Morning," Feb. 6, 1994.

As initially devised, the NDP welfare scheme...benefit. Ontario Ministry of Community and Social Services, *Turning Point: New support proposals for people with low incomes* (Toronto: Queen's Printer, 1993).

By January, 1994, Finance Minister Floyd Laughren...anticipated. Leslie Papp, "Laughren hints at layoffs for public sector workers," *Toronto Star*, Feb. 25, 1994. The shortfall was later projected at $2.1 billion after Ontario decided to follow Ottawa and lower cigarette taxes.

Word began to leak...cash. Kelly Toughill, "NDP to fall short on ambitious plan for welfare reform," *Toronto Star*, Jan. 25, 1994.

On March 2, an outraged Rae...reform. Leslie Papp, "Welfare reform plan fizzling, NDP admits," *Toronto Star*, Mar. 3, 1994.

"I guess we can't do it." Thomas Walkom, "Can Ontario's NDP save itself?" *Toronto Star*, Mar. 26, 1994.

It was an unmemorable document...months. See Ontario Ministry of Finance, *1994 Ontario Budget*, May 5, 1994.

"A major reform of the tax system...time." William Walker, "Laughren fails to implement Fair Tax Commission ideas," *Toronto Star*, May 6, 1994.

As an economics instructor...taxation. Unless otherwise indicated, all statements attributed to Floyd Laughren in this chapter are from an interview with author, Oct. 12, 1993.

In 1982, for instance, Rae...loopholes. Bob Rae et al. "Pre-Budget Statement and Proposals of the Ontario New Democratic Party," May 6, 1982, pp.10, 17-19.

In 1989, Laughren released...sales. Floyd Laughren, "Made in Ontario: A Fairer Tax System," May 12, 1989. The NDP also called for the elimination of OHIP premiums (a move announced by the Liberals five days later), expanded tax credits for the elderly and poor, elimination of income tax for the working poor and an expanded sales tax to cover certain kinds of services such as stock brokers' commissions.

The split reached a crescendo...ways. Ontario Fair Tax Commission, *Treatment of*
Real Estate Gains, Working Group Report, Mar. 1992.

The second set...property tax. Ontario Fair Tax Commission, *Fair Taxation in a*
Changing World (Report of the Ontario Fair Tax Commission, 1993), pp. 677-681.

As commission vice-chair Neil Brooks...decisions. Ontario Fair Tax Commission
[1993], pp. 1030-1033; Interview with Neil Brooks, Dec. 12, 1993.

"I was told by the NDP...upper class." Thomas Walkom, "NDP's Windsor castle
crumbles," *Toronto Star*, Sept. 15, 1993.

CHAPTER 11

The premier's uncle...Humperdinck. Ken Waxman, "This Songwriter's Life Began at
40 — and he's going strong," *Canadian Composer,* Apr. 1978, pp. 26-46.

As a bemused Jim Coyle...stalwarts. Jim Coyle, "Premier's bardic obsession sounds
like swansong for a foundering ship," *Ottawa Citizen*, Jan. 8, 1994.

Rae, then leader...debut. Bob Rae, "Communiqué," Apr. 10, 1990.

"I think it...opinion." Rae to Roth, Dec. 24, 1993.

"Some folks come...now." Quoted in Coyle, Jan. 8, 1994.

A growing number of black activists...institutions. See Juan Williams, "Why King's
dream still matters," *Guardian Weekly* Feb. 6, 1994, for a summary and critique of
voluntary segregation.

...June Callwood...non-white women. See Philip Marchand, "Callwood denounces
'bullying' by self-defined weak," *Toronto Star*, June 26, 1993.

Yet his ministers..."black-focused" schools in Toronto. See Jim Rankin, " 'Black'
schools split community," *Toronto Star*, Dec. 14, 1992; John Deverell, "Give
blacks bigger role in society, report says," *Toronto Star*, Nov. 21, 1992. Municipal
Affairs minister Ed Philip insisted that the credit union would be open to anyone,
of whatever colour, who happened to have a Caribbean or African ethnic heritage.
Ed Philip, "Credit union is not just for blacks," *Toronto Star*, Aug. 9, 1993.

"a lot of people to turn to." Interview with Janet Solberg, Nov. 11, 1993. Solberg was
in charge of finding political aides during the NDP's transition to power.

In their book....clinics. George Ehring and Wayne Roberts, *Giving Away a Miracle:*
Lost Dreams, Broken Promises and the Ontario NDP (Oakville: Mosaic Press,
1993), pp 101-108.

...an illegal blockade...logging. Rae wasn't charged. Others, including New
Democrat Dennis Drainville, who would a year later become an MPP, were.

"The meaning of the phrase...settlement." Bob Rae, "What We Owe Each Other"
(Jan. 10, 1990), pp. 42-43.

Key activists...such as Judy Rebick...NDP. For Rae and Rebick, see Ehring and
Roberts, *Giving Away a Miracle*, pp. 177-181.

Similarly, the rights of gays...position. Thomas Walkom, "Rae ready to take risky
step on same-sex rights," *Toronto Star*, Apr. 16, 1994.

Yet Rae himself attended Miss Saigon...pickets. See "Crowd of 40 seeks boycott,"
Toronto Star, May 27, 1993.

Traditional NDP allies...back. Kelly Toughill, "Ontario pay equity bill up for intense
scrutiny," *Toronto Star*, Feb. 1, 1993; "63,000 may get pay equity cheque," *Toronto*
Star, Jan. 19, 1993.

"I've never seen...mess." Interview with Julie Mason, Mar. 4, 1994.

Most union contracts...fired. The final regulations maintained seniority in the crucial
areas of lay-offs and recall. See Ontario, Ministry of Citizenship, "A Guide to Bill
79, The Employment Equity Act" (Dec. 1993), p. 3.

"Juanita wanted to...boots." Interview with Julie Mason, Mar. 4, 1994.

"I had come in...do." Ibid. Borovoy himself testified to a legislative committee that it made no sense to discriminate against white able-bodied males today in order to rectify injustices perpetrated by their ancestors in the past. See William Walker, "Job equity law not a cure-all, province told," *Toronto Star*, Oct. 2, 1993.

The final regulations...muted. For the employment equity bill and its critics, see Kelly Toughill, "Ontario passes job equity law—the first in Canada," *Toronto Star*, Dec. 10, 1993; Avvy Go, "Equity formula isn't strong enough," *Toronto Star*, June 25, 1993; Barbara Aarsteinsen, "Women's groups slam employment equity bill," *Toronto Star*, June 23, 1993; Derek Ferguson, "NDP official attacks party's job equity law," *Toronto Star*, Aug. 24, 1993,

The government also..."positive measures program"...heightened. Thomas Walkom, "Barring jobs to white men unjustifiable," *Toronto Star*, Nov. 13, 1993.

"While it is obviously true...others." Lewis to Rae, June 9, 1992. See pp. 2-3, 29-30, 36.

Karen Mock...Directorate. Interview with Karen Mock, Feb. 18, 1994.

Opinion in the Toronto black...*Show Boat*. For the *Show Boat* controversy, see "Pianist Peterson endorses Show Boat," *Toronto Star*, Oct. 26, 1993; Kellie Hudson, "Protestors hurl insults at gala Show Boat opening," *Toronto Star*, Oct. 18, 1993. *The Star* was one of the sponsors of *Show Boat*.

"...the worst year of my life." Interview with Julie Mason, Mar. 4, 1994.

One grant worth...arts. Interview with Jeff Henry, Feb. 25, 1994.

"One didn't tie...short-sightedness." Ibid.

When only 135...disappointment. Alan Barnes, "Show Boat policing called too costly at $26,857," *Toronto Star*. Nov. 9, 1993.

"The new government...office." Ontario, Premier's Office, "Speech Given by Premier Bob Rae at the Swearing-in Ceremony at Convocation Hall, University of Toronto, Oct. 1, 1990."

"We're hoping to service...bases." Interview with Leo Lessard, Mar. 8, 1994; Interview with Terry Fink, Mar. 8, 1994; Apr. 29, 1994.

On August 5...pay. Ontario Court (General Division) Divisional Court, In the Matter of an Application to the Divisional Court Pursuant to the Judicial Procedures Act Between Carlton Augustus Masters and Her Majesty the Queen in the Right of Ontario, "Affadavit of Carlton Augustus Masters" pp. 8, 33, 32, 24, 26, 27-33. In May 1994, the Divisional Court rejected Masters's request for a judicial review into his case. See Thane Burnett, "Master loses bid for hearing," *Toronto Sun*, May 31, 1994.

The report concluded...women. "Final Report on Carlton Masters," p. 71.

Rae's only public comment...courts. Derek Ferguson, "Premier denies giving assurances in Masters case," *Toronto Star*. Mar. 31, 1993.

Akande...Martin Luther King. Cal Millar, "'Province failed me,' Masters says," *Toronto Star*, Apr. 4, 1993.

"For a while there...possessed." Interview with Howard Hampton, Dec. 15, 1993.

Aboriginal leaders were adamant...them. Thomas Walkom, "Nothing's going to happen without a fight," *Toronto Star*, Sept. 28, 1991.

Other premiers were cool...too. Thomas Walkom, "Rae shows he's flexible as unity game resumes," *Toronto Star*, June 10, 1991.

faced with opposition from Romanow...principles. Thomas Walkom, "Rae takes hold of constitutional reins," *Toronto Star*, Dec. 7, 1991.

Rae had agreed to an equal and elected Senate...countenance. Thomas Walkom, "Will Rae blink or call Mulroney's bluff?" *Toronto Star*, Jan. 15, 1992.

Significantly, the new native governments...females. Thomas Walkom, "Between a native rock and a hard place," *Toronto Star*, Oct. 10, 1992.

Judy Rebick...interest group.) Paula Todd, "Rae denounces call for No vote," *Toronto Star*, Sept. 15, 1992.

"You know, trust...judgement." Thomas Walkom, " 'Trust us' a peeved Rae asks voters," *Toronto Star*, Oct. 23, 1992.

But most New Democrat...hands. Thomas Walkom, "Basic reason Yes is losing: Too few people like the accord," *Toronto Star*, Oct. 22, 1992.

CHAPTER 12

Donegan specialized...election. Georgette Gagnon and Dan Rath, *Not Without Cause: David Peterson's Fall from Grace* (Toronto: HarperCollins, 1991), pp. 144-145.

Dodds would later claim...him. See Thomas Walkom, "Public gained little from Martel affair," *Toronto Star*, Apr. 29, 1992.

"I put her into bed...big time." Unless otherwise indicated, all statements attributed to Kathleen O'Hara in this chapter are from an interview with the author Nov. 15, 1993.

"no basis in fact and were unfounded." Derek Ferguson, "Premier refuses to fire minister who made smear against doctor," *Toronto Star*, Dec. 11, 1991.

...the press interpreted Martel's statement...lied. See, for example, Derek Ferguson, "Rae may call probe in Martel affair," *Toronto Star*, Dec. 17, 1991.

"There was concern...further." Interview with Lynn Spink, Mar. 18, 1994.

"hardships for many members." Bob Rae, "Memo to cabinet ministers...[re] conflict of interest," Feb. 12, 1991.

...Rae kicked Toronto MPP Tony Rizzo...earlier. Jane Armstrong and Kevin Donovan, "Riding tells Rizzo to apologize," *Toronto Star*, Jan. 11, 1991.

To many New Democrats such as Janet Solberg...done. Interview with Janet Solberg, Nov. 11, 1993.

"He came along...round." Interview with Sue Colley, Dec. 8, 1993.

"I really think...jelled." Ibid.

In late 1992, Ferguson approached Piper . . . Dawson. See Kelly Toughill, "Ferguson cleared of conflict over record," *Toronto Star*, June 24, 1993; Kelly Toughill, "MPP admits Piper plot role but won't quit," *Toronto Star*, Mar. 10, 1993.

...sexually abused...reform school. The school, Grandview, had been closed in 1976. Harris did not claim that Ferguson had abused her, just helped her escape. In fact, she said, she always liked him. See Peter Edwards, "NDP cabinet minister quits," *Toronto Star*, Feb. 14, 1992.

"Anita is extremely bitter...inflexible." Interview with Janet Solberg, Nov. 11, 1993.

"Bob ain't got many friends left." Interview with Lenny Wise, Oct. 27, 1993.

Piper himself...big mistake. Kelly Toughill, "Was asked to release crime file, Piper says," *Toronto Star*, Apr. 6, 1993.

...Michele McLean...hand." See Thomas Walkom, "Unnatural acts exposed in NDP's scandal interruptus," *Toronto Star*, Nov. 18, 1992.

The denouement...independent. William Walker, "On-again, off-again North flees NDP for Tories," *Toronto Star*, Aug. 28, 1993; Leslie Papp, "Tory Caucus put Peter North entry on hold," *Toronto Star*, Sept. 21, 1993.

CHAPTER 13

If Maurice Strong... Most of the information on Strong's background comes from
Elaine Dewar, "Mr. Universe," *Saturday Night,* June 1992, pp. 17-83; Rick
Boychuk, "How Green was his valley," *Saturday Night,* Nov. 1991, pp. 24-66.

Many of these New Agers... Denver. Boychuk, Nov. 1991. Strong resigned from
the water-pumping company in 1989 and donated his shares to a foundation.
However, as Dewar says, "Just because Strong gave his water shares to the non-
profit Fetzer Foundation... doesn't mean he lost control of the transaction."
Dewar, June 1992, p. 74.

This caused... $100,000 to find a new Hydro head. See Derek Ferguson, "Hydro hunt
a waste, MPP says," *Toronto Star*, Nov. 4, 1992.

"mingling of public... policy." Dewar, June 1992, p. 73.

Within weeks... privatizing... utility. Anne Dawson "For sale signs at Hydro?,"
Toronto Sun, Dec. 3, 1992.

Energy Minister Brian Charlton was not amused... government. Ian Bailey, "Charlton
rules out privatizing Hydro," *Financial Post*, Dec. 4, 1992.

"Marc was not an easy person... did." Interview with Brian Charlton, Apr. 15, 1994.

... when Rae was asked about Eliesen's salary... premier. Matt Maychak, "Rae's
choice to run Ontario Hydro asks $400,000," *Toronto Star*, Sept. 5, 1991.

But Strong was a man of many interests... minister. Interview with Brian Charlton,
Apr. 15, 1994.

One anecdote is telling... died. Leslie Papp, "Jungle purchase still possible Strong
says," *Toronto Star*, May 19, 1994; Thomas Walkom, "Mere ministers are no
match for Mo of the jungle," *Toronto Star*, May 19, 1994; Maurice F. Strong,
"Jungle project criticism is petty," *Toronto Star*, May 26, 1994; Sean Conway to
author, June 2, 1994.

"Proponents of neo-liberalism... wagon." Bob Rae "The threat of privatization,"
Speech to the New Directions Conference, Washington, D.C., May 3, 1986.

"This is mistaken... wealth." Robert Rae, "The social and political thought of Sidney
and Beatrice Webb" (University of Oxford Bachelor of Philosophy Thesis, 1971),
pp. 14, 87; emphasis in original.

By April 1994... backed off. Thomas Walkom, "Revised road map keeps highways in
public domain," *Toronto Star*, Apr. 12, 1994.

Those who favoured privatizing... supply it. Interview with Bud Wildman,
Apr. 25, 1994.

"We're looking at everything... criticism." Thomas Walkom, "NDP idea conjures up
vision of Thatcher," *Toronto Star*, Jan. 23, 1993.

Two camps had formed... elsewhere. Interview with Michael Decter, Nov. 21, 1993.

"The way I put it... world." Ibid.

"My advice Mike... through." Quoted in ibid.

In March 1993... 4,500 employees. Geoff Scotton, "Ontario Hydro on a private
path," *Financial Post*, Mar. 13, 1993.

Analysts inside and outside... privatization. Geoff Scotton, "Ontario Hydro votes on
breakup," *Financial Post*, Apr. 13, 1993.

... Rae himself seemed to be hinting at privatization.... way. Thomas Walkom,
"Strong nudges NDP toward privatization of Hydro," *Toronto Star*, Nov 25, 1993;
Geoffrey Scotton, "Rae agrees to review law governing Hydro," *Financial Post*,
Oct. 28, 1993.

... the premier seemed reluctant to privatize... election. Interview with Michael
Decter, Nov. 21, 1993.

"I don't think Bob came to any conclusion." Interview with Bud Wildman,
    Apr. 25, 1994.

In early 1994, Wildman . . . Hydro. Martin Mittelstaedt, "Strong survives stormy year,"
    Globe and Mail, Jan. 24, 1994.

"At no point . . . it." Interview with Bud Wildman, Apr. 25, 1994.

"I do not think . . . fire sale . . . sense." Martin Mittelstaedt, "Rae rules out Hydro
    'fire sale', " *Globe and Mail*, Feb. 8, 1994.

"We were not interested . . . partnership." Interview with Brian Charlton,
    Apr. 15, 1994.

CHAPTER 14

A new name . . . problem. "Federal NDP plans face-lift," *Toronto Star*, Mar. 2, 1994.

"Let's not kid ourselves . . . party." Rae to Ontario NDP Convention, Mar. 3, 1991.

"There's a whole . . . done." Unless otherwise indicated, all statements attributed to
    Janet Solberg in this chapter are from an interview with the author, Nov. 11, 1993.

"What are people's records . . . now?" Quoted in Thomas Walkom, "Rae will be judged
    on whether he delivers," *Toronto Star*, Mar. 9, 1991.

"We're not going back . . . 1990." Quoted in "The Course of Politics: 1993-1995,
    Feature Interview: Ross McClellan." *GPC Ontario Quarterly* (published by
    Government Policy Consultants, Sept. 1993), p. 32.

"As a party activist . . . past." Interview with Frances Lankin, Apr. 12, 1994.

"Those that have known . . . haven't." Interview with Ruth Grier, Mar. 16, 1994.

"They're not doctors . . . media." Unless otherwise indicated, all statements attributed
    to Julie Davis are from an interview with the author, Oct. 29, 1993.

"You can't take on . . . Ontario." Interview with Evelyn Gigantes, Dec. 9, 1993.

"There's no choice . . . have]." Interview with Floyd Laughren, Oct. 12, 1993.

"hard choices." Interview with Michael Decter, Nov. 21, 1993.

"The only difference . . . party." Interview with Sue Colley, Dec. 8, 1993.

. . . labour would have to re-evaluate . . . nationally . . . Interview with Julie Davis,
    Oct. 29, 1993.

"Once a visonary . . . bellies." Ehring and Roberts, *Giving Away a Miracle,* p.9.

"intellectually decapitated . . . purge." Interview with Sue Colley, Dec. 8, 1993.

. . . Mel Watkins . . . was offered a job . . . Interview with Mel Watkins, Aug. 4, 1993. By
    the time the U of T was agreeable, the government had instituted its social contract
    and Watkins was no longer interested.

Canadian Autoworkers. . . . down. Interviews with Lynn Spink, Dec. 3, 1993; Bob
    White, Apr. 28, 1994. White went to head the Canadian Labour Congress instead.

"There was not much coherent thinking . . . priority." Interview with Chuck Rachlis,
    Mar. 9. 1994.

"Going into government . . . it." Interview with Kathleen O'Hara, Nov. 15, 1993.

Loyal New Democrats . . . enthusiasm. Interview with Stephen Lewis, Jan. 30, 1994.

"It destroyed hope." Interview with Judy Darcy, Apr. 27, 1994.

Index